PETER L. BERGEN

The Osama bin Laden I Know

An Oral History of al Qaeda's Leader

FREE PRESS

New York London Toronto Sydney

ƒP

FREE PRESS
A Division of Simon & Schuster, Inc.
1230 Avenue of the Americas
New York, NY 10020

Copyright © 2006 by Peter L. Bergen

Manufactured in the United States of America

10 9 8 7 6 5 4 3 2 1

Library of Congress Cataloging-in-Publication Data is available.

ISBN-13: 978-0-7432-7891-1
ISBN-10:   0-7432-7891-7

For information regarding special discounts for bulk purchases,
please contact Simon & Schuster Special Sales at
1-800-456-6798 or business@simonandschuster.com

For Juliana Silva, with love

The ink of the scholar is worth more than the blood of a martyr.

—the Prophet Muhammad

Contents

Dramatis Personae

Adel, Sayf al. The military commander of al Qaeda since 2002. Former Egyptian special forces officer who joined the Afghan mujahideen in the struggle against the Soviets in the 1980s. Escaped to Iran after the U.S. offensive in Afghanistan in late 2001. Suspected of masterminding al Qaeda's attacks in Riyadh, Saudi Arabia, in May 2003.

Anas, Abdullah. His less frequently used real name is Boudejema Bounoua. An Algerian born in 1958, he studied to be an imam (cleric) before traveling to Pakistan in 1984. There he helped run the Services Office to raise funds and recruits for the war in Afghanistan with Abdullah Azzam and Osama bin Laden during the eighties. Married Abdullah Azzam's daughter in 1990.

Atef, Mohammad, commonly known as Abu Hafs. Al Qaeda's second military commander (1996–2001) and cofounder of al Qaeda. Former police officer who was connected to the Egyptian Islamic Jihad group. In 2001 his daughter married bin Laden's son Mohammed. He was killed by a U.S. air strike in Afghanistan in November 2001.

Atta, Mohammed. The Egyptian studying in Hamburg, Germany, who became the lead 9/11 hijacker.

Atwan, Abdel Bari. Editor of *Al Quds al Arabi,* a leading Arabic-language newspaper based in London. Interviewed bin Laden in Afghanistan in November 1996.

Awdah, Sheikh Salman al. Saudi cleric who was sharply critical of the Saudi government's decision to invite U.S. troops into the Kingdom in 1990. His arrest and imprisonment in 1994 was one of the reasons bin Laden turned against the Saudi government. He was set free in 1999.

Azzam, Abdullah. In 1984 he founded the Services Office in Peshawar, Pakistan, to take on the mission of coordinating Arab volunteers coming to participate in some way in the Afghan jihad. Born in 1941 in the West Bank, he was a member of the Muslim Brotherhood and earned a doctorate in Islamic jurisprudence from Al Azhar University in Cairo. He was assassinated in Peshawar in November 1989.

Azzam, Hutaifa. Abdullah Azzam's son. Born in Egypt in 1971, he first went to Afghanistan in the mid-eighties, where he attended military training camps from the age of thirteen. He has known bin Laden since 1984.

Banjshiri, Abu Ubaidah al. Egyptian who was instrumental in the founding of al Qaeda and was its first military commander. Moved with al Qaeda to Sudan in 1992; in 1996, he drowned in a ferry accident on Lake Victoria in Kenya.

Batarfi, Khaled. Bin Laden's boyhood friend and next-door neighbor in the Musharifa neighborhood of Jeddah, Saudi Arabia.

Bentoman, Noman. Former member of the Shura Committee of the Libyan Islamic Fighting Group. Traveled from Libya to Afghanistan in late 1989 at the age of twenty-two. Took part in the battle of Khost in 1991. Trained in the al-Farouq camp in Afghanistan. Left Afghanistan in the summer of 1994 and went to Khartoum, Sudan, where he lived until October 1995, when the Sudanese government pressured Libyan militants to leave. He subsequently moved to London.

Bin Ladin, Bakr Mohammed. The present head of the Bin Ladin family. He also runs the Saudi Binladin Group.

Bin Ladin, Mohammed. Osama bin Laden's father. Born in 1908 in the village of Rubat, Hadramaut, in what is now a southeastern province of Yemen. Worked as a porter after emigrating to Jeddah, Saudi Arabia, in 1930. Built the Saudi Binladin Group into one of the top Middle Eastern construction companies. Died in a plane crash in Saudi Arabia in 1967 at the age of fifty-nine. In all, he married about twenty wives and fathered twenty-five sons and twenty-nine daughters.

bin Laden, Osama. Leader of al Qaeda. Born in Riyadh, Saudi Arabia, in 1957.

Binalshibh, Ramzi. 9/11 planner who failed to gain a visa to the United States and who subsequently acted as a point man between the 9/11 plot members in the United States and the al Qaeda leadership in Afghanistan.

Deraz, Essam. Egyptian army officer who became a filmmaker and spent more than a year with bin Laden on the frontlines in Afghanistan during the 1980s.

Fadl, Jamal al. An early member of al Qaeda. Testified as a prosecution witness in the 2001 trial of four men implicated in the 1998 American embassy bombings in Africa.

Faisal, Prince Turki al. Head of the Saudi intelligence service from 1977 to August 2001. Was responsible for funneling Saudi funds to the Afghan mujahideen and met bin Laden in Islamabad in the mid-1980s. In 1998 he personally attempted to pressure the Taliban leader Mullah Omar to hand over bin Laden.

Fauwaz, Khaled al. A Saudi who worked both as bin Laden's media representative in the United Kingdom and for the Advice and Reformation Committee, a political organization founded by bin Laden in 1994. Arrested in London following an American extradition request that alleged he had a role in the 1998 U.S. African embassy bombings.

Fouda, Yosri. Al Jazeera's chief investigative reporter. Interviewed the 9/11 planners Khaled Sheikh Mohammed and Ramzi bin al Shibh in the spring of 2002. His documentary, *The Road to September the 11th*, was aired on Al Jazeera on the first anniversary of 9/11.

Fyfield-Shayler, Brian. Taught bin Laden English during the 1968 school year at the Al Thagr School in Jeddah. Oxford-educated, he was recruited at the age of twenty-two to run the English department at Al Thagr. He did so from 1964 to 1968. During that time he taught a number of the Bin Ladin boys. He lived in Jeddah until 1974.

Ghanem, Alia. Osama's Syrian mother. She had one child with Mohammed Bin Ladin—Osama—in 1957. She visited her son several times in Sudan in the mid-nineties to try to persuade him to return to Saudi Arabia. She attended the wedding of bin Laden's son Mohammed in Afghanistan in 2001. Now living in Jeddah, Saudi Arabia, she has three sons and a daughter from her second marriage, to Muhammed bin Umar al Attas.

Haqqani, Jalaluddin. Pashtun Afghan warlord and a key ally of Mullah Omar and al Qaeda, who helped bin Laden set up camps in the mid-nineties in his stronghold in the Khost region of eastern Afghanistan. Joined the Taliban in 1995 and was made minister of tribes and frontiers before being given charge of Taliban military operations in 2001.

Hawali, Sheikh Safar al. Saudi cleric who was sharply critical of the Saudi government's decision to invite U.S. troops into the Kingdom in 1990. Audiotapes of his sermons became influential with jihadists across the Arab world. His arrest in 1994 along with that of Sheikh Al Awdah radicalized bin Laden. Released from prison in 1999.

Hekmatyar, Gulbuddin. Afghan Pashtun warlord. Nominally became prime minister of the Afghan coalition government that replaced the Afghan communists in 1992. But after a breakdown in this agreement with other Afghan factions he shelled Kabul repeatedly until the Taliban took Kabul in 1996. He then fled to Iran, where he later helped al Qaeda members reorganize after the U.S. offensive in Afghanistan in 2001.

Ismail, Faraj. An Egyptian journalist who covered the Afghan jihad for the *Al Muslimoon* newspaper, a newspaper that focused on Muslim movements. First met bin Laden in Jeddah in 1985.

Ismail, Jamal. Al Jazeera television correspondent who interviewed bin Laden in 1998. Worked for the Services Office's *Jihad* magazine during the eighties.

Jandal, Abu. Real name is Nasir Ahmad Nasir Abdallah al Bahri. Became bin Laden's chief bodyguard in Afghanistan in 2000. Born in Jeddah, Saudi Arabia, in 1972 to Yemeni parents. Left Saudi Arabia in 1993 to wage jihad in Bosnia, Somalia, and Tajikistan. Recruited personally by bin Laden into al Qaeda in 1997 in Jalalabad, Afghanistan. In 2000 helped to arrange bin Laden's marriage to his fifth wife, Amal al Sadah, a Yemeni. Left Afghanistan in August 2000 to return to Yemen.

Jouvenal, Peter. Veteran freelance combat cameraman. Left the British Army in 1979 and traveled to Afghanistan to cover the war against the Soviets. Has extensively covered the country since. Filmed CNN's interview with bin Laden in 1997 and was the first Western cameraman into Kabul after the fall of the Taliban.

Julaidan, Wael. Born in Medina, Saudi Arabia, in 1958. Met bin Laden socially in Jeddah between 1981 and 1983, before attending the University of Arizona. Recruited by Abdullah Azzam on a trip to the United States in 1984 to help the Afghan jihad. Worked for the Muslim

World League in Pakistan, a Saudi charity that aided Afghan refugees. Left Pakistan in 1994 to return to Saudi Arabia.

Khalifa, Jamal. Born September 1, 1956, in Medina. Bin Laden's closest friend at King Abdul Aziz University in Jeddah, where he studied biology from 1975 to 1980. Married bin Laden's half sister Sheikha in 1986. Traveled to Afghanistan in 1985 to wage jihad against the Soviets. Moved to Pakistan, where he worked for the Muslim World League helping Afghan refugees. Says he fell out with bin Laden in 1986. Subsequently moved back to Jeddah in Saudi Arabia, but also traveled extensively in Southeast Asia, where he is alleged to have been involved in financing al Qaeda affiliated groups.

Khashoggi, Jamal. Saudi journalist who knew bin Laden slightly when he was living in Jeddah. Was one of the first journalists from a major Arab media organization to cover the mujahideen's efforts against the Soviets when he was invited to Afghanistan by bin Laden in 1987.

Khawaja, Khalid. Joined the Pakistani Air Force in 1971. In 1985 seconded to ISI (Pakistan's military intelligence agency). Fought at the battle of Jaji in 1987. Became close to bin Laden and developed ties to the Taliban regime.

Kherchtou, L'Houssaine. Moroccan al Qaeda member who testified as a U.S. government witness in the 2001 trial of four men accused of a role in the bombing of two U.S. embassies in Africa in 1998. Moved to Afghanistan in 1991 and trained at the al Farouq training camp. From 1993 was al Qaeda's point man in Nairobi, Kenya.

Massoud, Ahmad Shah. Kabul University engineering student turned Afghan military leader who played a leading role in driving the Soviet army out of Afghanistan. His exploits earned him the nickname the "Lion of Panjshir." In 1992 he became Afghan defense minister under President Burhanuddin Rabbani. Following the collapse of Rabbani's government and the rise of the Taliban, Massoud became the military leader of the Northern Alliance, a coalition of various Afghan armed factions opposed to the Taliban. Assassinated on September 9, 2001, on the orders of bin Laden.

Miller, John. ABC News correspondent covering legal issues. He interviewed bin Laden for ABC in 1998 in Afghanistan. Before working for ABC, Miller was the deputy police commissioner of the New York City Police Department in charge of public affairs.

Mir, Hamid. Founding editor of the Urdu-language *Ausaf* newspaper in Pakistan. Interviewed bin Laden three times: in Jalalabad in March 1997 near Kandahar airport and in May 1998; and, in November 2001, he conducted the first and only print interview that bin Laden gave after the 9/11 attacks. Bin Laden asked him to become his biographer.

Misri, Abu Walid al. Egyptian sent to cover the Afghanistan war in 1979 for an Emirates newspaper and who remained in Afghanistan until 2001. Became a confidant of bin Laden and several top al Qaeda figures. Was chief editor of the Taliban's Arabic-language newspaper, *Al-Imara* (The Emirate), and was close to Mullah Omar. After the collapse of the Taliban wrote a book, *The History of the Arab Afghans from the Time of their Arrival in Afghanistan until their Departure with the Taliban* that was sharply critical of bin Laden.

Mohamed, Ali. Egyptian-American who was a key military trainer for al Qaeda. Born 1952 in Egypt. Became involved with the Egyptian Islamic Jihad organization in the early 1980s. Served as a major in the Egyptian army before moving to the United States, where he served in the U.S. Army at Ft. Bragg, North Carolina, between 1986 and 1989. During the early and mid-nineties, provided training to members of al Qaeda in Afghanistan and trained bin Laden's bodyguards in Sudan. In U.S. custody since 1998.

Mohammed, Khaled Sheikh. The key operational planner of the 9/11 attacks. Of Pakistani heritage, he grew up in Kuwait. Joined the Jihad against the Soviets. In 1996, he met bin Laden in Tora Bora, Afghanistan, and presented the outlines of what would become the 9/11 plot. Arrested in March 2003 in Pakistan.

Mojdeh, Vahid. Afghan who worked in the Services Office in Peshawar during the 1980s, where he encountered bin Laden. Held several positions in the Taliban Ministry of Foreign Affairs between 1995 and the fall of the Taliban in 2001.

Muttawakil, Wakil Ahmed. Taliban Foreign Minister. Part of the more "moderate" wing of the Taliban. Surrendered to U.S. military authorities at Kandahar airbase in 2002.

Omar, Mullah Mohammed. De facto leader of Afghanistan 1996–2001. Born 1959. A Pashtun who fought with the mujahideen in the Afghan war, losing an eye. Founded the Taliban movement in the southern Afghan city of Kandahar in 1994.

Qatada, Abu. Militant Jordanian cleric who moved to London in 1993. The spiritual mentor of Abu Musab al Zarqawi, now the most feared insurgent commander in Iraq.

Rahman, Sheikh Omar Abdel. Known as the "Blind Sheikh." Egyptian cleric and the spiritual leader of two Egyptian terrorist organizations: the Jihad group and Gamma Islamiyya (Islamic Group). Convicted in 1995 of plots against New York landmarks.

Rida, Abu al. Syrian, born 1961, who was a founding member of al Qaeda. U.S. court records allege that when he lived in Sudan during the mid-nineties, he purchased uranium, tractors, and automatic weapons for al Qaeda.

Ridi, Essam al. Egyptian-American who lived in Kuwait and Pakistan before gaining a piloting license from an aviation school in Texas. In the early 1980s he was recruited by Abdullah Azzam on a trip to the United States to join the Afghan jihad.

Rushdi, Osama. Former member of the Egyptian terrorist organization Gama'a al Islamiyya, the Islamic Group, who was jailed with Ayman al Zawahiri in the early 1980s after the assassination of Egyptian President Anwar Sadat. In 1989 he moved to Peshawar.

Sanoussi, Ibrahim al. Assistant to Hassan al Turabi, the Sudanese leader who between 1989 and 1999 introduced Sharia law into Sudan and invited in Islamist militants such as bin Laden. Met bin Laden regularly when he was living in Sudan.

Surayhi, Hasan Abd-Rabbuh al. Saudi who traveled to bin Laden's *Masada* training camp in eastern Afghanistan in 1987. Says he did not join al Qaeda himself. Visited bin Laden in Sudan. Was the former imam of the Ibn Baz Mosque in Mecca. Was imprisoned in Saudi Arabia in 1995, but released in November 2001 under a general amnesty.

Suri, Abu Mousab al. Real name, Mustafa Setmariam Nasar. Syrian jihadist who participated in the Afghan war against the Soviets, during which he met bin Laden. In the early 1990s he moved to Spain and then in 1995 to London. In 1997 he traveled to Afghanistan, where he arranged CNN's interview with bin Laden.

Turabi, Hassan al. Founder of Sudan's National Islamic Front, which helped bring President Omar Bashir to power in 1989. Lost out to Bashir in a power struggle in 1999 and was placed under house arrest and then imprisoned.

Yousef, Ramzi. Real name, Abdul Basit. Masterminded the attack on the World Trade Center in 1993. Arrested in Pakistan in 1995. Nephew of 9/11 planner Khalid Sheikh Mohammed. Born in Kuwait in 1968, of Pakistani origin.

Yusufzai, Rahimullah. One of Pakistan's leading journalists. Interviewed bin Laden twice in the late 1990s and Taliban leader Mullah Omar on several occasions.

Zaidan, Ahmad. Syrian-born journalist. Had contact with bin Laden in Peshawar between 1987 and bin Laden's departure for the Sudan in 1992. In October 2000 he interviewed bin Laden in Kabul. In January 2001 he was invited to a wedding party in Kandahar celebrating the marriage of Osama's son Mohammed and the daughter of Abu Hafs, which he videotaped for Al Jazeera. In 2002 he published the Arabic book *Bin Laden Unmasked.*

Zarqawi, Abu Musab al. Jordanian-born insurgent leader in the Iraq war, and from 2004 the leader of al Qaeda in Iraq. Left Jordan for Afghanistan in 1989, fighting in the battle of Khost. Returned to Jordan in 1993 and founded al Tawhid, a terrorist group made up principally of Jordanians. Imprisoned in Jordan from 1994 to 1999 for a plot to attack an Israeli target. After his release he returned to Afghanistan, where he received some al Qaeda assistance in setting up his own camp in Herat, near the Iranian border. Fled to Iran in December 2001 and later to Kurdistan, in northern Iraq.

Zawahiri, Ayman al. Bin Laden's deputy and an intellectual driving force of al Qaeda. Born June 19, 1951, in Cairo. In the 1970s led a cell of jihadists in Egypt. Imprisoned after Sadat's assassination in 1981. On release in 1984 moved to Saudi Arabia and then Peshawar, Pakistan, where he built up his Jihad organization. Met bin Laden in 1986 and encouraged him to split away from Abdullah Azzam. In the early 1990s moved to Sudan from where his group launched a series of attacks on

Egyptian targets. Relocated to Afghanistan in 1996 and allied his Jihad group with al Qaeda in 1998. Completed his autobiography *Knights under the Prophet's Banner* in 2001.

Zayyat, Montasser al. Egyptian lawyer from Cairo who has represented many Islamists facing trials in Egyptian courts. He also served as spokesman for Gama'a al Islamiyya. The group led an intense terrorism campaign in Egypt from the mid-1970s until 1997. In 2002 he wrote *The Road to Al-Qaeda,* a critical biography of Zawahiri, whom he first met in an Egyptian prison following the assassination of Anwar Sadat.

Osama bin Laden Timeline

1957	Born in Jeddah, Saudi Arabia.
1967	Mohammed Bin Ladin, father of Osama, dies in a plane crash.
1968	Attends Al Thagr High School in Jeddah.
1974	Marries first wife, Najwa Ghanem.
1976	Attends King Abdul Aziz University in Jeddah.
1980	Makes first trip to Pakistan after Soviet invasion of Afghanistan.
1984	Helps to found Services Office. Makes first trip to Afghanistan.
1986	Sets up first military base in Jaji, eastern Afghanistan.
1987	Fights in Battle of Jaji. Gains reputation as fighter.
1988 May 29	Eldest brother Salem Bin Ladin dies in a plane crash.
1988 August	Founds al Qaeda.
1989 February	Soviet forces leave Afghanistan.
1989 November	Leaves Pakistan and returns to Saudi Arabia.
1989 November 24	Assassination of Abdallah Azzam.
1990 August 2	Iraq invades Kuwait.
1991 Early	Returns to Peshawar, Pakistan.
1992 Early	Moves to Khartoum, the capital of Sudan.
1994 April	Family disowns him. Stripped of Saudi citizenship.
1996 Mid May	Pressured to leave Sudan. Returns to Afghanistan.
August 23	Issues fatwa declaring war against the United States.
Mid	Khalid Sheikh Mohammed floats plan that becomes 9/11 plot.
1997 May 10	First television interview airs on CNN.
1998 February 22	Forms World Islamic Front against the Crusaders and the Jews.
August 7	Bombing of U.S. embassies in Kenya and Tanzania.
September	Mullah Omar turns down Saudi extradition request for bin Laden.
2000 October 12	Attack on the USS *Cole*.
2001 September 11	9/11 Attack.
2001 October 7	Bin Laden videotape airs after 9/11. U.S. campaign against Taliban starts.
2004 April 14	Offer of truce to European governments airs on Arab television.

October 17   Abu Musab al Zarqawi pledges allegiance to bin Laden and
                renames his group al Qaeda in Iraq.
October 29   Videotaped address to American people just before U.S.
                election airs on Al Jazeera. Publicly admits to the 9/11 attack
                for the first time.

MEDITERRANEAN SEA

SYRIA

LEBANON
★Damascus

Tel Aviv
Jerusalem
ISRAEL JORDAN
★Amman

Cairo★

EGYPT

Nile

KURDISTAN   Tehra

Tigris

Euphrates   ★Baghdad

IRAQ

KUWAIT

Persian

BAHRAIN
QATAR

Medina○

Riyadh⊛

SAUDI
ARABIA

Jeddah○ ○Mecca

Port Sudan○

Red Sea

SUDAN

HADRAMAU○

Sanaa
★ YEMEN

Khartoum⊛

ERITREA

●Aden Gulf of Aden

DJIBOUTI

0 Miles   500

0 Kilometers   500

ETHIOPIA

SOMALIA

CENTRAL
AFRICAN
REPUBLIC

DEMOCRATIC
REPUBLIC
OF CONGO

UGANDA   KENYA

★Mogadishu

Lake
Victoria

★Nairobi

RWANDA

BURUNDI

Indian Ocean

TANZANIA

★Dar es Salaam

© 2005 Jeffrey L. Ward

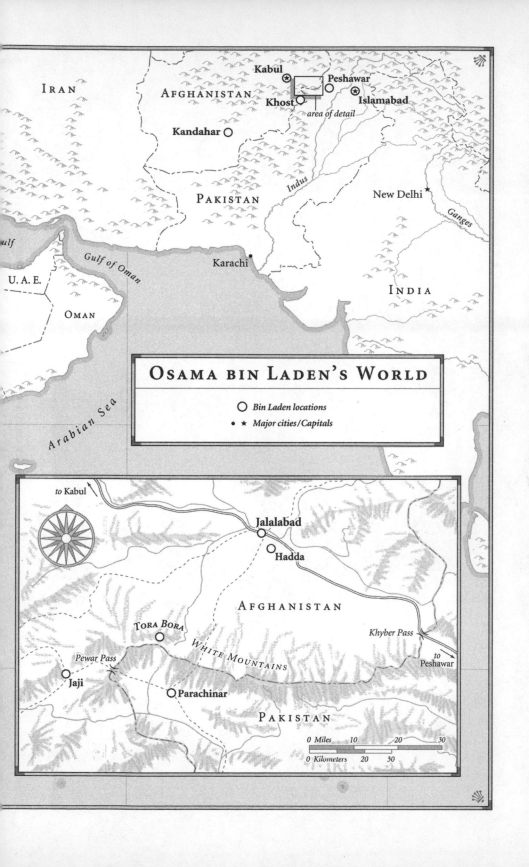

Introduction

Osama bin Laden first registered as a substantial threat within the U.S. government in January 1996 when a specialized bin Laden unit was established at the CIA. It was the first time any unit focusing on a particular individual had been set up within the agency. A year later bin Laden gave his first television interview, declaring war on the United States on CNN. Rarely have our enemies warned us so publicly of their intentions. Imagine for a minute that starting in 1937 the Japanese High Command had repeatedly publicized its goal of attacking the United States. Surely the U.S. Navy would then have been more prepared for the Japanese attack on Pearl Harbor on December 7, 1941.

Within four years of bin Laden's interview on CNN, al Qaeda had carried out the bombings of two U.S. embassies in Africa, an attack on the USS *Cole* in Yemen, and the 9/11 attacks, inflicting more direct damage on the United States than the Soviet Union had done during the nearly five decades of the Cold War. To a large degree, this exponentially increasing campaign of violence was the result of the vision of one man: Osama bin Laden.

Just as an account of Nazism and its impact on Europe would be nonsensical without reference to the persona and worldview of Hitler, or a history of France after the Revolution of 1789 would make no sense without an understanding of the goals and personality of Napoleon, so too our understanding of al Qaeda and the ideology it has spawned would be incoherent without reference to Osama bin Laden's personal story and his view of the world.

Despite bin Laden's importance to the al Qaeda organization and to the larger ideological movement it has spawned, the conventional wisdom now is that tracking bin Laden down won't make much of a difference to the larger war on terrorism. At a March 2002 press conference, President George W. Bush referred to bin Laden as "a person who's now been marginalized."[1] Some have even joked that bin Laden is, in fact, Bin Forgotten. Although it is certainly the case that the global jihadist movement will carry on whatever bin Laden's fate, it would be danger-ously wrong to assume that it doesn't really matter whether or not he is apprehended.

Finding bin Laden remains of utmost importance for two reasons: First, every day that bin Laden remains at liberty is a propaganda victory for al Qaeda. Second, although bin Laden and his deputy Ayman al Za-wahiri don't exert day-to-day control over al Qaeda, they do continue to supply broad strategic guidance for the group's actions and for those of its affiliates. Statements from bin Laden and al Zawahiri have always been the most reliable guide to the future actions of jihadist movements around the world. This has remained the case even while both men have been on the run. Indeed, since the 9/11 attacks, bin Laden has released at least eighteen statements on video or audiotape, which have reached audiences of tens of millions as those statements are relayed around the globe by the BBC, CNN, Al Jazeera, and other television networks.

Arresting the spread of bin Laden's ideas will prove more problematic than arresting or killing al Qaeda's leaders. One indicator of this is a worldwide opinion poll undertaken by the Pew Global Attitudes Project in March 2004. The Pew poll found that bin Laden is viewed favorably by large percentages in Pakistan (65 percent), Jordan (55 percent), and Morocco (45 percent), all key allies in the war on terrorism.[2] The results of the 2004 Pew poll are similar to a 2003 Pew poll in which Indonesians, Jordanians, Pakistanis, and Moroccans all expressed more "confidence" in bin Laden than in President Bush, by large pluralities.[3] Indeed, not since Egypt's president Gamal Abdel Nasser galvanized the Middle East in the 1950s and 1960s with his vision of Arab nationalism married to so-cialism has an Arab political figure had as much impact on the world. An indicator of bin Laden's continued ideological importance to the militant jihadists is that in 2004 the most feared insurgent commander in Iraq, Abu Musab al Zarqawi, pledged his allegiance to al Qaeda's leader.

Given the impact that bin Laden has had on the recent history of the world, there is surprisingly a good deal that remains mysterious about him. For instance, how did he develop into the leader of the world's most deadly terrorist organization? How did he conceive of the religious-political ideology that will be his legacy? Is he a rich, wannabe jihadist who became the pawn of Egyptian Islamist militants, or is he his own man? To what extent has al Qaeda functioned as a top-down organization run by bin Laden, and to what extent has it always been more of a loose ideological movement? Is bin Laden's fight against the West the petulant act of a quixotic millionaire, or the carefully thought-out strategy of a man who believes he is fighting for the very survival of true Islam? Is he attacking the United States because of its freedoms or its foreign policies? Finally, what does bin Laden really want: the overthrow of the Saudi regime, or the restoration of the caliphate across the Muslim world?

I do not pretend that this book will definitively answer all those questions. After all, the interior life of any person is something of a mystery. And writing about bin Laden is complicated by the fact that he grew up in one of the most closed societies on the planet, the Kingdom of Saudi Arabia, and is himself a scion of one of the kingdom's most secretive families. Moreover, he has seemingly deliberately avoided revealing much of his personal story when he has been interviewed. However, I hope I have elicited, through scores of interviews and a search of many archives and databases, something that will help the reader develop a fuller picture of the man and his organization.

My intent is not to perform an exercise of what the French term *Tout comprendre, c'est tout pardonner* (To understand everything is to forgive everything). What bin Laden has done is unforgivable. But bin Laden is a man and we need to understand him neither through a fog of our own propaganda—he has never, for instance, expressed an interest in attacking the West because of our "freedoms"—nor through the mythomania of his supporters, who style him as the defender of Islam, despite the fact that the Koran is full of injunctions against the killing of civilians. As you read this book, maybe bin Laden will remain forever a sphinx without a riddle, an enigmatic smile playing on his lips, or perhaps he will emerge as something fuller.

In an effort to try to fill in some of the information gaps about bin Laden, I decided to write an oral and document-based history of al Qaeda's leader using the words of those who have some personal insights about him, whether through one chance meeting, or years of deep friendship. Everyone quoted in this book, with a few exceptions that are noted in the text, has actually met bin Laden, thus ensuring that their stories are firsthand accounts and are filtered neither through the recollections of others nor through the tsunami of nonsense that has been written about him, such as the assertion that as a teenager he was partying in Beirut, or that al Qaeda had an alliance with Iraq's former leader, Saddam Hussein.

My decision to limit the people we hear from in this book to those who have met bin Laden is something of a device, but I believe it is a useful one. The fact that someone has actually encountered bin Laden is an indicator that the person probably has something insightful to say about bin Laden himself or al Qaeda's roots, history, and future. Of course, this book is not a series of dozens of accounts of someone's first meeting with bin Laden, which would become boring quickly. Rather, the meeting with bin Laden is, in most cases, simply a launching point for a wider discussion of bin Laden's character, the personalities of his inner circle, and al Qaeda's history and goals.

I hope this history of bin Laden will illuminate worlds of which the reader is likely to have little experience—for instance, the time and place where bin Laden grew up—Jeddah, Saudi Arabia, in the seventies; where al Qaeda slowly took shape—Afghanistan during the Soviet war in the eighties; where bin Laden became more radicalized—Sudan in the mid-nineties; also, Afghanistan under the Taliban in the late nineties; and, finally, the secretive world of al Qaeda itself."

To tell the stories in this book I have relied on interviews I have conducted over the past eight years in Afghanistan, Pakistan, Saudi Arabia, Jordan, Egypt, Yemen, and the United Kingdom. I have also incorporated testimony given by people who know bin Laden in legal cases in the United States, Canada, Italy, France, Bosnia, Belgium, Spain, Germany, and Egypt. Finally I have mined books written by al Qaeda's leaders and former Taliban officials; thousands of pages of transcripts of U.S. military tribunal proceedings for prisoners held at Guantánamo Bay; firsthand accounts of bin Laden from newspapers around the Muslim world; documents from the Saudi BinLadin Group; and a trove of al Qaeda–related documents and publications going back to the mid-eighties that I have collected.

A key discovery among those al Qaeda–related publications was several thousand pages of *Jihad* magazine, which was the in-house organ of the Arab jihadists based in Pakistan during the 1980s. West Point's Counterterrorism Center also made available its translation of thousands of pages of the *Encyclopedia of Jihad*, al Qaeda's vast internal training manual that was largely written during the 1990s. I have also used statements from bin Laden himself, such as those he made to me and to CNN's Peter Arnett in March 1997 when we interviewed him in Afghanistan for his first television interview, the only time that I met al Qaeda's leader.

The personal detail that most forcefully struck me when we met bin Laden was how he presented himself as a soft-spoken cleric, rather than as the fire-breathing leader of a global terrorist organization. During the course of our interview, bin Laden's tirade against the West was delivered in a voice that barely rose above a whisper. It was also clear that bin Laden was well informed about world events. He mentioned, for instance, that the former IRA terrorist leader Gerry Adams had recently met with President Clinton at the White House. This off-the-cuff comment, made in the middle of the night in a hut on a cold Afghan mountaintop, has always stayed with me as an example of bin Laden's intense interest in world politics. It's these kinds of insights and anecdotes about bin Laden that I hoped to elicit in my interviews with those who have spent time with him. At the same time I also wanted to derive a better account, from the inside, of the nature of the al Qaeda organization.

As I was gathering interviews and material for this book, I realized one theme had started emerging rather forcibly: The whole history of al Qaeda, much of Afghanistan's history over the past two decades, and even the events of 9/11 itself, reflect in part the ideological and military struggles between bin Laden and the legendary Afghan commander, Ahmad Shah Massoud. Not only was there personal enmity between the two men, but they are also both representative of the ideological civil war that is taking place today in the Muslim world between those who like bin Laden want to install Taliban-style theocracies from Indonesia to Morocco, and those who, like Massoud, aim to create Islamic states that enjoy friendly relations with the West, are tolerant of other religions, and are amenable to women having a role outside the home.

In 1993 during Afghanistan's civil war I met Massoud at his headquarters north of Kabul and, like so many others, I was struck by his intense integrity and charisma. Massoud was arguably the most brilliant military strategist of the late twentieth century, surviving six major Soviet operations during the eighties aimed at defeating him in his sanctuary in the Panjshir Valley in northern Afghanistan. Yet in person Massoud projected a kind of gentle fragility and a disarming sense of humor. The experience of meeting Massoud was quite a powerful sensation and was very different from the experience of meeting bin Laden, whom I found opaque and hard to read.

Massoud and bin Laden never met, but as one of the interviewees in this book perceptively observes, if they had done so, the recent history of the world might well have turned out differently. While Massoud was what most Westerners would term a fundamentalist, his was a moderate kind of fundamentalism, which was leavened by an interest in the poetry and mysticism of Sufism, tolerance for others, and an orientation towards the West. Beginning in the late eighties, bin Laden and the Egyptians who would form the core of al Qaeda began to turn against Massoud as they embraced a more highly radicalized Islamism that branded Muslims who did not share their militant jihadism as "apostates."

Beginning in the late eighties, al Qaeda allied itself with Massoud's bitter rival, the Afghan commander Gulbuddin Hekmatyar. And in the late nineties al Qaeda also joined forces with the Taliban, which faced its only serious opposition from Massoud's forces. Massoud had resisted the Taliban for more than five years. The story of the enmity between bin Laden and Massoud climaxed with Massoud's assassination on September 9, 2001, which historians will record as the curtain-raiser for the 9/11 attacks two days later. The assassination was personally ordered by bin Laden. It was a gratuity to the Taliban leader Mullah Omar, whom bin Laden did not clue in on his 9/11 plans, which Mullah Omar would have likely opposed on the grounds that such an act would threaten his regime.

Another theme that emerged as I was reporting this book is the extent to which bin Laden acts on impulse, often overreaching and paying little attention to the potential consequences of his actions. In some cases this trait might indicate decisiveness. Most of the time it indicates foolhardiness and egotism. Bin Laden, for instance, did not wait for a fatwa to be issued about the necessity of fighting the Soviets when they invaded Afghanistan on December 25, 1979. At the age of twenty-two, bin Laden went to Pakistan within weeks of the invasion and started fund-raising for the Afghan war effort. While other Arabs involved in the jihad against the Soviets saw it as their mission to play a supporting role to the Afghan mujahideen, between 1986 and 1987 bin Laden set up his own entirely Arab military force. That force took on the Soviets at the battle of Jaji in the spring of 1987.

However, while the Arab military engagement at the Jaji battle, much like the 9/11 attacks a decade and a half later, brought a great deal of publicity to bin Laden, neither turned out to be smart strategy. Which brings us to an important point: Bin Laden certainly attempts to think strategically. For instance when he created his Arab force that would not retreat from the Soviets, or later when he attacked the "far enemy" the United States, in an effort to destabilize the "near enemy" Saudi Arabia. But what are the fruits of his strategic thinking? The battle of Jaji showed the Arabs could hold off a larger number of Soviets for a period of a few weeks. Nothing more. September 11 showed that al Qaeda could attack the United States itself, but it turned out to be something of a kamikaze mission for bin Laden's organization, as the American response to the attacks was to decimate al Qaeda and destroy its Taliban partners.

Similarly, in 1989 bin Laden insisted on participating in the attack on the city of Jalalabad in eastern Afghanistan, despite the fact that such an attack did not play to the strengths of his small guerrilla army. The attack turned out to be a fiasco, and around one hundred of his Arab mujahideen were killed. And against the advice of several of his associates, as the war against the Soviets was winding down, bin Laden set up his own organization to continue fighting jihads around the world: al Qaeda.

Bin Laden continued to act impulsively after the war against the Soviets. When Saddam Hussein invaded Kuwait in 1990, bin Laden immediately offered to set up his own mujahideen force to defeat the Iraqis, an idea the Saudi government dismissed out of hand. After 1996, while bin Laden was based in Afghanistan, he gave interviews to several international media organizations calling for attacks on the United States, despite the fact that the Taliban had repeatedly put him on notice not to do so. And then, of course, he presided over the 9/11 attacks, which had the unintended effect of obliterating the Taliban regime and destroying al Qaeda's extensive infrastructure in Afghanistan.

Perhaps because we constantly hear that Islamist terrorists are bound together by their common dislike of the United States, we tend to assume that they must also be united by common tactics, strategies, and ideology. In fact, they often resent one another as much as they do the

Bush administration, and the global jihadist movement is split by squabbles over personnel and strategy. That is another key theme I hope emerges from this book: how fissured and split the jihadist movement has been historically—and how those fissures became even more pronounced as a result of the 9/11 attack, which many Islamist militants have concluded did damage to their cause.

☙

I have tried to exclude materials from the book that are either of questionable authenticity or impossible to verify. There is, for instance, a marvelous gossipy interview with bin Laden's fifth wife, a Yemeni, that was published in the Saudi *Majallah* magazine in 2002.[4] The article claimed that bin Laden's former wife had returned to Yemen from Afghanistan after the fall of the Taliban, a claim that is dismissed by Abu Jandal, bin Laden's chief bodyguard, who has proved a reliable source of information about al Qaeda's leader.

Likewise, a lengthy screed, which first surfaced in November 2002, "Osama bin Laden's Letter to America," purports to be from al Qaeda's leader. The letter decries everything about the United States, from its stance on global warming to its supposed toleration of incest.[5] However, it is dismissed as a fake by those familiar with bin Laden's style, such as the Palestinian journalist Jamal Ismail, who has known al Qaeda's leader since 1984. It is also my judgment that the letter is not from bin Laden, as it rants on about a number of issues, such as AIDS, gambling, and the American sex trade, which bin Laden has never discussed in any of his scores of other statements. Moreover, unlike a bin Laden audiotape or videotape, a letter posted on a Web site claiming to be from al Qaeda's leader, as this one was, cannot be independently verified.

Obviously, some of the people I am quoting in the book may have self-serving versions of events, and some may even be lying. Where that is the case readers should be able to detect it, either because of the circumstances in which those statements were made, or because of information supplied by other interviewees elsewhere in the book. Clearly a detainee held at Guantánamo is likely to put an innocent gloss on his activities, for example, while former officials in the Sudanese government may have developed amnesia about the close relations they enjoyed with bin Laden during his four-year sojourn in Sudan.

⚜

I have excerpted a variety of documents in this book. They are generally from court proceedings around the world, but there are also a myriad of other sources, such as U.S. State Department cables, and books written by al Qaeda insiders. In the interests of clarity and narrative flow I have generally edited these down, and I have not added ellipses to those edited texts so as not to clutter the book further. I have followed a similar procedure with statements made by bin Laden and Ayman al Zawahiri. For those readers who wish to consult the original documents and statements, the footnotes are a road map to where those can be found. In some cases those documents and statements are available on the Internet. Others are less accessible, but in all cases the original source is indicated.

Where an interview in the book was conducted by a news organization, such as the *Al Quds al Arabi* newspaper, that is made clear on first reference, and then it is footnoted if the interview appears again later in the book. The rest of the interviews in the book were largely conducted by me, and details of the dates and places of those interviews can be found in the footnotes. Interviews undertaken by three people who helped me research the book—Paul Cruickshank, Sam Dealey, and James Meek—are similarly footnoted. (Note that some interviewees chose to speak in English, their second language.)

Arabic names have been transliterated in a manner that is the most standard for Western readers. Thus, I have used Osama bin Laden and al Qaeda rather than Usama bin Ladin and al Qaida. I have also used the spelling Binladin when referring to the family construction business, as this is how it generally appears in English. In the case of references to Arabic names that appear in official documents that are written in English, I have retained the original spelling that was used in the document.

I have tried to be as accurate as possible about dates, cross-referencing the dates of events offered by interviewees in the book either with other people's accounts of the same event or with contemporary documents where that is possible. In the course of reporting this book I noticed, however, that because of the differences between the Western and Islamic calendars, sometimes interviewees in the Muslim world made mistakes when transposing dates between the two calendars. Additionally, because fundamentalist Muslims do not celebrate birthdays, it is hard, particularly in Saudi Arabia, to be absolutely certain about a person's birth date in the same manner that one can be in the West. With those caveats, I have endeavored to make the dates in the book as accurate as is possible.

The
Osama bin Laden
I Know

1

Arabia

Osama bin Laden grew up during the 1960s and 1970s in what was then the sleepy city of Jeddah, a port on the Red Sea, which for the past millennia and a half has served as a gateway to the holy city of Mecca, thirty miles away. It was in Jeddah's port that Osama's father, Mohammed Bin Ladin, would get his start in 1930 working as a porter for pilgrims on their way to Mecca.

Bin Laden came of age as the Muslim world was experiencing an Islamic awakening known as the *Sahwa*. This awakening came after Egypt, Syria, and Jordan had suffered a devastating defeat in the 1967 war with Israel, so exposing the ideological bankruptcy of Arab nationalism/socialism, which had been the dominant intellectual current in the Middle East since the 1950s. And that defeat came a year after the execution of the Egyptian writer Sayyid Qutb, whose writings and "martyrdom" would also play a key role in the burgeoning Islamist movement.

This period of Islamic awakening peaked in 1979—the first year of a new century on the Muslim calendar—with four seismic events that would profoundly influence bin Laden and other future members of al Qaeda: the overthrow of the Shah of Iran by the cleric Ayatollah Khomeni; the armed takeover of Islam's holy of holies, the mosque in Mecca, by Saudi militants; Egypt's historic cease-fire agreement with Israel; and, finally, the Soviet Union's invasion of Afghanistan. It was a thrilling time to be a deeply committed Muslim, as the twenty-two-year-old bin Laden already was.

This chapter traces bin Laden's first two decades. It was during this period that bin Laden first married, attended university, and started working intensively in the family business.

☙

Osama bin Laden speaking to Jamal Ismail, a correspondent for Al Jazeera television in an interview that aired in 1999.[1]

God Almighty was gracious enough for me to be born to Muslim parents in the Arabian Peninsula, in al Malazz neighborhood in Riyadh, [Saudi Arabia] on March 10, 1957. Then God was gracious to us as we went to Holy Medina six months after I was born. For the rest of my life I stayed in Hejaz [a Saudi province], moving between Mecca, Jeddah, and Medina.

As it is well known, my father, Sheikh Muhammad bin Awad Bin Ladin, was born in Hadramaut [in southern Yemen]. He went to work in Hejaz at an early age, more than seventy years ago. Then God blessed him and bestowed on him an honor that no other building contractor has known. He built the holy Mecca mosque and at the same time—because of God's blessings to him—he built the holy mosque in Medina. Then when he found out that the government of Jordan announced a tender for restoration work on the Dome of the Rock Mosque [in Jerusalem], he gathered engineers and asked them: "Calculate only the cost price of the project." When they did, they were surprised that [my father], God have mercy on his soul, reduced the cost price in order to guarantee that God's mosques are well served. He was awarded the project.

Because of God's graciousness to him, sometimes he prayed in all three mosques [in Mecca, Medina, and Jerusalem] in one single day. May God have mercy on his soul. It is not a secret that he was one of the founders of the infrastructure of the Kingdom of Saudi Arabia.

Afterward, I studied in Hejaz. I studied economics at Jeddah University, or the so-called King Abdul Aziz University. I worked at an early age on roads in my father's company, may God have mercy on his soul. My father died when I was ten years old. This is something brief about Osama bin Laden.

Brian Fyfield-Shayler is a British citizen who lived in Saudi Arabia between 1964 and 1974, where he taught English to a number of the bin Laden boys.[2]

The old man Bin Ladin only had one eye. He was very much a rough laborer-looking kind of person. He could never be smart and elegant.

One of the things about Hadramaut [in Yemen], it's not a classless society. A lot of it goes on whereabouts in Hadramaut you come from. If you came from Wadi Hadramaut, no one could criticize you because that's where the two ruling dynasties came from. But I suspect the people in Wadi Do'an [Bin Ladin's home valley] were quite low down the pecking order. And of course, there is another reason for this, and that is that your occupation depended on which area you came from. Different valleys and different villages supplied laborers and others supplied jewelers and others supplied people into import and exports; other areas supplied cloth merchants. So it was a bit like a medieval market in Western cities, that where you came from influenced the kind of profession you were likely to move into. So there is a pecking order within the Hadramis and although, of course, they were all aware that they were all one notch down from the top Saudi classes, within them there were infinite gradations.

Mohammed Bin Ladin was from a laboring class, but of course as the Bin Ladins made more and more money, they became more and more acceptable. It's a bit like the new money in England: after twenty, thirty, fifty years, it becomes much more acceptable.

The mothers of [Mohammed Bin Ladin's] children were very simple women from the villages around the construction camps where he developed. There are a lot of stories about how he acquired some of his very young wives. And they were, I think, primarily chosen, one, because they were Saudi Bedouin and, two, because they were young. That was his interest. All the sons are very good looking and they are quite striking. I don't think that I have ever met any ugly Bin Ladins. Osama's mother, I am told, she was a great beauty.

Since his father never had more than four wives at any one time, he was constantly divorcing the third and the fourth and taking in new ones, I don't know how many different mothers there are.[3] And there's only one more family in Saudi Arabia you can compare that with. This was an anachronism even in the 1950s and '60s, when bin Laden was doing this. The only family that was behaving like this was, in fact, King Abdul Aziz's and King Saud's. I think Bin Ladin probably even outnumbered King Abdul Aziz's children and number of wives.

The British are terrible snobs about class and the Saudis also have their sensitivities, and one of them, in fact, is color, which no Saudi will ever admit to. But, of course, when anyone gets married in Saudi Arabia, the first question the women ask is: "What color? What shade?" And there is a great hierarchy—the people who are white, which is beautiful, down to black, which is not beautiful. And so any great brain or terribly able person in Saudi Arabia who tends to be in the darker spectrum tends to be passed over for promotion and other things. Bin Laden is quite fair.

I was born in 1942 in Reading, near London. I went to university at Oxford, studied English there, got a degree, and my first job when I graduated in 1963 was in Ghana teaching English. I looked around for more jobs in the teaching world. And so I applied for three jobs: one in Saudi Arabia, one in Libya, and one in Ethiopia, and the Saudi interview was the first to come up. I was interviewed in the embassy in London in the spring/early summer of '64. I arrived in Saudi Arabia about the end of August, and was based in Al Thagr School.

The Al Thagr School was a prestige school, had hundreds of visitors every week. There were presidents of all sorts of countries arriving, parliamentary delegations from England came. In the secondary school there were perhaps twenty students in the first class, and I think sixteen, seventeen only in the top third class. So it was, in fact, a very small school. I had a fleet of Jordanians, Egyptians, Syrian, and a Sudanese teacher of English, who were all very good indeed. They were hand-picked from their countries.

King Faisal (who became king in 1964), one of the first things he did was to order that all the princes should educate their children in Saudi Arabia, and this was a tremendous upheaval because a number of his brothers and cousins had been in the habit of sending their sons to schools abroad. So from 1964 onwards there was a huge influx of young Saudi princes who had been educated in all sorts of ridiculous schools abroad—some of them couldn't even read and write Arabic—who were brought back forcefully to Saudi Arabia, kicking and screaming in some cases. It became known that it was no longer socially acceptable to send all your children abroad for education, so the top business families had to follow the example of the princes and consider putting their sons in schools in Saudi Arabia.

The pupils [at Al Thagr] were the elite in all ways. First of all, the sons of the princes and the ministers who were based in Jeddah. And then, of course, there were the top business families. So if you looked along King Abdul Aziz Street, which was the main shopping street in those days, and you looked at the names over the shops, many of them second generation Hadrami businessmen, then those were the names that formed a very big slice of the school; a roll call of the school register.

The school has been criticized for being just for the toffs, but in fact it wasn't. My taxi driver's son was at the school. And so it tended to be that the cleverest boys in each class were in fact not from the princely families and not even always from the top business families, but were just extremely bright kids from middle-income or very low-income families.

The school didn't owe much to the old Koranic madrassas of Arabia. The headmaster had toured schools in England and picked up some ideas. The curriculum was constantly in a state of development. The school prided itself on its science. I heard no criticism of the curriculum, no criticism at all of the scientific bias of the syllabus while I was there—remember the fundamentalists were not known to be a major influence in Saudi society in the 1960s.

We had this theater, which we built in the school, that was mostly used as an assembly hall for the great and the good of Jeddah, who would come to be addressed by the Crown Prince Faisal, who was chairman of the board of governors. It was his school. And at the end of my first year in the school the headmaster said that he was sitting on a committee to form a new university in Jeddah. This was what became King Abdul Aziz University (which bin Laden would attend a decade later). So in my second year in Saudi Arabia [in 1965], I began to attend these meetings of the founding committee of King Abdul Aziz University. By the end of that year, it was decided to have a grand meeting of all the wealthy people in Jeddah—businessmen, bankers, princes—who would pledge money to set up King Abdul Aziz University. And so this huge meeting was held inside our school. It was one of many occasions in which [Mohammed] Bin Ladin was present. All the businessmen were vying with each other to pledge more of their money. Of course, when the first person pledged a million riyals that was a big event. A huge applause went up in the hall. Bin Ladin was in his element there and was thoroughly enjoying himself; outbidding people and upping the ante. So he was a very familiar figure around the school.

From an official history of the Saudi Binladin Group that was once published on the Internet, disappearing after the 9/11 attacks.[4]

The history of Binladin began in 1931 when Mohammed Binladin founded the company. From its humble beginnings as a general contractor, the company has grown and prospered in parallel with the growth and prosperity of the Kingdom of Saudi Arabia. Over the years the company has been entrusted with many major construction projects, projects that helped the Kingdom to develop its resources and expand its infrastructure.

Under the leadership of the late M. Binladin, the company diversified into other areas and became an international conglomerate with interests ranging from its traditional construction business [to] industrial and power projects, petroleum, chemicals and mining, telecommunications, operations and maintenance, manufacturing and trading.

The 1967 Six-Day War that Israel fought against Egypt, Syria, and Jordan, when bin Laden was ten, had a profound impact effect on the Arab world. The Egyptian government had promised a quick victory against Israel; instead it was a spectacular defeat that called into question the very basis of Egyptian President Gamal Nasser's regime, which was built on secular Arab nationalism and socialism. The defeat would energize the Islamist movement around the Arab world. Essam Deraz, an Egyptian army officer who would spend more than a year with bin Laden on the frontlines in Afghanistan during the 1980s, recalls what the '67 defeat meant to Deraz and his fellow Islamists.[5]

I can tell you what the war of '67 did to the region. I was a reconnaissance officer, so I was moving in front of troops, so I saw this whole war as a movie. The Egyptian officers and soldiers saw their colleagues burned by napalm. We saw the army of our country destroyed in hours. We thought that we would conquer Israel in hours.

I discovered that it wasn't Israel that defeated us, but it was the [Egyptian] regime that defeated us, and I started to be against the regime. It wasn't a military defeat. It became a civilizational defeat. We didn't know that we were so backward, we were so retarded, so behind the rest of the modern civilization. There was an earthquake in the Arab-Islamic personality, not only in Egypt, but in the entire Arab world.

Brian Fyfield-Shayler.

The 1967 war (between Israel and Egypt) had a big effect on the school. Many of the children wanted to get on buses to go and join the good cause, but the school made a lot of effort to keep them in the classrooms and told them the best way to fight their cause was to get a good education.

Hutaifa Azzam is the son of bin Laden's mentor, the Palestinian cleric Abdullah Azzam. Abdullah took up arms against the Israelis during the 1967 war.[6]

When the Jews took the area of Jenin [in Palestine] and my father's village of Seilah al Harthai, my father took some of his friends, followers, and relatives, and they took their guns and they were trying to make resistance against this. [At the time he was] twenty-six, teaching in a high school.

They decided to transfer to Jordan and to restart their mission from Jordan. He made [training] camps [known as] "the camps of the real Muslim religious people," on the border of Palestine. They continued their movement until 1970.

My father wrote a special book. It's called *Palestine from Heart to Heart*. You could say the title means we don't want to lose Palestine forever.

Hamid Mir, a Pakistani journalist who is writing a biography of bin Laden.[7]

[Bin Laden] said that his father was not a very well educated man, and that's why [following the 1967 war] he called all the engineers of his Bin Ladin construction company and he asked them, "How many bulldozers do we have?" So they counted the bulldozers, and they said that we have more than two hundred and fifty bulldozers. So Mohammed Bin Ladin asked the engineers, "Can you convert these bulldozers into two hundred and fifty tanks." So one engineer asked, "Why?" [Bin Laden's father] said, "I want to use these tanks against the Jews because they have captured our land."

[Bin Laden's father] was very, very, very anti-Israel, anti-Jewish because he was of the view that the land of Palestine belongs to [the Arabs]. You can understand his love for *Al Quds* (the Arabic name for Jerusalem) through an example told to me by Osama bin Laden. He said that that was a routine of his father, once or twice in a month; he used to offer his morning prayers in Medina, afternoon prayers in Mecca, and then the evening prayers in Jerusalem because he had a plane.

Brian Fyfield-Shayler recalls teaching Osama bin Laden English in the year after the death of his father, Mohammed.

This was my fourth year teaching, when [Osama] came along [in 1968 when he was aged eleven]. Osama was one of thirty students. He [used to sit] two-thirds of the way back on the window side that looked out onto sports fields and playing grounds. Why did I remember Osama? First of all, I would have noticed because of his name, because of the family, and of course, when you walked into a class of anyone of his age, he was literally outstanding because he was taller than his contemporaries and so he was very noticeable. His English was not amazing. He was not one of the great brains of that class. On the other hand, he was not in the bottom. But this does not necessarily mean that he is middling because it was one of the top two schools in the country. So to be in the middle of the top class at the top school really puts you in the top fifty students in the country. So although he did not shine at that particular school, nationally, he would be one of the top fifty students of his age education-wise.

It's most important to put this particular student in context. He did not start as a monster. Something I have subsequently been very interested in, how much can you tell of a person's personality from how they were at eleven? Sometimes I have thought that people don't change; that these things are formed very early in life. On the other hand, how much of the man can you tell from an eleven- or twelve-year-old?

[He was] extraordinarily courteous, but this, of course, is also a characteristic of students in Saudi Arabia in general, but I think he was, in fact, more courteous than the average student, probably partly because he was a bit shyer than most of the other students. For example, when the teacher asked questions, a forest of hands [would go up]. "Ask me! Ask me!" And Osama would not do that. It's one of the things I do remember about him. [He] would sit quietly with a very confident smile on his face, but he would not push forward to display his knowledge. And of course, if you actually asked him, then he was usually right, but he didn't push himself forward. He wasn't one of the students who sat in the front row and demanded the teacher's attention and nor was he one of those who slunk away in the back row. And so he was not pushy in any way.

It was big news, it was national news, when Mohammed (Osama's father) was killed (in a plane crash in 1967). I remember getting the news. I was in Taif when I got the news and of course [Mohammed Bin Ladin] built the road to Taif, which was a road from Jeddah bypassing Mecca to Taif. The news came through that Mohammed Bin Ladin had been killed. And of course everyone was very shocked.

Hamid Mir, bin Laden's Pakistani biographer.

Osama told me that when his father died, [Saudi] King Faisal wept for many days, so they were close.

Brian Fyfield-Shayler.

And for the next year at least, the future of the [Bin Ladin] business [hung in the balance]. There were a lot of projects that were not completed and it was the major construction company of Saudi Arabia, so it was of huge importance; so there was great deal of anxiety for the finances and for the running of the company, and there was probably only Salem (Osama's eldest brother) and three or four brothers at that period who were of an age even to take on the mantle.

Salem was educated at Millfield (a boarding school in England). Salem was a fraction younger than me. I was introduced to him by mutual friends. Nothing at all to do with the school or his much younger brothers who were in the school; just on a social level. Most of my contacts with Salem would have been in '73, '74. He was very Westernized.

His English was beautiful; it was very fluent, very characterful. He played the guitar; he had lots of Western friends and was a great socialite in Jeddah.

A relative of the Bin Ladin family who knew Salem and asked to remain anonymous because the family is wary of talking to outsiders.

Salem was a unique individual by any standard. By Saudi standards he was off the charts. Very charismatic, amusing, no facial hair. He played guitar—sixties hits like, "Where Have All the Flowers Gone?"

He acted as sort of a court jester to King Fahd and was part of Fahd's inner circle. Sometime he overstepped with the king. One time he buzzed the king's camp in the desert with one of his planes, which went down badly, but he was always taken back into the fold.

Salem took control of the business beginning in '73–'74. The links to the royal family that his father had cultivated had subsided by then. Salem was very successful at rekindling that relationship. If King Fahd wanted a palace built, Salem would build it for him.

He was twenty-one when his father died in 1967. King Faisal, the most respected of all the Saudi monarchs, arranged for the Bin Ladin company to be put into trust until the children were older. Salem was personally responsible for distributing the dividends. Some brothers, such as Ali, who lives in Paris, cashed out of the business.

This raises the question of how much money bin Laden inherited from his family. Certainly far less than the figures of 200–300 million dollars mentioned in the media after 9/11. In fact, according to someone designated by the family to speak to me, bin Laden benefited from the distribution of his father's estate according to Sharia law, which meant that the sons received twice as much as daughters.[8] However, with fifty-four children even Mohammed Bin Ladin's vast fortune did not go too far. Until bin Laden's family cut him off in 1994, over the course of the two decades or so that he benefited from the distribution of his father's estate, he would have received something like 20 million dollars.

In the years following his father's death Salem visited Sweden to establish business relationships for the family firm and to purchase a fleet

of trucks from Volvo. During this period Salem got to know the small
town of Falun, known for its iron mine and a local nightclub called
Ophelia. Christina Akerblad is the former owner of the Hotel Astoria in
Falun. She says that in 1970 Salem bin Laden and his younger brother
Osama came to visit.[9]

[The Hotel Astoria] was just a small bed and breakfast. They [Salem
and Osama] just came to sleep with us and to have breakfast. On the
other side of the street there was a huge hotel and they took food from
this hotel and they took the food up to their rooms and sat in the Astoria
to have their dinner. They didn't want to eat at the bigger hotel. I don't
know why. We had this hotel in 1970 and 1971 and they came to us both
years. The two of them came in the first year, Osama bin Laden and his
elder brother [Salem].

What I remember very well is that they came with a big Rolls-Royce
and it was forbidden to park the car outside the building in this street.
But they did it and we [my husband and I] said to them you have to pay
[a fine] for every day and every hour you are staying outside this hotel,
but they said, "Oh it doesn't matter, it's so funny to go to the police station and to talk with the police. We will stay where we are." It was like a
joke to them. They had so much money, they didn't know how much
money they had. They came with their own flight to Copenhagen because I asked them how they had managed to come to Sweden with this
enormous Rolls-Royce. They said, "We have our plane and the plane is
staying in Copenhagen, and then we have driven through Sweden because we want to make contacts in Sweden." I asked them, "What sort of
contacts?" But they didn't answer my question.

They stayed one week. It was in the winter of 1970. I think it was in
January. There was a lot of snow outside the street. It was a very cold winter that year. They came like two very elegant boys. They were dressed
very exclusive. They were very nice and they had very lovely eyes, I remember, especially Osama. His eyes, it was streaming love from his eyes.
My two sons [Anders and Gerk] admired them because they were so
nicely dressed and they had curly black hair and they were very friendly.
When they saw our boys in the corridor, they said hello to them and they
played a little bit with them.

They had two double rooms. They slept in one bed and on the other bed they had their bags. On the Sunday I had no cleaner at the hotel so I took care of the room myself and I was shocked because in the big bag they had lots of white, expensive shirts from [Christian] Dior and Yves St. Laurent. When they had [used] the shirt once, they dropped it. So the cleaner had taken these shirts to wash them, but they said [to her], "No, we are just using them once, so you can take them if you want." In the smaller bag, they had lots of jewels, for shirts. Very exclusive diamonds and rubies and emeralds and so on. It was fantastic to see.

[Salem and Osama] said that they were about sixty children altogether. When they said good-bye to us, they said, "Next year we will see you again and I hope we will take the whole family with us. We will [get in] touch with you when we are coming." The year after they came [again]. I think there were twenty-three children [on the second visit].

That following year Hans Lindquist, a reporter for Falun's newspaper, the *Dalarnes Tidningar,* was asked to do a feature piece on a large family visiting from Saudi Arabia. An excerpt of his story from September 7, 1971, follows:

ARAB CELEBRITY VISIT

Yesterday Salem bin Ladin visited Falun on a combined business and pleasure trip through Europe. He was accompanied by 22 members of his family, which in total consists of 54 children. The young sheikh, who is 26 years old, arrived in his private jet to Borlange airport, while the rest of the family arrived by car. He has visited the Club Ophelia in Falun. The young sheikh is reportedly a big fan of discos and has visited the discos of Falun at various times in the past, however, not together with his family.

The sheikh is said to be the owner of a big and successful construction company in his home country, Saudi Arabia. In Gothenburg, it is said that he surprised Volvo by entering their office and ordering a large number of trucks for his company. The family is now traveling to Stockholm, where they will visit AB Nitro Nobel. The sheikh's private jet has been sent to London.

Khaled Batarfi was bin Laden's next-door neighbor when they were growing up in Jeddah. Bin Laden was sixteen, three years older than Batarfi, when they first met in about 1973. For those in the West who

have heard erroneous tales of bin Laden's huge fortune, in fact, the Musharifa neighborhood where he grew up is a typical middle-class Jeddah neighborhood.

The houses are relatively modest and are nothing like the enormous mansions that Jeddah's rich have built for themselves along the water-front "Corniche," the main highway along the Red Sea. The neighborhood sits behind the five-star Mövenpick hotel and is anchored by the intimate mosque in which Batarfi and bin Laden would make their five daily prayers, and a playground the size of a city block where the two friends would play soccer after school.

Batarfi gave me a tour of the Musharifa district in Jeddah where he has lived for the past three decades, and where he first befriended bin Laden. After her divorce from Mohammed Bin Ladin, Osama's mother married Muhammad al Attas, who is from an old Jeddah merchant family. The couple continues to live in the Musharifa district where Osama grew up. When he showed me around the neighborhood Batarfi was careful not to point out bin Laden's mother's house because he said he wanted to protect her privacy and that of her family.[10]

When we came here first, it was mostly desert; most of these buildings were built in the last decades. And our houses were some of the first [in] the neighborhood. Still there was no paved road here. The nearest street was Al-Medina Street, and you had to drive through dirt roads to get here. We moved here in 1970. Osama, his mother, stepfather, and half-brothers moved [into the neighborhood] three or four years after that.

We were very close neighbors so we went together to the mosque. We went to places around the district to talk or just drink tea and coffee. Entertainment options then were very limited.

We used to come out of school about 2:00 p.m. and then we had lunch and a rest. When the sun went down about 4:00 to 5:00, [we played soccer]. I was the captain even though Osama was older than me. Because he was tall he used to play forward to use his head and put in the goals. He was a good soldier; send him anywhere and he will follow orders.

There was a funny story: his [half] brother, Ahmed, came to me running and said, "Look: Osama is about to be hit." And I looked back and I saw one of the rough guys—we were in a rough neighborhood playing a match—trying to hit Osama, talking abusively. So I ran back to him and I pushed the guy away and I solved the problem. Osama said, "I was going to solve it peacefully."

So I was a tough guy then and Osama was the peaceful one. So that's the kind of Osama he was then. He was very shy, very observant. He weighs his words a lot before he says anything. And you feel that he's watching very observantly, very carefully, listening very carefully to what's going on. And then when he says something, you understand that he was watching and observing everything around him.

He liked western movies. One of the series he liked was *Fury*. (*Fury* originally ran on NBC from 1955 to 1960. The stallion Fury also appeared in other TV shows and movies). He used to watch that, and he liked karate movies. Bruce Lee [especially].

He liked to go climbing mountains in the area between Syria and Turkey. He loved horse riding. He loved horses since he was a young boy. He had a farm in south Jeddah and twenty-something horses. One of them was [named] al-Balga. Al-Balga is the name of the horse used by one of the Companions of the Prophet.

I was close enough to come to his bedroom and wake him up for prayer [just before dawn]. In the morning I would go to his windows and knock on the windows, "Osama, you know, it's time." Even after he gets married, I used to do that. Osama used to do all his prayers in the mosque. He was a very religious guy, and everyone else was behaving like there is a sheikh (religious figure) around. You know how kids joke—[in Osama's presence] we watch our words, don't use bad words, because it's like [having] a priest around. You watch your mouth and your behavior.

He was a natural leader; he leads by example and by hints more than direct orders. He just set an example and expects you to follow, and somehow you follow even if you are not 100 percent convinced. I remember I was driving my car going to play soccer and I saw him standing near his door, so I had to stop because he saw me. So the problem was I was wearing shorts, [which is not strictly Islamic]. So I was trying to avoid him seeing me, and then when I had to stop, I had to get out and kiss him. So he saw me and I was very embarrassed, talking small talk while I was thinking, what I'm going to say if he said, "So why you are wearing shorts?" Finally at the end he just looked at my legs and said, "Good-bye." And from that day on, I didn't wear shorts. So he has this charisma.

I wouldn't go with him in every prayer, but he was intriguing to me. He would fast every Monday and Thursday. [Monday and Thursday] fasting is an extra thing because it's what the Prophet used to do. But you don't have to do it. And I saw a man who could have the world, he's very rich, and everything he spends is spent on poor people. Every Monday and Thursday he would go and bring poor people and take us all in cars to north of our district, which was almost desert, near the Pepsi-Cola factory. And they don't have much entertainment options, so [Osama] provided them with entertainment. We would sit in groups of three or four and he asked us questions [such as] where the Prophet was born. And if you answered a question, "Yeah," you get a mark. And then he counted the marks and decided who's the winner.

And we used to go to his house and sing religious chants about Muslim youth and Palestine. [His view was,] "Unless we, the new generation, change and become stronger and more educated and more dedicated, we will never reclaim Palestine." He was saying that all the time, whenever the subject arose.

[Osama's mother] is a moderate Muslim. She watches TV. She [has] never been very conservative, and her [present] husband is like that; their kids are like that. So Osama was different. But then he was different in a quiet way. He would bother his brothers sometimes for looking at the maid or things like that. He was kind of trying to influence his brothers. Of course, he woke them for the prayers in the morning, and that was good—nobody complained. But sometimes he was kind of upset if something is not done in an Islamic way. "Don't wear short sleeves, don't do this, don't do that." But they all loved him. I was like that in my house, not as much as he was, but I was trying to advise, sometimes forcibly, my brothers and sisters.

[When he was] seventeen he married his cousin in Latakia [Syria]— a beautiful resort, I hear [she was] the daughter of his uncle, the brother of his mother. And then he went to the university and I saw less of him.

In her book *Inside the Kingdom: My Life in Saudi Arabia*, Carmen Bin Ladin provides a vivid, if not especially flattering, account of Jeddah in the mid-1970s. At the time, she was married to Osama's half-brother Yeslam.[11]

I discovered the city of Jeddah when we went to the Swiss embassy to register for our imminent marriage [in 1974]. Driving through Jeddah, staring from behind the tinted windows of the Mercedes, I watched a roadside scene from another millennium. Saudi Arabia was still emerging in those days from the crushing poverty of its traditional way of life. People had become less poor after oil was discovered in the 1930s, but the crazy bonanza of wealth that would sweep the country after the 1973 oil embargo lay in the future. Donkey Square was a crisscross of dirt tracks where people came to buy water from men leading donkeys with barrels on their backs. Shimmering waves of heat rose off the city's few tarmac roads. I saw one or two squalid little shops. Scattered across the endless sand dunes were the houses—invisible behind tall concrete walls that protected their women from view. At first I wasn't even aware of what seemed so strange about this country, but then it hit me: Half the population of Saudi Arabia is behind walls, all the time. It was hard to fathom a city with almost no women. I felt like a ghost: Women didn't exist, in this world. And there were no parks, no flowers, not even trees. This was a place without color. Apart from the sand, which covered the roads with a soft, dusty carpet, the only colors that stood out were white and black-and-white. The men's white thobes, and a very few stark black triangles of cloth: the shrouded women.

Jamal Khalifa became bin Laden's closest friend at King Abdul Aziz University in Jeddah.[12]

In '76 I met Osama. He's one year younger [than me]. I can't remember the first meeting. He was in a different college, in economics. I was in science, but our activities were the same. [At the time] King Abdul Aziz University was small, a few hundred people. I was almost twenty, and he was nineteen. At that time we were religious and we were very conservative; we go to that extreme side. When I met him, he was religious already. We don't watch movies. Some of the scholars in Saudi Arabi were saying that music is *haram*, it's prohibited. So we believe that it's prohibited. When we want to watch the news there is some music, and at that time there is no remote control. So I used to let my son stay beside the TV so when it came to music, he knows that he will turn the sound down. Of course, no girls, don't even talk about it. And no photo-

graphs. That's why I don't have any pictures with Osama. I was pho-
tographed in high school, but when I became religious, I threw everything away.

We had mutual interests together. We would go to the [Red] Sea
swimming, sometimes fishing. We also went riding Jeeps to the mountains and deserts; have some adventures. He's a very good driver. Together we would go fast, mostly the two of us, so that made us very close.

The [Bin Ladins] have a very big land in the desert; in a place we call
Bahra. It's between Jeddah and Mecca, around 25 kilometers from Jeddah. The Bin Ladin family have like a farm there. Osama pointed to that
area and said, "This is our land." I told him, "Who came here? Who's the
crazy person who came to this place and owned the land?" He said, "My
father." And so Osama decided to have a portion there and we made a
place for horses and planted some trees.

He likes his father [Mohammed Bin Ladin] very much. He considered him as a model. He was not with his father much, because his father
died when he was ten years old. And also, the father didn't meet his children much. He was very busy—a lot of children, a lot of houses, so he
just met them officially. There are fifty-four children [25 sons and 29
daughters] and he had twenty-plus wives. Osama's mother is Syrian; he's
the only child from his mother and Mohammed Bin Ladin.

Osama heard a lot about [his father]. He's a person who built [his com-
pany] from nothing. He was not a person who sits down behind the desk
and gives orders. [Similarly] Osama, when he used to work with his
brothers in the company, he used to go to the bulldozer, get the driver
out and drive himself. [At that time] he was twenty-two. He never graduated [from university]. He just went to work with his family.

We [discussed] polygamy—late '70s we started to talk about it—and
we recalled how our fathers practiced polygamy. We found that they
were practicing it in a wrong way, where they are married and divorced,
married and divorced; a lot of wives and sometime they don't give equal
justice between all of them.

Some of those practicing polygamy will, if they marry the second one,
neglect the first one. That's not the Islamic way at all. You have to be fair,
you have to give equal justice between all of them, and you have to divide
the time, to give each one what is enough for her. And we look at
polygamy as solving a social problem, especially when it's confirmed that

there are more women than men in the society. So if everyone marries one wife, so it means that there are many women that are not married: So what they are going to do? They need a man. So this is the solution. So it's not fun. It's not a matter of just having women with you to sleep with— it's a solution for a problem.

So that's how we looked at it and we decided to practice it and to be a model. I never divorced; he also never divorced, except he divorced one [wife] because she didn't adapt herself to his life, so she decided to leave. That's the only one he divorced. So we really did it in, I thank God, a very good way. For myself, I'm really very happy with my wives. They are very happy with me. They love me. I love them all. I thank God I don't have a problem at all. Osama, I'm sure that he also doesn't have any problem with his wives. You imagine, now they are with him in his situation, so it means that he is really practicing this [polygamy] well.

It's hard to underestimate the impact that the Egyptian writer Sayyid Qutb had on Islamists around the world.[13] In his many books Qutb argued that Islam was not simply the traditional observation of the five pillars of Islam—the profession of faith, the Haj pilgrimage to Mecca, the giving of alms to the poor, fasting during Ramadan, and the five daily prayers—it was a whole way of life. Qutb's writings, which were widely distributed after his execution in Cairo in 1966, together with the Arab defeat in the 1967 war with Israel, provided much of the ideological underpinnings that shaped the emerging Islamic awakening in the Muslim world; the *Sahwa.*

Like the countercultural hippie revolution in the 1960s in the United States, which, of course, from an ideological perspective was profoundly different, the Islamic awakening shared one key feature: it was a movement of the young against an ossified establishment. And both the countercultural movement in the West and the Islamic awakening had revolutionary features because Qutb's writings not only explained that Islam was a whole way of being, they also contended that most Muslim governmental systems were mired in *Jahiliya,* a state of pre-Islamic ignorance and even barbarism. Qutb never named names in his writing. But what he wrote was clearly directed against authoritarian Middle Eastern regimes. So not only did Qutb profoundly influence the

Islamist movement in his beautifully written, massive masterpiece, *In the Shade of the Koran,* but in his much shorter polemic *Milestones,* he provided the handbook for jihadist movements across the Muslim world.

Jamal Khalifa, bin Laden's university friend, was a student when he started reading Qutb.

It was a tradition in my father's generation: They go to pray, and the understanding of Islam it's only the five pillars of Islam. So that's that generation before. This *Sahwa* [Islamic awakening] came and [it became clear that you] have a responsibility to advise others to reach Islam everywhere, to make the *Dawa* [preaching of Islam.]

In '76, '77 we used to read [Qutb's books] *Milestones* and *In the Shade of the Koran.* So Sayyid Qutb was concentrating on the meaning of Islam that it's the way of life. It influenced every Muslim in that period of time.

Mohammed Qutb [Sayyid Qutb's brother who was a visiting professor at King Abdul Aziz University in the late 1970s] used to give [myself and bin Laden] lectures. He was giving us very good lessons about education—how to educate our children.

In his 2001 autobiography, *Knights under the Prophet's Banner,* Ayman al Zawahiri, al Qaeda's second ranking leader, explained his intellectual debt to Qutb.[14]

Sayyid Qutb's call for loyalty to God's oneness and to acknowledge God's sole authority and sovereignty was the spark that ignited the Islamic revolution against the enemies of Islam at home and abroad. The bloody chapters of this revolution continue to unfold day after day. Sayyid Qutb played a key role in directing the Muslim youth to this road in the second half of the twentieth century in Egypt in particular, and the Arab region in general.

A passage from Sayyid Qutb's book *Milestones* explains that jihad must not only be defensive in nature, but it must also be waged offensively.[15]

As to the persons who attempt to defend the concept of Islamic jihad by interpreting it in the narrow sense of the current concept of defensive war . . . they lack understanding of the nature of Islam and its primary aim.

Essam Deraz explains that Qutb's execution in 1966 was a key impetus for the emergence of Islamic opposition to the Egyptian government.

When Qutb was executed everybody was sad, even people who didn't agree with him. People had suffered so much from socialism under [Egyptian dictator Gamal] Nasser's rule. [Qutb] rejected socialism and he rejected dictatorship. It came out in a religious form. His books are sold by the millions now.

Yeslam Bin Ladin, bin Laden's older half brother talking to Al Arabiya television on May 28, 2005, remembers that what marked the young Osama out was his religiosity.[16]

From a young age, many of us were sent overseas to study. I left for Lebanon at the age of six or seven, and returned only after graduating from university in America. Osama was one of those who did not leave Saudi Arabia. I think there were four or five brothers who didn't leave. [Between 1978 and 1981] I met Osama bin Laden three or four times. Osama was more religious than the rest of us. Those of us who went to Lebanon had other things on our mind. He did not like to listen to music or to watch TV, and he prevented his children from doing so. I thought that was odd.

Carmen Bin Ladin, the former wife of Yeslam Bin Ladin, writing in her 2004 book, *Inside the Kingdom*.[17]

One day, Yeslam's younger brother Osama came to visit. Back then he was a young student attending King Abdul Aziz University in Jeddah, respected in the family for his stern religious beliefs, and recently married to a Syrian niece of his mother's. Osama was perfectly integrated into the family, although he didn't live in the neighborhood where most of the Bin Ladens lived on the outskirts of Jeddah—at Kilometre Seven on the road towards Mecca, at the very edge of the desert. He was a tall man, despite the slightness of his build, and he had a commanding presence—when Osama stepped into the room, you felt it. But he was not strikingly different from the other brothers, just younger and more reserved. That afternoon, I was playing with [my daughter] Wafah in the hallway when the doorbell rang. I, stupidly, automatically, answered it myself, instead of calling for the houseboy.

Catching sight of Osama and his (adult) nephew Mafouz, I smiled and asked them in. "Yeslam is here," I assured them, but Osama snapped his head away when he saw me and glared back towards the gate. "No, really," I insisted. "Come in." Osama was making rapid back-off gestures with his hand, waving me aside and muttering something in Arabic, but I truly didn't understand what he meant. Mafouz could see that I was seemingly lacking in the basics of social etiquette, and he finally explained that Osama could not see my naked face.

In Saudi culture, any man who might one day become your husband is not supposed to see you unveiled. The only men who may look at you are your father, brother and husband, or step-father. Osama was among those men who followed the rule strictly. So I retreated into a back room while my admirably devout brother-in-law visited my husband. I felt stupid and awkward.

Jamal Khashoggi is a Saudi journalist who knew bin Laden when he was living in Jeddah.[18]

Osama was just like many of us who become part of the [Muslim] Brotherhood movement in Saudi Arabia. The only difference which set him apart from me and others, he was more religious. More religious, more literal, more fundamentalist. For example, he would not listen to music. He would not shake hands with a woman. He would not smoke. He would not watch television, unless it is news. He wouldn't play cards. He would not put a picture on his wall. But more than that, there was also a harsh or radical side in his life. I'm sure you have some people like that in your culture. For example, even though he comes from a rich family, he lives in a very simple house. He had no appreciation of art. He sees art as contrary to a Muslim. [He lived a] very simple, basic life. [He] doesn't attach himself to extravagant [or] to good living.

Khaled Batarfi, bin Laden's close childhood buddy, explains that his friend was not anti-American as a young man; in fact, he owned a Chrysler car that he crashed at some point. Batarfi even says that bin Laden visited the United States on a brief trip shortly after he was first married, an account that has not been independently corroborated.[19]

Did you know he went to America? He took his son Abdallah because Abdallah had problems with his head; it was deformed, so he took him for a medical trip. He was telling [me] about when people looked at him, his robes and his wife. [They were] taking pictures of them, so sometimes he joked about this.

Even after his marriage, for a year or so he was still living in his mother's house. Later on, after he got his first child, it seems like it was too tight a place for him, especially since he was planning to marry another woman. So they moved to a building in the Al Aziziyah district. He gave each wife an apartment. I visited him once, and I saw that they were bare apartments. I mean, I wouldn't live there myself. Very humble.

We weren't as close as before, especially [because] he went on to join King Abdul Aziz University and I was still in high school. And then he was involved with his family business. That's the way the bin Ladins are. They study and work, all of them, all the people I know, but he was different because he used to work with his own hands, go drive tractors and like his father eat with the workers, work from dawn to sundown, tirelessly in the field. So he wasn't the rich boy.

He was responsible for some project in Mecca for the bin Ladins, and he used to go from dawn to sundown; he works hard—really hard. And then, he would be busy at nights doing social activities, visiting friends, meeting with his families, and at night, he would be doing prayer. He would sleep then wake up a few hours later and do more prayers. This is optional. It's just following the example of the Prophet. And then he would sleep a couple of hours and wake up for morning prayer and then start his day. So it must have been tough for him.

He moved later to Medina to be a supervisor of bin Ladin projects in al Medina [the second holiest site in Islam]. And there he has a farm and he married a woman from al Medina and lived for a few years there until [he moved to] Afghanistan.

Bin Laden was twenty-two years old when Juhayman al Utaybi and several hundred Islamist militants seized the Al Haram mosque in Mecca, the holiest site in the Muslim world, on November 20, 1979. King Fahd conferred with Saudi religious leaders and, after several weeks, ordered the mosque retaken. Saudi security working with French special forces did so, and sixty militants were later publicly beheaded. Bin Laden subsequently reflected on this event, which seems to have precipitated an early distrust of the Saudi regime.[20]

[King] Fahd defiled the sanctity of Al Haram [the holy mosque in Mecca]. He showed stubbornness, acted against the advice of everybody, and sent tracked and armored vehicles into the mosque. I still recall the imprint of tracked vehicles on the tiles of the mosque. People still recall that the minarets were covered with black smoke due to their shelling by tanks.

The picture that emerges of bin Laden in this past chapter is of a shy, pious, even priggish, young man admired by friends and family alike for his piety, but at the same time regarded, even within his own family, as someone who was a little bit *different*. However, during this period there was little to suggest that he was anything more than a hardworking scion of the bin Laden family whose only quirk was his intense religiosity.

That would all change after the Soviet invasion of Afghanistan in late December 1979.

2

The Afghan War

The Soviet invasion of Afghanistan in December of 1979 was a profoundly shocking event for bin Laden, as it was for thousands of other devout young Muslims from around the world, who were drawn to the Afghan jihad during the 1980s. It was the first time since World War II that a non-Muslim power had invaded and occupied a Muslim nation. Indeed, for bin Laden it was the most transformative event of his life, uncoupling him from his tranquil domestic life of work and family in Saudi Arabia, and launching him into what would become effectively a full-time job helping the Afghan resistance.

A key to this transformation was bin Laden's encounter with the charismatic Palestinian cleric Abdullah Azzam. Azzam was the critical force both ideologically and organizationally for the recruitment of Muslims from around the world to engage in the Afghan struggle against the Soviets. Azzam would become bin Laden's mentor and together they would found the Services Office in 1984, an organization that was dedicated to placing Arab volunteers either with relief organizations serving the Afghan refugees who had flooded into Pakistan after the Soviet invasion of their country, or with the Afghan factions fighting the Soviets on the frontlines.

Osama bin Laden in 1977 to CNN.[1]

The news was broadcast by radio stations that the Soviet Union invaded a Muslim country; this was a sufficient motivation for me to start to aid our brothers in Afghanistan. In spite of the Soviet power, God conferred favors on us so that we transported heavy equipment from the country of the Two Holy Places [Saudi Arabia to Afghanistan] estimated at hundreds of tons altogether that included bulldozers, loaders, dump trucks and equipment for digging trenches. When we saw the brutality of the Russians bombing the mujahideen positions, by the grace of God, we dug a good number of huge tunnels and built in them some storage places.

In 1982, around the time that bin Laden was starting to do something about the plight of the Afghans, I was a student at Oxford. With a couple of university friends, George Case and Barney Thompson, we decided to make a film about the refugees then pouring out of Afghanistan. Six million Afghans had been forced out of their country by the Soviets, creating the largest refugee population in the world. About half were in Pakistan, and half were in Iran.[2]

We knew little about filmmaking (particularly myself) but our ignorance of the actual difficulties of doing such a project provided a spur to getting the project completed. In the summer of 1983 myself and my two colleagues set off to Pakistan with an Afghan cameraman who was based in London. He proved to be a somewhat difficult person, given to titanic tantrums. I took these volcanic displays of temper to be normal professional behavior. In fairness to our cameraman, we knew next to nothing about making documentaries, working in Pakistan, or the Afghan jihad. We would get a crash course in all of those subjects during the several weeks we spent in the North West Frontier Province and Baluchistan, regions of Pakistan that border Afghanistan.

We documented the lives of the Afghan refugees there and the generosity of their Pakistani hosts who had taken them in with little complaint on the basis that they were brothers in Islam. The subsequent documentary, *Refugees of Faith,* was shown on Britain's Channel 4 in 1984.

At one point during our research we traveled into Parachinar, a region of Pakistan that sticks like a finger into Afghanistan, from which the mujahideen would often begin their travels into the war zone. There we were greeted by more than a hundred cheering fierce mujahideen from one of the seven Afghan factions battling the Soviets. The whole experience made a powerful impression on me and would launch me down the road to meet bin Laden almost a decade and a half later, not far from the place where I had first set eyes on the Afghan mujahideen.

Hutaifa Azzam is the son of Abdullah Azzam, bin Laden's mentor during the mid 1980s. He first met bin Laden through his father, Azzam, in Saudi Arabia.[3]

Anyone who wanted to know anything about Afghanistan connects with my father. They met in the summer of 1984 in Jeddah. Their relationship was very strong.

I was very close to Osama. I still remember him driving a Land Cruiser, desert color in 1984; he took us to his farm forty kilometers from Jeddah. We used to go there for hunting, whatever we find in the desert.

He's really nice to his kids; treating them like they are friends. He was teaching them how to be tough, how to be a *mujahid* [holy warrior], trying to grow them up on jihad, on jihad thinking, and trying to build their bodies for this mission. I never saw him shouting at his kids, hitting his kids. Even his wives, they never say that he has treated them bad. I can say his wives, they like him so much.

We're brothers in Islam and we were very close to him. We used to stay in his house in Wadi Bisha Street in Al-Aziziyah District in Jeddah. He had a building with four flats for the three wives and one for the guest. It's very simple, building—you can't believe that these guys are millionaires.

Jamal Ismail was studying engineering in Pakistan in the early eighties when he met the Palestinian cleric Abdullah Azzam. He would also meet bin Laden on a number of occasions throughout his later career as a journalist.[4]

Sheikh Abdullah Azzam came in September '81 as a lecturer, from King Abdul Aziz University in Jeddah to Islamic University in Islamabad [Pakistan's capital].

Abdullah Azzam was a religious scholar. He was committed to his belief and very strict in religious affairs. He used to be popular among Arab religious scholars, especially [among] members of the Muslim Brotherhood. He was the one who introduced the Afghan issue to all Muslims.

[Azzam] started his contacts with one of the Afghan mujahideen groups while he was residing in Islamabad in the university up to the summer of '86 when he quit the university. During the period from '81 to '86 he was a visitor to Peshawar [the headquarters of the Afghan mujahideen in Pakistan].

In the summer of '84, when Azzam went for Hajj [pilgrimage to Mecca], at that time he wrote the fatwa [religious ruling] "Defending

Muslim Lands." Azzam announced that this fatwa was signed by late Sheikh bin Baz, the grand mufti of Saudi Arabia, and some other religious scholars from Saudi Arabia, Syria, and Yemen.

Abdullah Azzam, from his 1984 book *Defense of Muslim Lands*.[5]

Defensive Jihad: This is expelling the Kuffar [infidels] from our land, and it is Fard Ayn, a compulsory duty upon all. It is the most important of all the compulsory duties and arises in the following conditions: if the Kuffar enter a land of the Muslims.

We have to concentrate our efforts on Afghanistan and Palestine now, because they have become our foremost problems. Moreover, our occupying enemies are very deceptive and execute programs to extend their power in these regions. The people of Afghanistan are renowned for their strength and pride. It seems as if the Glorified and Exalted prepared the mountains and the land there especially for jihad. The Afghan people say: "The presence of one Arab among us is more loved by us than one million dollars."

Pay close attention to the hadith [sayings of the Prophet Mohammed]: "To stand one hour in the battle line in the cause of Allah is better than sixty years of night prayer."

Jamal Ismail, the journalist.

Azzam came [to Pakistan again] in the fall of '84. He started his Services Office and he started calling Muslims from America, from Europe, and from Arab countries to come and join the [Afghan] mujahideen.

Jamal Khalifa was bin Laden's close friend in university in the late seventies. Khalifa later went on to marry bin Laden's half sister Sheikha in 1986. He fought against the Soviets and later worked with the Muslim World League to help Afghan refugees.[6]

Osama invited me to his house in al Aziziyah [in Jeddah]. He has a building there, he was twenty-five, twenty-six, he's already married a couple of times. He told me that Abdullah Azzam [was coming]. I knew Abdullah Azzam from his books. He's a very good writer and he's real educated so I was really very eager to hear him when he started to talk about Afghanistan.

Dr. Abdullah Azzam, I can really call him the Koranic person because when you heard him reciting the Koran, it's really different than anybody else. It's coming from his heart. It's a matter of the feeling, the way how he's reciting it, it's totally different. And sometimes he's forgetting himself when he's reciting the Koran. He is a person who has light so you will be influenced immediately; immediately any person will meet him, he will love him. He's unique.

After I met with Abdullah Azzam I went one time to Afghanistan in '84 and I came back and I went back again in '85.

Hutaifa Azzam, Abdullah Azzam's son.

The first time I went into Afghanistan was 1984 [when I was thirteen]. At that time, I spent two months in Sada training camp and took antiaircraft training. In 1985, we went to the camps for six months and in 1987 was the last time we went to the camps.

Boudejema Bounoua is an Algerian, known as Abdullah Anas, who was one of Abdullah Azzam's first Arab recruits to the Afghan jihad.[7]

[In 1984] I found a newspaper that said a group of *ulema*—religious scholars—are saying that Afghanistan is occupied by the Soviet Union and they are going to cancel Islamic life and replace it with atheism. In this situation they [the *ulema*] explained the fatwa, that if one meter of land of Islam is under occupation, it's the duty of every Muslim to liberate it. [That fatwa was] signed by the group of ulema. Among them was Abdullah Azzam.

So I decided to go to Afghanistan. I had no idea at all where Afghanistan is, how to go there, which language they speak, which airlines go there—a hundred questions. I had decided to go to Hajj pilgrimage [in Saudi Arabia], but I went with this idea, if I find a way to go to Afghanistan, I will go.

Once I was walking around the K'aba [the sacred site at the center of Mecca] and I found Abdullah Azzam with his children and his wife. I asked him, "Are you Abdullah Azzam? I've read the fatwa. I'm from Algeria and I saw your signature among the *ulemas* saying that jihad in Afghanistan is a duty. And if I decide to go, what can I do?"

He told me that after fifteen days, I would be in Islamabad [the capital of Pakistan]. "If you come to Islamabad, just call me from the airport and I will give you the address to come to my home." I took the flight. I found Sheikh Abdullah. And he told me: "There is a group of guests here in my house. We will wait for you to have dinner with us." One of them was Abdullah Saadi. He was the constructor for Osama bin Laden. He was an engineer to guide the bulldozers. Osama borrowed him from the [bin Ladin family] company to work for him in Afghanistan.

The second day, Sheikh Abdullah told me, "I'm going to Peshawar after three days. We will go together." The flight was at 4:00 p.m. and around 1:00 p.m. we were having lunch. Somebody was sitting on my right and Sheikh Abdullah told me, "This is your brother, Osama [bin Laden]." I told him, "Welcome. Nice to meet you." I remember the guy who was introduced to me—very shy and very, very well-mannered. Speaks very slowly. After one hour in that meeting, I can't remember that I heard two or three words from that guy Osama. He was [in his mid-twenties].

I'm the fourteenth of the Arabs [who arrived in Pakistan to help the Afghan jihad]. It was a very small group and all of us were under the control of Sheikh Abdullah Azzam. Sheikh Abdullah has this reputation to push people. That's what he did with Osama later. He sees what talent you have, journalist or organizer or fighter. Sheikh Abdullah was really an angel inside.

Late '84, beginning '85, the founders of the Services Bureau [also known as the Services Office] were Osama, Sheikh Abdullah, and me. Sheikh Abdullah told me that "We have found this bureau to gather the Arabs and to send them inside Afghanistan instead of going to the guest-house of [someone like Afghan leader Gulbuddin] Hekmatyar. It's better to save them from the political games of the Afghans. So we need to stay in a separate guesthouse. We are here as servants. We are proud to serve the boots of the mujahideen inside Afghanistan. We are not here to guide them, to tell them what to do. We are here to serve them, to liberate their land."

It's one of our aims to get deep information about what is happening inside Afghanistan. I told Sheikh Abdullah I would like to go with this caravan to Mazar-i-Sharif [in the far north of Afghanistan]. We were maybe three hundred Afghan mujahideen and that trip took forty days walking. I lost my toenails on the way. And [when the villagers] hear that among the caravan there was an Arab, all the village's people come out of their home to see this Arab because they remember that the Arabs speak the language of the Prophet; they came from the land of Mecca and Medina.

We started learning [the local language] and we found it very, very necessary. When we used to cross the villages, the people would come from everywhere and they used to ask us to give speech in the mosques. When we would speak, people just crying, *"Allahu Akbar!"* [God is Great!] Hundreds of people would come, some of them from three hours away, bringing their grandson or granddaughter. The feeling which I used to touch, up to now I can't find it anywhere. I used to feel that I am an angel. I am walking in the air. I'm doing my duty, making my God happy, helping brother Muslims, and no pressure of life, sitting with the Afghans. These simple people all were loving the Prophet, all loving Koran, making jihad to liberate land. Very exciting in a positive way.

We stayed in Mazar-i-Sharif for two months. I think these months give me the experience of five years; pushed me to act in a responsible way. I decided that our participation in Afghanistan was not just to take a Kalashnikov [rifle] and to fire on the Soviets and be *shaheed* [martyred] and that's it. This is a very, very, very small part of our duty. I recognized that these people needed to be educated; these people needed to stay at their home, not to be refugees to Pakistan. In order to do that, you had to fund salaries for the *ulema* [clergy] to stay inside Afghanistan, and you needed to build schools, you needed to build hospitals.

When I went back to Peshawar, I went to Sheikh Abdullah. He was eager to welcome a group who had come from deep inside Afghanistan. Sheikh Abdullah told me, now you have to go to the Hajj [in Saudi Arabia] with me. Sheikh Abdullah saw it as useful and beneficial to bring me to Saudi. [I went in 1985.] We stayed in Mecca. And Sheikh Abdullah used to give speeches because in that period he was the star of jihad. Every year people were waiting for Abdullah Azzam, what statement is he going to give when he comes to Saudi Arabia? Sheikh Abdullah finished his speech, and said, "We have a young man with me who just recently came from Mazar-i-Sharif, the furthest front inside Afghanistan, and he saw exactly what is happening inside Afghanistan. I call him to come to the stage to speak." I couldn't. Too shy.

And so we spent three or four days there, and we lived in the house of Osama in Mecca. The entire bin Ladin family were hosting people. And they had food and buses to take people. And Osama was very polite in his dealings and very generous.

Wael Julaidan, a Saudi from a Medina family involved in real estate, was a student in the United States as the war in Afghanistan heated up in the mid-eighties. Julaidan's account illustrates the effectiveness of Abdallah Azzam's recruiting tours.[8]

I lived in Jeddah for three years from '81 to '83. Osama, we see him from time to time in our social activities, but then in '85 in Pakistan, that's when I went I start to create some relationship [with him]. We were all there to serve the Afghans. For such a power like the Soviet's Red Army to come and attack such a poor country like Afghanistan, everybody was unhappy. [Osama] was so much feeling responsibility toward the Afghan issue and he wanted to extend whatever help he can to the Afghans.

Sheikh Abdullah Azzam had given that issue a lot of effort, to show how this invasion could be dangerous to all the region. And he also came to the States in December '84 and he talked about Afghanistan. I listened to his lecture. He talked about how much people there are in need of everything and I felt the responsibility at least to go and visit there [to see] if I can be of any help. Finally, I decided to visit Afghanistan. That was in April '85. I was twenty-eight.

I was doing my Master's degree at that time, in range management—developing the range for animal grazing—at the University of Arizona in Tucson. I was really appreciating the American system, the respect for the individual and the freedom we had been given, the chance to talk about anything that we are interested in.

I came to Saudi Arabia, visited my family, and then I went to Pakistan. I found that the size of the problem—it's so big, so large, and that's why I agreed with Dr. Azzam, I would like to mainly concentrate on relief work. So from '85 to '94 I lived [in Pakistan].

A key project of Azzam and bin Laden's Services Office was the *Jihad* magazine that the organization started publishing in the fall of 1984. The Arab language magazine appeared monthly carrying news of the war in Afghanistan and a focus on Arab efforts to help the Afghan jihad. Over time the magazine became increasingly professional. In its first six months the magazine was an amateur production in black-and-white, while subsequent issues were well laid out and featured a wealth of color photographs. The magazine proved to be vital for fund-raising and for recruiting Muslim volunteers from around the world for the Afghan jihad.

In the summer of 2004 I was browsing in a bookshop in central Kabul, looking for books about jihadist movements, when I was approached by the owner Shah Muhammad Rais. As I was chatting with him I realized that he was "Sultan Khan," the central character in *The Bookseller of Kabul*. It was an international bestseller that portrayed a man who had heroically saved thousands of books from destruction by the Taliban, yet who treated much of his own family harshly, particularly his first wife, whom he had recently displaced with a much younger new wife.[9]

Khan took me into a dusty back room piled high with mounds of books and pointed to a dozen or so volumes bound in gold, green, and brown. "That," he said, "is ten years of the *Jihad* magazine." As I leafed through thousands of pages of the Arabic-language magazine I realized I had stumbled upon a gold mine. This was effectively the in-flight magazine of the Services Office, an organization that would morph, in part, into al Qaeda, and in these pages was a decade of their own history as they recorded it contemporaneously.

Jamal Ismail, a Palestinian student living in Pakistan during the 1980s, was one of the first journalists to work for *Jihad* magazine.

In 1984 I was a student in Peshawar Engineering University. My studies were all in English. The Arabs, none of them were able to speak or read English. They asked me to help them in translation of some news items from the Pakistani daily newspapers, some news which they used to get from the Afghan groups. We were receiving the news [from Afghanistan] in a magazine called *al Mujahid* [the Holy Warrior]. When it stopped [publishing], Sheikh Abdullah Azzam picked up the idea and changed the name from *al-Mujahid* to *al-Jihad*. Initially, the first one, two, three, or fourth issues, was printed on a printing press in Peshawar.

Extracts from *Jihad* magazine will appear throughout this book, the first time that it has appeared in English.
***Jihad* magazine, Issue 1, December 28, 1984, lead article.**

To the Supporters of Jihad.

To all the supporters of the Jihad on Earth. We remind you that the Afghan Jihad is a necessity for the Muslims, even if the number of Russian enemies and others are double your number. And, in God's name, you will defeat your enemies. Because one of you is superior to ten of your enemies, and even in the worst case, you are double them.

The call to Jihad in God's name is a part of this Earth and it is the satisfaction of the conscience. And it leads to eternal life in the end, and is relief from your earthly chains.

Abdullah Anas, one of the cofounders of the Services Office.

The main aim of Sheikh Abdullah in creating the *Jihad* magazine was to inform the Arab world what is happening in Afghanistan; informing them, help funding, recruit people. [Eventually we printed] seventy thousand copies [an issue]. Most of them go to the United States because we had fifty-two centers in the United States. The main office was in Brooklyn, [also] Phoenix, Boston, Chicago, Tucson, Minnesota, Washington DC, and Washington State. Every year [Azzam] used to go to United States. The wealthy of the United States can help much more than Muslims who are living in poor countries or under dictatorship.

***Jihad* magazine, Issue 29, April 1987.**

To Our Community in America.

The magazine is receiving a warm welcome from Muslims in the United States, and so the magazine is looking to increase its circulation in a massive way. This is done with the help of God and our good brothers who assisted in making this happen. And they have tried their best to make sure circulation increases to anyone who is interested in knowing the latest news about their Mujahideen brothers.

Due to increased demand from the United States, we will be sending them our magazines from our office in the United States by the 31st of the month—God willing—and we hope that our brothers who are interested in subscribing will send their request to our American office whose address is on page 3, so that the magazine can be received more quickly, God willing.

And we ask all our brothers who are able to help support the magazine's efforts to increase its readership. And we ask Islamic centers also to help us in this endeavor, as well as to ask God to bless us and look after us.

Jamal Ismail.

I think after the issue 25 or maybe 30 [*Jihad* magazine] was printed in Lahore. After that we shifted printing to Karachi for commercial reasons, because instead of bringing it from Lahore by truck, we were sending it abroad from Karachi directly. Mostly, it was circulated in Saudi Arabia, Kuwait, United Arab Emirates, Jordan, the United States, and some European countries. There were some subscribers in northern Africa. It was available in all the markets in Saudi Arabia. It was not expensive. The magazine was not commercial. The main purpose is to tell Muslims all over the world what is happening in Afghanistan and to generate funds for Afghan mujahideen.

Initially, we were four: the editor, the typist, me, and someone who was going on a motorbike to bring the news from here and there. Sheikh Abdullah Azzam asked us to make it better. We were in need to recruit more people. Sheikh Abdullah Azzam started campaigning for the magazine among the Arabs, saying that if you work for the magazine inside Afghanistan, maybe in the eyes of Almighty Allah, your achievements will be more important than carrying a Kalashnikov [rifle].

***Jihad* magazine, Issue 27, February 1987, "Jihad . . . Not Terrorism," by Abdullah Azzam.**

Thanks be to God and we thank him and ask him for his help and forgiveness. Every time the word Jihad is mentioned, sin springs up and runs away. And every time the Muslims talk about defending their rights, the Western Media comes in and libels the name of the Muslims, and portrays them as extremists and beasts.

Maybe the Muslims forgot the wars that occurred in the last century between France, Britain, and other European countries. And maybe the Muslims forgot the hardships of two world wars, created by the West and lasting twenty-five years, which killed fifty million people, and left people injured, maimed, and wounded. It was a gruesome war, built on greediness and small hopes. And maybe the Muslims are not aware of the cultural war being waged on them to libel the name of Jihad, in order to portray the Muslims as bandits and bloodthirsty warriors, and in order to make the Muslims leave Jihad, and so they create stories about killing hostages so that they can portray Muslims as killers.

America is the New World leader, or better yet, a country that has built its empire on the backs of its original inhabitants [the Native Americans] who they wiped out and who now number less than a million, who have been put into little reservations as if they were museum pieces. And they still use kerosene lamps instead of electricity in the Midwest. And those were the red Indians who were the original inhabitants of America. We are not ashamed of our religion or the order given to us by God. We say it frankly without playing with words or deception. Plain and straight:

1. That Jihad is a religious duty for the Umma [Muslims around the world], so as to free the people and give them Islamic justice and protection of the religion.
2. That the religion of God and the blessed religion is that of all of humanity, and we want to spread it all over all four corners of the world.
3. Jihad in God's will means killing the infidels in the name of God and raising the banner of His name. And we do not want to make this great Jihad only words to be said on podiums, or articles to be published in newspapers. Jihad is done in the will of God only if you fight the infidel with the sword until he submits to Islam.

And nothing is left to block you from the Afghan Jihad.

Abu Walid al Misri is a confidant of bin Laden's who wrote a history of the Afghan Arabs, those Arabs who traveled to support the Afghan jihad.[10]

Jihad magazine was among the most important projects established by Azzam. This magazine was the main means of communication between Arab youth in various places and the Jihad network in Afghanistan. The intellectual edifice built by Dr. Azzam through this magazine is still the supplying factor for the migrating Arab volunteers, most of them from Saudi Arabia, the Gulf states, and Yemen. These volunteers have traveled the fields of jihad [around the world].

A sense of *Jihad* magazine's global distribution can be found in this list of cover prices from an issue in late 1989.

Country	Price	Country	Price
Afghanistan	R 20	Kuwait	Fils 500
Algeria	AD 3	Lebanon	L 5
Argentina	NP 70	Libya	PS 50
Austria	SH 30	Malaysia	M$ 3
Bahrain	FHs 500	Morocco	D 8
Bangladesh	Ta 20	Nigeria	N 1
Belgium	FR 100	Oman	Fils 500
Brazil	CR $2,500	Pakistan	Rs 15
Canada	C$ 3.00	Philippines	Pp 20
Cyprus	Ms 400	Portugal	ESC 150
Denmark	Dkr 15	Qatar	Ris 5
Egypt	EF 1	Singapore	S$ 3
France	FF 5	South Africa	R 1.50
Germany	DM 4	Spain	Pts 150
Greece	Dr 90	Sudan	SF 1
Hong Kong	HK 15	Sweden	Kr 15
India	Rs 10	Syria	SF 5
Indonesia	R 15	Tanzania	Shs 16
Iran	Ris 1	Thailand	BT 40
Iraq	Fils 500	Tunisia	Tu 600
Italy	L2,500	Turkey	TL 120
Japan	¥ 500	UAE	DH 5
Jordan	F 300	UK	P 1.25
Kenya	Sh 20	USA	$2.60
Saudi Arabia	R 5		

The following comments in *Jihad* magazine, Issue 68, June 1990, indicate how widely distributed it was in the United States.

FROM THE OFFICE OF SERVICES OF THE
MUJAHIDEEN IN AMERICA
The office would like to thank every Muslim who has supported the Jihad in spirit, monetary contributions, and good words that has shepherded this religion and its defense of Muslim lands. And we would like to thank and wish God's praise upon the Islamic Centers and the devoted brothers that work in them. And in addition, we would specifically like to thank these centers among many others—Michigan, Georgia, Florida, California, Texas, Missouri, New Mexico, Arizona, New Jersey, and Tennessee.

So stay with us, our Muslim brothers, in spirit, financially, with your good words, your valuable advice, and your opinions, with your prayers and with all your heart and soul.

Contact us . . . consult with us . . . we are at your service.
Letters should be addressed to the following:
Al-Kifah Refugee Center
552 Atlantic Avenue
Brooklyn, NY 11217, U.S.A.

OR:
1085 Commonwealth Avenue, Suite 124, Boston, MA. 02215
P.O. Box 95244 Atlanta, GA. 30347
P.O. Box 157889 Chicago, IL. 60615-7889

Jihad Magazine, Issue 81, August 1991, "With a Young Cadet" [a regular feature of the magazine].
This interview conducted with a five-year-old boy shows how the militants based in Peshawar encouraged even young children to embrace jihad.

Q: What is your name?
A: Saleh.

Q: What is your family name?
A: Sayf al Rahman.

Q: What is your country of origin?
A: Palestine.

Q: How old are you?
A: Five years old.

Q: Do you go to school?
A: I go to Hadana Al Ansaar School and the Center for memorizing the glorious Koran in Peshawar.

Q: Who do you like?
A: I like God and Muhammad, the messenger of God, praise be upon him, and I like my mommy and daddy and the mujahideen.

Q: Trivia question—the Stinger missile is used against what?
A: Airplanes!

Q: And rocket-propelled grenades?
A: Against guerrillas!

Q: What is the name of the weapons held by the defender?
A: Kalashnikov!

Q: And after you kill the Communist infidels in Afghanistan, what next?
A: I want to go with daddy and the mujahideen to Palestine and fight the infidel Jews.

In 1991 Basil Muhammad, a Syrian journalist, published *Al Ansar al Arab fi Afghanistan,* "The Arab Volunteers in Afghanistan." For his authoritative account Muhammad interviewed key Afghan Arab leaders during the jihad against the Soviets. According to Muhammad's book, bin Laden ventured into Afghanistan for the first time in 1984. Bin Laden explained to Muhammad:[11]

I feel so guilty for listening to my friends and those that I love to not come here [to Afghanistan] and stay home for reasons of safety, and I feel that this delay of four years requires my own martyrdom in the name of God.

Like many others who met bin Laden in this period, the Palestinian journalist Jamal Ismail did not find the young Saudi, now in his mid-twenties, to be particularly striking.

Coming to Peshawar on a visit in 1984, I was in the office of *Jihad* magazine and we were having prayer there. Osama came and we met him—Mr. Osama bin Laden, one of the main financers of the Services Office. I was at that time twenty-three. He did not talk so much—"Hi, how are you? How is everything? From where are you?" Just a few sentences. We offered prayers and then he left. [He was] maybe twenty-seven. Not a big impression. He was a little bit quiet. He did not talk much.

I knew from the beginning that [bin Laden] was not willing to drink any soft drinks from American companies, Pepsi, Coca-Cola, Sprite, 7-Up. He was trying to boycott all American products because he believed that without Americans, Israel cannot exist.

Sheikh Abdullah Azzam was praising [bin Laden] so much in every speech, praying for him, for his family. According to Abdullah Azzam, when they started the Services Office, Osama agreed to finance the presence of fifty or sixty Arab families, anyone who was chosen by Sheikh Abdullah Azzam.

Faraj Ismail, an Egyptian journalist who covered the Afghan jihad for the *Al Muslimoon* newspaper, also did not find bin Laden to be of any particular significance during this period.[12]

My newspaper focused on Islamic movements. At the time the Afghan jihad was looked on positively, and it was happening at the same time as there was an Islamic revival in the Muslim world. I met with Abdullah Azzam in Jeddah, Saudi Arabia, and I met bin Laden at the same time, in 1985. I was living in Jeddah at the time. In 1986 at the *Muslimoon* newspaper the main issue was the Afghan jihad. Bin Laden used to visit our offices in Jeddah. He had no leadership charisma and a weak voice.

I remember a discussion with Azzam when someone asked him, "You are Palestinian, shouldn't you be fighting in Palestine?" He said, "This is an experiment [fighting the Soviets in Afghanistan] that will allow us to create a generation of young men. If it succeeds they will go on to Palestine."

Azzam was always smiling a lot, not a gloomy person. The relationship between bin Laden and Azzam was the relationship of a student to a professor. I felt that Azzam was the religious reference for bin Laden. Bin Laden read Azzam's books. The writings of Azzam were very inspiring to young men including bin Laden.

Vahid Modjeh is an Afghan who worked at the Services Office in Peshawar during the eighties. He too remembers Azzam completely overshadowing the younger bin Laden.[13]

I was working in the translation office, translating mostly religious books. The main office was in University Town [a suburb of Peshawar]. The first time I saw bin Laden I thought he looked very similar to [the late Saudi] King Faisal; he has a narrow face. At the beginning I thought he was a Saudi prince. At that time he was not an important person in the jihad. I never heard bin Laden delivering a speech in Peshawar. He was not considered clever or intelligent. Azzam, on the other hand, was a powerful speaker, and a declaimer of poems. Azzam met bin Laden in Saudi Arabia and completely held sway over him in the mid-eighties.

Around the time a young Osama bin Laden first ventured into Afghanistan, Arab volunteers were beginning to engage the Soviets. "Together on the Road," by Abdullah Azzam (_Jihad_ magazine, issue 4, March 22 1985) provides an account of perhaps the first Arab to be killed.

Every time I visited the camps I would meet a young, just man who was mingling with the Afghans, helping them, and benefiting from every minute of his life. I asked about him from the people around me, and they told me that Abu Hamza was the first Arab Muslim to mix with the

Afghans and to live among them, and the harsh life they lived. I would see him, in the house coming to serve us with tea and food. He would serve us, and sit respectfully, and wait for us to eat and finish so that he could clean up after us.

And so Abu Hamza died, like lightning. He was a dear brother, a true martyr, and a reserved man. Martyrdom is a high honor that God will not bestow upon someone unless they deserve it. You passed away quickly, and you left us brokenhearted, and you received the joy of meeting God.

Jamal Ismail, the Palestinian journalist.

Arabs started growing in numbers in Peshawar after '84 and '85. Hundreds of Arabs started coming from different affiliations; from Muslim Brotherhood, from Jihad groups in Egypt. Saudi Arabia was announcing even some incentives for its citizens—75 percent discount on Saudi Airlines for anyone who wants to join the mujahideen.

Jamal Khashoggi, a Saudi, was the first journalists from a major Arab media organization to cover the Afghan jihad.[14]

Altogether, I don't think the [number of] Arab mujahideen [during the jihad against the Soviets] at one time ever exceeded two thousand, three thousand. But altogether, people who spent six years and people who spent six days, maybe the number will come up to ten thousand. Because there was even jihad tour. Jihad vacation.

Abdullah Anas was one of the cofounders of the Services Office.

Up to '84 we were thirteen Arab mujahideen. By the end of '85, it was up to 90 or 100. So then the peak came between '87 and '89. We're not more than 3,000 to 5,000. The people who were inside Afghanistan active permanently, no more than 10 percent, 300, 400, 500 people. But 90 percent were teachers, cooks, accountants, doctors [over the border in Pakistan].

We had the three categories [of recruits]: People who did not speak Arabic, from Malaysia, Indonesia, India, Burma, the Philippines. Normally they were really poor. The other kind of people came from the non-Gulf area. Algeria, Egypt, Morocco, people normally between middle-class and a little bit poor. The wealthy people were from the Gulf area, Kuwait, Emirates, Saudi. Most of the mujahideen were Saudi. They had money and sometimes they used good hotels, good restaurants. Some of the Saudis used to come and go as a trip, as a holiday. Most of them are coming for the holidays, but Islamic holidays. For example, rich people, instead of going to Switzerland, would go spend a few days or weeks with the Afghan refugees; sharing their suffering, bringing some clothes, some money.

Abdullah Azzam's speaking tours and magazine brought contributions and volunteers to the jihad against the Soviets. Azzam's powerful rhetoric would resonate among young Muslims across the Arab world and further afield. The following is the lead article by Abullah Azzam in *Jihad* magazine, issue 3, March 22, 1985.

To All Muslims in the World.

In the name of God the merciful.

To my dear brothers. Peace be upon you. I was hoping I could be able to convey this to you in person, but since we could not meet in person, I would like to convey my feelings so you can share our passion, that encompasses our life and our work.

Dear brothers, God was kind to me when I visited the fighters attacked by the Russians. And thank God that the Russians were badly defeated in this battle. They lost seven hundred men whereas the Muslims lost only seven martyrs. And thank God that Russia tried, but did not succeed, to block even one road connecting Pakistan with Afghanistan used by the Mujahideen.

My brothers, The Afghan Jihad is at the crossroads. It lacks the resources, and we have been asking for a long time for help from Muslims to come forward, and only a few have responded.

My brothers, the door is still open and the chance is still available to implement God's religion in the land of Afghanistan. If the Afghan Jihad fails, God forbid, then all the Muslims will be responsible for this failure. And also they will be responsible for the loss of this golden opportunity that is unprecedented. We missed the opportunity in Palestine, and now it may be lost in Afghanistan. The historical responsibility is great and time is not on our side.

Other authors, including the unusual case of a woman named Khawla Bint al Azoor also used powerful language to win recruits to the Afghan war. The following is her article in *Jihad* magazine, issue 29, April 1987.

To the young men, I urge you in the name of God the powerful, and in the name of the Prophet, to raise the flag of Islam as our ancestors did in the beginning of the religion. We all have learned that Islam began weak, and gained ground little by little, until it spread from East Asia to Western Europe. This was done through the holy Islamic Jihad, which raised the name of God high.

Oh ye young men wake up, and realize the Soviets and the Red Army desecrate Islamic land and destroy it. Yes, they carry out acts in the pure land of Afghanistan, that are against our Islamic beliefs. I urge you, oh young men, to undertake Jihad and martyr yourselves beside your Afghan brothers who are fighting against oppression. I only wish I could give my life and my spirit as a gift to this pure land as a martyr. But I am a girl and not able to do anything.

Essam al Ridi is an Egyptian pilot who was one of the earliest Arab recruits to the Afghan jihad. He testified in early 2001 in the New York trial of four men accused of playing a role in al Qaeda's attacks on the two U.S. embassies in Africa in 1998. The following extracts from his testimony illustrate the powerful impact of a speech delivered by Abdullah Azzam in Texas. (Conversely, arriving in Pakistan, al Ridi treated the still-minor figure of bin Laden with suspicion.)[15]

I was born in Cairo, Egypt, 1958. I moved to Kuwait and stayed there for the next 23 years. I went to Karachi, Pakistan, [to] study engineering [in 1976]. There was civil unrest in Pakistan so they closed the universities for a month. I could not stay any longer. I resolved to come to the States and finish my aviation [training], which was always my desire. [In 1979] I went to Texas, a school by the name of Ed Boardman Aviation School.

Must have been 1982 or '83 I'm not sure, but it was the MAYA convention. Muslim American Youth Association. I was helping in organizing part of the convention since I resided in Fort Worth [Texas] where the convention was held. [Abduallah Azzam] was one of the guest speakers. He spoke about jihad in Afghanistan. He indicated to Muslims attending the convention that it is an obligation upon Muslims to help in any way they could to help the Afghan jihad.

1983. I went to Pakistan. We met Sheikh Abdullah [Azzam], spent the night at his house. The following morning we went to Peshawar to meet Abdul Rasool Sayyaf, who at the time was the leader of the Afghanis. It was very important to me to make sure that my help will be actually needed to the extent of residing in Peshawar, rather than just giving them some help from the States. So I had the liberty to ask Sayyaf himself.

[I was] basically traveling and getting [the mujahideen] items that they needed: range finders, night vision goggles and night vision scopes. I bought the range finders from England. The scuba diving equipment also from England. The night vision scopes were from the U.S.

I was one of the people invited to special meetings with Sheikh Abdullah to organize the work of the Arabs and the visitors in Peshawar. One of the main sticking issues was I was totally opposing the fact that any rich individual [such as bin Laden] would control the decision making. I don't think he have the experience to be involved in the day-to-day running of the business in Afghanistan. I was very much opposed to that and my voice was very well heard out. But nobody really acted on it. I think I was right and I took a stand on that.

Jamal al Fadl is a Sudanese member of al Qaeda who testified for the prosecution at the same New York trial. Edited extracts of several days of his testimony, which took place in early February 2001, are included throughout this narrative. In this extract he describes the impact of reading Azzam's _Jihad_ magazine that encouraged him to travel from the United States to Afghanistan.[16]

[During the 1980s] I lived in Atlanta, Georgia, North Carolina [and] Brooklyn. I work for grocery and food market; I work for Farouq Mosque [in Brooklyn]. At that time they help Afghans during the war against Russia, and we tried to help them bring money from the Muslim brothers in New York. It's part of [the] Services [Office] in Peshawar.

'87 when I work in Brooklyn the [Jihad] newspaper come, and that time we know who is bin Laden. At that time I work in Farouk Mosque and they tell me go to Afghanistan. I work in grocery and two guys came and start talking, tell me come to the mosque, there [is] lecture something about Afghanistan. They tell me about the fatwa [to go to Afghanistan] I say, "Well, that's a good idea, because Abdullah Azzam make lecture in *Jihad* magazine, and we read the magazine in Brooklyn, and we see, well, this is fatwa." Fatwa means when the people tell you [to go] the jihad in Afghanistan means you have to leave everything and go.

Our Emir (leader in Brooklyn) Mustafa Shalabi tell me we need you and other brothers to go to Pakistan and Afghanistan to help the brothers over there. He made the tickets and the visa for us and give us some money. We went to Karachi Airport, and from there we went to Peshawar and we stayed in hotel for two nights. We went to the hotel for two days and somebody come, he give us a little lecture about jihad. We went after that to the guesthouse and they give you nickname. Nickname mean when you go inside Afghanistan you not going to use your true name.

We went to Khalid ibn Walid camp with other brothers and the camp is for training new people. I got training for regular weapons, like the Kalashnikov, RPG (rocket-propelled grenade). It's a weapon used against tank and against helicopter. They teach you how to use it and they give you chance to fire it. They got math to tell you if the tank go 20 miles an hour, that means you [aim] 200 meters in front of the tank. Because helicopter goes faster than tank, if the helicopter go 200 miles an hour, that means you need 2,000 meters in front of the helicopter.

I met [bin Laden]. He talk about the Soviet Union army come to Afghanistan and kill people and we have to help them, and you have to be patient, you have to follow the rule of the emir (leader). I work with bin Laden nine years.

The training takes forty-five days. I went to the guesthouse Bait al Ansar (House of the Supporters) and after that we went to Miran Shah City. It's the border between Pakistan and Afghanistan. We spend one night, and the next day we went to the camp. It's in Khost area. We went to Jihad Wal camp. We got general training about how to use explosive, TNT and C4.

Mektab al Khidmat is [the Services] Office run by Dr. Abdallah Azzam and Abu Abdallah, Osama bin Laden, and it helps the new people when they came to Afghanistan help the Afghani people against Russia. This office helps them for training and gives them some money and some support. The office in Farouq Mosque [in Brooklyn], it's branch of Mektab al Khidmat (Services Office). In beginning, they worked together because Abdullah Azzam, he runs office, and bin Laden; he gives them the money for that, for running the Mektab al Khidmat. But later on they split.

Jamal Khalifa, bin Laden's university friend, describes his impressions of the Afghan war and his marriage to bin Laden's half sister.

In '85 I went to Jaji [a military camp in eastern Afghanistan]. It was in a jungle. I woke up early morning start to go around the camp. At that time I really had the impression that those people they don't need fighters. They need a lot of education. Yes, I came to die, actually, but at the same time, my understanding, the goal—it's not to be a *shaheed* [martyred]. The goal is to help. It's not a matter to be killed.

We saw the [Afghan] refugees in Pakistan. You know the emotions, the feeling that you are coming for a noble cause, you are helping your brothers, you are going to do the same what you read about the Prophet and his Companions, what they used to do. It's emotional, but it's kind of a good feeling. All that period of time, we were really flying; life it had a meaning.

The first [wife] I married was at university. Then the second was Shaikha, Osama's sister. She is very close to Osama because she is religious and he is religious, and they are the two [most] religious [people] in the family. And she is alone; she doesn't have a brother from her mother, so he was really taking care of her.

[It was] at Osama's suggestion; we were really very close off and on. I love him very much. When we decided to work in Afghanistan, early '85, he told me, "What if you marry my sister, Shaikha?" I told him, "Osama, we are going to war. We are going to die and you're asking me about marriage?" He insisted and I told him, "Okay, look, If I came back and did not die I will do it."

So imagine how close we are. We never disagreed about anything, we were always together, always laughing, always going out together. This person, you're forced to respect him. He would never raise his voice. You would never hear from him anything bad. He would force you to love him from his attitude and the way he is dealing with you.

In 1986 I married [Shaika bin Laden.] The family of my wife did not accept [my old] house. So Osama has his villa where he's in the ground floor, his mother on the second floor. He divided that house by two, even the kitchen; half for me, half for him, and he built a wall and separated [us]. He has his [first wife] Um Abdallah [the mother of Abdallah] with him. Abdallah also was an infant at that time. [Bin Laden later married] Um Ali from the Sharif family. They are descended from the Prophet. And then Um Hamza from the Sabar family.

Abdullah Anas recalls what seems to be one of the few jokes told by his friend bin Laden.

[Osama] told stories, not only religious ones. Osama had his own jokes [for instance] saying, I don't understand why people take only one wife. If you take four wives you live as a groom. With a small group he has a sense of humor.

Beginning in 1986 bin Laden's close relationship with his mentor Abdullah Azzam would gradually fray as the young Saudi militant millionaire was becoming preoccupied with personally fighting the Soviets on the frontlines rather than simply supporting the activities of the Afghan mujahideen.

Jamal Ismail, the Palestinian journalist.

Abdullah Azzam was having the idea that we have to work under Afghan mujahideen, because we have to support their unity. He was dealing with them in Peshawar more and more. Osama was dealing with the frontline people more, because in '85, '86 Osama was spending most of his time on the Afghan frontline with commanders, especially [the Afghan] general Jalaluddin Haqqani in Khost [in eastern Afghanistan].

Abdullah Anas, the Algerian cofounder of the Services Office.

We passed through stages of coalitionship with Osama. Osama used to love Sheikh Abdullah [Azzam] and he loved mujahideen and loves jihad. He ate what we ate; slept in what we sleep in.

We became very [good] friends, because Osama is very, very well brought up. We were working under the leadership of Sheikh Abdullah as a group, and people who loved Sheikh Abdullah and obeyed his orders and his policy are automatically the Arab family. And the relationship between us and Osama, it went deep year by year and month by month. It's really friendly, intense. So this Osama, in this period, my judgment, he's just an angel.

The second part of [our relationship with] Osama is when he started in '86 to take distance from Abdullah Azam, but not in a rude way, or in an unacceptable [way]. Externally [the relationship] seemed very fine. Very, very few people [knew otherwise], no more than five or six people. We were not allowed to say it. In that period, Sheikh Abdullah did continue his policy without consulting Osama and Osama continued on his own way.

I think Osama started to believe in himself. [He was] twenty-eight. He wasn't happy with the group very close to Sheikh Abdullah. We were not under his orders.

Our relationship as a friend continued, but our relationship as a colleague of work completely stopped.

Khalid Batarfi, bin Laden's childhood friend, continued to encounter bin Laden when he would return home to Saudi Arabia during the 1980s. By this time Batarfi had started his career as a journalist.[17]

He invited me every time he saw me to go to jihad in Afghanistan. And he was telling me that, "You don't have to fight with your gun. You can fight with your pen. Come as a journalist and write about us. I'll grant you access to anybody you need. And you go to any area you want to." I was reluctant. Once I decided to go, but then my son was born, so— there was always something. Maybe three times he asked me and each time I failed [to go]. Then he stopped asking.

[I noticed a] gradual change [in him]. He became more assertive, less shy, more talkative. He [started] making speeches [in] mosques and gatherings.

That change happened as bin Laden was developing from the retiring, rich young man who was supportive of the Afghan jihad into someone who would soon resolve to form his own military force to fight the Soviets.

3

From Donor to Holy Warrior

War changes men. The Afghan war certainly changed bin Laden. The humble, young, monosyllabic millionaire with the open checkbook who first visited Pakistan in the early 1980s would, by the middle of the decade, launch an ambitious plan to confront the Soviets directly inside Afghanistan with a group of Arabs under his command. That cadre of Arabs would provide the nucleus of al Qaeda, which was founded in 1988 to wage jihads around the Muslim world.

Bin Laden's military ambitions and personality evolved in tandem. He became more assertive, to the point that he ignored the advice of many of his old friends about the folly of setting up his own military force. That decision would also precipitate an irrevocable (but carefully concealed) split with his onetime mentor, the Palestinian cleric Abdullah Azzam.

Between 1986 and 1987 bin Laden established a base near a Soviet garrison in Eastern Afghanistan for several dozen of his Arab fighters, located near the village of Jaji in eastern Afghanistan, about ten miles from the Pakistani border. The base was known as *al Masada,* the Lions' Den. From this base, bin Laden fought a military engagement with the Soviets during the spring of 1987. This was a critical turning point in his career, when he left behind his former role as a donor and fundraiser for the mujahideen and launched his career as a *muhjahid* or holy warrior.

Bin Laden's decision to found his own military force was an odd one. Informed estimates of the number of Afghan soldiers fighting the Soviets at any given time vary between 175,000 and 250,000.[1] By contrast, the largest number of Arabs fighting the Soviets inside Afghanistan at any given moment amounted to no more than several hundred.[2] To assemble those fighters in one force did not make much sense from a military standpoint, as they could not possibly have any strategic impact on the war. Indeed, despite bin Laden's subsequent hyperventilating rhetoric, his "Arab Afghans" had no meaningful impact on the conduct of the war, which was won with the blood of Afghans and the billions of dollars and riyals of the United States and Saudi Arabia.

Abdullah Azzam was opposed to the idea of a separate Arab military force because he saw the presence of Arabs scattered throughout all of the Afghan factions functioning as morale boosters who could simultaneously teach the Afghans about Islam, aid them with education and medicine, and bring news of the Afghan jihad to wealthy donors in the Middle East. A single Arab military force would end this effort, and in any event could have no impact on the conduct of the war.

Bin Laden saw matters rather differently. He believed that an Arab military force would stand its ground against Soviet attacks because his recruits were eager to martyr themselves, unlike the Afghans who had a much more pragmatic approach to fighting. They might leave the battlefront if they faced serious opposition, or sometimes simply because they had to go home to their villages to plant fields or to attend weddings and funerals.

Bin Laden felt that his Arab force could deliver an important psychological victory for the Afghans and the entire Muslim world if it stood up to the Soviets. To some degree that happened because bin Laden's stand against the Russians at Jaji in 1987 was lionized not only in *Jihad* magazine, but also in the mainstream Arab press, turning bin Laden into an authentic war hero, and providing a boost to recruitment efforts for Muslims around the world to come to the Afghan jihad.

Jaji would be bin Laden's first brush with publicity, and over time the shy millionaire would increasingly come to appreciate the spotlight. But the battle of Jaji was only a public relations victory, no more. It was not a battle of strategic significance to be compared with Ahmad Shah Massoud's resistance to several major Soviet offensives against his stronghold in the Panjshir Valley in the 1980s.

At the same time that bin Laden was building up his small military operation in Jaji he was also growing closer to the militants of Egypt's Jihad group, first to Abu Hafs and Abu Ubaidah, who fought with him at Jaji, and later to Ayman al Zawahiri, at that time working in Peshawar as a surgeon.

Jihad **magazine, issue 53, April 1989. (In this period bin Laden
was generally known as Abu Abdallah, the father of Abdallah, his oldest son.)**

When Abu Abdullah [bin Laden] created "Masada al Ansar" [the
Lions' Den of the Supporters] a young man called Abu Hanifa joined it
and was very pleased by this group. Abu Abdullah [bin Laden] asked him
to represent the group [in Saudi Arabia] and to preach about the Lions'
Den. Therefore a group of young men departed [from Taif in Saudi
Arabi for Jaji]. This was the first year of the inception by Abu Abdallah of
the Lions' Den [in 1986]; and this was very hard for the souls because it
started during the winter; and snow covered the mountains; and you
could not even go out during the sunny days because the cold was
stronger than the sun's heat.

**Jamal Khalifa, bin Laden's closest friend from university, was not im-
pressed by his plans to set up a military operation right next door to a
Soviet military post at Jaji. Not only did Khalifa know that bin Laden
had absolutely no military experience, he was also concerned that his
friend was sending idealistic young Arabs to the Afghan frontlines on
kamikaze missions. He confronted bin Laden inside the Jaji base in
1986.[3]**

I decided to go myself to see what's going on there. I stayed three days
in the *Masada*. I started to ask the people how it's going. They said every
day we have plenty of *shaheeds* [martyrs]—people dying. I said "Why?
They are not trained and they are very young. They don't have experience and they are facing the Soviets. It's not a joke."

Then I went to Abu Ubaidah; he was the chief of staff [for bin Laden].
I asked Abu Ubaidah: "Is this the right place to have this kind of camp
everybody can see?" He said, "No." I said, "You are a person who knows
the danger of this place." I was really very angry. You know, in Islam—
blood, it means something. You can throw away the Koran, but not drop
the blood of a person.

So I said, "Okay, I am going to face Osama." So I sat down with Osama
in his tent. I told him "Osama—everybody is against this idea, why you

are here? Don't you know that this is very dangerous?" He said, "We came to be in the front." I said, "No, we did not come to be in the front. We came to [act as supporters of the] Afghans." I told him, "Every drop of blood bleeds here in this place; God will ask you about it in the here-after. Everybody is saying this is wrong, so Osama, please leave the place right now." Everybody was hearing our argument, our voices become hard. I was really very angry; this is our first time to be like this. I told him, "Look, you will leave the place or I will never see you again." He told me, "Do whatever you want." So I left.

Demonstrating the zeal of a fanatic, bin Laden told the Syrian journalist Basil Muhammad that he hoped his new base would draw heavy Soviet firepower.[4]

God willing, we want the Lions' Den [in Jaji] to be the first thing that the enemy faces. Its place as the first camp visible to the enemy means that they will focus their bombardments on us in an extreme manner.

Hasan Abd-Rabbuh al-Surayhi was an early Saudi recruit to the jihad in Afghanistan who joined bin Laden in the *Al-Masada* near Jaji. He recalled that experience when he was interviewed by Hasin al-Banyan of the *Al Sharq al Awsat* newspaper in the fall of 2001.[5]

Those who were going for jihad [from Saudi Arabia to Afghanistan] were many [in 1987]. When I went to buy my ticket to Islamabad, I realized that many had preceded me to the reservations office. There were about twenty young Saudis from various cities on the same flight. I found out that conditions in Peshawar airport were different from the first time [that I went to Afghanistan for jihad]. This time, I saw individuals greeting and welcoming the seekers of jihad. They were facilitating their entry and providing them with transport buses. [Leading this effort] was Abdullah Azzam.

I had heard about him [bin Laden] but I did not ask any questions about him. At the time, he was known by his alias of "Abu-Abdullah." I found out that he was inside Afghanistan and not in Peshawar like Abdullah Azzam. [After I left Azzam's camp] I went to the fighting fronts inside [Afghanistan]. We saw that there was only one camp for the mujahideen. It was called "Camp Al-Madinah" and bin Laden was its amir (leader). When we arrived there, bin Laden was not there. This camp had started with only five individuals: Osama bin Laden and four of his schoolmates. We then joined them. As more and more young Saudi mujahideen began to arrive, the number of the camps also rose and then they gave the whole area the name of "Al-Masada" (The Lions' Den").

I went to meet him (bin Laden) with other young men from Taif [in Saudi Arabia] and he introduced himself to us. He addressed us as follows: "We want this site to be only for the Saudi mujahideen and not for anyone else. We want to stay away from anything that might harm our reputation and the reputation of our families as Saudi mujahideen." I liked what he said.

Jamal Ismail.[6]

Osama and some others were having the idea—let's liberate one area and after that do liberation of other areas one by one. Jaji was chosen because of its geographical location—close to Parcahinar (a finger of Pakistani territory that extends into eastern Afghanistan).

Edward Giardet was one of a handful of Western reporters who repeatedly traveled into Afghanistan during the 1980s.[7]

Bin Laden had an operation going up in Jaji. I actually walked by the construction often. This would have been '87, '88. I saw bulldozers, which were bin Laden's bulldozers. They said they were building an underground hospital. It was more substantial than that.

Ahmad Zaidan reported on the jihad in Afghanistan for _Al Sharq al Awsat_ newspaper.[8]

[Bin Laden's] personality as a businessman: he's calculating each and every thing. The psyche of businessman is not like the psyche of others. He was very much organized and he was very much calculating things. And that's why he brought some heavy machinery to make bunkers and roads to help mujahideen because he was of the view that if there are good caves, if there are good bunkers, so there will be good jihad.

Abu Walid al Misri is an Egyptian close to bin Laden who has written a book about the "Arab Afghans," excerpts of which were published in *Al Sharq al Awsat* in December 2004.

Bin Laden built roads and hospitals and started fortifying a chain of mountains on the front lines that restricted the enemy's positions. Consequently, the warning bells rang in Kabul to start a large-scale Soviet operation to mop up the region and recover it. A tough battle took place, and the Soviet special forces reached *al Masada* (the Lions' Den). But they could not consolidate their position for a long time. The Soviets lost many soldiers. Some of them were killed by the Arabs during close confrontations, ambushes, and smart and daring encirclements led by Abu Hafs and Abu Ubaidah [two of bin Laden's key Egyptian allies who would later take prominent positions in al Qaeda.].

Jihad magazine, issue 31, June 1987, "With Our Four Automobiles against the Warsaw Pact." [An article about the battle of Jaji.]

Beginning the night of Ramadan, the enemy tried to take over, but every time they tried, our men hit them with weapons. And they tried again for another hit with their commandos, but we hit them with our rocket-propelled grenades. And we saw them retreating with our telescopes. Russia lost many of their well-respected commandos to the mujahideen.

Hutaifa Azzam, then in his mid-teens, was with his father, Abdullah Azzam, and bin Laden as they battled the Soviets at Jaji. Abdullah Azzam was perfectly happy to take on the Soviets personally, despite his later opposition to bin Laden's plan to set up his own separate Arab military force to fight the Communists.[9]

Father was there, bin Laden was there, and my brother-in-law was injured. He was kept in the hospital for more than fifteen months. The mountains [surrounding Jaji] were like a jungle. The airplanes were dropping bombs: [containing] napalm. One and a half tons of bombs, every five or ten seconds, and after one month, you couldn't find a single tree on those mountains. After more than one week of bombarding that area the Russian special forces started coming. We were waiting. The Afghans left the area and seventy Arabs [stayed].

We got some prisoners. Some Russians were killed. All the Afghans started talking about the Arabs and the bravery of the Arabs defending that area. We lost seventeen Arabs in one battle.

Essam Deraz, an Egyptian writer and filmmaker, covered the battle in Jaji in 1987. He explains that Jaji was the making of bin Laden.[10]

I went to Afghanistan in 1986. I knew that some Egyptian journalists visited before me. But they went as journalists; you know, two weeks, make interviews, and visit places. I am different. I want to live the question. Write from inside. I must go to the camps of refugees to sleep with them, to eat like them. I must [be] with them, and attack with them. I went about five times and every time for between three or four months.

They picked the site at Jaji because it was on the front lines. In '87, it was a very important battle. The Arab group fought against Russian commandos. Not more than fifty or sixty young Arabs, twenty-one, twenty-two- [years old]. Most of them students at the universities. [Bin Laden] fought in this battle like a private. The Russian bombing went on for one week.

They discovered that Russian commandos were encircling them. Abu Hafs and Osama decided to come out of the *Masada* [Lions' Den]. The Russians thought they were all dead.

Two or three months [I was] with him daily under the bunker, fighting. It was clear now he'd be the leader. I was near him in the battle, many months, and he was really brave. That's why he got respect from Afghans and Arabs.

Khalid Khawaja, a former Pakistani Air Force officer, fought with bin Laden.[11]

In 1987 I participated in the Jaji battle. I was introduced to Abu Abdallah [bin Laden]. First of all he's not a genius. He was thirty when I met him. He prayed a lot, always smiling. As a personality I never thought he would make a place in history; he is not charismatic. He is not very intelligent, but he is the most dedicated and self-sacrificing person to a degree that is unparalleled. He would spend money like water. No one sacrifices like him. [At the time] he did not love publicity; he used to hide himself.

Jihad magazine, issue 53, April 1989, "The Martyr Abu Khalil." This entry gives a sense of the difficult conditions the mujahideen faced in Jaji.

He stayed a whole year in the *Masada* (the Lions' Den) and everyone that visited *Masada* could see the struggle of staying there for even four months. The snow was covering the earth face, and the mujahideen could not even see the sun at midday because of the cold. They were putting water in plastic bottles and would wake up and see them frozen. In this environment where the body extremities were freezing Abu Khalil swore not to go down. Abu Khalil burned the enemy's back with projectiles. And the mortar was his musical instrument.

Wael Julaidan is a Saudi who was present at the battle of Jaji.[12]

When that big attack came from the Soviets on Jaji [bin Laden] was alone there [without the help of the Afghans] and he believed that by staying there, by resisting that attack that area has been saved [from the] the Soviets. And that's when everybody started to know about Osama, that he confronted this attack and defended Jaji. We were all there at the beginning of the fight. But that took twenty-two days, the fight. So Osama was there until the end and he came out with a victory. That made him think forward more—what is next?

Basil Muhammad, the Syrian journalist, interviewed bin Laden after the battle of Jaji. Bin Laden recalled the battle.[13]

At 7 a.m. on the 27th morning of Ramadan 1407 (April 1987) most of the people were sleeping in the camp because it was Ramadan. Then, I saw things that by God I have never seen before. A Soviet airplane, a MIG I believe, passed by in front of us, when a group of our Afghan Mujahideen brothers grouped together [and attacked]. The plane then broke to pieces as it fell right in front of our eyes. This battle is what gave me the strong will to continue with this war.

For bin Laden it would not have been a coincidence that this key battle took place on the 27th of Ramadan, an especially sacred day in the Muslim calendar, known as *"Lailat al Qadr,"* the Night of Power. Muslims believe that on this day is when destiny is decided and the gates of heaven are opened and Allah will listen to the lucky ones. It is praised in the Koran: *"Lailut al Qudr* is better than a thousand months. The angels and the Spirit descend therein, by the permission of their Lord, with all decrees. [The night is] p]eace until the rising of the dawn." [14]

Jihad **magazine, issue 53, April 1989, explained that accounts of the Jaji battle were a tremendous recruiting device for Arabs drawn to the Afghan jihad.**

After the victorious battle of *Masada* [in Jaji] in 1987 the youths started coming in waves. The number of young Arabs arriving in Afghanistan was getting much bigger.

It was during the period of the Jaji battles in the spring of 1987 that bin Laden discovered for the first time the power of the press to burnish his image as a holy warrior. One of the first journalists from the mainstream Arab media to cover bin Laden was Jamal Khashoggi, a Saudi.

Khashoggi was studying in the United States as the Afghan war intensified during the early eighties. [15]

I was introduced to political Islam and I become an activist in a sense. It was after 1980, with the Iranian revolution and the rise of Islamic awareness throughout the world. I was still living in Terre Haute (Indiana) at that time and I begin to attend Islamic conferences and meetings. I met [Abdullah Azzam] in the States once. Seven months after my graduation [from college in Indiana] I ended up in working in a [Saudi] newspaper. I was about twenty-four or twenty-five. I was religious at that time.

In late '87 I had a scoop. I was invited to write about the role of Arab mujahideen in Afghanistan and I liked the idea. It was Osama [who invited me]. I knew him slightly in Jeddah. We are from the same generation, same background. I went to Peshawar and then I traveled inside Afghanistan with him to Jaji area. [I found a] very enthusiastic bunch of Arabs who believe in what they are doing, very proud of what they are doing. I interviewed Osama.

Khashoggi published an article, titled "Arab youths fight shoulder to shoulder with Mujahideen," in the Saudi magazine *Al Majallah,* on May 4, 1988. An English version of the article was also published in *Arab News* on the same day. Excerpts from that story follow.[16]

As many as 1,000 Arab youths are in Afghanistan. They are actively involved in the war and activities such as teaching, medical service, and relief work. Most come from Saudi Arabia, Egypt, Yemen, Syria, Algeria, Libya, and Morocco. Some of the Arab Mujahideen are from affluent families. For example, Osama Benladen, known as Abu Abdullah, is a famous Saudi contractor and comes from the renowned Saudi business family of that name.

Abu Abdullah decided to contribute his experience and capabilities to the Mujahideen and he played a vital role in the construction of Maasada camp, home to mainly Arab Mujahideen in Afghanistan. The Russian and Afghan government forces launched a fierce attack [on the camp] at the end of May [1987] and its effects can still be seen throughout the region. A massive number of trees and all plants in the vicinity were burned in extensive bombing and missile attacks for three weeks.

Describing the harrowing situation during these days, Abu Abdullah said: "We sometimes spent the whole day in the trenches or in the caves until our ears could no longer bear the sound of the explosions around us. War planes continually shrieked by us and their crazy song of death echoed endlessly. We spent the days praying to God Almighty. Despite the massive Russian onslaughts, one of us had to come out from our shelter regularly to see the enemy's movements."

When the attack abated or the mujahideen received word from their observation centers that Russian and government forces were approaching, they attacked them. "Three attacks were made during a period of three weeks, and each time we were able, by the grace of God, to inflict a crushing defeat on the Russians," Abu Abdullah said.

During this bitter campaign some seventy Afghan Mujahedeen and thirteen [Arab] supporters fell martyrs. They stand in mute testimony to the sacrifices which must be made if Afghanistan is to win back its freedom.

[Abu Abdullah] is optimistic about the mujahideen achieving a great victory in the next campaign, since they are now equipped with more weapons and better facilities that ever before. However, Abu Abdullah noted that their numbers and supplies are nothing compared to the well-equipped Russian forces. "It was God alone who protected us from the Russians during their offensive last year. Reliance upon God is the main source of our strength and these trenches and tunnels are merely the military facilities God asked us to make. We depend completely on God in all matters."

As the Afghan war intensified, bin Laden's boyhood friend Khaled Batarfi remained in touch with bin Laden's mother. He explains her growing concerns about her son, especially after bin Laden supposedly suffered the effects of a Soviet gas attack some time in the late 1980s.[17]

The situation became worse when [Osama] went to jihad [in Afghanistan]. In the beginning, it wasn't for jihad, it was going there just to support, so that was starting to worry his mother, and then he decided to become a fighter and his mother—oh, God, it went from bad to worse. And then she heard about the gas, the chemical gas Russians used against mujahideen, and her son was affected. Since then, she was [watching] TV and [listening to] radio, waiting for bad news.

Jamal Ismail, the Palestinian journalist who worked at *Jihad* magazine, says that during the mid-1980s bin Laden was careful to distance himself from more radical Arab elements in Pakistan who opposed the ruling regimes of the Middle East.

In '86 when [Saudi] King Fahd visited Britain, he was given a medal like a cross by Queen Elizabeth. Many scholars in Saudi Arabia, they say he wears that cross, which is prohibited according to our teachings of

Islam and whoever wears this cross declares himself a non-Muslim. And some people [in Peshawar] they were saying it is a cross which represents the British ideas about Christianity and therefore [King Fahd] is not Muslim.

[Osama] asked all of them, "For God's sake, don't discuss this subject. Concentrate on your mission. I don't permit anyone to discuss this issue here." He was not criticizing the leadership of Saudi Arabia [at that time].

Indeed, bin Laden maintained cordial relations with the Saudi government during this period. Prince Turki al Faisal, the director general of the Saudi General Intelligence Directorate, met bin Laden on several occasions in Afghanistan and Pakistan during the Afghan jihad. In November 2001, Jamal Khashoggi, then deputy editor-in-chief of *Arab News,* interviewed Prince Turki, excerpts of which follow.[18]

When jihad started in Afghanistan, I used to travel to Pakistan and sometimes to Afghanistan to follow up on the developments. It was there that I met him [bin Laden]. Once or twice he was invited to the Saudi Embassy [in Islamabad]. The first time I met him was during one of these occasions. [He was] a gentle, enthusiastic young man of few words who didn't raise his voice while talking. [We discussed] the condition of the mujahideen and what he [bin Laden] was doing to help them. I did not know him thoroughly enough to judge him or expect any other thing from him. His behavior at that time left no impression that he would become what he has become.

As you know, at that time there were many volunteers, Saudis and non-Saudis, and he [bin Laden] was one of them. He did not enjoy special status that made us focus on him. We had no information that he had contacts with any foreign government agencies [such as the CIA], except the Pakistanis.

Allow me to take a quick detour here to discuss the question of the CIA's complicity, or rather lack thereof, in the rise of bin Laden and the Afghan Arabs. The agency directed around three billion dollars to the Afghan mujahideen during the war against the Soviets, but there is no evidence that any of that money went to the Afghan Arabs, nor is there

any evidence of CIA personnel meeting with bin Laden or anyone in his circle. However, the notion that bin Laden is a CIA creation, and that the 9/11 attacks were some form of "blowback" from the CIA operation during the Afghan jihad is a boilerplate analysis among leftists and conspiracy theorists around the world.

The Indian novelist Arundhati Roy, for instance, has written that bin Laden was "among the jihadis who moved to Afghanistan in 1979 when the CIA commenced its operations there. Bin Laden has the distinction of being created by the CIA."[19] The American filmmaker-author-blowhard Michael Moore similarly believes, "WE created the monster known as Osama bin Laden! Where did he go to terrorist school? At the CIA!"[20] The theory that bin Laden was created by the CIA is invariably advanced as an axiom with no supporting evidence. The real problem is not that the CIA helped bin Laden during the 1980s, but that the Agency simply had no idea of his possible significance until the bin Laden unit was set up within the CIA in January 1996.[21]

Since 9/11 al Qaeda insiders have responded to the erroneous assertions that the CIA had some kind of relationship with bin Laden.[22]

Ayman al Zawahiri, from his autobiographical *Knights under the Prophet's Banner,* published in December 2001:[23]

The truth that everyone should learn is that the United States did not give one penny in aid to the [Arab] mujahideen. Is it possible that Osama bin Laden who, in his lectures in the year 1987, called for the boycott of U.S. goods as a form of support for the Intifada in Palestine, is a U.S. agent in Afghanistan?

Abu Musab al Suri, long an associate of bin Laden's, released a 1,500-page book titled *The International Islamic Resistance Call,* which was posted on the Internet in November 2004.

It is a big lie that the Afghan Arabs were formed with the backing of the CIA, whose minions were bin Laden and Azzam. The truth is that Saudi intelligence agencies did have involvement with bin Laden, and elements of their apparatus did send assistance from Saudi Arabia. Yet the accusation that bin Laden was an employee of the CIA [is false.]

Hutaifa Azzam, Abdullah Azzam's son.

You could say that bin Laden separated from my father in 1987. Bin Laden said that he wanted to make special camps for the Arabs only, where we can start our own jihad and we give the orders. We will gather all the Arabs in Afghanistan in one area in Jalalabad [in eastern Afghanistan]. My father was against that. He was shocked.

So in 1987 Osama decided to separate and create special camps and special forces for the Arabs. Osama decided to move all of his troops into Jalalabad. [The question was] how he could transfer his troops there? There is no way from Pakistan. That's impossible.

At that time he started opening the road with bulldozers from Jaji to Jalalabad; it goes directly through the mountains of Tora Bora. [It took him] maybe six to seven months to build this road. Only four-wheel drives could drive on it.

This seems to be the first time that bin Laden became familiar with the mountains of Tora Bora. The half-year he spent building the road through the Tora Bora mountains in 1987 would be knowledge that would serve him well almost a decade and a half later when he fled there after the fall of the Taliban in November 2001.

Wael Julaidan, who headed the Saudi Red Crescent Organization in Pakistan in the mid-1980s, was also a key player in the Services Office.[24]

Abdullah Azzam was insisting that we were only here to help the Afghans. I'm saying the same thing—always trying to remind Osama that we are here to solve the Afghan issue. He felt that he can do more. One day in Peshawar we meet together and we try to solve this problem. Abdullah Azzam made it very clear: "You are there to serve the issue through the Afghans. There is no other agenda."

Jamal Ismail, the Palestinian journalist.

Osama was not having any involvement in the Services Office since late '87 or maybe early '88. In '88 his financial support for Services Office was stopped by mutual understanding between him and Abdullah Azzam.

Osama was willing to contribute and finance anything which is related to jihad which means "fighting." Services Office by '87, '88, it was becoming more of an NGO [nongovernmental organization]. They were having a printing press in Peshawar. They were helping with orphans and schools, mosques and dispensaries. Osama wanted to put all his wealth and financial support for fighting inside Afghanistan.

It was not an accident that bin Laden's split from Abdullah Azzam began around the time of his first meeting with Dr. Ayman al Zawahiri in 1986. For bin Laden, the slightly older, cerebral Zawahiri likely presented an intriguing figure. Zawahiri had first joined a jihadist group at age fifteen and had by 1986 recently served three years in Egypt's notorious prisons for his jihadist activities. So, Zawahiri was far more experienced politically than bin Laden.[25] For Zawahiri, bin Laden likely also presented an interesting opportunity: someone who was on his way to becoming a genuine war hero, whose deep pockets were well known.

In 1987 Zawahiri was setting up his own jihadist group, which within a couple of years was being supported by bin Laden. At the same time Zawahiri increasingly turned bin Laden against Abdullah Azzam and also aligned him with the hardline Islamist Afghan leader Gulbuddin Hekmatyar, the bitter rival of the Afghan commander Ahmad Shah Massoud. In short, the late 1980s marked the beginning of the symbiosis between bin Laden and Zawahiri that continues to this day.

Jamal Ismail.

In '86 [Ayman al Zawahiri] came to Peshawar for a few months. They met at a function which was organized by a Kuwaiti Charity Organization and Osama was asked to deliver a sermon there, and when Ayman Al-Zawahiri listened to bin Laden he introduced himself to bin Laden, and that was the first meeting.

Ayman al Zawahiri, from his 2001 autobiography, *Knights under the Prophet's Banner*.

I remember that [bin Laden] visited us in those days at the Kuwaiti-funded Al Hilal Hospital in Peshawar and gave us lectures.

My connection with Afghanistan began in the summer of 1980 by a twist of fate, when I was temporarily filling in for one of my colleagues at Al Sayyidah Zaynab Clinic [in Cairo]. One night the clinic director asked me if I would like to travel to Pakistan to contribute, through my work as a surgeon, to the medical relief effort among the Afghan refugees. I immediately agreed because I saw this as an opportunity to get to know one of the arenas of jihad that might be a base for jihad in Egypt and the Arab region, the heart of the Islamic world, where the basic battle of Islam was being fought. I left for Peshawar, Pakistan, in the company of a colleague who was an anesthetist. We were soon followed by another colleague who specialized in plastic surgery. We were the first three Arabs to arrive there to participate in relief work among the Afghan refugees.

When Zawahiri returned to Egypt from Pakistan he was imprisoned with three hundred other militants in the wake of the assassination of the Egyptian president Anwar Sadat on October 6, 1981. His experience in prison would radicalize him.[26] Zawahiri recalled the torture inflicted on the imprisoned militants.

The treadmill of torture and repression turned at full speed, writing a bloody chapter in the history of the modern Islamic movement in Egypt. The brutal treadmill of torture broke bones, stripped out skins, shocked nerves, and killed souls. Its methods were lowly. It detained women, committed sexual assaults, called men feminine names, starved prisoners, gave them bad food, cut off water, and prevented visits to humiliate the detainees. The treadmill of torture has devoured thousands of victims since the killing of Sadat.

Zawahiri's command of English and uncompromising stance made him a spokesman for his fellow prisoners when they made their appearances in court. On December 4, 1982, the three hundred accused Islamists were held in cages in a temporary courtroom built in the Cairo Exhibition Center for the first day of the Sadat assassination trial. In a film made that day, detainees are chanting and holding up their Korans,

and a man shouts, "This is our word by Dr. Ayman Zawahiri." The room quiets, and Zawahiri addresses members of the international press covering the trial in English.[27]

We want to speak to the whole world. Who are we? Why did they bring us here and what do we want to say? We are Muslims. We are Muslims who believe in our religion and hence we tried our best to establish an Islamic state and an Islamic society. We have sacrificed and stand ready for more sacrifice. We are here the real Islamic front and the real Islamic opposition [prisoners chanting]. And now as an answer to the second question, why did they bring us here? They bring us for two reasons. First, they are trying to abort the expanding Islamic movement, which threatens the dishonest agents of the regime [more chanting]. And secondly, to complete a conspiracy of evacuating the area in preparation for the Zionist infiltration. Such a conspiracy was declared by the stupid agent Anwar Sadat [more chanting].

Humiliation and torture regarding Egyptian jails: We discovered the various inhuman treatment. There they beat us, they kicked us, they worked with electric cables, they shocked us with electricity! They shocked us with electricity! And they used the wild dogs! And they hanged us over the edges of the doors with our hands [he demonstrates with his hands]. They arrested the wives, the mothers, the fathers, the sisters and the sons in a trial to put psychological pressure over these innocent prisoners [more chanting].

We are here in this jail after fourteen months. So where is democracy? Where is freedom? Where is human rights? Where is justice? Where is justice? We will never forget! We will never forget what these criminals have done! [more chanting].

Montasser al Zayyat never met bin Laden, but he has some unique insights into Egypt's Jihad group, which would form the basis of al Qaeda. Al Zayyat first met Ayman al Zawahiri when they were both jailed following Sadat's assassination. As a Cairo lawyer, al Zayyat would later represent many Islamists facing trial in Egyptian courts. He would also serve as a spokesman for Gama'a al-Islamiyya, which led an intense terrorism campaign in Egypt from the 1970s until 1997. In 2002 al Zayyat wrote *The Road to Al-Qaeda,* a biography of Zawahiri,

excerpts of which follow.²⁸ (The book was published in English in 2004.)

The first session of the higher State Security Court that looked into the case known as the "Great Jihad." The hall was full of journalists looking to cover the great event that was shaking Egypt: the assassination of President Anwar al-Sadat. Ayman al-Zawahiri spoke of the torture that members of the groups accused of assassinating the late president suffered in prison.

Zawahiri held up, as an example of the ongoing torture taking place in the Citadel Prison during the months following the assassination of Sadat, the case of a young man held in solitary confinement in cell number three. Thus, Zawahiri called for the transfer of this young man: myself, Montasser al Zayyat. I have always remembered this incident and what Zawahiri did for me despite never having met me. When I met him in the Tora Prison afterwards, I expressed my gratitude for his support, which had relieved much of the pain of the torture and the cruel loneliness that I felt between the walls of the prison.

Zawahiri was born into an aristocratic family in 1951 in the Cairo suburb of Maadi. His family noticed his interest in reading, academic excellence, and studiousness from a young age. Whenever he got tired of studying, he would not spend time with children his age to play or watch television, but rather read books on religion and Islamic jurisprudence as a pastime. Because of this studious introversion, no group of childhood friends are to be found to tell stories about this time of his life.

Zawahiri joined the Faculty of Medicine at Cairo University in the academic year 1968–1969 and graduated in 1974, with a mark of *gayyid giddan*, the next highest mark possible. He then earned a Master's degree in surgery from Cairo University in 1978. When he was arrested on October 23, 1981, it turned out that he had led a clandestine cell before the age of 16.

During the three stages of the trial following the assassination of Anwar al-Sadat, the Egyptian authorities distributed us amongst different prisons. That is where I met Ayman al Zawahiri. It was there that I witnessed the debates regarding whether [the blind cleric] Dr. Omar Abdel Rahman should lead the newly born coalition between the various jihadi groups and the Gama'a al-Islamiyya [the Islamic Group]. This was the most violent crisis facing all the jihadi activists spread among the city's prisons. One of the strongest opponents of Abdel Rahman's leadership was Zawahiri [because the cleric was blind]. In the end Abdel Rahman persisted in his bid for leadership and the difference eventually led to the break-up of the coalition between the jihadi groups and the Gama'a al-Islamiyya.

Osama Rushdi is a member of the Gama'a al Islamiyya who was also jailed with Ayman al Zawahiri in the early eighties.[29]

Zawahiri had three years of jail. They destroyed Zawahiri from inside. The torture for Zawahiri was very very bad. They pushed him to become a witness against his friend in jail. In [Egyptian] jails in 1981 the situation was very very bad. If you want to give one [person] a lot of responsibility for the front of bin Laden [set up in 1998 together with Zawahiri] then that's [Hosni] Mubarak [Egypt's president since 1981].

Zawahiri escaped from Egypt in 1985. I was the first man to meet him in Saudi Arabia [where he went after he was jailed]. Al Zawahiri after that was planning to go to Peshawar [Pakistan]. In 1987 he made this [al Jihad] group with other Egyptians.

There was a big difference between Ayman al Zawahiri in 1985 and Ayman al Zawahiri in 1989. The difference is that he has found a good situation and he is trying to build this organization. And now he was trying to build a special ideology for this organization. Because if you want to do something different, you should be different. McDonald's is not like Burger King. Everybody likes to do something different and say my burger is the best. Because somebody ask you: "Why do you do Burger King if McDonald's is available here beside you?" So you decide to build your ideology, your organization, your movement [differently].

Ayman al Zawahri went at an early time to Peshawar. There wasn't another Egyptian group in Peshawar so he took about two or three years alone to build his group. And in this period he had a good relationship with bin Laden through [the Egyptians] Abu Ubaidah and Abu Hafs. Abu Ubaidah and Abu Hafs were with bin Laden when they were fighting the Russian forces at Jaji [in 1987].

Abu Jandal became bin Laden's chief bodyguard in 1998.[30]

At the time of Sheikh Azzam's presence in Peshawar, Sheikh Omar Abdel Rahman [the spiritual leader of Egypt's Jihad group] was also there. Although both their jihad thinking met at some points, there were many points where they differed. Sheikh Omar Abdel Rahman's arguments were totally different from those of Sheikh Abdullah Azzam. In Peshawar, there were also several Islamic organizations who did not agree with the ideas of Sheikh Abdullah Azzam. Among them were the Egyptian al Jihad group.

Osama Rushdi, the Egyptian militant, was living in Peshawar in 1989.

Al Zawahiri changed his ideology when he went to Peshawar. If you read books from the al Jihad organization of Ayman al Zawahiri you will find a lot of *Takfir* [i.e., declaring other Muslims apostates] in these books. And this ideology is new for al Zawahiri. This ideology grew inside the isolated atmosphere in Peshawar. In these conditions if you have any moderate opinion you would be [marginalized].

The bad chemistry [between bin Laden and Abdullah Azzam] began because the Maktab al Khadamat [the Services Bureau] had a lot of bureaucracy problems; the administration was not good and projects were not completed. Abdullah Azzam made some mistakes, but they were normal mistakes because he did not work with professional people. Ayman al Zawahiri [was frustrated about this]. He made a lot of [noise] about it and pushed bin Laden to be not happy with this [situation]. [Zawahiri told him] "Spend your money yourself, [do] not give it to Abdullah Azzam."

Ayman al Zawahiri invited people not to pray with Dr. Azzam and that is a grave thing in Islam. Because in Islam it is correct to pray with any Muslim.

Faraj Ismail, an Egyptian journalist, covered the Afghan jihad for the Saudi *Al Muslimoon* newspaper in the late eighties.[31]

I met Ayman al Zawahiri in Peshawar around this time. He didn't seem like a doctor, he was very strict in his views. He had a lot of anger.

Bin Laden and Ayman were very close friends. Ayman was more mature politically and religiously than Osama. Ayman was the one who got Osama to focus not only on the Afghan jihad, but regime change in the Arab world.

Abdullah Anas, a confidant of Abdullah Azzam's, recalls Zawahiri maneuvering against Azzam and Afghan leader Ahmad Shah Massoud.[32]

In Peshawar, we didn't count Zawahiri as a *mujahid*. He was just sitting in Peshawar trying to recruit people to fight against Egypt. Osama became part of this Egyptian group and they used to sit in Osama's guest house. They wrote communiqués against Sheikh Abdullah [Azzam]. Sheikh Abdullah—one time he told me inside Afghanistan in an unhappy way, "What is Osama doing gathering these people around him in Peshawar?"

A group of people brought a statement of ten pages and translated it into Arabic, English, Urdu, and gave it to the guesthouses in Peshawar and sent it to all newspapers, saying that Massoud was banning Sharia [Islamic] law inside Afghanistan. At the time I was with Massoud, organizing training for the commanders.

One letter came from Sheikh Abdullah saying you have to come to Peshawar quick. After two days, another message. "Did you move or not? Peshawar is burning. Come quick! I need you!" I went to Peshawar and Sheikh Abdullah told me, "You know the people who signed the communiqué against Massoud are twenty-one Arabs." Sheikh Abdullah said, "I don't know these crazy people and what happened to them. They are trying to make rumors against Massoud."

Osama Rushdi.

That was the negative thing that Ayman [al Zawahiri] used against Dr. Abdullah Azzam: the good relationship between Abdullah Azzam and Massoud. Because he described Massoud in this period as an agent for the French. And they used some statements from some Arabic people who were with Massoud who sent letters to say he is a bad man, that he had a lot of French women there [in his base], so they sent very negative reports about him and they distributed these reports. And [they said] Abdullah Azzam is a liar when he said Massoud is a good man.

Zawahiri tried to keep his relationship with bin Laden secret. He didn't tell me. I heard from my friend Mohammed Shawq Islambouli [the brother of the assassin of Egypt's President Anwar Sadat] in Peshawar that bin Laden, gave [Zawahiri's] Jihad organization $100,000 to begin work.

An unidentified Guantánamo detainee testifying before a U.S. military tribunal.[33]

I met him [bin Laden] before 11 September. I met him maybe 14 or 15 years ago, while on Jihad, in the war against Russia. I followed some of the leaders of the mujahideen in the past. [Ahmad Shah] Massoud: I liked him and thought he was a very good man. I said to the [Arab] mujahideen, "That he is good and God bless him." They got mad when I said I liked Massoud. If I had known they didn't like him, I wouldn't have spoken. For saying that, they punished me; they bothered me; they beat me; they hit me very badly. They accused me of being a spy.

Abdullah Anas, one of the cofounders of the Services Office.

Sometimes we had a council to decide how much money I would take to Massoud. Osama was a member of the *shura* (council) and I was a member. Every time I tried to persuade them to give me much more money for Massoud. But my problem was always with Osama [he didn't want Massoud to get the money.] The last time I went to Massoud I took $500,000.

***Jihad* magazine, issue 12, October 1985, "A Letter of Invitation" by Abdullah Azzam.**

In the name of God the most merciful and great. From Abdullah Azzam to his brother the Mujahid, [Ahmad Shah] Massoud, the leader of the Panjshir front, may God save him:
Peace be with you
To Massoud, God was kind to you in granting you an honorable position, and he made Jihad second nature for you. And God was good to you by making you one of the Mujahideen in the battlefield. And because God is with you, you will be victorious.

Hutaifa Azzam.

My father wrote a book about Massoud—*One Month among the Giants.* He visited him twice in 1988 and 1989.

Abdullah Anas.

The only way to visit Massoud was via the Hindu Kush Mountains. It was fourteen days' walking. Seven mountains, every mountain takes two days. So once Sheikh Abdullah [Azzam] went to Panjshir [valley in northern Afghanistan and], he met Massoud. He said, "Massoud is a phenomenon that will never be repeated."

I found Massoud greater than Napoleon, because Napoleon was defeated in his military life, but Massoud never faced defeat in his military life. Massoud organized the battle against the Soviets in a good way. Massoud, was the man who took Kabul [in 1992] after all the mujahideen in Afghanistan failed. And I used to say this story to Osama and Osama told me in one meeting, "I don't need you to exaggerate about Massoud. Nothing happened inside Afghanistan." He was under the influence of Gulbuddin Hekmatyar, who hated Massoud.

On May 29, 1988, Salem Bin Ladin, the head of the Bin Ladin family, crashed a microlight aircraft he was piloting shortly after takeoff from Kitty Hawk airfield in San Antonio, Texas, dying on impact.[34] It was an eerie echo of how the patriarch of the family, Mohammed, had died more than two decades earlier. Although Salem had not seen much of Osama because he was busy running the family business and, in any event, was far more fun-loving and Westernized than his austere younger half-brother, Salem's death was a blow to Osama.

Alia Ghanem, Osama bin Laden's mother.[35]

His older brother Salem, who was killed in a plane crash in America, was like a father to him after the death of their father, Mohammed. Salem's death saddened Osama a great deal.

Jamal Khalifa, brother-in-law to both Salem and Osama bin Laden.

Salem was a very nice guy; very social. You will get along with him very fast.

A relative describes Salem's central role in the family construction business.

Salem is the person in the family who generated the big projects; for instance, the billion-dollar contract in the early eighties to renovate the mosque in Medina. The marble bill alone was 200 million dollars. He also got the $90 million contract to convert a 747 into King Fahd's private plane between 1987 and 1988. He was working on this with the Dee Howard Aircraft Maintenance company in San Antonio, Texas. They did the refurbishment. There was a throne room, a dining room for thirty, and an elevator inside the plane.

Salem's first Saudi wife, Sheikha, was an al Attas [the same Jeddah family that Osama's mother would marry into after her divorce from Mohammed bin Laden]. His second wife was English [Caroline Carey]. He married her at age thirty-eight.

Salem was great fun, incredibly generous and not the least snobby. He had a lovely boat that he would take to Bodrum (a resort in Turkey). He would give hippies rides in the boat. He did not need sleep. At the drop of a hat he would decide at three in the morning—let's go to Bodrum [from Saudi Arabia]. Life was very exciting with him. He would go skiing in Courchevel (Switzerland). He had a fleet of planes, a 707 jet, and two Lear jets. They were also for the use of the family and the company. He also flew gliders and hot air balloons. He had a house called "Desert Bear" in Orlando, Florida, and he spent a lot of time there.

Salem did not talk about Osama. He was not part of Salem's entourage. The two brothers Salem was closest to were Tariq and Ghalib. The striking thing was how little Osama's brothers knew about him personally.

Salem was killed May [29th] 1988, in San Antonio, Texas. He was forty-three. He was flying a microlight plane. It was a peculiar crash, as Salem, a very experienced pilot, took off in the direction of some visible high-tension electric cables and crashed. He was a fantastic pilot—he would fly his Lear jet upside down at 38,000 feet and had logged more flying hours than full-time commercial pilots. He flew 24/7. So there has always been a huge question about the crash. Did he black out? It was such an inconceivable accident.

The body was brought back to Saudi Arabia. He was buried in Medina. There was a massive funeral, sort of like a wake for two days. All the brothers including Osama were in a receiving line for the guests at the funeral. It took place on a playing field full of chairs with an imam chanting prayers periodically.

Salem had little to do with Bakr [who became the head of the family after Salem's plane crash]. They were like chalk and cheese. Bakr is a crossing the *t*'s and dotting the *i*'s kind of guy. Bakr and another brother Yahia called the shots for the family company after Salem's death.

If Salem had still been around no one would be writing books about Osama bin Laden. Salem had a volcanic temper and had no problem about rocking the boat. He would have personally flown to Sudan [where bin Laden lived in the mid-'90s]. Salem would have grabbed Osama by the lapels and taken him back to Saudi Arabia.

Three months after the death of his eldest brother, Salem, bin Laden would take what would turn out to be a momentous step: secretly founding his own jihadist group, al Qaeda.

4

The Birth of al Qaeda

The founding of al Qaeda marked an irrevocable split between bin Laden and his former mentor Abdullah Azzam. This split would have fateful consequences. Azzam advocated a concept of jihad that was essentially a traditional fundamentalist interpretation of the nature of jihad: the reclamation of once-Muslim lands from non-Muslim rule in places such as Palestine, what was then the Soviet Union, and even southern Spain, which had been under Muslim rule five centuries earlier.

The predominantly Egyptian militants who surrounded bin Laden at the end of the eighties advocated something more radical: the violent overthrow of governments across the Muslim world they deemed "apostate," a concept of jihad that Azzam and many of his followers rejected, as they wanted no part in conflicts between Muslims. The split between Azzam and the ultrajihadists around bin Laden may have even cost Azzam his life; he was assassinated by unknown assailants in November 1989, a year after al Qaeda had been secretly founded.

Osama bin Laden.[1]

Abu Ubaidah al Banjshiri established the training camps for our mujahideen against Russia's terrorism during the 1980s. We used to call the training camp al Qaeda. And the name stayed.

What follows is a passage from *Jihad* magazine, which seems to be the first discussion of al Qaeda, "the base." In this passage Abdullah Azzam was writing about a base that would serve as the foundation of an Islamist vanguard. He was *not* using the word *al Qaeda* in the military sense of a base.

"Al Qaeda al Sulbah" ("The Solid Base") by Abdullah Azzam from *Jihad* magazine, issue 41, April 1988.

Every principle needs a vanguard to carry it forward and, while forcing its way into society, puts up with heavy tasks and enormous sacrifices. There is no ideology, neither earthly nor heavenly, that does not require such a vanguard that gives everything it possesses in order to achieve victory for this ideology. It carries the flag all along the sheer endless and difficult path until it reaches its destination. This vanguard constitutes the solid base (al Qaeda al Sulbah) for the expected society.

Four months after Azzam wrote about the need for a "solid base" for the creation of the perfect Islamic society, bin Laden founded "al Qaeda," an explicitly military organization that was created to be quite different in purpose from Abdullah Azzam's Services Office, which had increasingly taken a role in non-military activities, such as schooling.

In March 2002, Bosnian authorities seized documents in the Sarajevo offices of Benevolence International Foundation, a Muslim charity long supportive of jihads around the world.[2] They discovered a substantial number of electronic files and documents stored on a computer. One of the computer files was titled "Tareekh Osama" ("Osama's History"), a collection of bin Laden's correspondence, minutes of meetings, and other documents, which details his activities during the Afghanistan jihad and the formation of al Qaeda in 1988.[3] Some of these documents would be entered into evidence in the trial of Enaam Arnaout, an employee of Benevolence International living in Chicago who pled guilty to charges of racketeering in February 2003.[4]

In some circles it has become fashionable to suggest that bin Laden has not been especially significant to the global jihadist movement, or that al Qaeda has always, in reality, been only a loose-knit collection of like-minded Islamist militant groups, or even that al Qaeda is an organization that was fabricated by U.S. law enforcement. The fullest exposition of this point of view was made in 2004 in the three-hour BBC documentary *The Power of Nightmares,* directed by Adam Curtis, which argued that "Beyond his small group, bin Laden had no formal organization, until the Americans invented one for him."[5]

Curtis claims that al Qaeda was first "invented" in 2001 when U.S.

prosecutors put four men involved in the 1998 plot to blow up two U.S. embassies in East Africa on trial in New York.[6] During the trial they drew heavily on the testimony of former bin Laden aide Jamal al Fadl, who Curtis explains spun a story about the Saudi militant that would make it easier for U.S. prosecutors to target bin Laden using conspiracy laws that had previously put Mafia bosses behind bars. Curtis says: "The picture al-Fadl drew for the Americans of bin Laden was of an all-powerful figure at the head of a large terrorist network that had an organized network of control. He also said that bin Laden had given this network a name, al Qaeda. . . . But there was no organization. These were militants who mostly planned their own operations and looked to bin Laden for funding and assistance. He was not their commander. There is also no evidence that bin Laden used the term al Qaeda to refer to the name of a group until after 11th September, when he realized that this was the term the Americans had given it."[7]

All of these assertions are nonsense. There is overwhelming evidence that al Qaeda was founded in 1988 by bin Laden and a small group of like-minded militants, and that the group would eventually mushroom into the secretive, disciplined, global organization dominated by bin Laden that implemented the 9/11 attacks. That evidence can be found in the documents in this chapter, which were recovered in Bosnia in 2002, and can also be found in the interviews throughout this book.

The following are translated copies of handwritten correspondence between bin Laden (alias Abu al Qaaqaa) and Mohamed Loay Bayazid, a Syrian also known as Abu Rida al Suri.[8] Some of the letters bear bin Laden's signature at the bottom of the originals. Bayazid, a founding member of al Qaeda, had responsibility for procuring weapons and other equipment.[9]

TAREEKHOSAMA/33/TAREEKH OSAMA.99

In the name of God, the most Compassionate, the most Merciful.

Dear brother Abu al Rida, may God protect him.

God's peace, mercy, and blessings be upon you.

I hope that you and all of the brothers are well and enjoying the approval of God the Almighty. It disappoints me that your news reached us very late, knowing that travelers come to us frequently. I also hope that after Abu Anees reaches you that you move toward us immediately in anticipation of the attack on the Russians as the time has come. One of the brothers whose name is Abu Abdel Lateef is with Abu al Nasr, and if he wants to come tonight, take care of him so that he comes to us tomorrow, for his plane [departs] on Thursday from Karachi to Yemen.

I request that you ask the Yemeni embassy if a Saudi needs a visa to enter Yemen. If so, I hope you work on a visa for me so I can go with him. I ask that you communicate my greetings to Abu al Hasan al Madani and I hope that he will visit us if he has returned from Hijaz [a Saudi province], and I also hope that you bring 500,000 Rupees at a minimum [about 10,000 US dollars].

And God's peace, mercy, and blessings be upon you. Do not forget us in your prayers.

Your brother

(Osama bin Laden's signature)

(1407 Hijriyya) 1987

This letter refers to Abu Ubaidah al Banjshiri, a founding member of al Qaeda who became its first military commander. Bin Laden instructs Abu Rida to pay Abu Ubaidah and Abu Hafs al Masri, two Egyptians who would play a crucial leadership role in al Qaeda, a monthly salary and to treat them as if they were a part of the Mektab al Khidmat (the Services Office).[10]

TAREEKHOSAMA/34/TAREEKH OSAMA.100

In the name of God, the most Compassionate, the most Merciful.

Brother Abu al Rida.

Peace be upon you.

Please arrange the statuses of brother Abu Ubaidah Al-Banjshiri, and brother Abu Hafs Al-Masri, as married, and on a monthly basis, and peace and God's mercy be upon you.

Both are to be treated like Maktab al Khadamat [the Services Office].

Osama bin Laden

[Signature]

9000 RS. Monthly [around $200 a month]

Starting with month (1) 1987

4500 to each of them

This document, dating probably from 1988, illustrates how from its earliest days al Qaeda had an interest in recruiting Americans.[11] Wadei al Haj, a Lebanese-American, would become bin Laden's personal secretary when al Qaeda was based in Sudan in the mid nineties. Al Haj was born in Lebanon in 1960 and in 1978, he settled in Lafayette, Louisiana, where he studied urban planning at the University of Louisiana.[12] He is serving a life sentence for his involvement in the 1998 attacks on the two U.S. embassies in Africa.

TAREEKH, AL MUSADAT, 86, 87, 88
   Name: Wadei al Haj [sometimes referred to as Wadih el Hage]
   Alias: Abdel Saboor
   Age: 28 years old
   Address: Tucson, Arizona, America
   Training: Salman al Farsi, Afghani fronts, five years, trained on most
      types of weapons, mines, explosives and booby traps.
   Time spent previously in Jihad: A total of three years
   Time I will spend now: Three weeks, starting from 15th of Ramadan
   Work skilled at: Carrying out orders
   Time spent previously in Jaji: Two and a half months

What follows are excerpts of a key document: the minutes of the first meeting about the establishment of al Qaeda on August 11, 1988. This document outlines the discussion between bin Laden, referred to as the "the Sheikh," and Abu Rida, or Mohamed Loay Bayazid, to discuss the formation of a "new military group," which would include "al Qaeda (the base)." Abu Rida refers to a disagreement with Abdullah Azzam, with whom bin Laden had founded the Mektab al Khidmat (Services Office).[13]

TAREEKHOSAMA/50/TAREEKH OSAMA 122–123
8/11/1988

Between Abu al Rida and the Sheikh [bin Laden], a discussion regarding the establishment of the new military group

--> general camp
--> special camp
--> Qaeda (base)

Abu al Rida:
a. Did you take the opinion of Sheikh Abdullah [Azzam]
--> knowing that the Sheikh's military gang has ended.
b. This future project is in the interest of the Egyptian brothers. [An apparent reference to Ayman al Zawahiri's Jihad group.]
The Sheikh [bin Laden]: I am one person. We have not started an organization or an Islamic group. It was a period of one year and a half, it was a period of education, building energy, and testing the brothers who came. Starting all these matters, in the darkest of circumstances, and the period is very short, we took very huge gains from the people in Saudi Arabia. We were able to give political power to the Mujahideen; gathering donations in very large amounts.

As for our Egyptian brothers: Their standing with us in the darkest of circumstances cannot be ignored. (Another apparent reference to Ayman al Zawahiri's Jihad group.)

Abu al Rida:
We did not reach the primary goals and we did not follow the plan.
We did not expect the events that happened.
Our work moves according to capability; we lost a lot of time.

In conclusion:

Abu al Rida:
a. Establishing a staged plan.
b. Establishing a time-frame for this stage.

Initial estimate, within 6 months of al Qaeda (the Base), 314 brothers will be trained and ready.

A week later there was a more formal discussion of the formation of al Qaeda. What follows are some of the minutes of a three-day meeting, starting August 18, 1988, in bin Laden's house. The participants, including bin Laden, Abu Ubaidah, al Qaeda's military commander and Abu Hajir, al Qaeda's religious adviser, established an advisory council and a list of requirements and an oath of allegiance for new members in al Qaeda.[14]

TAREEKHOSAMA/54/TAREEKH OSAMA 127–127a

In the Name of God, the most Compassionate, the most Merciful.

The brothers mentioned attended the Sheikh (bin Laden's) house. Most of the discussion was about choosing an Advisory Council. [There is also] a summary of what happened [with the] Maktab al Khadamat (the Services Office). The meeting was held for two days in a row and the Advisory Council [met] on Friday, with the following brothers:

1. Sheikh Usama (bin Laden).
2. Abu Ubaidah al Banjshiri (Al Qaeda's military commander).
3. Abu Burhan.
4. Sheikh Tameem.
5. Abu Hajir.
6. Abu Anas.
7. Abu al Hasan al Madani.
8. Abu al Hasan al Maki.
9. Abu Ibraheem.

The meeting [was] summarized in 2 points by the Sheikh [bin Laden]:

*   The complaints.
*   Mismanagement and bad treatment in Maktab al Khadamat (the Services Office).

The Sheikh decided to engage the Council in making a change. The meeting stayed from sunset until two at night. And on Saturday morning, 8/20/1988, the aforementioned brothers came and started the meeting, and the military work was suggested to be divided in two parts, according to duration:

- Limited duration: They will go to Sada Camp [a camp on the Afghan-Pakistan border], then get trained and distributed on Afghan fronts, under supervision of the military council.
- Open [ended] duration: They enter a testing camp and the best brothers of them are chosen to enter Al Qaeda Al Askariya (the Military Base).

Al Qaeda is basically an organized Islamic faction; its goal will be to lift the word of God, to make His religion victorious.

Requirements to enter Al Qaeda:
- Members of open duration (an apparent reference to an open-ended commitment).
- Listening and obedient.
- Good manners.
- Referred from a trusted side.
- Obeying statutes and instructions of Al Qaeda.

The pledge [to join al Qaeda]:
The pledge of God and his covenant is upon me, to listen and obey the superiors, who are doing this work, in energy, early-rising, difficulty, and easiness, and for his superiority upon us, so that the word of God will be the highest, and His religion victorious.

The meeting ended on the evening of Saturday, 8/20. Work of al Qaeda commenced on 9/10/1988, with a group of fifteen brothers, including nine administrative brothers.

Almost exactly thirteen years after al Qaeda was first launched on September 10, 1988, the organization carried out the 9/11 attacks.

Jamal Khalifa, bin Laden's brother-in-law, explains his theory of why bin Laden, by all accounts a humble, retiring, young man, would have agreed to become the leader of the al Qaeda organization.[15]

Especially when you come to a religious issue—Osama is very sensitive and he really likes to implement Islam. And he's very much at the same time afraid that if he does not, God will punish him. He saw Abu Ubaidah, Abu Hafs in the battle—they were very brave, and they have [religious] knowledge. Abu Ubaidah is memorizing all the Koran, and when you see him most of the time, he is fasting, and in the night, he is praying the night prayer, which is very difficult. He is really a very good religious Muslim.

[Abu Ubaidah and Abu Hafs] came and they said, "Look, Osama, we are thousands of persons and we are a party. We have this background, we have this profile, and we saw that you are the leader which we can trust." In Islam we call it *Baiyah*—"We appointed you as our leader and we will follow you." This is [my] theory. There is no other way to convince Osama to be a leader. He doesn't like being a leader, because he's a humble person, he's not a person who wants to show off at all.

Jamal Ismail, a Palestinian who edited *Jihad* magazine for the Services Office.[16]

Al Qaeda is different than other organizations. Their target is to spread the soul and the idea of jihad among Muslims, to spread the understanding of the importance of jihad; their idea of jihad, which means fighting infidels and to establish a truly Islamic government all over the world. They were recruiting people from different countries, from Saudi, Yemen, Sudan, Iraq, Egypt, Palestine, Jordan, elsewhere, but they were very, very, very careful about choosing or recruiting anyone.

Abu Musab al Suri, who first met bin Laden in 1988, offers his explanation of the founding of al Qaeda in his history of jihadist movements, *The International Islamic Resistance Call*.[17]

Islam needed al Qaeda. Al Qaeda came from the first example of Abu Bakr (one of the Companions of the Prophet) when he joined the Prophet Mohammed in war [in the period following 622 A.D.]. And this Army was able to win against the greatest powers of the world—Rome and Persia. This is the inspiration for al Qaeda.[18]

In its early days al Qaeda may have been largely financed and nominally led by bin Laden, but both its ideological outlook and its key personnel derived from Egypt's Jihad group.

Hasan Abd-Rabbuh al Surayhi was an early Saudi recruit to the Afghan jihad.[19]

The establishment of al Qaeda was discussed in the home of Osama bin Laden in Peshawar following the departure of the Russians from Afghanistan and the end of the Jihad. I was one of those who witnessed the birth of al Qaeda. The idea of al Qaeda is an Egyptian one by the Islamic Jihad group led by Abu-Ubaidah al Banjshiri and Abu-Hafs. They are the ones, especially al Banjshiri, who proposed the idea to Osama bin Laden after the end of Jihad. Al Banjshiri was with us in the al Masada camp in 1987 to repulse a sweeping Russian assault when he was hit in the leg. He is a former officer in the Egyptian army.

Bin Laden's finances were not a secret to anyone and I think the Egyptians wanted to exploit this angle. After the end of the jihad, the Egyptians began to gather and meet in bin Laden's residence in Peshawar. They began to invite journalists and the representatives of relief agencies to bin Laden's residence in order to put him in the spotlight because they began to operate under his umbrella. Bin Laden liked the idea of al Qaeda and he also liked the media spotlight. One day, I went to Osama's home and saw al Banjshiri, Abu-Hafs, some others, and a group of journalists.

After the journalists left, only al Banjshiri, Abu-Hafs al Masri, and Osama were left in the gathering. Al Banjshiri was talking. Al Banjshiri was a sedate and soft-spoken man; he also had a strong personality. Al Banjshiri addressed his words to me. "You are aware of brother Osama bin Laden's generosity. He has spent a lot of money to buy arms for the young mujahideen as well as in training them and paying for their travel tickets. Now that the jihad has ended, we should not waste this. We should invest in these young men and we should mobilize them under his umbrella. We should form an Islamic army for jihad that will be called al Qaeda. This army will be one of the fruits of what bin Laden has spent on the Afghan jihad. We should train these young men and equip them to be ready to uphold Islam and defend Muslims in any part of the world. The members of this army should be organized and highly trained." As Al Banjshiri was addressing his words to me, I looked at Osama bin Laden to see his reaction.

I said "Let me be frank and clear with you. I joined the jihad after one of our ulema [clergy] issued a fatwa. I also came for a specific purpose. I am not inclined to support what you are saying about the formation of an organization and an Islamic army." As I was talking, I noticed that Osama bin Laden raised his head, smiled, and turned to me. He stood up, looked at me, and asked that we talk in private in a place close by. He emphasized to me that they very much wanted me to join them because they are looking for someone with traits that can influence the young men. He said that young men usually gather around someone they love.

Osama had noticed these traits when I was working under his command in the al Masada camp in which I spent about four months. He asked me to respond to this wish and he tried to persuade me. However, I declined and told him: "Brother Osama, you will be rewarded by God Almighty for what you have spent for the sake of Jihad and not by anyone else as brother Abu Ubaidah al Banjshiri is saying. Do not expect to reap the fruit of what you spent here by forming such an army to continue to train the young men on the use of arms. These young men came to wage jihad in Afghanistan following legal fatwas that gave them permission to wage jihad in the name of God." I told him "I do not want to stand against you. However, I will give my opinion if anyone asks me because I do not see a Muslim legitimacy for such an organization."

[After al Qaeda was formed] they established arms training camps. The majority of the instructors were Egyptians who were paid their salaries by bin Ladin. It seems that these instructors, who used to work in Azzam's camps before he was assassinated, had past experience in the Egyptian army or security organs. During the training period, there were some Egyptians whose task was to screen the young men well. They looked for certain specific qualifications among these young men. The most important criteria were that the ones who are chosen should be young, zealous, obedient, and with a weak character that obeys instructions without question. This period of scrutiny went on for one to two weeks in closed and guarded locations which were accessible only to al Qaeda. Sometimes, only very few were selected and were asked whether they wanted to join. If these accepted to join, they were asked to leave and bid farewell to their families and then to return for higher training in the camps on specialized military curricula (preparatory level, middle level, and final level).

Jamal Khashoggi is a Saudi journalist who covered the Afghan jihad.[20]

Al Qaeda was founded almost the same time when I first heard it from Osama himself. Bin Laden saw that Afghan Jihad would be over soon, the Soviet have withdrawn, and it's just a matter of time. He predicted that the mujahideen would be victorious in weeks or months. So what we will do with those Arab mujahideen? They will go back to their countries, but the flame of jihad should continue elsewhere, so he saw that there would be opportunities in places like Central Asia. It will be called al Qaeda. I was surprised, and I discussed it with him, and I said, "But Arab regimes will not like that."

Radicalism came to Afghanistan after '89 when the Afghan cause became a popular cause. When I went to Afghanistan [first in 1987] what Osama had in mind and Abdullah Azzam had in mind is to use me somehow to tell about the opportunity waiting for the Arabs in Afghanistan so they could invite more Arabs. And Abdullah Azzam, when he used to travel to America, he was inviting Arabs. But Abdullah Azzam was kind of selective. He wanted people whom they would come under his guidance, to work within his system. But Afghanistan become so popular so everybody began to go there; independent Muslims and radical Muslims; people who were a drug addict a couple of months ago and then they're sober, and now they like a newborn Christian. And I remember us making jokes about those people, like I remember this Belgian Muslim who came to Afghanistan and six months before he was a bouncer at one of the bars there.

So after '89, floodgates open to Afghanistan of all kind of Arab adventurists and that's when radicalism starts creeping in. Abdullah Azzam was selective. Osama was more in the mind-set that this is a jihad and we must open it to everybody. And Abdullah Azzam did not like that.

This letter, discovered in the "Tareekh Osama" file in the Sarajevo offices of Benevolence International Foundation in 2002, shows how already in the late 1980s bin Laden's name and largesse were becoming known not only in the Middle East, but around the Muslim world. This is an undated letter, probably from around 1989, from a jihadist group based in the eastern African country of Eritrea addressed to bin Laden.[21]

TAREEKHOSAMA/43/TAREEKH OSAMA.110–12

In the name of God, the most Compassionate, the most Merciful.

To our Mujahid prince and reviver of the spirit of Jihad in our Islamic world, brother in God, Mr. Abu Abdallah Osama bin Laden.

We greet you with the greeting of Islam, peace and God's mercy and blessings be upon you.

We come to you with the following requests which we believe to be important at the present time:

1. Facilitating the travel of the youth to the field of Jihad so that they can benefit from the training possibilities, by providing them with tickets and entry visas.
2. Dedicating two individuals on a temporary basis to follow up on transporting the youth and to facilitate their travel and movement.
3. Opening a Maktab Al-Khadamat [Services Office] in Northern Yemen and Sudan.
4. Providing a number of vehicles for transportation and movement inside Sudan and Eritrea.
5. Providing a number of the following equipment:
   A typewriter, a video recorder, and a photocopier.
   And peace and God's mercy and blessings be upon you.

Presented by: Mr. Mohamed Othman

Jamal al Fadl, an early al Qaeda recruit.[22]

When the Russians decide to leave Afghanistan, bin Laden he decide to make his own group. Al Qaeda, it's established to do jihad. You have to make bayat. "Bayat" means you swear [an oath of allegiance to bin Laden].

At that time our general emir [is] Osama bin Laden. Under the emir it's something called shura (consultative) council. Under shura council we have different committee. We have committee for military purpose. The emir of the military committee, his name Abu Ubaidah al Banjshiri. We got money and business committee. Under the money committee, we got office for immigration stuff. Like if you want to travel. We got another committee for media reporting and the newspaper. There was a daily and a weekly publication.

※

On February 15, 1989, after occupying Afghanistan for a decade, the Soviets finally withdrew. All sides anticipated that the Afghan communist government in Kabul would collapse relatively quickly after the withdrawal of the Soviets. Jalalabad, a city near the border with Pakistan, was the most obvious candidate where the Afghan mujahideen might win a quick victory. Arabs under bin Laden's command were also eager to take part in the siege of Jalalabad, which began in March 1989. This battle illustrates bin Laden's military incompetence. It was a virtual bloodbath for his men. This did not quell their enthusiasm.

Jihad **magazine, issues 57 and 58 (July and August 1989), "The Battle of Jalalabad."**

One of the first to come to the land of jihad [in Afghanistan]. Abu Qutayba found his place in the Masada [the Lions' Den] and became the closest escort to Abu Abdallah [Osama bin Laden]. And it was as if his passion was serving Abu Abdallah. He was Abu Abdallah's right hand who loved him like the spring.

The fire of the battle started to burn on the land of the heroes around Jalalabad; and the role of the Arab "Ansar" [supporters] became visible; and the battle started to intensify and the hand of death was kidnapping souls. A tank rocket killed three brothers, including Abu Qutayba. It slashed them in pieces.

And Abu Abdallah [bin Laden] was talking and suddenly when he came to talk about Abu Qutayba, his throat became dry and his eyes became wet and he couldn't find his words anymore. He tried again to talk and the dry throat and the wet eyes came back again. And the third time, he couldn't talk anymore and the whole audience stayed silent.

The hot fights started in Jalalabad; and Abu Abdallah took charge of the closest front lines to the enemy and he started attacking with every hero that God gave him. Their number increased in view of their desire of taking part in the deliverance of Jalalabad under the command of Osama bin Laden. The Arab mujahideen lost eighty and more than one hundred were injured.

Steve McCurry is an American photographer who visited Afghanistan throughout the 1980s. His *National Geographic* portrait of a twelve-year-old Afghan girl with luminous green eyes is one of the iconic photographs of the past two decades. In the spring of 1989 he was on assignment for *Time* magazine in the Jalalabad area.[23]

We all ran into these Arab types, particularly Saudis, throughout that period. And I can think of four separate encounters in Kandahar, Khost, around Jalalabad where you were kind of wondering if they were just going to shoot you right there on the spot, and they were very nasty and kind of felt that they owned Afghanistan.

My encounter with bin Laden: There was fairly heavy fighting going on around Jalalabad, particularly around the airport, about as heavy a fighting as I ever experienced in Afghanistan. The [mujahideen] thought [the seizure of Jalalabad] was going to be a walkover, and they basically had a daytime attack, like in the middle of the morning on the airport in Jalalabad. We were getting bombed by mortars and artillery and small arms, really kind of frightening. It must have been about 10:00 in the morning. We were getting shelled not only from the guys in the airport, but also from other bases and artillery. It was a major battle with mortars and artillery. It was just amazing.

The Arabs were clearly into this whole thing. They were clearly willing to be on the front lines, willing to sacrifice. There were these Arabs that were actually taking pretty heavy casualties. And one of these Arabs got hit, and they were dragging him feet first down a path, and he was probably dead. And I jumped out from behind a wall. We were probably twenty people just sort of cowering there. And I went over to photograph this guy they were dragging down the path. And one [Arab] guy picked up a stone and we were like eyeball-to-eyeball and he was screaming at me. And he was going to bash my brains. And for whatever reason, he didn't.

That night or the next day, these Arabs were kind of grouped together in a house, [around] this really tall guy with this white thing on his head, a white kind of cloth. And we had come up on them unexpectedly. As we approached, they came up and they wanted to know why this kaffir [infidel] was in Afghanistan, and I had no business being there, and it was a jihad, a guy with a pistol stood up—basically if you don't shove off, there's nothing I'd like better to do than just to blow you away. It was one of [bin Laden's] hangers-on. [Bin Laden] seemed totally indifferent, like we were stray dogs who had come into the perimeter, and we were being shooed off.

I first went to Afghanistan in '79, and had been in probably a dozen times up to that point and always felt very much at home. The Afghans are really friendly people, and I could basically just kind of walk around with one person, even unarmed. For the [Arabs] to come in and act as though this was their war, their country, and they were treating the Afghans like they were just these sort of uneducated, uncouth, illiterate sort of bumpkins [who] didn't really get it. These guys, they're really, really nasty and very aggressive and very condescending, and just hateful. And the Afghans, actually it was their country being basically slowly destroyed, and they were often very good-humored.

Jamal Ismail.

A lot of Arabs were there [in Jalalabad] and they were supporting the idea to have control over any major city. Unfortunately, it was a disaster.

***Jihad* magazine, issues 57 and 58 (July and August 1989).**

Here is how the heroes of the Masada [Lions' Den] died and the land of Jalalabad swallowed one lion after another. And Abu Abdallah Osama [bin Laden] had pain every time he would say good-bye to one muhjahid and every time he would say good-bye, a new rocket would come and take another one and it would leave him in pain and sorrow. And before the healing of his injury, a new arrow would hit his wound, reopening the injury that was healing, Abu Zaheb died and Abu Abdallah [bin Laden] told me: I never had pain for anyone before like I had for Abu Zaheb; and then followed him Khaled el Kerde [the Kurd]; and Abu Abdallah said I never had sorrow before like for Khaled.

***Jihad* magazine, issue 53 (April 1989).**

[Around the time of the siege of Jalalabad, Afghan leader Gulbuddin] Hekmatyar [whose party had received at least $600 million in U.S. aid][24] was asked during a press conference by a Western journalist about his position on the Arab groups trying to spread Wahabbism. Hekmatyar answered: "It's none of your business and we won't accept anybody to interfere in our internal affairs. We are against the Western organizations that spy on us and the Christian organizations that come here under a humanitarian pretext. We won't let them come to Afghanistan."

Edward Giardet, a reporter, was covering the siege of Jalalabad.[25]

The incident with bin Laden was in February '89. About fifteen kilometers outside Jalalabad you had the [Communist] government forces entrenched, and the Muj and the Arabs were on a ridge. One of the Afghans took us to the frontlines, and there were about fifty, sixty Arabs in the trenches there, and then a tall man came out and he spoke in English. I was trying to think where he went to school. It was sort of an American accent. Very tall. That's what struck me immediately. And he wants you to have respect for him. He was clearly the boss. When I asked him his name, he wouldn't give me his real name. Of all the people crowded around him, there wasn't a single Afghan among them. It was clear that he was the Arab Man. And later on I asked an Afghan and he said yeah, they have lots of money and cars and such.

[Bin Laden] came out demanding what we were doing there—saying, "This is our Jihad not your Jihad." Then I went into a thing about how "We've been coming here for quite a number of years, and we've never seen you guys."

After that we had a delightful conversation. I stopped going through the interpreter, and we had a direct conversation [in English]. The best description I can give is that he sort of came across as being a rather spoiled brat, like he was sort of "playing at jihad." Kind of an "I'm here now, look at me" sort of thing. Of course, by then the conversation was getting more and more hostile, and many of his men came, and many of the Muj came over. At this point my translator was translating everything into Pashtun for the Afghans. They were all snickering. There was obviously no love lost between the two sides.

We actually did get into a rather interesting conversation in the end. He was warming up to be a rather congenial fellow. We started talking about religion and I said, "Look, I respect Islam, but you've also gotta respect us." And this went on for about forty-five minutes, and he actually seemed to be quite understanding of that. But that all changed toward the end when I said, "Look, I gotta go." And then when I made a move to leave I held out my hand for him to shake it, but he refused to take it. I'd traveled a lot in Afghanistan, and Afghans give a lot of respect to others; they would always accept my hand. And then he said, "If you ever come again, I'll kill you." Then he said I should leave the country. And I said, "I will leave the country when my hosts wish me to leave, just as I'm sure you will leave when they wish you to leave." And you could see he really resented that. But, I tried to make sure he could save face, wanted to make sure I didn't force him into being aggressive.

[A day or so later] suddenly we hear this guy from over our shoulders: "I TOLD YOU NOT TO COME BACK HERE," and it was bin Laden again. We were probably with about fifty Afghans. And we tried to film, but bin Laden's guys noticed the lights. "Switch that off! We told you!" And then one stuck his gun up to the camera guy's back. And they kept creeping closer and closer. And suddenly I realized, these guys didn't care. They were totally obsessed with bin Laden's yelling. And I began trying to talk to bin Laden, saying the Afghans wanted us there. And then an Afghan got between the two groups saying, "You've got to stop; this is bad for Islam. This is jihad. We have to stop fighting amongst ourselves." So all this was going on, and it was all getting closer and closer. Finally, I said "We've gotta go. We're gonna get killed."

And as we're driving away two mortars started hitting by the side of the truck. And they all started screaming, they all had AK-47s. So a little way down the road I tell Tom [the cameraman] to stop and I said, "Look, we've got to tell whoever is coming up the road not to go into the camp. They're going to get killed." So these two Swiss guys, just arrived, get out and they say, "No, no, no. It's OK. We're ICRC (International Committee of the Red Cross)." And I tell them, "Look, I don't think these guys give a *shit* who you are. They're gonna kill you if they see you." And I heard they did eventually drive up there, and they got shot at.

So we get back to the Peshawar base [in Pakistan]. And the [Afghans] were outraged. Utterly outraged. The commander said, "The guy you met was Osama bin Laden," which meant nothing to me at all. I was scared shitless. I actually wrote a short story about all of this. It was never published. I was thirty-eight at the time.

Despite the setback during the battle of Jalalabad, the journalists at *Jihad* magazine emphasized the glorious martyrdoms of the dead in the issue of April 1991 in an interview "With a Young Cadet."

The magazine was contacted by the young cadet Hassam, son of the martyr Abi Hassam al Suri, who was martyred in Jalalabad in 1989. Cadet Hassem is fourteen years old and is from Hama, Syria. He now lives with his mother and his six siblings and studies in the academy.

Cadet Hassem says: "Jihad in Afghanistan is an obligation on Muslims, to sacrifice with their blood to free the land of Muslims. First we were sad that my dad was martyred, but it was done for the will of God, so his martyrdom is a blessing to us and the world and is honorable in the end. And I want to live happy and die a martyr in the name of God."

The failure to win the battle of Jalalabad in 1989 was a defeat for the Afghan mujahideen and their Arab allies. It set the stage for a lingering war of attrition between the Afghan communist regime and the various Afghan armed factions that would drag on until April 1992, when the Afghan commander Ahmad Shah Massoud would finally take Kabul. By then many of the Arabs had left the Afghan battlefield seeking other jihads.

🔱

The assassination of the Palestinian cleric Abdullah Azzam on November 24, 1989, in Peshawar is a pivotal point in this story. Over the years bin Laden had drifted way from Azzam, establishing his own military organization that would evolve into al Qaeda. Meanwhile, Azzam became increasingly convinced that Ahmad Shah Massoud represented the future of Afghanistan, a conclusion that was not shared by the Islamist hardliners who surrounded bin Laden.

Who killed Azzam remains a mystery and will likely remain so. There are several candidates that have been floated, such as KHAD, the intelligence agency of the Afghan communists who were then still in power in Kabul, which had ample reason to bump off one of the leaders of the Afghan resistance. Mossad, the Israeli intelligence service, might also have wanted Azzam dead, as the influential Palestinian cleric played a role in the emergence of Hamas in the late eighties and was recruiting and training Hamas fighters along the Pakistan-Afghanistan border.

However, the more I looked into Azzam's death, the more plausible it looked that it was not Hamas or the Afghan communists that killed him, but rather a coalition of Egyptian hardliners and the Afghan leader Gulbuddin Hekmatyar, who had the strongest motives and inclination to murder Azzam. With Azzam dead Hekmatyar eliminated a key advocate for his principal opponent, Massoud, while the Egyptian jihadists got rid of the leader of the "Afghan Arabs" who did not share their views about the necessity of overthrowing Middle Eastern regimes.

Bin Laden was not in Pakistan at the time of Azzam's assassination, but his closest allies benefited from Azzam's death as only Azzam had the spiritual authority and moral weight to rein in the ultrajihadists.[26] With Azzam gone there was little intellectual counterweight to al Qaeda's ideas among the Afghan Arabs. And support for the view that Egyptian radicals, possibly in an alliance with Hekmatyar, likely killed Azzam comes from an unlikely source: Arab militants and journalists based in Pakistan at the time.

Faraj Ismail, an Egyptian journalist, covered the Afghan jihad for the *Al Muslimoon* newspaper beginning in 1986.[27]

A few months before Azzam was murdered there was some sort of bad vibration between bin Laden and Ayman al Zawahiri against Azzam. Azzam wanted unity between the Afghan groups, but by 1989 bin Laden and Zawahiri hated Ahmed Shah Massoud. Azzam felt that the Arabs should not take sides in the Afghan conflict.

At this time Azzam no longer gave lectures in Bait al Ansar [the House of Supporters, which would morph into al Qaeda], and Azzam started doing shuttle trips to see Massoud [in the Panjshir Valley, northern Afghanistan].

Wael Julaidan ran the Saudi Red Crescent relief organization in Peshawar. He knew both Azzam and bin Laden well.[28]

Abdullah Azzam continued to talk good about Massoud, writing books about Massoud, giving speeches about Massoud. Sheikh Abdullah Azzam said, "Massoud is the hope of the whole nation." And he swore, by God, Massoud is the hope of the whole nation. This is my last meeting with Abdullah Azzam. That was on Tuesday. He was assassinated on Friday.

"A Millionaire Finances Extremism in Egypt and Saudi Arabia," is an early profile of bin Laden that appeared in the Egyptian weekly magazine *Ruz al Yusuf*.[29]

"At that juncture [in 1989] the seeds of conflict among the different Afghan factions began to show on the scene. Gulbuddin Hekmatyar (the hard-line Islamist Afghan leader) and his followers were of the opinion that those Arabs with their wealth and weapons and youthful fervor were a winning horse worth betting on, especially since some of them had previous military experience, such as the young men from Egypt and Syria.

By contrast, Burhanuddin Rabbani's party and the commander of his forces in those days [Ahmad Shah Massoud] expressed strong reservation with regard to the participation of those Arabs and the roles of Osama bin Laden. Actually they completely refused to let them share in the fighting, arguing that those Arabs were disorganized and were only seeking to become martyrs. They also felt that Osama bin Laden's aims were somewhat obscure.

This drove bin Laden even more into the arms of Hekmatyar.

Hasan Abd-Rabbuh al Surayhi was an early Saudi recruit to the Afghan jihad.[30]

In 1989 there was friction between the Egyptians and Azzam. They hated him due to differences in theological beliefs and they wanted to give a chance to bin Laden's star to rise. I doubt that bin Laden was involved in Azzam's assassination. I suspect the Egyptians because the killing of Azzam coincided with the idea of establishing the al Qaeda organization.

Osama Rushdi, a member of Egypt's Islamic Group, was in Peshawar at the time of Azzam's assassination.[31]

We [started to hear] about al Qaeda from 1989. They gave people good military training and they arranged it themselves. In this period it was not against America or any other regime. I think they began that after the differentiation with Sheikh Abdullah Azzam. Ayman [al Zawahiri] had a severe conflict with Dr. Abdullah Azzam. He called him an agent of America, an agent of Saudi Arabia. I have spoken to Dr. al Zawahiri many times. [He said to us] why do you have a good relationship with Dr. Azzam? Al Zawahiri [tried to maneuver] bin Laden away from Dr. Azzam. Two days before Dr. Azzam [was assassinated] I am in conversation with al Zawahiri [for] two hours, and trying to change his mind, but he was very angry. I met al Zawahiri again at the funeral for Dr. Azzam. And Dr. al Zawahiri was very affected and sad. But before [Azzam was] dead he [was saying Azzam] is a spy.

Kamal Halbawi, a leading member of the Egyptian Muslim Brotherhood, was in Peshawar at the time of Azzam's assassination.[32]

I believe that [Azzam's] killers are from the local and domestic environment and not from abroad, neither Zionists, nor Russians nor Americans. It was not the [Soviet] Communists: they were defeated already. I think it was domestic. I mean it was either the Arabs or the Afghans. With Azzam maybe some of the factions of the mujahideen were not happy with him. The guns are there, the environment is there, they have easy access to him so you don't need a plot by the Israelis, Russians, Americans to do that. Before [Azzam] was killed there were many statements and leaflets distributed in Peshawar saying he is not a good Muslim.

***Jihad* magazine, issue 63 (January 1990), "Bloody Friday: the Assassination of Sheikh Abdullah and his two kids."**

On November 24, 1989, Azzam was going to the Mosque of the Martyrs [in Peshawar] where he used to preach every Friday. He took a car with his sons. It was the first time they had used this car. His son, Mohammed, was driving it. While he was taking a right in a narrow street a 20 kg bomb exploded. Since it was the first time he had used this car, the assassins were probably following him from his home. The bomb was in a main street close to a gas station. It was linked to the detonator through a fifty meters long cable hidden in the sewerage system. The way they built the bomb shows that they did not intend to kill other people. They did not put any metal in it. They did not want to kill any Pakistanis in order not to have any investigation.

Hutaifa Azzam, Abdullah Azzam's son.[33]

Twenty kilograms of TNT—my brother Mohammed was found 17 meters from the car. My father went out of the car directly into the road, my brother Ibrahim went into the electric wires [overhead]—his hands were found in another area.

Jihad **magazine, issue 63 (January 1990). The wife of the martyr Sheikh Abdullah Azzam.**

The way he raised our children is for them to become martyrs of God. From their upbringing, it is evident that he wants our children to follow in the footsteps of their father, the Jihadi martyr.

As for me, I hope to continue helping my Afghan brothers in any way I can; sewing, teaching, nursing, and I will stay here in Peshawar with my Arab brothers until victory.

To my Muslim sisters, I ask that they raise their children in the true Muslim way, so that those kids can bear the responsibility of continuing the Jihad and the will of God and to give themselves as martyrs of God for the religion.

Abdullah Anas is the Algerian whom Azzam had recruited to the Afghan jihad. In 1990, Anas married one of Azzam's daughters.[34]

You can't imagine [the reaction to Azzam's murder]. We used to receive calls from everywhere in the world, people are just calling and crying, because they can't speak. Ladies and gents. From Palestine, from the United States, from Algeria, from Saudi, from everywhere and three, four telephone lines, twenty-four hours for more than one month—people calling and crying. It's without exaggeration, an earthquake.

Ahmad Zaidan is the author of the Arabic-language book *Bin Laden Unmasked*, which is based, in part, on his own meetings with bin Laden.[35]

It's very much difficult to figure out or to assess who was behind the killing of Abdullah Azzam—Mossad [the Israeli intelligence service] because Abdullah Azzam had a hand for establishment of Hamas. The other view is that maybe KHAD [the Afghan communist intelligence service]. I rule out totally that bin Laden would indulge himself in such things, after all, Osama bin Laden, he's not type of person to kill Abdullah Azzam. Otherwise, if he be exposed, he would be finished, totally.

Jamal Khashoggi.

[Who killed Azzam?] It could be Hekmatyar, it could be the KHAD, it could be the Mossad, the Egyptians [around Ayman al Zawahiri]. One of the theories I developed later [is that] Abdullah Azzam had a strategic mind. And he saw where the problem lay in Afghanistan. It was a problem between [the Afghan commanders] Massoud and Hekmatyar. If you bring those two together, then the problem of Afghanistan would be solved, then we can secure the future of establishment of the Islamic state. So he put so much effort on that front. Osama was reluctant. Osama was torn between two ideologies: radicalism and moderate Islam. So maybe if Massoud met Osama, he could have influenced Osama and strengthened the weight of moderate Islam in Osama.

I met with Hekmatyar, an arrogant, self-centered person. I think Hekmatyar had a secret organization to eliminate his enemies. Hekmatyar was obsessed with the concept that he is the legitimate leader of the Afghan jihad movement because he is the one who started jihad in the '70s. From an early time some of the secret assassinations which took place against certain Afghan mujahideen were done by Hekmatyar [it was suspected].

Jamal Ismail.

Abdullah Azzam was assassinated on the 24th November 1989. Osama was forced to leave Pakistan in the month before that. There was a no-confidence motion [on November 2, 1989] in the Pakistan National Assembly against the government of Benazir Bhutto (Pakistan's first female prime minister). [The money that was used] to purchase the votes of some members of the National Assembly was given by Osama. Benazir came to know before the no-confidence motion that was raised in parliament that they were trying to purchase some votes from her party members. When the date of the no-confidence motion came, the opposition failed to produce the majority that the parliament doesn't trust their government and therefore it has to resign.

When [Benazir] came to know about Osama's role, she called King Fahd [of Saudi Arabia] and told him that either you call your man from here or we have to arrest him and interrogate him. And we have free media. They will talk and they will speculate many things about Saudi interference in our own internal affairs. Osama went [back to Saudi Arabia] for some consultation. When he went back, his passport was snatched by Saudi officials and they banned him from traveling.

Despite the fact that bin Laden was now back living in Saudi Arabia, his al Qaeda organization continued to train recruits for the jihad against the Afghan communist regime that had replaced the Soviets.

Noman Benotman, a Libyan, was one of those recruits.[36]

I came from a wealthy or bourgeois family; ministers, in the intelligence service, they are very wealthy. First of September '69 the Qadaffi regime [took over]. They believed in the revolution with the whole world and they like took sides with the Soviet Union. It was a ruthless regime. I'll give you just one example. I was in the university in political science in college. And I can tell you I was one of the best. After the fifth day they kicked me out because they are classifying people by their family name. So it's a lot of problems like this, and I have two brothers, they had to leave the university. One of them is now living in Miami and the other is living in London.

In late '87, early '88—in Arabic we call it, *Sahwa,* the Islamic Awakening—started to be noticeable in society. Hundreds of my friends [were affected by it]. In early '89 the security service decided to launch a huge attack against the Islamists. Out of the blue you found like hundreds of your friends had disappeared.

I left Libya late '89. January 1990 I arrived in Islamabad Airport, and from there. [I went to Peshawar to] a guesthouse. As if you're coming to a hotel—it's a huge villa with about 150 people everywhere. And there were huge tents. It was well prepared.

Then I go to Khost [in eastern Afghanistan]. There is a [training] camp called Farouk. Every week you find some [people] left the camp because they believe that because they are being trained by Islamists, it is going to be like somewhere in heaven, in paradise, and, like, angels hanging around. But when they come to the reality of the facing the music—to have people shouting at them, waking them at 2:00 a.m., they found it very difficult. It was very difficult and strenuous. My God, you just slept like in the middle of nowhere. If you go out of the camp, you can't find nothing.

All of the [trainers] are members of al Qaeda. It was very hard training. It is all about the basics, if you like. And the most important thing is for transferring people from one life to another, from a civilian to be a guerrilla warrior.

Benotman fought in the siege of the city of Khost in eastern Afghanistan. The Afghan communists defended the strategic city furiously for two years between 1989 and 1991.

We stayed there for a long time, months and months. In certain areas, the frontline between us and the enemy—it's just 100 meters. And we shoot each other. The Communists; not easy to beat them. My God. It was a huge army! They are thousands and thousands of people, and tanks.

The Arabs [went there] to die. The Afghans, they are there to get their country back. That is the difference. We want to die there. We don't want to come back. So if you need, like, a very hardcore fight in certain places or to do something very stupid. [then you asked the Arabs to do it].

It's something very interesting you know, fantastic. I liked it.

L'Houssaine Kherchtou is an al Qaeda member who testified as a U.S. government witness in the 2001 trial of four men accused of a role in attacking two U.S. embassies in Africa in 1998. Excerpts of his testimony follow. Like Benotman, he was drawn to the jihad against the Afghan communists and would train with al Qaeda.[37]

My name is L'Houssaine Kherchtou. I was born in Morocco in May 15, 1964. When I finished my high school I went to catering school for three years. I learn English in high school. In 1989 I moved to France. I found a job in bakeries and later on in Corsica. I work for about six or seven months. I left Corsica. I sneaked to Italy. I didn't had a visa to go to Italy. I settled down in Milano, or Milan.

January 23, 1991, I left Italy to Pakistan. At that time many people they were coming from all over the world towards Afghanistan to help Muslims there, and I was one of them. We reach Karachi. Then we took another plane to Islamabad, and from Islamabad we took another plane to *Bait al Ansar,* Peshawar. Bait al Ansar [House of the Supporters] was a guesthouse. The first thing you do is you take all your valuable things like passports, money; they put it in a safe place, and they let you know many things about Afghanistan, how long you have for training, and which camp you are going to be trained in.

The *Encyclopedia of Jihad,* al Qaeda's massive how-to manual, explains the set up at the *Bait al Ansar,* "House of Supporters," in its section on Security and Intelligence. An extract follows that gives a flavor of the bureaucratic side of the jihad.[38]

[The *Bait al Ansar* complex included] a guards' tent, a visitors' room, a room for newcomers arriving from camps and fronts, a safe room, a phone booth, a room for the passport section, a sick room, a dining room, a prayer room, a kitchen, a mosque, and a laundry room.

The safe room is where passports and valuables are kept. It is the center for rest and sleep for members of the management. S. is in charge of the mail and departure from the camp. Sh. is responsible for treasury and accounting. Q. is responsible for transactions and for the safe. The official hours of the management are from 8:00 a.m. until the noon prayers and from 5:00 p.m. until the evening prayers.

The [monthly] salaries of the members of the management:

1. Q gets 6,000 rupees [around $100].
2. Sh gets 6,000 rupees.
3. T gets 4,000 rupees.

The social status of the members of the management:

1. S. is married with kids. He is 35 years old.
2. M. is married and has a 1.5 year old son. He is about 30 years old.
3. Q. is married and he is 27 years old.
4. Sh. is married. He has two boys and a girl and he is 30 years old.
5. T. is married with no kids. He is 25 years old.
6. D. is single and he is 19 years old.
7. S. is single and he is 23 years old.
8. D. is single and he is 22 years old.

Visitors' room (the big room): at least fifty people sleep in the room. This room is used for prayer in the winter and for lessons and lectures.

The room for newcomers from the camps and fronts: it is a room that is about seven by five meters, in which about 20 people sleep.

The passports section. Brother W and Y work in the room. Y works for an hour in the morning and an hour in the evening and most of the afternoons. Most of his work is outside the office, at the foreign ministry and Passports' Administration. W opens the place at 8:00 a.m. until 1:00 p.m. The work of this room is to get visas and exit permits and other matters related to passports.

L'Houssaine Kherchtou's testimony continues.[39]

I choose al Farouq [training] camp. We arrived there around 6 o'clock in the afternoon. Then they told me to spend the night in the mosque with other people and during the night there was a shooting and it was around 1 o'clock. Then we came out from the mosque and all people were in the meeting there. It was a welcome to the camp. They want us to know that you have to be prepared. Don't think that you are coming to sleep in the camp.

We spent in the first part almost a month and we trained on light weapons, like AK-47, M-16, Uzi. Then we moved to the second place in which we learned how to use explosives like C3, C4, dynamite. They had two types of detonator, electric ones and explosive ones. Then you go next to the third part. We were trained about antiaircraft weapons. In Farouq camp you have exercise every morning after the first prayer, exercising for one hour and one hour and a half, sometimes two hours. Myself I lost a lot of weight. Approximately twenty kilograms (44 pounds).

The emir of Farouq camp he told us if you need more details about al Qaeda and how to join it in Peshawar you will learn a lot of things there. *Bait al Salaam* (House of Peace) is al Qaeda guesthouse. Everybody is talking about al Qaeda there. We ask many people. We made the decision to join them. So we arrived to Miran Shah guesthouse we met a guy called Abu Ahmed al Harbi. He explained many things about joining al Qaeda, and he gave us a paper written in Arabic. It's [an oath] to join al Qaeda. He told us that al Qaeda is a group of Muslims join[ed] to fight for Islam, and to do good things for Islam and Muslims all over the world.

He said that the emir—is Islamic word for the manager but, more religious than that—you have obey that man and you have to follow his orders as far as they are to benefit Islam and as far as they are not against Islam. I made the *bayat* (oath). At that time I didn't know many people in al Qaeda, but I knew that Osama bin Laden is the emir and Abu Banjshiri is number two, and Abu Hafs is the third one.

Abu Hafs called me with some other people for us to attend another training session in Osama bin Laden's house in Hayatabad, Peshawar. It was approximately 1992. Abu Hafs didn't tell us anything about the type of training, but he told us that the trainer is a severe man. He is very, very strict. It was Abu Mohamed al Amriki. The American. (Ali Mohamed, an Egyptian-American who served in the U.S. army as a sergeant at Ft. Bragg, North Carolina, in the late eighties).

The trainer [Ali Mohamed explained] how to make surveillance of targets and how to collect information about these targets. We trained how to use different cameras, especially small cameras, and how to take pictures in the guesthouse in which we were living. After taking pictures we go back to our place and we develop that film, using a machine, fixer and developer and water.

We started [surveying] small things, like bridge, like stadium, like normal places in which nobody is, and then in the second stage we went to police stations, for example, and in my group we were trained to go to Iranian consulate and Iranian cultural center in Peshawar.

During the training, Mohamed explained us that this job is the first part of [the] military part. You collect the information about this certain target, and whenever you finish your work, our group, we just leave, we send our reports to our bosses and we leave. Those people, they go through this report and they read all the information, and everything. Then they make some decisions how to attack that target, and then they send another group who supply everything so as to attack that target. Whenever that third group finish [its] job, [it] has to leave. At the end the fourth group who can do the job come so as to do the final job.

Ali Mohamed was a key trainer for al Qaeda, despite the fact that he was enrolled in the U.S. Army from 1986 to 1989 and was married to an American. Extracts from Mohamed's U.S. military record follow. The record indicates the range of training and skills Ali Mohamed could pass on to al Qaeda's recruits.[40]

Name: Mohamed Ali Aboualacoud
Date of Birth: 6/3/52
Place of Birth: Alexandria, Egypt
Education:
  1. Military Academy, Cairo, Egypt, BS '73
  2. Univ. of Alexandria, Egypt, BA in Psychology '80
Military Occupational Specialty—76C10, Equipment Records:
  Home of Record: Santa Clara, Calif.
  Last Rank: E-5, Sgt.
  Place of Enlistment: Oakland, Calif.
  Date of Enlistment: 8/15/86
  Reserve Obligation until: 8/94

SERVICE INFORMATION:

11/86	Basic Training	A Company 4th Bn 1st Basic Training Brig. Fort Jackson, S.C.
2/87	Casual	Fort Lee, Va.
4/87	Equip. Rec./Parts Specialist	Headquarters, Headquarters Co. 1st, Special Operations Command Fort Bragg, N.C.
5/87	Material Supply Spec. Service Co.	5th Special Forces Group Fort Bragg
11/89	Active duty fulfilled, to Individual Ready Reserve. Army Reserve Personnel Center, St. Louis, Mo.	

Awards: Army Lapel Button/Parachute Badge/M16 Expert Badge/
Army Service Ribbon/Army Achievement Medal/Army Commen-
dation Medal.

༈

**After the Soviet withdrawal from Afghanistan in 1989, the Afghan fac-
tions, which were fragmented by internal bickering and outright fighting, made little headway in seizing Kabul. The most pronounced
conflict was between the longtime rival commanders Gulbuddin Hekmatyar and Ahmad Shah Massoud.**

**While bin Laden had left Pakistan in November of 1989 and had
moved back to Saudi Arabia, by early 1991 he was back in Pakistan,
making efforts to mediate between the Afghan factions. However, as
Afghanistan slipped into civil war in early 1992, bin Laden washed his
hands of the place and decided to move to Sudan.**

**Wael Julaidan remembers that he and bin Laden tried to placate the
warring Afghan leaders during the early nineties.**

Osama for one year and a half, from '89 to '91 was in Jeddah. Then he
decided to go to Medina because he's working with his family's project
and also he can be in the holy place where he can be nearby the mosque.
And at the time developing the whole city [of Medina] was taking place.

Bin Laden returned to Peshawar in early '91 and he stayed until early
'92 and I see him from time to time because I was there. We used to visit
the Afghan leaders to solve disputes, because at that time the disputes of
the Afghan leaders is getting more serious. From time to time we go together to talk to the different Afghan leaders, to calm them.

**Abdullah Anas had helped to run the Services Office with Abdullah
Azzam and bin Laden. He recalls that during this period bin Laden had
a poorly conceived plan to take Kabul.**

Osama, he had to create an organization and to keep everything under
his control, but as an organizer, I think he had many mistakes during this
period. In 1991 he had a project to enter Kabul [then under the control
of the Afghan communists] and he spent 100 million rupees (more than
1.5 million dollars) and after a few weeks, everything collapsed and the

people took his 100 million rupees. Osama as an organizer—completely a catastrophe, I consider him.

Haji Deen Mohamed was a mujahideen commander during the war against the communists in Afghanistan. He also recalls bin Laden's plan to attack Kabul.[41]

I saw bin Laden in 1991. Because he was spending a lot of money, he was an important personality. Bin Laden had a plan to attack Kabul. When I met bin Laden in Peshawar he brought money for the mujahideen to attack Kabul. We worried about how such a plan would work. I was the representative of Afghan leader Younis Khalis. We had a debate about this because Khalis did not want to attack Kabul. We had a two-hour debate with bin Laden in Peshawar, which led nowhere.

To be honest we didn't care about bin Laden. We didn't notice him much. The only thing he did have was cash. The only thing was that he was rich. When Osama was in Peshawar people were thinking the Americans were supporting him.

Ahmad Shah Ahmadzai was acting Afghan prime minister from 1995 to 1996.[42]

I have seen [bin Laden]. Why should I say no? He was a normal man. Today he is a very a big man. He was a normal man; he was coming with donations for us like thousands of other Arabs. Those days there was a motivation that the Soviet Union should be blocked in its borders.

After the defeat of the Soviet Union, we sent a message to all Arabs that were in Afghanistan: "We thank them for their cooperation with us in fighting the Soviet Union. Now that the Soviet Union is defeated, please do not participate in any factions in Afghanistan to fight against us. And please go back to your home countries." This was announced by all of us to the Arabs. Because all the Arabs were fighting along side [the Afghan hard-line Islamist] Gulbuddin Hekmatyar.

Hekmatyar, nominally the prime minister in the Afghan coalition government that replaced the Afghan communists who lost Kabul to Massoud in 1992, would shell Kabul on an almost daily basis between

**1992 and 1996 during the civil war that followed the fall of the commu-
nist regime. Hekmatyar would never defeat Massoud.**

**Abdullah Anas, Abdullah Azzam's son-in-law, kept in touch with bin
Laden, even though they had long since parted ways ideologically.**

In 1992 Osama came back to [Pakistan to] see if he can organize the
mujahideen but I remember he failed. Most of the Arabs had become
part of Hekmatyar's group. I remember the people who were with Hekmatyar warned Osama. You are not anymore a leader. And after that, he
immediately decided to go to Sudan.

Osama supported Hekmatyar before. Not only Osama, 90 percent of
the Arabs invested in Hekmatyar because the charisma of Hekmatyar
and the media machine of Hekmatyar was very, very strong, helped by
the ISI [Pakistan's military intelligence agency]. So the Arabs in Peshawar exaggerated about Hekmatyar: when they came to the moment
of the truth, they found Hekmatyar was nothing. A failure. I can't remember any victory of Hekmatyar inside Afghanistan, even though he's
the first man who received arms from the West. [Hekmatayr would
receive at least 20 percent of the U.S. aid that flowed to the Afghan
groups fighting the Soviets. Hekmatayr's share was a minimum of $600
million.][43]

Osama Rushdi.

Before [Osama] decided to go to Sudan, he decided that everything is
finished [in Pakistan]. This is 1992. They sell everything in Peshawar and
they said al Qaeda is finished. I have seen that. The Pakistani government [exerted] a lot of pressure against Arab people. So most of the
Saudi Arabia people went to their country. Some of them went to Bosnia.
Osama bin Laden didn't order them to go to Bosnia or Chechnya or any
other place. He ordered the people that can go peacefully back to their
country to go back, but the problem is for the people who cannot go back
to their own country, and bin Laden [felt] some responsibility about
those people.

**Those members of al Qaeda who could not return to their own
countries—particularly the Egyptians, Algerians, Libyans, Syrians, and**

Iraqis who would have faced governmental persecution in their own countries—would regroup in Sudan, where in 1989 the Islamist party, the National Islamic Front (NIF), had come to power. Al Qaeda and the NIF would enjoy a convenient symbiosis. Bin Laden provided money and men to build up the desperately poor country, while Sudan provided a safe haven for al Qaeda.

5

Al Qaeda Goes Global

In the period between the Soviet's final withdrawal from Afghanistan in February 1989 and bin Laden's return to Afghanistan in May 1996, al Qaeda became increasingly globalized. Al Qaeda's focus in this period would gradually widen from the Afghan conflict to operations in the Middle East, Africa, Europe and even in the United States.

A sense of al Qaeda's global ambitions can be seen in bin Laden's offer of the services of his Afghan veterans to the Saudi government after Saddam Hussein seized Kuwait in August 1990. In its new base in Sudan during the early nineties al Qaeda would also attempt to insert itself in the war in Somalia to oppose the U.S. humanitarian mission there beginning in December 1992. Al Qaeda would also send mujahideen to fight in Bosnia against the Serbs in 1993, and graduates of its camps bombed the World Trade Center in New York the same year. In 1995 members of the Egyptian wing of the group attempted to assassinate the Egyptian president Hosni Mubarak in Ethiopia.

For bin Laden, the first order of business as the Afghan jihad wound down was to dislodge the socialist government of southern Yemen, which had ruled over bin Laden's ancestral land in Hadramaut since 1967, when the British protectorate of Aden was replaced by a government that aligned itself with the Soviets.

Abu Musab al Suri, a Syrian jihadist.[1]

I had occasionally trained militants at al Qaeda's camps from 1988 till 1991. While the Afghan Jihad was under way, bin Laden was focusing on recruiting for the Jihad in the Arab peninsula, in Yemen. Osama's main passion was the Jihad in South Yemen. He worked tirelessly to garner the support to stage a jihad against the "infidel" government there. Sheikh

Osama established al Qaeda for Jihadi goals in Afghanistan and abroad, to support Jihadi causes and organizations in many regions. Sheikh Osama didn't have any direct special project except Yemen [at that time].

Abu Walid al Misri, an Egyptian journalist close to bin Laden.[2]

Bin Laden's program was not secret either. He talked frankly about the need to liberate South Yemen from the communist rule, the Afghan way. All his moves and preparations were within that framework. To him, the Afghanistan arena was just one for training, or preparing for the decisive confrontation on the land of Yemen. He wished to Islamize the cause internationally, after the Afghan example, so as to have a massive Muslim presence in Yemen similar to the one in Afghanistan. It is for this purpose that he established the al Qaeda organization to internationalize jihad. He meant specifically the internationalization of jihad in Yemen.

Norman Benotman is the Libyan who fought with al Qaeda in Afghanistan in the early nineties.[3]

The main focus of bin Laden is Yemen. Even when he was in Afghanistan he would spend a lot of money [on the jihad in Yemen] in '88, '89, '90.

In '89 and '90 a lot of people from the jihadi movement—they considered [bin Laden] as a non-Muslim—He doesn't care about the [Arab] regimes. He doesn't declare [Saudi King] Fahd a non-Muslim. He didn't care to fight in India or Egypt or Algeria. And he started to be involved in a clash with the Egyptian Jihad. I heard from the leaders of Egyptian Jihad: "Spoiled Saudi with a lot of cash; that's it; a decent soft guy. Nothing more. He's not a Jihadist; he doesn't know anything about how to launch war. He's still thinking about the Saudis as if they are a legitimate regime."

He found himself in a critical situation. The majority of al Qaeda members—they were from Saudi Arabia. And you're talking about hundreds of people. These people, when they were in Afghanistan, they didn't have any ideology about clashes with the government and the religious bodies in Saudi Arabia. The main concern was how to liberate Muslim nations from their enemies.

Bin Laden decided to send them back to Saudi Arabia back to normal life, not as sleeper cells, but to study Shari'a (Islamic) law. That's why a lot of people said to him: "How come you have hundreds and hundreds of trained members, and then you just decide to send them back to the country to study Shari'a law. That's means you haven't got a plan and can't be considered a real jihadi leader."

Back in Saudi Arabia, bin Laden was widely seen as a war hero. Yet bin Laden, like many veterans of foreign wars, could not settle back into a comfortable domestic life when he returned home. Essam Deraz, the Egyptian filmmaker who covered bin Laden during the Afghan jihad, visited him in Saudi Arabia in 1990 as he delivered what appears to have been his first anti-American speech in public.[4]

I was there when [bin Laden] changed. He get permission to make a speech in the mosque in Saudi Arabia, after Afghan war finished. It was about the Israeli question and the supporting of USA to [bring] a million immigrants from Russia to Israel and this [made] the Palestinian question more complicated. [It was] in Jeddah, Saudi Arabia, he told me, "Please Essam. I want you to be with me for this speech. It is very important, you must be with me." In this speech he attacked America very hard. And he asked all Arab people to cut off their relationship with American people. [He said] "We have to make a stand against America because it helps Israel."

In 1990 Jamal Khalifa had not spoken to his old university buddy and brother-in-law bin Laden for four years, since they had had the bitter argument about bin Laden's military operation in Jaji in eastern Afghanistan in 1986.[5]

We met after that in '90 when he came back [to Saudi Arabia]. I was very angry with him. We were very formal; we are polite, we just talk about families, the children, sometimes we talk about horses. No politics, no jihad. Not even "what's going on, what's happening?"

[I noticed] he was very busy. Many people coming, many people going. He was a hero. Everybody talking, "Osama is great." Everybody in the street saying he is a big hero.

For me he was making a very big mistake, not only me; those who know him very closely: Wael [Julaidan], Abdullah Anas, all his friends from [the Saudi cities of] Jeddah, Medina. They left him between '86 and '88. They have been removed and the Egyptians took their place. He did not listen to anybody. He went with those Egyptians. I don't know what exactly they did, how they are able to manipulate him, how they are able to brain wash him.

When I really start to talk to him, he is not the Osama I knew. The difference: [before] we were sitting down analyzing things, talking nicely, quietly, and we came to a conclusion. But [now] he said, "No. It's like this. It's true. You are wrong."

The relationship, or lack thereof, between bin Laden and Saddam Hussein has long been a matter of debate. Yet it's clear from these accounts of what bin Laden was saying around the time of Saddam's invasion of Kuwait in 1990 that al Qaeda's leader has long been an opponent of the Iraqi dictator.

Jamal al-Fadl is the Sudanese member of al Qaeda who testified for the prosecution in the New York trial of several men implicated in the attacks on the U.S. embassies in Africa in 1998.[6]

Saddam [Hussein] he don't believe most of Islam. He got something called Ba'ath [Arab socialist political party]. I remember even bin Laden himself in '88 he make lecture against Saddam. He say Saddam is a Ba'ath [ist] and Saddam one day he going to take all of Gulf area. I remember that in '88 he make lecture in Pakistan and everybody listen to that lecture.

Khaled Batarfi, bin Laden's old friend, recalls that bin Laden was predicting Saddam Hussein's invasion of Kuwait months before it happened in August 1990.[7]

Last time I saw him was 1990, six months before the Iraqi invasion of Kuwait. It was in Mecca in a friend's house where a group of intellectuals meet every Friday. And he came and talked about jihad in Afghanistan and told us then that he'd speak to us about Saddam. He said, "We should train our people, our young and increase our army and prepare for the day when eventually we are attacked. This guy [Saddam] can never be trusted."

He doesn't believe [Saddam is] a Muslim. So he never liked him nor trusted him.

Prince Turki, the former head of Saudi intelligence, recalled bin Laden's offer of help against Saddam Hussein in an interview with *Arab News*.[8]

[After Iraq's invasion of Kuwait in August 1990] it was not [bin Laden] alone who offered their services [for jihad against Saddam Hussein]. Other personalities in the Arab world did the same. They wanted to show that there are Arabs capable of fighting and defeating Saddam.

[Bin Laden] believed that he was capable of preparing an army to challenge Saddam's forces. Secondly, he opposed the Kingdom's decision to call friendly forces, [the U.S. military]. By doing so, he disobeyed the ruler and violated the fatwa of senior Islamic scholars, who had endorsed the plan as an essential move to fight [Saddam's] aggression.

I saw radical changes in his personality as he changed from a calm, peaceful and gentle man interested in helping Muslims into a person who believed that he would be able to amass and command an army to liberate Kuwait. It revealed his arrogance.

Abu Jandal is a Saudi who became bin Laden's bodyguard in Afghanistan. He recalls bin Laden's opposition to Saddam Hussein.

[Bin Laden] called on the Saudi Government to allow for the recruitment of youths and to open the door of jihad in the land of the two holy mosques [Saudi Arabia] in order to defeat the Iraqi invasion and expel the invaders from Kuwait. Bin Laden had many reasons to call for jihad. His intentions were geared toward ending the Iraqi occupation of Kuwait and rescuing the Iraqi people from the domination of the Ba'th Party (Saddam Hussein's nationalist-socialist organization). Sheikh Osama bin Laden was dreaming of this. Therefore, he asked the Saudi Government to open the door for him. He said he was ready to prepare more than 100,000 fighters in three months. He used to say: "I have more than 40,000 mujahideen in the land of the two holy mosques alone." These were trained in Afghanistan. He said he was ready to prepare them within a few days. The number of other mujahideen outside Saudi Arabia was many times more.

According to bin Laden, he proposed this to a senior official in the Saudi Government. He told him: "We are ready to get the Iraqi forces out of Kuwait." But the state policy at that time showed that the issue had already been decided and U.S. forces were called in to get the Iraqis out of Kuwait.

The Saudi government's decision to allow the introduction of some 500,000 U.S. troops into Saudi Arabia in the summer of 1990 was a defining moment for bin Laden. In the late eighties bin Laden had instructed Arab militants living in Pakistan and Afghanistan to avoid criticism of members of the Saud royal family. In the early 1990s he would turn against the royal family, partly because of its corruption, but primarily because of its decision to rely on non-Muslims to defend the holy land of Arabia.

Abu Jandal became bin Laden's chief bodyguard in 1998. In a series of interviews with Khaled al Hammadi, the Yemeni correspondent of the *Al Quds al Arabi* newspaper, he provides a unique insider's account of al Qaeda. Those interviews appeared in the *Al Quds* newspaper in August 2004 and are woven throughout this book.[9]

Sheikh Osama bin Laden's departure from Saudi Arabia was not direct. He left Saudi Arabia for Pakistan and stayed there for some time. During that time, he was looking for a more suitable country to receive his followers, because the Saudi authorities were giving them a hard time. Sheikh Osama himself was given a onetime-passport, to be used to exit Saudi Arabia and return once only. He used this passport for a final exit from Saudi Arabia and never returned. He was given that passport because of his personal connections with some members of the royal family [so he could] travel to Pakistan to liquidate his investments there and then to return to Saudi Arabia and live under house arrest. But he used this permission to exit Saudi Arabia and never return.

Noman Benotman.

The first thing he did when he left for Pakistan, he wrote a letter to his brother saying: "Sorry, I will never come back." And I think that's when bin Laden started to reshape his view about Saudi Arabia. He started to think, oh, it's real business. You can't be a leader for jihad and at the same time be allied to Arab governments.

Abu Musab al Suri first met bin Laden in 1988. In his book *The International Islamic Resistance Call,* published on jihadist Web sites in December 2004, he explains how bin Laden, who had firmly allied himself with the Saudi government during the 1980s, would gradually change his views, and in challenging the Saudi government how he also would come to oppose the American government.

The methodical and intellectual change of Osama bin Laden, may God keep him, which was reflected in his and al Qaeda's attitude towards the USA is one of the issues that had not been discussed by media or publications. The two essential factors that caused this attitude were (by order of importance):

1. Sheikh Osama had fundamentally built al Qaeda by the efforts of Egyptian al-Jihad organization militants and others who participated in training the Jihadi movement's cadres in other regions. Those were not all members of al Qaeda, but cooperated with it on the basis of mutual benefits. Those mujahideen, and I was one of them for a period of time, began preaching their Jihadist ideas. Fighters were trained to fire at [targets of Saudi] King Fahd and senior Saudi princes' pictures. As time passed by, the jihadists influenced the youth base of al Qaeda, through their books, lectures, methods and discussions. This influence was later transmitted to Sheikh Osama. He, like most Saudis, had come for Jihad in Afghanistan, carrying the method of the Islamic Awakening which is a mixture of the views of the Muslim Brotherhood and Wahabbi [Saudi] official preachers.

[At the time] Sheikh Osama and most Saudi mujahideen believed that the Saudi government is legitimate, that King Fahd and the Saud family are Muslims and legitimate rulers, despite their depravity and oppression. They deeply respected official [Saudi] Islamic scholars, and adhered to their fatwas. The general aspects of Islam and support for the Afghan Jihad constituted the only common ground between those brothers including Sheikh Osama, and us, the Jihadists. On the other hand, our differences in Jihadi thought were clear. With time, Sheikh Osama, may God keep him; gradually digested, accepted and adopted the Jihadist thought and became one of its symbols. I believe that what helped in this, in addition to mingling with Jihadists, was the second factor:

2. The Saudi government, its ruling institutions and official clergy-men's stance about the [1990] Kuwait war aftermath and the presence of U.S. troops in Saudi Arabia. The changes that followed this war exposed the infidel's great role in the Arabian Peninsula and the depth of the religious institutions' hypocrisy (which had given their blessing to the presence of U.S. troops in Saudi Arabia).

Bin Laden understood the strategic reasons behind the American presence in the region. His long stay in Sudan (1992–1996), gave him enough time for contemplation. His rhetoric changed from his lenient media opposition to the Saudi royal family to calling for serious reforms through harsh speeches and criticism of the government as well as the hypocritical official religious institutions.

With God's help, Osama bin Laden arrived at the correct political equation:

1. Islamic clerics give legitimacy to the Royal family (the Saudis).
2. The Saud Family gave legitimacy to the American presence in the Arabian Peninsula.

There were therefore two methods to confront the Saud family:

1. Either by confronting the Sauds, thereby necessitating confrontation with the Islamic clerics to unveil their hypocrisy, in order to overthrow the Sauds' legitimacy. This is a losing battle in the eyes of the people due to the size and influence of the Saudi religious establishment that has planted legitimacy and prestige in the minds of people for the past seventy years or more.

2. Or a safer route, which is to attack the American presence [in Saudi Arabia]. Thus the Sauds will be forced to defend them, which mean they will lose their legitimacy in the eyes of Muslims. This will lead the reli-

gious establishment to defend [the Americans] which in turn will make them lose their legitimacy. Then the battle will be on clearer grounds in the eyes of the people.

Sheikh Osama chose the second option, and I think he was right to a large extent. Furthermore, Sheikh Osama had studied the collapse of the Soviet Union and of the dictator governments in the Warsaw Pact countries and, as had happened in East Germany, Romania, Poland and other countries; he was convinced that with the fall of the United States, all the components of the existing Arab and Islamic regimes will fall as well. Therefore he was convinced of the necessity of focusing his effort on fighting Jihad against America. He then started to call upon those around him to the idea of fighting the war against the "Head of the Snake," as he would call it, rather than against "its many tails" (i.e. the authoritarian governments of the Middle East).

Paulo Jose de Almeida Santos is a Portuguese convert to Islam and an early al Qaeda recruit, who met bin Laden on a number of occasions in Pakistan when al Qaeda's leader had returned from Saudi Arabia in early 1991.

In November 1991 Santos was dispatched by al Qaeda to Italy to assassinate Zahir Shah, the seventy-seven-year-old king of Afghanistan, who had lived in exile in Rome for decades. The assassination attempt against the king appears to be the first time that al Qaeda had engaged in an act of international terrorism. The king was popular among ordinary Afghans, and the militants within al Qaeda were concerned that the king, who they viewed as a secularist, might be brought back from exile to be the titular head of a new Afghan government.

Posing as a journalist Santos was able to enter the king's heavily guarded villa, where he stabbed the king in the heart with a dagger. Only a tin of Café Crème cigarillos in the king's breast pocket, which deflected the dagger's blade, saved the aging monarch from death. The king was hospitalized and later recovered. (A decade later, al Qaeda assassins also posing as journalists would succeed in killing another popular Afghan leader, Ahmad Shah Massoud, a hit ordered by bin Laden himself.)

**After the assassination attempt against the king failed, Santos was
arrested and sentenced to ten years. He was released from Italian
prison in December 1999. Jose Pedro Castanheira of the Portuguese
magazine *Expresso* tracked Santos down to a location in East Africa
where he gave an interview in April 2002 about his time in al Qaeda, excerpts of which follow.[10]**

When I went to Afghanistan, al Qaeda was just starting to take shape,
in about 1989 or 1990; I was one of its first members. It was during the
Umrã, the lesser pilgrimage to Mecca, that I met some Afghans. When
they found out that I was a recently converted Muslim, they invited me
to take part in the war against the Soviets.

I accepted and set off for Pakistan, from where I entered Afghanistan.
I went to a training camp in Paktia (a province of Afghanistan). There
were people of various nationalities: almost from all the Arab countries,
Americans, Britons and other western countries. I asked to be trained in
that camp and after three months the person in charge invited me to discuss my becoming part of the group. The objective, at the time, was to
train Muslims in martial arts. At that time I was in very good physical
shape. We managed to run twenty-four kilometres a day, in the mountains, heavily laden. There were black Muslim Americans [there].

I took an oath of loyalty to [al Qaeda]. Our final aim was to establish
the caliphate and Islamic government and combat oppression. The immediate aim was to train Muslims in the art of warfare.

I was capable of making explosives from a pile of aspirins. The science
is in knowing how to separate acids and then mix them with other sub-
stances. I also learned how to make explosives with the mercury of ther-
mometers. I even managed to make nitroglycerine, the handling of
which is very dangerous. Very often as a result of copies of manuals intended for the American Green Berets! (U.S. Special Forces manuals
provided to al Qaeda by its main military trainer, the Egyptian-American
Ali Mohamed, who was a U.S. army sergeant at Fort Bragg, South Carolina, the headquarters of the Green Berets between 1986 and 1989.)

[I arrived in in Afghanistan in March 1990 and left in] October '91.
My group used my services on several occasions because I had a clean
European passport and could therefore travel and contact certain peo-

ple. I went to India, Egypt, Turkey as part of my work. In Afghanistan, we all used an alias, "kunya," in Arabic. Most people were called Abu something. I was called Abdullah Yusuf. No one used their real name.

When [bin Laden] had to leave Saudi Arabia [in 1991] some of the al Qaeda people got together—including me—to welcome him [to Pakistan]. It was in one of our houses in Peshawar; bin Laden arrived, shook hands with all of us, sat down and began to speak. I recall that when he arrived, we were all seated and remained so. I said, "but wouldn't it be better if we stood up?" The person next to me replied, "If no-one stood up for a man like the Prophet Mohammed, why should we have to stand up for bin Laden?"

He was an extraordinarily humble person. He was not the typical Arab who has photographs of himself everywhere. I think he desires only one thing and that is martyrdom. It doesn't bother me in the slightest to think that bin Laden could die at the hands of the Americans. I believe this is what he wants.

He spoke about jihad being the top. I remember an oral tradition passed on by the Prophet which says that up until the Final Judgment there will be a group of Muslims who will wage war against oppression. [Bin Laden said] al Qaeda was one of the groups the Prophet Mohammed was speaking of. He he said that jihad was like the summit of a mountain; the longer we were in jihad, the longer we would be at the top of the mountain. I considered them normal words spoken by a normal guy. I can love him, symphathize with him, but it's not as if I in any way venerated bin Laden.

We had been divided into several groups. There was a technological group. I did a test to become part of that group, but the person in charge, who was an Egyptian electronics engineer, did not like what I did and failed me. They put me in the analysis group where I had to read all the newspapers and give my analysis about what to do.

Abu Hafs (the Egyptian Mohamed Atef, one of the group's military commanders) was the real chief of al Qaeda. Bin Laden was very humble. I could ask him for advice in particular circumstances and he would simply say: "Go and ask Abu Hafs, who is more intelligent than me."

After the fall of Khost, capital of Paktia [in March 1991] our analysis was that the fall of Kabul was near. It was logical in so far that Khost was on the road to Kabul. There were several mujahideen groups that were fighting. Some felt that the king [of Afghanistan] was better than nothing, that at least during his time the country had enjoyed some stability. Those groups were thinking of bringing the king back. Other groups, the more hard-line Muslims, said that this king had never been a good Muslim. One of those groups was Hizh-e-Islami, led by [Gulbuddin] Hekmatyar, who said: "If the king comes back, we will fight him and will wage war against those who want to establish a monarchy."

So I made a proposal to eliminate the king. In our group, there wasn't a well-defined hierarchy, we were rather disorganized; you could give a try to whatever entered into your head. After having described the project, I was invited in Peshawar to meet bin Laden—or Abu Abdallah, which means "father of Abdallah." No one in Afghanistan called him Osama bin Laden. He wanted to know why I was so sure the king had to be killed.

They asked how I could carry it out, with whom, what my plan was. I very much liked asking questions as a way of testing my interlocutor, so I asked him, "If a woman were to be near the king, and I were to use a bomb or a weapon that could injure or kill the person next to him, would I be allowed to continue?" The answer was: "If it were the king's wife, she shares with the king the same responsibilities; she may, therefore be eliminated." Then I asked: "And if it happened to be a grandson of the king, a child?" Bin Laden said "No, no, in no way!" He became angry: "What are you saying? We are Muslims, we do not eliminate children!" Bin Laden said that if a child was [present during the assassination attempt] you could not attack the king. He would rather have the king return and have a civil war than to kill a child."

Bin Laden once said that any adult Israeli citizen, man or woman, could be assassinated. Because [Israeli] women could also serve in the army. There was an American there who asked: "But the Americans are also our enemies, so can we eliminate American civilians?" Bin Laden answered: "No. The American government is one thing, the majority of Americans don't even vote, they are totally apathetic."

At one time they proposed increasing (al-Qaeda's) finances through the use of drug money. I know that bin Laden answered that "We Muslims carry a message of hope to humanity and can therefore in no way use drugs—which destroy families in Europe and the West—to obtain money." That is the bin Laden I know. Someone who refused to dirty his hands with the blood of innocent people. He is a very moral person.

We went to eat at [bin Laden's] house where [a few al Qaeda members] were invited to have lunch to get to know each other. Whether he gave the green light [to kill the king] or not is not important. Bin Laden, at that time, did not give any orders. He was the guy who gave money to keep the organization going, he had a reputation for being very courageous, but he didn't give many orders.

Often, I have thought that I probably experienced a moment of weakness [in my attempt to kill the king]. I spent one hour with him, in his house; I drank the coffee he offered me, I was his guest; we talked and he was friendly, pleasant. I believe that subconsciously I failed in my attempt because at the last moment I felt pity for the old man.

I do not repent! At the Italian trial I asked for the case to be over quickly. I did not defend myself. No defense was possible: it was an act of war in a country that was not at war, so I had to pay the consequences.

In my time [in al Qaeda], operations against Western governments were not popular. It was at the embryonic stage [of al Qaeda]. The bin Laden who I know is a man I can admire, for whom I pray, that his wishes may be fulfilled and that God may accept his martyrdom.

Al Qaeda began rebasing itself far from Afghanistan after 1989, taking advantage of the conditions in the weak and failed African states of Sudan and Somalia. Former Egyptian army officer Sayf al Adel, now al Qaeda's military commander, is quoted in the book *Al-Zarqawi: The Second al Qaeda Generation* by Fuad Hussein, a Jordanian journalist. *Al Quds al Arabi* started serializing the book in May 2005. Al Adel outlines al Qaeda's shift toward Africa.[11]

After God granted the Muslim mujahideen in Afghanistan victory against the Russians and when disagreements began to emerge among factions of the Afghan mujahideen, many of our Arab brothers were thinking of returning to their native countries, including the Saudis, Yemenis, and Jordanians, who had no problems with the security services in their homeland. On the other hand, we, the Egyptians, and our

Syrian, Algerian, and Libyan brothers had no alternative other than to stay in Afghanistan, fight on the frontlines of jihad, or go to safe places where there were no powerful central Governments. Therefore, we chose Sudan, Somalia, and some underprivileged African countries. Some fraternal brothers had already left to the countries that won independence from the disintegrating Soviet Union while others spread to the four corners of the world.

Jamal al Fadl is a Sudanese citizen who became an early member of al Qaeda. He was a government witness in the 2001 trial of the four men accused in al Qaeda's bombing of two U.S. embassies in Africa in 1998. Extracts from his testimony are woven throughout this book.[12]

[In 1989] I remember in a guesthouse for al Qaeda members, they start[ed] talking: "In Afghanistan we don't have too much work because the Russians, they left." And they talk[ed] about the government change in Sudan, and [how] the Islamic National Front runs the government over there, and [that] they [are] very good. And they want to make [a] relationship with al Qaeda, [and that] if we move over there it's better because it's near [the] Arab world. Afghanistan is too far.

Bin Laden decide[d] to send some people to Sudan at that time to discover what [was] going on over there. And when they came back I remember I was in Khost area in Farouq camp [in eastern Afghanistan]. Some of the al Qaeda members in the camp got lecture[d] by Abu Hajer al Iraqi. He said he went over there and [met] some of the Islamic National Front in Sudan and they are very good people and they [are] very happy to make this relationship with al Qaeda, and he [said] I have some books from the scholar in that group, named Dr. Hassan al Turabi.

I went with some members [of al Qaeda] and we start [to] rent houses and farms in Khartoum, we rent[ed] houses for the single people and some houses for the people that got family. And also we bought farms for [a form of military] training. The first farm I bought for $250,000. I bought in my name [a] salt farm in Port Sudan; it's around 1,100 kilometers from Khartoum, the capital city, [for] around $180,000.

Jamal Ismail worked at *Jihad* magazine.[13]

The Sudan government extended an invitation for [bin Laden]. They opened the borders for Arabs and Muslims to invest and to visit Sudan. And I think Sudanese, especially Dr. al Turabi, played a very, very important role in convincing [Sudanese President] Omar Bashir [to] bring Osama because by bringing Osama, others will come with him, Ayman al Zawahiri and al Jihad group. And you don't have anyone better than Osama at that time to raise funds and to help the government.

Hassan al Turabi was released from prison in Sudan in July 2005 after falling out with the regime in 1999. The de facto leader of Sudan during the 1990s, Turabi today plays down his once close relationship with bin Laden.[14]

I met bin Laden in this chair once. I never invited him for dinner here. It was only to chat, to visit for a while. And I then visited his home, but it wasn't for dinner or lunch or anything. He wasn't present in public life—not in the mosque and not in the papers. He was just investing here. His temperament is very cold and very gentle. Just very cool. We spoke a little bit about his country, about Saudi Arabia, and a little bit about investing.

The people who knew him in Afghanistan came from all parts of the world to fight against the Russians. But they couldn't go back home. The war was over, and retroactively they became "terrorists." They can't go to Egypt, they can't go to Saudi Arabia, they can't go to Algeria.

Wisal al Turabi, the wife of Hassan al Turabi.[15]

[My husband] didn't bring bin Laden to the Sudan. Bin Laden thought that the Sudan was attractive to him and [he could] use his money for building the Sudan. He was planting, he was making chicken farms. He was building roads for the Sudanese people.

You know, Muslim women don't meet Muslim men. And when they come to our houses, we don't see them. We don't converse with them. I didn't see bin Laden at all in my life. And he was not such an important figure in the Sudan. Nobody knew him because he was only planting [at his farms] in Damazine. He was planting sunflowers to make oil, and he built the road from Khartoum to Damazine. He built the Port Sudan airport and he was supposed to be given money [for that] by the government.

I met [one of bin Laden's wives], Um Ali (mother of Ali), in her house. I didn't see her children, but she said the children were in another room trying to learn the Koran. I saw one room only. It was furnished, with European furniture, of course. She was a university lecturer. She was very knowledgeable because she studied in Saudi Arabia. She used to go to Saudi Arabia and come during her holidays to stay in Khartoum. She was teaching Islam to some families in Riyadh (an upscale neighborhood in Khartoum). I [went] once to hear what she was saying. She was saying things about the relation of Islam to the woman's status in the family.

Three of his wives are university lecturers; the first one is not. He has four wives. And he married the other three because they were spinsters. They were going to go without marrying in this world. So he married them for the word of God. In Islam we do this. If you have a spinster, if you marry her, you will be rewarded for this in the afterworld, because you will bring up your offspring as Muslims. And when they become Muslims they will be merciful, they will be lawful, they won't drink, they won't kill, they won't commit adultery.

I [also] met [bin Laden's first wife]. She lived in Riyadh [in Khartoum]. She was Syrian. She cared for her children and she wasn't complaining of her husband marrying three other wives. Not like the modern trend now in the Muslim world. Now a husband marries over his wife, she becomes very prudish and very angry and she may even ask for a divorce. I invited her for supper here in the house. We just talked about how many children we have, and about social subjects. You see you don't speak in the Muslim world about how you met your husband. She was very pretty, tall, very tall. I didn't care for her. It was just a social occasion to invite somebody who came to your country, and we are very well known in Sudan. I had to do something to recognize her. Well, Sheikh Osama was not such an important person in the Sudan. So we had a very small dinner upstairs.

Abu Jandal, bin Laden's chief bodyguard.[16]

His wife Um Ali (the mother of Ali) asked Sheikh Osama for a divorce when they still lived in Sudan. She said that she could not continue to live in an austere way and in hardship. He respected her wish and divorced her in accordance with the Koranic verse, "Husband and wife should either live together equitably or separate in kindness." The other wives stayed with him, however, although they come from distinguished families and are highly educated. His wives Um Hamza and Um Khalid [the mothers of Hamza and Khalid] both have doctoral degrees, one in Arabic language and the other in Islamic sharia.

Ibrahim Mohammed al Sanoussi was the assistant to Hassan Turabi. They were two of the most powerful people in Sudan when bin Laden was living there in the mid-nineties.[17]

I have known Hassan al Turabi since we were at secondary school together [in] 1954. He was very brilliant and intelligent during intermediate school and secondary school. He went to the faculty of law and then went to do his Master's in the UK and then his Ph.D. in Paris in constitutional law. Since then I have had a relationship with him. I eventually became a governor [of a province in Sudan].

Osama bin Laden came to the Sudan offering his help making roads and they assigned him to make a road north of Khartoum. And he began to make canals and cultivating soil, and sunflower oil. It was very successful. I remembered he showed us [a sunflower] it was thirty centimeters, a very big one. In this way we knew him for the first time. He was a very decent man, he was always silent and he [was] very religious and generous and he never had the appetite for the luxurious.

At that time Dr. Turabi and Osama were friends. We used to sit together and were chatting about his agricultural schemes and how he made the roads and the kinds of stones [he used]. I didn't think he was the right man to speak to about politics. [Osama] just came to my country and helped me and at that time I was grateful to him. At that time still we thought he was a religious man and not a politician because sometimes we would be meeting and he never speaks to us about politics. He asked Dr. Turabi especially about his ideas about Islam [for instance] Islam [and its view on] mortgages.

The Egyptians sent their security men to Sudan. They were able to penetrate the circle of these Islamists around Osama and the Egyptians. They recruited the son of one of them and they gave him a microphone.

The security men of the Sudan knew that and arrested the boy (the 15-year-old son of Muhammad Sharaf, an Egyptian Jihad member living in Sudan). The father of the boy came to the security men and asked to [have] his son back. They give him [the son and] then [the Egyptian Jihad group mounted a court hearing]. They tried him in their own courts and convicted him [and executed him]. This is the reason why the [Sudanese] government [wanted to expel the Jihad group]. They said, "You are practicing the power of a state within a state within our state so you have to go out. Now you are [acting like] a government. You make a trial and execute people without permission."

Montasser al Zayyat is the Egyptian lawyer who became friendly with Ayman al Zawahiri in the early 1980s when they were both in prison in Cairo. Zayyat and Zawahiri have in recent years become vocal critics of each other.[18]

Zawahiri became so cruel that he killed the son of one of his closest confidants in front of his father. When Zawahiri was living in Sudan [in 1994] with Osama bin Laden along with hundreds of Jihad members, the [Security] committee noticed that information was being leaked to the Egyptian government. The boy was condemned by a shari'a court that Zawahiri formed. The court said that he harmed the group by spying on its activities for the Egyptian authorities. The boy, 15-year-old Mos'ab Mohamed Sharaf, was executed in front of a number of leading figures within the group in order to deter others from committing the same crime. This incident shows how the cruel life that Zawahiri has lived has affected his character. In Zawahiri's mind Jihad has turned from being a means to an end into being an end in and of itself.

Hassan Abd-Rabbuh al Surayhi is a Saudi who fought with bin Laden in Afghanistan.[19]

I visited him in Sudan. He owned two buildings. He used one as his residence and the second as his company headquarters. I found him with his Egyptian cronies—Abu-Ubaidah and Abu Hafs—and some Sudanese who were working in his company. I invited him to return to Saudi Arabia and told him, "I advise you to return instead of staying with this bunch." We were alone in the room. He said that he owned companies that were operating in Sudan. I told him, "You can run your companies from your country." He said, "I am tired. I miss living in Medina [in Saudi Arabia]. Only God knows how nostalgic I am."

Jamal al Fadl.[20]

[The] first company we establish [was] Wadi al Aqiq and we establish Ladin International Company. Al Hijra construction built roads and bridge. They build a road 83 miles between Damazine City and Kormuk City.

Mohamed Zeki Mahjoub, an Egyptian who had worked for bin Laden's businesses in Sudan during the mid-1990s, submitted this affidavit in the matter of _Minister of Citizenship and Immigration and Mohamed Zeki Mahjoub,_ Federal Court of Canada, September 6, 2000. He describes what it was like to be employed by bin Laden.[21]

I am an agricultural engineer by profession. I arrived in Canada in 1995 and immediately made claim to refugee status.

While working and living in Sudan I some time heard the name "al Qaida" mentioned. Individuals some time mentioned, in casual conversation, this name and admitted belonging to this organization. I have never been a member, associate or supporter of the organization known as al Qaida.

With respect to Osama bin Laden, I wish to state the following: Prior to leaving Egypt, I had no relationship with Osama bin Laden whatsoever. From Egypt, I went to Saudi Arabia and, from there I went to Sudan. For the first five months in Sudan I had no employment and I was trying to find a job as an Agricultural Engineer. In Sudan, I lived in Khartoum. While looking for work in Sudan, I approached several prospective employers; however, the salaries being offered were very low. Also as a non-Sudanese, I was expected to have a certain number of years experience which I did not have.

Osama bin Laden owns a company in Sudan, Al Thimar al Mubaraka Agricultural company. This company is one of many branches of a larger company involved in irrigation, agriculture, commerce, roads and bridges, etc. The company employs ten thousand people approximately. In the branch that I ended up working in there were approximately 4000 employees and approximately 85% were Sudanese.

When I was looking for work in Sudan, there was intensive media coverage of Osama bin Laden's presence in Sudan. As well, the media ran daily reports about his business activities and various business projects. One Friday, I went to the mosque for the regular Friday prayer and met an individual whom I got to know and told him that I was looking for a job as an agricultural Engineer. I also told him that my academic training was in land reclamation. I later came to learn that the man I met in the mosque was an employee of one of Osama bin Laden's companies.

One of Osama bin Laden's large projects in Sudan at that time, involved making the soil ready for the cultivation of corn, sunflowers, wheat and some vegetables. The man whom I met in the mosque told me that he would try to speak with Osama bin Laden about getting me a job with one of his companies.

The appointment was arranged for me to meet Osama bin Laden at his office in Khartoum. Osama bin Laden met me personally and told me that he had interviewed several people with my academic qualifications but not in the same field of specialization. He further told me that he needs to assess the persons personally and that it is not enough to assess the person's academic qualifications. My first interview with Osama bin Laden lasted one and half to two hours. He asked me many questions about my field of specialization and about my previous work experience. I was honest and told bin Laden that I had no experience but that I would be willing to study the project and tell him if I was able to do the job or not. Bin Laden told me to take one week to study the project and report back about whether I could do the job.

After one week, I met with the general manager of bin Laden's company and provided my decision to him in writing and also discussed technical aspects of the project. It was this way that I began to work as the deputy general manager of the Al Damazin Farms project in Sudan. I had approximately 4000 people under my supervision the majority of whom were temporary or seasonal workers. The area of the project that I was in-charge of was approximately 1 million acres. I held this position until May 1993.

During this period of my employment, I met Osama bin Laden three additional times. I met him once in Khartoum and two additional times on location at the project that I was working on. The meeting in Khartoum was solely for the purpose of reporting to him about the day-to-day operations of the project. This meeting took place in his office in Khartoum and lasted approximately 1½ to 2 hours. The two meetings on location at the project took place when Osama bin Laden visited the project.

I made a personal decision to leave my employment with Osama bin Laden's company. While I had agreed on a salary with Osama bin Laden after I began working for his company, I learned that others working on other projects, with a lower job titles and level of responsibility were getting paid more money that I was. During the course of my employment, I worked a 10-hour shift but regularly worked 8 hours of overtime as well.

In the end, I decided that, if bin Laden agreed to pay equity I may stay, otherwise, I would resign. I resigned as the answer to my request came back in the negative through the Director General of the company. After I resigned I never saw or talked with Osama bin Laden again. Later, Osama bin Laden realized that he needed me to come back offering a higher salary and benefits. However, I did not return because I had told bin Laden, during our previous discussion, that if I resigned I would not come back.

During the time I worked on the project in Sudan I heard the following about Osama bin Laden's reputation from other office employees. I heard that bin Laden had been in Afghanistan and that he had a large number of employees in Afghanistan and Sudan. I heard that he was supporting the mujahedeen in Afghanistan and that his relationship with Saudi Arabia was not good. During the approximately one year that I worked for his company, I never heard that he was involved in any terrorist activities.

At around August 1995, the relationship between Egypt and Sudan was deteriorating especially due to the attempted assassination of Egyptian President Mubarak in Ethiopia during the summer of 1995 (an attack carried out by Egyptian militants based in Sudan). At this time, I began to look for a way to come to Canada safely. I began looking for a passport which would allow me to enter Canada without a visa. I was told that a passport from Saudi Arabia does not require a visa to Canada and

I eventually bought a Saudi Arabian passport in Sudan for 2500 US dollars.

Abdullah Anas was bin Laden's friend in Peshawar during the mid-1980s.[22]

I met Osama twice [in Sudan]. I think more than 95 percent of his time was for business. He failed completely. He was very angry about the Sudanese. I remember when we were in his car he told me "I am facing problems with the Sudanese people. They told me they never imagined in their life somebody can work eight hours. They come for work two-three hours, and then they go."

Jamal al Fadl.[23]

We talked [with] bin Laden and we asked him if we have to make money because the business is very bad in Sudan. [Bin Laden] say our agenda is bigger than business. We not going to make business here, but we need to help the government, and the government help our group, and this is our purpose.

Wael Julaidan had known bin Laden in Jeddah since the early 1980s and had worked with him in Pakistan during the mid-1980s. He visited him in Sudan in 1993, the last time he would speak with bin Laden.[24]

Until 1992, there was nothing serious [about], "al Qaeda" or a real front. It's more of an idea.

One day he disappeared, just disappeared [from Pakistan]. That was in '92, maybe mid-'92. Then later we have heard he's in Sudan.

I met Osama in '93 in Sudan because at that time there was land given to the Muslim World League [with which I am associated] to establish their own office in Khartoum. So I went there for an official visit for three days. I visited Osama and I talked to him. I said "Do you believe that your family are happy? As long as you are out [of Saudi Arabia], everybody is unhappy."

Most of the family members went to him in Khartoum and tried to convince him the same—come back. I talked to some of his family. I said

"Why is Osama not back?" They said we are all trying, even we have asked our uncle who is a very old man, Abdullah (Mohamed bin Laden's brother), he went there. We thought if the eldest of the family would go there, he would surely come back. But Osama did not pay any respect to [his uncle.]

Really, the big question here is: What happened? Is he the same Osama?

Essam al Ridi is the Egyptian pilot who met bin Laden in Pakistan in the mid-1980s. A decade before the 9/11 attacks, while bin Laden was based in Sudan, he reached out to al Ridi to ask him to purchase a jet in the United States, the first time that bin Laden had interested himself in American aviation. Ridi testified about that purchase in a New York terrorism trial in 2001. Excerpts of his testimony follow:[25]

[In 1992] there was quite a few communications between me and Wadih El Hage (bin Laden's Lebanese-American personal secretary) about the interests of Osama acquiring an airplane [to be] used in Khartoum. The price range within 350,000 U.S. [dollars] and a [flying] range of about a little bit over two thousand miles. Once I located an airplane with that price and that range, I've called Wadih and specifically told him, it's 350,000 and I'll be offered 9 percent from the dealer, the owner of the airplane. This is a customary commission when you buy or sell an aircraft in the U.S.

This part did not really go through. They came later with a different price. They wanted something within the 250,000 [dollars] or less, and my response was, you'll never get a used jet aircraft for that price that will do the range that you want.

They [had] some goods of their own they want to ship from Peshawar [Pakistan] to Khartoum—[U.S.] Stinger missiles (a highly effective anti-aircraft missile).

With the reduction in the price and the range I had limited options, one of which was a military aircraft under the designation of T389 which is the equivalent of a civilian aircraft called Saber-40. The airplane was in storage, what we call "boneyard" in Tucson, Arizona. So we pulled the aircraft out of the storage and we had to go through certain checks mechanically to make it acceptable by the FAA [Federal Aviation Administration]. [I spent] about a total of 230 thousand dollars. I refurbished it completely.

We took off from Dallas–Fort Worth to Khartoum. The airplane had a range of about 1500 miles. You cannot really cross the Atlantic with that range. The first [flight] was Dallas–Fort Worth to St. Marie at the Canadian border. From there on to a place 67 lat[itude] north [in]Canada and then to Iceland, to Rome, Cairo, Khartoum. It should have taken two days at the most, but actually we had some technical problems due to the bad weather in [Canada]. It was minus 65, so we lost hydraulics and we had a crack in the window.

I just parked the airplane [at Khartoum airport]. It must have been the same day, at night, we were offered dinner on [bin Laden's] behalf at his guest house. We had dinner and chatted. I gave the keys of the airplane to Osama bin Laden. We collectively agreed to come to the airport the next morning to look at the airplane. I went early morning to the airplane, got it ready, cleaned it from the previous flight, and waited for Osama. Then I was told to go to the office. I had few other receipts to finish with the accountant, and to meet with Osama. We were supposed to discuss an offer for me to work with [him].

The offer was earlier discussed over the phone with Wadih, and I said we will delay those things until I come there and see Khartoum itself. The offer was to work with him to fly that particular airplane and to also set up an operation of crop dusting because he's into the agriculture business.

Before we start discussing the offer I had few things to discuss with Osama on a personal level relating to the days in Peshawar [during the '80s] and relating to my stand that led me to leave Peshawar. I told him, "Regardless what you think I want you to hear it from me. I do oppose the fact that you are a rich man trying to be a military leader. At the time I did not think that you have any military background, nor did you have any military experience. Thus, I think that what you have done to some of the guys is flat killing, not jihad. Now, perhaps after so many years you have gained experience, and now it's a different situation." He said, "Well, thank you very much." He was very acceptable of the critiques. And later he said, "This is not jihad. This is strictly business, and this is an official certified company in Khartoum."

[Bin Laden offered me 1,200 dollars a month salary] I said: "This is to do what exactly of the three jobs? I mean flying the airplane, doing the crop dusting and the cargo. One thousand two hundred U.S. dollars." He said "That's the offer. This is the highest that I'm paying around the company for my highest officers." I said, "That's fine. I have heard enough about Khartoum. There is a high inflation in the country; schools are very expensive for expatriates. The furniture also is very expensive. It is not healthy environment at all, so I guess it's going to cost me much more than that. So if you are paying this price for your highest officers that does not mean that I should be paid equivalently because I do a different job."

Ridi turned down the job.

Jamal al Fadl describes bin Laden's living situation in Sudan.[26]

[Bin Laden's] guesthouse, it's in Riyadh City, [Khartoum]. It's a big house and three floors with a front yard and backyard. [Bin Laden] spend most of his time in the guesthouse. When we go over there we do the prayer together and sometime we take dinner together and we talk. [Bin Laden] liked to sit in the front yard and talk about jihad and about Islam and about the al Qaeda in general, in the second floor he got big room. It's only for him.

Sheikh Abdul Ghafar, the imam of the Khartoum mosque where bin Laden worshipped.[27]

He stayed here until 1996. He lived in this area. The weather here is very good. Also, all of the people here in the area, they are first-class. This mosque is the nearest mosque [to his house]. He used to come to the mosque for prayers five times a day, and he came to the mosque always very calm. He was a very, very decent man, and the very wisest man. And really a good Muslim. I asked him to address the Muslims in the mosque. He refused. He would just come to do his prayers. No more than that.

Osama and his kids and one of his guards would come to the mosque for two or three minutes [before prayer time]. And after they did their prayers, he would leave the mosque, again after two or three minutes also. He did not stay a long time.

He was very simple. Really, very simple. He put his blankets on the floor and he always slept on the ground. I visited him once or twice when he was sick or he asked for me from the mosque. And he always had his food in one dish. Very simple types of foods. It is not often that you find it like that, a rich family, as famous as his. You know that he is very rich? A Good Muslim! 100 percent, you know?

Mahjub al Aradi worked as a gardener for bin Laden when he lived in Sudan. In November 2001, the London newspaper *Al Quds al Arabi* published al Aradi's account of his time with bin Laden in Sudan. Excerpts from the *Al Quds* article follow.[28]

Bin Laden used to live in a two-story house in al Riyadh suburb, east of Khartoum, and would receive his guests at another house similar to the first one. He had an office on [Mc]Nimr Street. Al Aradi, 74 years old, worked for Osama bin Laden for four years up to the moment he left Sudan. Al Aradi said, "There were many guests who used to visit bin Laden during the daytime, including Egyptian and Yemeni men wearing the traditional long dress. Very often these people would bring their families, many of whom left with bin Laden to Afghanistan."

Al Aradi said bin Laden had four wives, four sons—Abdallah, Abd al Rahman, Ahmad, and Muhammad—and a very young daughter. His son Abdallah went to Saudi Arabia, where he married his cousin. Osama bin Laden made his three other sons leave school to attend lessons on the recital of the Koran by two teachers from West Sudan. Regarding his activity in Khartoum, al Aradi said Osama bin Laden was always escorted by special guards, in addition to guards in front of his house who would sit in a ground-level place where they could clearly see others. The guards carried machine guns to protect bin Laden's homes and would accompany bin Laden on his trips outside Khartoum.

Every day, bin Laden would go to the office and then to his guesthouse where he would stay until eight or nine o'clock in the evening after which he would return to his houses. He used to like farming and he contributed to planting vast areas with watermelon. This helped decrease the price of watermelon. He was also interested in training police dogs.

Al Aradi said bin Laden used to eat a little amount of food and would eat the leftovers from guests because he thought this was a blessing taught by the Prophet. Bin Laden used to dress simply. He often wore a long dress and long headdress and shoes open at the back.

Scott Macleod, a correspondent for *Time* magazine, interviewed bin Laden in the spring of 1996, while he was living in Sudan.[29]

He was at that time building a road in Sudan from Khartoum to Port Sudan, and he owned a sunflower seed plantation and owned a tanning factory. And he went to great pains to show me all this. Clearly he was trying to present the image that—look, I'm a businessman, I have my problems with the Saudi government, I won't deny them—and he ran through a litany of why the Saudi government was corrupt or illegitimate. But he said, "The way of fighting this is not violent. We're politicians." He was at pains to show me the non-military side of Osama bin Laden. If he was purely involved in business, this is what I would have seen. It was a very normal sort of Third World business setting.

Khaled al Fauwaz, a Saudi, worked both as bin Laden's media representative in London and for the Advice and Reformation Committee, a political organization founded by bin Laden in 1994 that ostensibly worked nonviolently to reform the Saudi regime.[30]

I visited him once at least in Sudan, and when I observed his house and his way of living, I couldn't believe my eyes. He has no fridge at home, no air conditioning, no refrigerator, no fancy car. He also took me to a large farm where he was doing experimental plantings of unusual trees. He wanted to encourage me to invest in Sudan. I was not convinced. I thought Sudan was difficult to invest in, because of their regulations. At that time I was in the food import-export business. Osama said: "You should grow food in Sudan and then export it to Saudi Arabia."

He's a millionaire, and he is keeping his money for the general Muslim cause and also for supporting reforms back home [in Saudi Arabia]. People can only respect him more and more because of that.

The Advice and Reformation Committee is not a new thing. It is simply a continuation of the reforming business [in Saudi Arabia], which was there for decades. We thought of uniting this effort. It's also going to make our project stronger because when individual people speak about reforms to the [Saudi] regime, they will think these are isolated individuals who are not happy with what's going on. But if an organization started to speak about this, then the regime should understand that this is something serious.

Abdullah Anas, bin Laden's old friend, visited Sudan in late 1994. Anas arrived around the time that a group of Takfiris, an ultra-Islamist group who considered bin Laden to be a heretic, mounted a serious assassination attempt against the Saudi exile.

I was in Sudan [when the attempt against bin Laden happened]. They just came straight to the house of Osama and they started to shoot. They fired on the walls of the guesthouse. They were Takfiris that considered bin Laden not sufficiently Muslim! Some of them were from Libya. Takfiris—very crazy, very crazy. They kill everybody.[31]

Sheikh Abdul Ghafar is the imam of the Khartoum mosque where bin Laden worshipped.

A lot of the neighbors of Osama bin Laden, they were against him being here in Sudan. We lived here for several years before Sheikh Osama joined this area. It was a very calm area. Those people tried to kill Osama bin Laden. Our area was closed for more than eighteen hours, as some people from the government tried to catch the group. It was a terrible accident for us in this area. And all of us, we asked Sheikh Osama to leave this area. We prayed that he would leave.

One of bin Laden's former neighbors is the landlord of a house that stands next to his old residence in Khartoum. (He refused to give his name.)[32]

They were members of the Takfiri sect. It was Friday, just before sunset, [one of the gunmen] appeared racing down bin Laden's street, spraying bullets at his house and the guards. He turned up the side road where a guard shot the tires [of the gunmen's car]. The whole thing lasted a quarter of an hour.

After the attack, security was stepped up. A large ditch was dug in the street, blocking passage from the main road, and additional armed guards were posted. The only entrance was by way of a small side street off the soccer field. There, too, a ditch was dug, but smaller so cars could still pass. The ditch gave cars a good, audible bump, so guards were alerted to unexpected visitors.

Bin Laden left several months later moving out quietly without warning. One morning bin Laden and his guards were there; the next they were gone. After Osama moved out, the Chinese embassy took it over as their residence.

Abu Jandal became bin Laden's chief bodyguard in 1998.[33]

According to what I heard about that case from Sheikh Osama himself, he had a licensed gun, which never left his pocket. A group of his followers were also armed. Sheikh Osama was ready to leave his home, heading to the office. But he was delayed by a talk between him and his son, Abdallah. During that period, he was readying his family for a more austere life, to be content with a simple life, away from all the luxuries. His son Abdallah opposed that idea. His point of view was that his father was a millionaire and that they were supposed to enjoy that wealth. That talk with his son delayed him, while his bodyguards had already left for the office. So his attackers were deceived, thinking that Sheikh Osama was in his office with his guards. They started firing directly at the office, while Sheikh Osama was still at home. He and his son were armed. When he heard the gunfire, he came out of the house and saw armed men shooting at his office, while at the same time attacking his guards. Sudanese security was also present. He and his son attacked them from the other side. So the attackers were besieged. Some were killed and others wounded, while the rest escaped. Later it became clear that the attackers were members of an Islamic group that had declared bin Laden an infidel.

In December 1992 President George H. W. Bush dispatched 28,000 U.S. troops for Operation Restore Hope, a humanitarian mission to feed hundreds of thousands of starving Somalis embroiled in a civil war sweeping their country. Al Qaeda saw the arrival of those troops in Somalia, two years after the introduction of hundreds of thousands of American troops into Saudi Arabia, as part of a larger American strategy to take over the Islamic world.

Jamal al Fadl.[34]

In Soba town we got big farm also belong to the group. Every Thursday after the sunset prayer, if any of al Qaeda's membership are in Khartoum that day, they have to come to the meeting in the farm. And it's lecture by bin Laden and other membership about jihad and our agenda. I was in the guesthouse and they talk after Iraq government took Kuwait (in 1990, following which 500,000 U.S. troops were posted to Saudi Arabia). After few months, they say American army now; they should leave the Gulf area. I hear from Abu Abdallah, Osama bin Laden himself: we cannot let the American army stay in the Gulf area and take our oil, take our money, and we have to do something to take them out. We have to fight them.

After that, also, we got another fatwa because they say the American army come to the Horn of Africa in Somalia. Also I was in the guesthouse and Abu Ubaidah al Banjshiri, he talk about that. He says the American army [is] in Horn of Africa in Somalia and now they already took off Gulf area and now they go to Somalia, and if they [are] successful in Somalia, the next thing it could be [the] south of Sudan and [other] Islamic countries.

In the big guesthouse [bin Laden] say about American army now they came to the Horn of Africa, and we have to stop the head of the snake. He said that the snake is America, and we have to stop them. We have to cut the head and stop them.

They sent Abu Hafs to Somalia to Mogadishu [the Somali capital] and he went to see if they can do something over there.

Abdel Bari Atwan, the editor of *Al Quds al Arabi* newspaper.[35]

Bin Laden told me that he was expecting the [Americans] to come to Somalia and he sent people a month before their arrival to be prepared.

And when they came actually he attacked them. But unfortunately, according to him, they ran away. And he wanted them to stay in order to fight them. He told me that the American soldiers were cowards in comparison with the Soviet soldiers. I think he was telling the truth about Somalia, he sent people from al-Jihad—the Egyptian al-Jihad troops.

Abu Jandal.[36]

The impact of international developments on Somalia and the entry of the U.S. forces into it were [Osama bin Laden's] justification for the entry of al Qaeda into [the country]. Al Qaeda viewed the entry of the Americans into Somalia not as a move that is meant to save the Somalis from [famine], but to control Somalia and then spread U.S. hegemony over the region. This will achieve several goals. First, it will strike the growing Islamic movement in Sudan. Second, it will set up a rear U.S. base in the Gulf, since Somalia was the closest point to the Arabian Gulf.

I did not take part in any battles in Somalia because when I entered Somalia, al Qaeda Organization itself had started to leave Somalia.

Mohammed Sadiq Odeh, who is of Palestinian heritage, joined al Qaeda in 1992. As a member of al Qaeda he traveled to Somalia in 1993 and 1997. FBI agents interviewed him in the Kenyan capital Nairobi from August 15 through August 28, 1998, following al Qaeda's attack on the U.S. embassy there. Excerpts of their report follow.[37]

Odeh stated that he left Palestine to attend Far Eastern University in Manila, Philippines, in late 1986 to pursue studies in engineering and architecture. Odeh became interested in the Jihad. Odeh is indoctrinated by watching video tapes and listening to cassette tapes of Abdullah Azzam, who is the leader of the Arabs fighting in Afghanistan." Odeh was attracted to Osama bin Ladin and the group al Qaeda because it did not matter what nationality you were. Odeh was first approached by al Qaeda while he was still at the basic training camp. Odeh's behavior, his ability to work with others, his knowledge of the religion and respect towards others were the reasons he was approached. Odeh stated that eventually one year passed before he decided to make *bayat* [an oath] to bin Ladin and al Qaeda. Odeh made *bayat* and officially joined al Qaeda in March 1992.

Odeh stated that he was ordered to Somalia [in March 1993] by Emir Saif el Adel [one of the Egyptian military commanders of al Qaeda] which was coming from Osama bin Ladin. Odeh was told by al Adel that jihad in Afghanistan was over and that they were moving to do jihad elsewhere. Odeh stated that his mission in Somalia was to train some of the tribes in fighting and to provide food and money. The position of al Qaeda regarding aid to Somalia by civilian organizations was that it was acceptable. It was, however, unacceptable for U.S. armed troops to be in Somalia. Bin Ladin/al Qaeda considered this colonization. Abu Hafs [Mohammed Atef] was sent by bin Ladin to assess the situation in Mogadishu. Somali leaders [General Mohamed Farah] Aideed and Ali Mani were fighting each other as well as the UN and U.S. Aideed's tribe (the Hawir) met with Abu Hafs. They agreed to cooperate with each other to take the UN out of Mogadishu by force in military fashion. Abu Hafs was happy about this meeting. In March 1997, Odeh was given a mission by Osama bin Ladin to go back to Somalia to evaluate the situation there.

Essam al Ridi is the Egyptian pilot who flew bin Laden's jet from Arizona to Khartoum airport in 1993, where it subsequently sat on the tarmac unused for more than a year. Al Ridi was asked to get the plane flying again.[38]

I had a call stating that the airplane is still parked outside for maybe a year and a half and Osama would like me to take it and try to do some business with it instead of just parking it there. I said I will try to check the market near Cairo and if there is any possibility that we could generate any business with it, I will call you back, but there is one other security matter here: The fact [is] by then Osama bin Laden was very much exposed in the Egyptian media. He was not, of course, accepted by the Egyptian government. So I indicated my concern.

I took a flight to Khartoum. We start discussing about the aircraft and checking it and make sure that it is in a flyable condition. I would say [it was in] a very terrible condition because we had melted tires from the heat, and standing in the same spot for a long time, the engine intakes and outtakes were full of sand due to sand storms in Khartoum. We had a problem finding the keys initially. We also needed to locate the batteries and charge them and then we cleaned the engine's intake and outlets. We inflated the tires. We asked the mechanic to charge the hydraulic systems.

We had the first engine start with a lot of fire coming out of the engine. It must have been due to some leftover sand. But anyway, after we managed to have a start, I decided to fly the aircraft and then after we do some other extensive checks relating to the avionics equipment. We took off. It flew fine. We had some problem with the power setting. I decided to make a touch and go, which is a land without a first stop, again took off again for another circuit, made another touch, took off for the number three circuit, and we decided to stop. I was satisfied then by the engine parameters that it would be flyable so decided to stop.

To my surprise I could not really stop the aircraft. We lost the main hydraulic or the main brake system. I tried the alternate brake system and I was actually talking to my first officer, who doesn't know anything about the aircraft, that "I'm doing this now" and "I'm doing this now" as a way of making sure that I'm doing the act and also making him up to speed with what's going on. So I said, "We've lost the main brakes, I'm using the alternate. We've lost the alternate brakes; I'm using the hand brakes." We basically lost all kind of brakes. We could not really stop the aircraft. The last option would be to turn off the engines to reduce the propulsion of the aircraft forward, So we shut down the engines.

We were still going on the runway, running out of runway, the speed we were [was] about 60 knots when we hit a sand pile off the runway. The first two things that came to my mind is, of course, the safety of the first officer. Secondly, is how to leave Khartoum as soon as I can. By then, of course, the tower and everybody else could see where the aircraft [was] going. This aircraft was very unique to Khartoum. There is no such private jet aircraft at Khartoum International Airport. So because of our take-off after a year and a half, everybody was really focusing on what we are doing.

This is a very explosive situation. It's an aircraft accident. I'm the only one who flew this aircraft. Everybody knows that it is Osama bin Laden's aircraft. I wouldn't like to be seen in association with Osama at the time.

So I was very concerned to leave. Went back to the Hilton, packed. I went to Addis Ababa [Ethiopia].

L'Houssaine Kherchtou is the Moroccan who testified in the al Qaeda trial in New York in early 2001. He explains how al Qaeda increased its focus on operations in Kenya in the years preceding its 1998 attack on the U.S. embassy in the Kenyan capital, Nairobi.[39]

In 1993, a member of al Qaeda told me that they need me to go to Kenya [from Pakistan] to study flying and one day I will be Osama bin Laden's pilot. After the registration [in the flying school] they gave me all documents that they need and I fill all the forms, and they told me to go to the immigration service to get the permit to study in Kenya.

I was helping other people of al Qaeda in Nairobi. Some people of al Qaeda they were in Somalia, and if somebody needs help while he's transiting Nairobi to travel to Sudan, if he needs a translator or any assistance I was there to do that. I met many people there. They were going to Somalia to train people there. They were against the presence of the United Nations in Somalia. They [the members of al Qaeda] helped some Somalis they wanted to put some explosives in a car and to put it inside a compound of United Nations, and they didn't succeed to do that. They told me that they were in a house in Mogadishu (the Somali capital) and one of the nights one of the [U.S.] helicopters were shot, they had some shooting in the next house where they were living, and they were scared, and the next day they left because they were afraid that they will be caught by the Americans.

Abu Mohammed Amriki (Ali Mohamed, the American). The first time he came with other people to my apartment [in Nairobi] probably the end of '94 or early '95, and they were using it to develop pictures and all their stuff of surveillance [of the U.S. embassy in Nairobi, Kenya].

A complaint against Ali Mohamed was filed in the Southern District of New York in September 1998. Key excerpts follow of an affidavit filed by FBI Special Agent Daniel Coleman, who is generally considered to be the most effective agent the bureau has ever had in its investigation of al Qaeda.[40]

DANIEL COLEMAN, being duly sworn, deposes and says that he is a Special Agent of the Federal Bureau of Investigation ("FBI"), and charges as follows:

Usama Bin Laden had a particular need for United States citizens to aid al Qaeda as persons with United States passports could travel freely without raising suspicion.

THE 1997 INTERVIEW BY THE FBI

During an October 1997 interview by the FBI, MOHAMED admitted that he trained Usama Bin Laden's bodyguards in the Sudan following an unsuccessful assassination attempt against Bin Laden. (I know from other investigations that such an attempt occurred in 1994.) MOHAMED advised that the Sudanese intelligence service provided perimeter security for Bin Laden but that MOHAMED had trained the guards who provided the inner security. MOHAMED stated that he lived in Bin Laden's house in Khartoum at the time of such training.

MOHAMED also advised that he was in Somalia during the United States intervention overseas and knew that Bin Laden's people were responsible for the killing of the United States soldiers in Somalia. MOHAMED further confirmed that in or about 1991 he went to Afghanistan to take Bin Laden to Pakistan, and on to the Sudan. MOHAMED stated that he did this because he loved Bin Laden and believed in him. MOHAMED further admitted that he had done training in Afghanistan. Still later, MOHAMED admitted that he had trained people in "war zones" and added that war zones can be anywhere. MOHAMED indicated that he knew lots of people and was well trusted and could put people together with people that they need.

Mohamed further stated that one did not need a fatwah to go against the United States since it was "obvious" that the United States was the enemy.

WHEREFORE, your deponent respectfully requests that the defendant ALI ABDELSEOUD MOHAMED, a/k/a "Abu Omar," a/k/a "Omar," be imprisoned or bailed as the case may be.

DANIEL COLEMAN
Special Agent,
Federal Bureau of Investigation

Ali Mohamed is a U.S. citizen of Egyptian origin. This is a partial transcript of his plea bargain hearing before Judge Sand in the Southern District of New York on October 20, 2000.[41]

Your honor, in the early 1980's I became involved with the Egyptian Islamic Jihad organization. In the early 1990's, I was introduced to al Qaeda—al Qaeda is the organization headed by Osama bin Laden—through my involvement with the Egyptian Islamic Jihad. In 1992, I conducted military and basic explosives training for al Qaeda in Afghanistan. In 1991, I helped transport Osama bin Laden from Afghanistan to the Sudan.

In late 1993, I was asked by bin Laden to conduct surveillance of American, British, French and Israeli targets in Nairobi. Among the targets I did surveillance for was the American Embassy. These targets were selected to retaliate against the United States for its involvement in Somalia. I later went to Khartoum, where my surveillance files and photographs were reviewed by Osama bin Laden. Bin Laden looked at the picture of the American Embassy and pointed to where a truck could go as a suicide bomber.

In 1994, bin Laden sent me to Djibouti [in East Africa] to do surveillance on several facilities, including French military bases and the American Embassy. In 1994, after an attempt to assassinate bin Laden, I went to the Sudan in 1994 to train bin Laden's bodyguards, security detail. I trained those conducting the security of the interior of his compound and coordinated with the Sudanese intelligence agents who were responsible for the exterior security.

I was aware of certain contacts between al Qaeda and al Jihad organization, on one side, and Iran and Hezbollah (an Iranian terrorist group) on the other side. I arranged security for a meeting in the Sudan between [Imad] Mugniyeh, Hezbollah's chief, and bin Laden. (Mugniyeh had masterminded the 1983 attack on the U.S. Marine barracks in Beirut that killed 241 U.S. soldiers.) Hezbollah provided explosives training for al Qaeda. Iran supplied Egyptian Jihad with weapons. Iran also used Hezbollah to supply explosives that were disguised to look like rocks.

I was involved in the [Egyptian] Islamic Jihad organization, and the Islamic Jihad organization had a very close link to al Qaeda. And the objective of all this, just to attack any Western target in the Middle East, to force Western countries to pull out from the Middle East, based on the Marine [barracks] explosion in Beirut [in 1983].

During the mid-nineties al Qaeda was primarily based in Sudan. However graduates of its training camps in Afghanistan had already spread around the world.

Ramzi Yousef was the mastermind of the bombing of the World Trade Center in 1993 that killed six people and that was intended to bring the Twin Towers down. Yousef had trained at an al Qaeda training camp (although it seems he may never have met bin Laden) and is the nephew of Khaled Sheikh Mohammed who oversaw al Qaeda's 9/11 operation. After fleeing Manhattan, following the attack on the Trade Center on February 26, 1993, Yousef was finally captured in Pakistan two years later. Following is the FBI report "Interview of Ramzi Ahmed Yousef," February 7, 1995.[42]

At approximately 10:37 a.m. on 2-7-95, Ramzi Ahmed Yousef, shortly after being arrested by Pakistani Military officials, was interviewed by FBI Special Agent Brad Garrett at a military station in Islamabad, Pakistan. Yousef was asked what his name is and he stated "I have many," but he stated he is presently using Ali Baloch, DOB 2-15-66. Yousef was asked if he is Ramzi Ahmed Yousef and he stated that he was Yousef and that the individual in the FBI wanted flyer is in fact him.

Yousef was fingerprinted at the military station with a preliminary indication that his prints match Yousef. Yousef stated that his real name is Abdul Basit, DOB: 4-27-68 and that he was born in Kuwait. Yousef was verbally advised of his rights and then [the] SA [Special Agent] wrote out in longhand his rights and read them to Yousef. Yousef advised he understood his rights, does not want an attorney and will voluntarily talk.

Yousef was asked if he committed the World Trade Center (WTC) bombing and he stated, "I masterminded the explosion." Yousef stated he purchased the materials to build the bomb from City Chemicals in Jersey City, NJ. Yousef stated the WTC bombing cost less than $20,000. Yousef stated he built the bomb used in the WTC bombing. Yousef declined to state who provided the money but he stated the money partly came from friends in Pakistan. Yousef said that because of a lack of funds, the WTC was not as successful as he desired. Yousef stated he was hoping for a quarter million causalities but could not obtain the funds to complete the bomb to his satisfaction.

Yousef stated the reason for the bombings was because of the U.S. military, financial and political support of Israel. Yousef talked at length about Israel being an illegal state and that Israel is committing criminal acts against Muslims. Yousef stated that the American people would need to convince Washington of changing Israeli policy and this would happen by bombing various locations in the U.S. Yousef stated that he was most affected by a BBC report, where Israeli soldiers broke the hand of a Palestinian using a rock. Yousef stated he has no personal agenda with the U.S., only the U.S.-Israeli policy.

Yousef stated the he was born in Kuwait and lived there for 20 years until the Iraqi war [against Iran] when his family moved to Pakistan. Yousef stated that his family was originally from Pakistan. He attended high school in Kuwait and from 1986 to 1989 attended the West Glamorgan Institute of Higher Learning in the United Kingdom. Yousef stated he earned a Higher National Diploma in Electronics and the course was called Computer Aided Electronics. In 1989 he returned to Kuwait and worked as a communications engineer at the National Computer Center for the Minister of Planning. After Iraq invaded Kuwait in August 1990, Yousef then moved to Pakistan.

After moving to Pakistan Yousef stated he went to various training camps in Afghanistan for a period of six months. Yousef described these camps as "a place Arabs can get training" in explosives, defensive tactics, weapons use, etc. These camps are located at various sites in Afghanistan but Yousef declined to provide their locations or any specific information about their funding or manpower. Yousef stated that after training in Afghanistan, he returned to Pakistan and continued to read about bomb building.

Yousef stated that during World War II the U.S. dropped nuclear bombs on Japan to force Japan to surrender. Yousef advised the same logic applies to him setting off explosive devices at U.S. targets to force the U.S. to change their policy toward Israel. Yousef stated that this is an extreme approach but believes it is the only way to force the U.S. to withdraw its support of Israel.

Yousef asked [the] SA [Special Agent] several questions about executions in the U.S. and asked the length of time before executions are car-

ried out after receiving the death penalty. Yousef stated he believes that
he will be executed in the U.S.

**The interrogation of Ramzi Yousef continued as he was flown from
Pakistan to the United States. What follows is the FBI's report on that
interrogation, which is listed under Yousef's real name: "Interview of
Abdul Basit Mahmoud Abdul Karim," on February 7–8 1995.**[43]

[On February 7–8, 1995] Abdul Basit Mahmoud Abdul Karim [also
known as Ramzi Yousef], hereafter referred to as "Basit," was interviewed aboard an aircraft en route from Islamabad, Pakistan, to the
United States. Basit advised that he could fluently speak, read and understand the English language. He was advised of the official identities
of the interviewing agents and was reminded that he was under arrest for
offenses concerning the bombing of the World Trade Center (WTC) in
New York City. He was, thereafter, advised of his constitutional rights by
reading them and having them read to him. Due to Basit's request, notes
were not taken in his presence, but were summarized during breaks in
the interview.

[In 1992 he traveled to New York City from Pakistan.] Upon entry at
John F. Kennedy International Airport, in New York, Basit utilized an
Iraqi passport in the name of Ramzi Ahmed Yousef. Basit explained that
he had purchased the Iraqi passport for $100 U.S. dollars in Peshawar,
Pakistan. He noted Peshawar is the easiest place to purchase Iraqi passports and further explained that these are genuine documents stolen by
Iraqi rebels who raid passport offices in Northern Iraq. When presenting
the Iraqi passport to U.S. Immigration Officials, Basit requested political
asylum, and was processed and released."[44]

Basit advised that in the fall of 1994 [after the WTC attack], he had
learned through various press accounts that President Clinton would be
traveling to Manila [the capital of the Philippines] in November. Basit
claimed that he traveled to Manila a few days prior to the President's arrival. Once in Manila, Basit determined the President's planned itinerary
through reported press accounts. Basit related that he thereafter traveled to each of the sites which the President would visit, in order to survey them for opportunities to attempt an assassination. He noted that
the level of security which he observed at each of these sites was very

high. Basit advised that the assassination attempt on Clinton was never carried out, due to the observations of high security, and his lack of time needed to plan and organize such an attempt.

The second option which Basit considered was a bombing attack of the Presidential motorcade while the motorcade was en route between sites in Manila. Basit indicated that he considered placing an improvised explosive device in a location along the motorcade route, designed to disable the lead car in the motorcade. He explained that by disabling the lead vehicle, the entire motorcade would be brought to a stop, enabling an explosive or poisonous gas attack on the Presidential limousine.

He related that he had considered using the chemical agent 'phosgene' in the attack on the limousine, and noted that he had the technical ability to readily manufacture that substance. According to Basit, the phosgene, in a liquid form, could be placed in a metal container, which could then be opened with a charge of explosive, rapidly dispensing the substance as gas.

He related that his associates had [also] been interested in the Pope, but denied that the Pope was an assassination target. Basit attributed religious articles and photographs of the Pope, found in [his] apartment in Manila, to the general interest of his associates [in the Pope].

He spoke of an incident which occurred in his Manila apartment in early January 1995, which had been reported in the media as a fire. He related that he had been demonstrating the burning of a mixture of [chemicals] when smoke produced by the burning began to fill the apartment. He was then questioned as to certain materials found in the Manila apartment which appeared to refer to U.S. airline flights. He noted that, if the incident at the Manila apartment had not occurred, there would have been several airline bombings within two weeks of that time [known as the Manila air plot].

Basit asked the interviewing Agents whether the Agents knew how the person who had been arrested in the Philippines, and who had subsequently escaped, had effected the escape. In discussing [this] individual, Basit acknowledged that this individual was known as Wali [Khan Amin] Shah [who was an early associate of bin Laden's]. Following Basit's descriptions of Wali as strong and intelligent, Basit was questioned as to whether Basit had been acting under the direction of Wali Shah. Basit would not further elaborate on that issue.

When questioned regarding a business card in the name of Moham-mad Khalifa [bin Laden's brother-in-law Jamal Khalifa], found in Basit's apartment in the Philippines, Basit stated that he did not personally know Khalifa, but that Khalifa's business card had been given to him by Wali Shah, as a contact in the event Basit needed aid. Basit acknowl-edged that he was familiar with the name Osama bin Laden, and knew him to be a relative of Khalifa's, but would not further elaborate.

Raghida Dergham of the Arabic newspaper *Al Hayat* interviewed Ramzi Yousef in a Manhattan jail after his arrest in 1995, the only time that he has spoken to a reporter. Excerpts of that interview follow.[45]

My [real] name is Abd al Basit. I was born in Kuwait. The family is from Pakistan, but I also descend from Palestinian origins. I carry a Paki-stani passport. I am Palestinian on my mother's side; my grandmother is Palestinian. A part of my family is in Pakistan, a part in Kuwait, and I have some relatives in Palestine.

I have no connection with Iraq or with other governmental circles. The Iraqi people must not pay for the mistakes made by Saddam. I only support the Liberation Army, which declared its responsibility for the World Trade Center bombing. It is an international movement con-cerned with affairs of the world's Islamic armed movements. I am not the brains. The movement has groups and military divisions, each of which takes care of Islamic movements' affairs in various countries.

I support this movement's objectives, which are to pressure the U.S. Administration by carrying out operations against U.S. targets so this ad-ministration will stop its aid for Israel. I believe that this movement, is entitled to strike U.S. targets because the United States is a partner in the crimes committed in Palestine, considering that it finances these crimes and supports them with weapons. The movement is also entitled because this money is taken from taxes paid by Americans. Logically and legally, this makes the American people responsible for all the killing, settlement, torture, and imprisonment to which the Palestinian people are subjected. It is no excuse that the American people do not know where their federal tax money goes.

One of the Liberation Army's goals has been to aid members of Egypt's Islamic Group and Jihad Group; Palestine's Hamas [Islamic Resistance Movement] and Islamic Jihad; and Algeria's FIS [Islamic Salvation Front] and armed Islamic movements.

The Liberation Army Movement was about to embark on retaliatory acts in Saudi Arabia in wake of the 1994 arrest of Sheikh Salman Fahd al Awdah and Sheikh Safar al Hawali.

The fatwas and fates of the militant Saudi clerics Salman al Awdah and Safar al Hawali would have an important impact on bin Laden and al Qaeda. Al Awdah and al Hawali were among the first Saudi clerics to issue cassette tapes of sermons against the U.S. presence in Saudi Arabia in 1991. Their subsequent arrests in September 1994 would have a radicalizing effect on bin Laden.[46]

Hamid Mir is bin Laden's Pakistani biographer.[47]

He said that Sheikh Salman Awdah is my ideal personality; a savior who was the first person to demand the withdrawal of U.S. troops from Saudi. And Salman al Awdah wrote some pamphlets for al Qaeda, but those pamphlets were not distributed in his name. They were on jihad.

Abu Jandal became bin Laden's chief bodyguard in 1998.[48]

Osama bin Laden respected Sheikh Salman al Awdah and Sheikh Safar al Hawali. The Saudi government had responded by arresting all of these Sheikhs and imprisoning them, and after he had learned that the government stifled all sources of the truth, Sheikh Osama bin Laden was forced to make himself heard. "By God, if the Saudi Government did not arrest the reform movement Sheikhs and preachers, I would not have raised my voice or spoken. When the Saudi Sheikhs were arrested and when the Government silenced all words of truth that were said against them, I was forced to speak and take this action. My words of course differ from that of others. Some speak through discussion, but I do it well with the rifle."

Ibrahim al Sanoussi, assistant to Hussan al Turabi, the de facto leader of Sudan in the mid-nineties.

After the invasion of Iraq [Desert Storm] some *ulema* [clergy] started to speak about this [U.S.] invasion and occupation of Iraq and the [U.S.]

bases in Saudi, especially al Hawali and al Awdah [the influential militant Saudi clerics]. These are the teachers of Osama bin Laden. They inspired his ideas and they gave him the arguments. [At this time bin Laden] started his interest of being a politician. And he began to speak about what should happen in Saudi and the reformation that you have to have [there]. It was maybe '93/'94 when he began to speak about that. Before that he was just a contractor, but now these speeches of al Hawali, they began to come all over the Arabic countries in cassettes, criticizing the [Saudi] royal family. And this [atmosphere] gave Osama bin Laden here in the Sudan the chance to speak. During this time the youth from all Arabic countries began to come to Sudan—Libyans, Saudis, Emirates. They gave [bin Laden] the title of "Sheikh Osama." Quickly he became very popular. They like him and they listen to him and especially [as] he has money. He can solve their problems.

And when [bin Laden's] activities became a nuisance to Saudis, Saudis announced that they have renounced his nationality and said that he is no longer Saudi and no longer has a passport. That wasn't a problem for him because the Sudanese gave him a passport.

Hamid Mir, bin Laden's Pakistani biographer.

Bin Laden pays a lot of respect to his mother. His mother tried her best to convince bin Laden that he should make a ceasefire with the Saudi regime; he should come back to Saudi Arabia. She went to see him in Sudan and she spent many days with him in Sudan. She was carrying a message of [the Saudi] King Fahd. At that stage, the differences between Osama bin Laden and the Saudi regime were entirely ego problems. No Islam, nothing. That was a problem between [Prince] Nayef [the minister of the Interior] and bin Laden. They had some ego problems. Bin Laden had an objection; "Why he shouts [at] me?" And Nayef said "Why he threatened me?"

So there was a problem between bin Laden and [Prince] Nayef, so his mother tried her best to calm down him. It was very difficult for her to understand that her son had a problem with Nayef. Now he is speaking against the king. He never spoke against the king in the past. Why he is speaking against the royal family? So he was going through a transformation period in those days and he said sorry to his mother, "Sorry, I'm not going to announce a ceasefire with the royal family. I'm going to oppose them."

Muhammad Atef [al Qaeda's military commander, told me] that "Sheikh bin Laden have lot of respect for the women. There is a misconception that we don't have any soft corner for women. He said that Sheikh bin Laden—"he is always very, very careful for his mother and he is in constant touch with his mother." He said, "I was present in that meeting in Khartoum: Sheikh bin Laden told his mother, "I can sacrifice my life for you, but right now what you are talking to me is against Islam. I'm fighting against the enemies of Islam and you want that I should announce a ceasefire with the enemies of Islam." And his mother said, "Okay, I will not repeat my demand again. Thank you very much." So I think that Sheikh bin Laden was successful in convincing his mother that you should not interfere in my ideological affairs. And his mother went back and she informed the Saudi authorities and after that they announced they canceled his citizenship.

Abdel Bari Atwan, the editor of *Al Quds al Arabi* newspaper, who spent two days interviewing bin Laden in Afghanistan in November 1996.

He loves his mother. You really can't imagine how he admires her. And even he loves his stepfather [whose family name is] Attas. He's a businessman in Jeddah. So usually in our culture, we don't like our stepfather, but he liked him a lot. And he said, "The Saudi government sent me, my mother, and my stepfather to see me [in Sudan]." The offer, as he told me, is the Saudis have frozen his share of the business in a bank account in Saudi Arabia. And he told me there were about $200 million in that account and they promised to double it if he comes back, and it's just on one condition: to say that Saudi government is applying the Sharia [rule of Islamic law]. He turned that down.

Osama bin Laden.[49]

They sent me my mother, my uncle, and my brothers in almost nine visits to Khartoum asking me to stop and return to Arabia to apologize to [Saudi] King Fahd. I apologized to my family kindly because I know that they were driven by force to come to talk to me. I refused to go back. [My family] conveyed the Saudi government's message that if you do not go back, they'll freeze all my assets, deprive me of my citizenship, my passport, my Saudi ID and distort my picture in the Saudi and foreign media.

They think that a Muslim may bargain on his religion. I said to them "Do whatever you may wish. It is with Allah's bounty, we refuse to go back. We are living with dignity and honor for which we thank Allah. It is much better for us to live under a tree here on these mountains than to live in palaces in the most sacred land to Allah."

In April 1994, the Saudi government officially stripped bin Laden of his citizenship. The same month Bakr Mohammed Bin Ladin, the head of the Bin Ladin family and a half brother to Osama bin Laden, issued the following statement to the Saudi press:[50]

[On behalf of] "all members of the family" [we express] "regret, denunciation and condemnation of all acts that Osama bin Laden may have committed."

The information below was gathered from the Saudi Binladin Group's (SBG) Web site before it was taken off the Internet after September 11, 2001. It gives you a snapshot of the diversity and extent of the Binladin holdings around the time that Osama was cut off financially from his extended family.[51] **(For additional information on the Saudi Binladin Group please refer to appendix C.)**

Infrastructure:
SBG [Saudi Binladin Group] has played a key role in building the Kingdom [of Saudi Arabia's] infrastructure, actively participating in successive government development programmes. The company's infrastructure projects include highways, expressways, bridges, flyovers, tunnels and underpasses built to link the two holy cities of [Mecca and Medina] with the rest of the Kingdom and neighboring countries. To date, roads built by SBG number [in the] thousands of kilometers.

SBG's skills in [infrastructure] have been recognized and utilized in the United Arab Emirates, Jordan, Yemen, and Sudan. SBG's impressive list of achievements includes construction of desalination plants, water storage reservoirs and one of the longest fresh water pipelines in existence. In the process of executing such heavy construction, SBG has built up one of the largest fleets of heavy equipment and tunneling drills in the world.

Public Buildings and Airports:

Over the years the Division has undertaken various challenging projects, large and medium scale, including complete airports and roads, hospitals and university complexes, housing facilities on a turnkey basis including all civil, electro-mechanical work for the Prophet's Mosque in [Medina], Armed Forces Hospital Extension in Riyadh, Port Sudan Airport, [and the] Al Musa Tower in Dubai.

Trading Division:

SBG is active throughout the Middle and Far East in the operation of large franchise ventures in the fields of food and catering, for example the distribution of "Snapple" drink and the distribution operations for companies like York International Corporation, Nortel, Schreder SA, Landis & Gyr, Audi, Porsche, [and] Volkswagen.

The flagship of SBG's trading activities is Mimar Trading Group, with its headquarters in Beirut. Mimar is a company operating in Saudi Arabia, the United Arab Emirates, Egypt, Lebanon, Syria, Turkey, France, Malaysia, Hong Kong and Singapore.

☙

L'Houssaine Kherchtou is the al Qaeda member who testified as a U.S. government witness in the 2001 trial of the four men accused of a role in attacking two U.S. embassies in Africa in 1998. Excerpts of his testimony follow, outlining how bin Laden's funding dried up as a result of the Saudi government freezing his assets in 1994. Kherchtou also explains that the Sudanese government started putting pressure on the Arab militants living in the country.[52]

There was a pressure from the Libyan government on the Sudanese government that all the Libyans must leave the country, and they informed Osama bin Laden that if you have some Libyans you have to let them get out from the country. And Osama bin Laden informed these guys, "You have to leave, because if you don't leave, you will be responsible for yourselves, and if somebody [is] caught, I am not responsible. What I can do for you is I can give you twenty-four hundred bucks, plus a ticket with you and your wife if you want to live somewhere," but the Libyans, most of them, they refused the offer of Osama bin Laden. They were very upset and angry because [he] couldn't protect them, and they had a meeting. At the end of the meeting they gave a letter to Osama bin Laden that they are leaving al Qaeda, and they took money and tickets and some of them they left. Some of them they joined the Libyan Islamic group.

Since the end of '94, '95 we have a crisis in al Qaeda. Osama bin Laden himself he was talking to us and saying he lost all his money, and he reduced the salary of people, and myself when I wanted to go to renew my flying license in Kenya he told me, "Just forget about it."

In December '95 my wife was pregnant and she has C section, so I booked in the hospital in Khartoum, and I needed money for the hospital; it was five hundred bucks I think, and I asked Sheikh Sayyid el Masry [a bin Laden aide]. I asked him if he can give me some money. At that time Osama bin Laden was in one of his projects in Kassala, another city in the Sudan.

[Sheikh Sayyid el Masry] told me "There is no money. We can't give you anything, and, why you don't take your wife to the Muslim hospital." I knew that if I take my wife there she will die the first day. And I told him, "If it was your wife or your daughter, you would take her there?" I tell him, "Listen, why don't you borrow money for me and I will give money back to you." He said, "I can't do anything until bin Laden come back." If I had a gun I would shoot him at that time.

Jamal al Fadl, an early member of al Qaeda.[53]

What I tell [bin Laden] some people complain because some people, they got high salary, some people, they got a little and they want to know if we [are] all al Qaeda membership, why somebody got more than others. [Bin Laden] say some people, they traveling a lot and they do more work. Some people, they got citizenship from another country and [if] they go back over there for regular life, they can make more money. And he says that's why he try to make them happy and give them more money.

[I stole from bin Laden] $110,000. When I find they know I take the money, I tell them yes, I pay around between 25,000 to 30,000 [dollars] back. [Bin Laden] told me, "I don't care about the money, but I care about you because you start this from the beginning. You work hard in Afghanistan, you are one of the best people in al Qaeda group, we give you everything, when you travel we give you extra money, we pay your medical bill—why you did that?" I tell him, "The reason we talk about before, the Egyptian people, they got a lot of money, they got more salary than other, and we told you some people, they joined the al Qaeda only a few years ago: Why they got [higher] salary?" He said, "If you need money, you should come speak with me and told me I want to buy house, I want to change my car, and you didn't do that, you just stole the money." And he say, "There's no forgive[ness] until you bring all the money back." I tell him, "But there's no money left," and he say, "I can't forgive you until you give all the money." After that, I feel like I have to leave the group; there is no hope and I think to leave Sudan.

[In 1996] I went to the American embassy in that [unidentified] country[54] and I went to the visa line. The person asked me, "Do you want visa?" I tell him, "No, I don't want visa, but I have information about people, they want to do something against your government." And he went inside, and 20 minutes later a lady opens the door and she point to me and tells me come inside. And she took me inside the room and she tell me, "What kind of information?" I told her, "I was in Afghanistan and I work with group and I know in fact those people, they try to make war against your country and they train very hard." And she tell me, "What kind of war?" I tell her, "I don't know, maybe they try to do something inside United States." And she tell me, "How you know that?" She give a lot of questions and she tell, "I need you to answer these questions and when you finish, I need you to focus what you believe and what you know what the group they going to do exactly to our government."

Al Fadl's "walk-in" to a U.S. embassy would be a critical break for the CIA and FBI; the first time someone inside al Qaeda could describe the inner workings of the organization.

In 1996, the Sudanese government was coming under increasing pressure to rein in or expel bin Laden from the governments of Egypt, the United States, and Saudi Arabia.

Prince Turki al Faisal was the head of Saudi intelligence at the time.[55]

[We monitored bin Laden] recruiting persons from different parts of the Islamic world, from Algeria to Egypt, from East Asia to Somalia, to get them trained at these [Sudanese] camps. It was an unacceptable activity. So remarks were made and the [Sudanese] authorities were informed and we were given assurances that Osama would not be allowed to harm Saudi interests. [Sudanese] President Bashir asked for guarantees regarding bin Laden's prosecution [if he were handed over to us] that he would not be tried by any legal authority in the [Saudi] Kingdom. Bashir was told that no one is above the law and that we could not give such guarantees [and we rejected this offer].

Abu Jandal, a Yemeni bodyguard of bin Laden's and a close confidant of al Qaeda's leader.[56]

The Sudanese were—until the very last moment, when bin Laden left Sudan—giving him the best treatment. His leaving Sudan was due to his political impact on the Saudi street through his effective speeches and statements. That led Riyadh (the Saudi capital) to pressure Khartoum to expel him from their country. Simultaneously, there were other Egyptian pressures, which went along with the American pressure on Sudan. So the ruling Islamic Front in Sudan, under the leadership of Dr. Hassan al Turabi, asked Sheikh Usama to leave the country. For bin Laden Turabi was always a nuisance.

Al Turabi himself exerted a great deal of pressure on Sheikh Osama to make him leave Sudan. He visited him for three consecutive days, holding long meetings and heated discussions with him, until late at night, to convince him to leave Sudan. Sheikh Osama tried to convince him of the opposite: that there was no need to expel him, that [he] had not committed any armed acts against Sudan, and that there was no other country ready to receive [his men]. But al Turabi told him that he had two options: Either keep silent or he leave the country. That was when Sheikh Osama decided to leave Sudan. He made arrangements with the Sudanese to leave the country with his followers and moved to Afghanistan.

Khaled Batarfi, bin Laden's boyhood friend in Saudi Arabia.

Bin Laden's family originated in this village, Rubat, in the Hadramaut region of Yemen.
Photo by Peter Bergen

Al Thagr School in Jeddah, Saudi Arabia, in the mid-1960s, around the time that bin Laden was a student there. *Courtesy of Brian Fyfield-Shayler*

Brian Fyfield-Shayler, bin Laden's English teacher at Al Thagr School. *Courtesy of Brian Fyfield-Shayler*

Khaled Batarfi, bin Laden's childhood friend pointing out the playground where they used to play soccer together in Jeddah, Saudi Arabia. *Photo by Essam al Ghalib.*

Jamal Khalifa, bin Laden's university friend and brother-in-law. *Photo by Peter Bergen*

Hutaifa Azzam, Ibrahim Azzam, Abdullah Azzam, and Abdullah Anas inside Afghanistan in the late 1980s. *Courtesy of Abdullah Anas*

Jihad magazine from 1989.
Abdullah Azzam is on the cover.
Courtesy of Peter Bergen

Peter Bergen with Afghan leader, Ahmad Shah Massoud in 1993. *Courtesy of Peter Bergen*

Bin Laden's house in Khartoum, Sudan, above and below. *Photos by Sam Dealey*

Housing outside Khartoum, Sudan used by bin Laden's men, above and below. *Photos by Sam Dealey*

Bin Laden in March 1997. *Photo by Peter Bergen*

Longtime bin Laden ally, the Afghan commander Jalaluddin Haqqani, in eastern Afghanistan in 1997. *Courtesy of Peter Bergen*

Peter Arnett, bin Laden, Peter Bergen, and Peter Jouvenal in Afghanistan in March, 1997. *Courtesy of Peter Bergen*

Ayman al Zawahiri, bin Laden, and Abu Hafs (Mohammed Atef) calling for attacks against the United States at a press conference in eastern Afghanistan in May 1998. *Courtesy of Peter Bergen*

Sheik Omar Abdel Rahman's fatwa urging attacks on American corporations, ships, and planes, which was distributed at al Qaeda's May 1998 press conference. *Courtesy of Peter Bergen*

Ismail Khan, bin Laden, and Rahimullah Yusufzai at al Qaeda's May 1998 press conference in eastern Afghanistan. *Courtesy of Peter Bergen*

An al Qaeda training camp destroyed by a U.S. missile strike in August 1998. *Courtesy of Peter Bergen*

A mosque that bin Laden was building in Kandahar, Afghanistan, in the late 1980s. *Courtesy of Peter Bergen*

Bin Laden's destroyed compound in Hadda, outside Jalalabad, Afghanistan. *Photo by Peter Bergen*

Commander Musa, a frontline commander at the December 2001 battle of Tora Bora in eastern Afghanistan. *Photo by Scott Wallace*

A cave in Tora Bora. *Photo by Peter
Bergen*

Bin Laden toy on sale in Kabul,
Afghanistan in 2003. *Photo by
Scott Wallace*

Muhammad Zahir, Yusuf Masada, and Peter Bergen in Tora Bora, Afghanistan, in 2003.
Photo by Scott Wallace

Tora Bora, 2005.
Photos by Peter Bergen

There was pressure on Sudan and finally the Sudanese kicked him out and then they took over his properties. From what I hear from his family, they took almost everything without compensation.

Ibrahim al Sanoussi, assistant to Sudan's then-leader, Hussan Turabi.

One day Osama came to me and he told me that the government told him to leave the Sudan. I said to him not to leave. Then he came and said to me farewell and that was the last time [I saw him].

Later on I found out Ali Osman Taha, at that time the Sudanese minister of foreign affairs, invited U.S. Ambassador [Timothy] Carney to his house for a dinner and he told him, "We can give you Osama bin Laden." Carney said "Let me consult Washington." And after a month or more he came and said, "They had no [legal] charges [filed] against him, so we don't want him."

Ambassador Timothy Carney, the former U.S. envoy to Sudan, responds.[57]

At no time did any Sudanese, Ali Osman Taha [the foreign minister of Sudan] or anyone else, ever say to me that they could give the U.S. Osama bin Laden. Taha and I talked about sending him back to Saudi in a mid-January 1996 chat. This was before the early February dinner at Taha's [referred to above]. No offer to give bin Laden to the U.S. figured there, either.

Indeed, the 9/11 Commission concluded that the Sudanese government had not offered to hand over bin Laden to the United States, and that, in any event, it would have been a futile gesture because during the spring of 1996 there was no legal basis to hold bin Laden, as he had yet to be indicted for any crime. Here is how the 9/11 Commission Report describes this episode.[58]

In late 1995, when bin Ladin was still in Sudan, the State Department and the CIA learned that Sudanese officials were discussing with the Saudi government the possibility of expelling bin Ladin. U.S. Ambassador Timothy Carney encouraged the Sudanese to pursue this course. The Saudis, however, did not want bin Ladin, giving as their reason their revocation of his citizenship. Sudan's minister of defence, Fatih Erwa, has claimed that Sudan offered to hand bin Ladin over to the United States. The Commission has found no credible evidence that this was so. Ambassador Carney had instructions only to push the Sudanese to expel bin Ladin. Ambassador Carney had no legal basis to ask for more from the Sudanese since, at the time, there was no indictment outstanding.

Vahid Mojdeh held several posts in various divisions of the Afghan Foreign Affairs Ministry between 1995 and the fall of the Taliban in 2001. Here he describes how bin Laden engineered his departure from Sudan.[59]

Some members of the Hezbi-Islami led by Younis Khalis [an Afghan faction] went to Sudan in '96 and made bin Laden the offer to go to Afghanistan. Two planes left Afghanistan for Sharjah [a tiny emirate in the United Arab Emirates] to bring bin Laden. One plane went to Khartoum and returned for an overnight stay in Sharjah. Bin Laden was on board. The next day he got off one plane and boarded the other plane. One [decoy plane went] to Kabul and the other carrying bin Laden went to Jalalabad. At that time Jalalabad was controlled by Haji Qadeer, of the Khalis faction, who treated him as an honored guest. The Americans contacted Haji Qadeer in order to get hold of bin Laden, but at that time the Taliban were speeding towards Jalalabad [which they seized on July 26 1996] and then bin Laden joined up with the Taliban.

Abu Jandal.[60]

Bin Laden left Sudan for Jalalabad [Afghanistan] on a private jet. On board there was only a Russian pilot, who spoke no Arabic. Bin Laden was also accompanied by two of his sons, Saad and Omar. There were also very few guards with him in the small plane, which held only twelve passengers. Brother Sayf Adel [an Egyptian former special forces officer who would become al Qaeda's military commander in 2003] was sitting next to the pilot. In his hands he held a map of the route, because they did not trust the pilot very much.

The departure was kept highly secret, and the security measures were very important for the success of bin Laden's departure for Afghanistan. His arrival in Afghanistan was coordinated with the field leader in Jalalabad, Engineer Mahmud, a leader of the Hezb-e Islami [the Afghan faction] which controlled Jalalabad. They welcomed Sheikh Osama there because they both were former acquaintances. They gave him a warm welcome, and then accompanied him to the headquarters of the Afghan leader, Mullah Yunus Khalis. That reception was a kind of payment for Sheikh Osama for everything he had offered the Afghan warriors.

6

Afghanistan, Again

Bin Laden has always had something of a romantic attachment to Afghanistan, sometimes referring to it by its ancient Muslim name of Khurasan, and on one occasion signing his declaration of war against the West with a notation that it was written in the Hindu Kush mountains. It was also a country bin Laden knew intimately, as he had fought the communists there on and off for seven years between 1985 and 1992.

In the years since bin Laden had moved from Peshawar to Sudan, an armed fundamentalist movement, the Taliban, meaning "religious students," had gradually taken over Afghanistan. The movement was an alliance between the graduates of Afghan and Pakistani madrassas, impoverished young Afghan refugees who had grown up in Pakistan, and leaders of the Pashtun tribal grouping (including, at least initially, Hamid Karzai, who become Afghanistan's president after the fall of the Taliban).

The Taliban first emerged in Kandahar in 1994 under the leadership of an enigmatic, reclusive leader, the one-eyed Mullah Omar. The Taliban enjoyed quite a high degree of popularity and legitimacy in their earlier years as they brought order and a measure of peace to a country that had suffered through a decade and a half of civil war. The Taliban also initially suggested that they might restore Afghanistan's monarchy, an institution that continued to enjoy great popularity. And the Taliban were also seen as incorruptible, and little interested in assuming power for themselves.

However, Lord Acton's maxim that "power corrupts and absolute power corrupts absolutely" is an almost perfect description of how the Taliban regime evolved over the years. The Taliban increasingly turned their law-and-order government into something that aspired to be a truly totalitarian Islamic state. The Taliban were neither modern enough nor competent enough to succeed in that project, but they certainly tried hard.

For bin Laden, the fact that the Taliban were consolidating their hold on Afghanistan just as he returned to the country was a fortuitous gift that he would exploit brilliantly, entering into a powerful symbiotic relationship with Mullah Omar. Al Qaeda would provide the Taliban some much-needed cash and zealous Arab fighters, while the Taliban would provide a sure refuge and carte blanche to build up the training camps of the al Qaeda organization.

Bin Laden would say that Afghanistan was destined to be the Medina of the twenty-first century, a reference to the Arabian city to which the Prophet Muhammad immigrated from his native Mecca in the year 622 to build up his Islamic army, which seized Mecca from its pagan inhabitants eight years later. Indeed, bin Laden saw his own immigration (or *hijra*) to Afghanistan as self-consciously replicating the *hijra* of the Prophet from Mecca to Medina fourteen centuries earlier.

Once in Afghanistan, under the patronage of the Taliban, bin Laden launched his holy war in earnest against the United States. A campaign that began with statements issued against "the Crusaders and the Jews" in 1996, that were then amplified by bellicose interviews on CNN, ABC News, and Al Jazeera, and that took concrete shape across three continents with the U.S. embassy attacks in Africa in 1998, the USS *Cole* attack in Yemen in 2000, and finally 9/11 itself.

Parallel to this, al Qaeda developed a number of training camps during this period that would churn out thousands of graduates, many of whom would simply be cannon fodder for the war against Ahmad Shah Massoud's reviled Northern Alliance, while more promising graduates would receive advanced training in terrorist tactics and the production of crude weapons of mass destruction.

The years between 1996 and 2001 were when bin Laden reached the apogee of his power. In Afghanistan he was able to create his own jihad kingdom, as if "The Man Who Would be King" had been remade as a jihadist epic. While he publicly professed fealty to the Taliban leader Mullah Omar, in practice bin Laden paid little attention to the Taliban's repeated efforts to stop his attacks on the West, doing pretty much as he pleased throughout his five-year stay in Afghanistan as the Taliban's "honored guest."

᭩

On July 18, 1996, the State Department's Bureau of Intelligence Research, which has a well-deserved reputation for the consistently excellent quality of its analysis, prepared a top-secret document titled "Terrorism/Usama bin Ladin: Who's Chasing Whom?" The document summarized the bureau's understanding of al Qaeda's leader after his departure from Sudan and its analysis of the implications of his likely relocation to Afghanistan. The documents were made public under a Freedom of Information Act request and were declassified in July 2005. Key excerpts follow.

Terrorism/Usama bin Ladin: Who's Chasing Whom?.[1]

Bin Ladin's homecoming

Bin Ladin would feel comfortable returning to Afghanistan, where he got his start as a patron and mujahid during the war with the former Soviet Union. Afghanistan may be an ideal haven as long as bin Ladin can continue to run his businesses and financial networks. His prolonged stay in Afghanistan—where hundreds of "Arab Mujahidin" receive terrorist training and key extremist leaders often congregate—could prove more dangerous to U.S. interests in the long run than his three-year liaison with Khartoum.

On the run?

With pressure against him mounting from the United States and some Muslim states, especially Saudi Arabia and Egypt, bin Ladin seemingly should be on the run. But his willingness to speak more openly to the press about his militant opposition to the Saudi regime and the West suggests more a man emboldened by recent events, whether or not he was involved in them.

Vahid Mojdeh is the Afghan who worked with Abdullah Azzam's and bin Laden's Services Office during the eighties in Peshawar. Between 1995 and the fall of the Taliban in 2001, he held several posts in various divisions of the Afghan foreign affairs ministry. He published an insider's account of his time as a Taliban official, *Afghanistan Under Five Years of Taliban Sovereignty* in late 2001.[2] Extracts from the book follow.

The Taliban movement was not initially a political organization. In fact, the movement was formed to remove the groups that had fomented civil war [in Afghanistan during the early '90s]. The Taliban disarmed armed groups. They removed all checkpoints on transit routes and brought security. It was precisely these sorts of actions that ordinary people were interested in seeing. By securing the roads, Taliban received financial aid from tradesmen.

Before entering Kabul in September of 1996, the Taliban alleged that they had no intention of ruling Afghanistan. The Taliban's greatest problem in forming a government was that they were rural people and when they entered Kabul, they faced open conflicts with urban values and requirements. As time passed it became evident that the Taliban's intention went well beyond the imposition of rural values in an urban setting. Women and girls were prohibited to work and to get an education. Women could only move about the city under the long burqah. Men were not allowed to shave their beards; it was considered a crime. Wearing turbans became mandatory in governmental offices and schools.

Recruitment and employment in the Taliban's governmental offices were also strange. The majority of the officials were titled "Mullah," an honorary religious title. Even in places where specialists were needed to carry out technical projects, the majority of employment belonged to barely literate Taliban, or those known as Mullah.

The Taliban movement initially had a consultative system, with Mullah Omar at the head, but after the invasion of Kabul, consultation faded as many members were assigned to government posts. The quiet dissolution of this council granted ill-defined but unlimited power and control to Mullah Omar as Amir-ul Mumineen (The Leader of the Faithful) and so he could rule the country by issuing whatever order he wished to.

The Taliban movement was not essentially political and its leaders were extremely religious individuals. In some instances such as with Mullah Omar, mystic inclinations were apparent. Many of them had no knowledge beyond a few religious books and their worldly perspective was limited to a couple of provinces in Afghanistan. Their understanding of political matters was completely auditory, the result of listening to radio news or talking with people. The majority of these leaders had no desire to study anything but the Holy Koran, and religious texts.

Osama and his loyalists were of course well aware of how to influence the Taliban, relying on their previous experiences with Mujahideen leaders. The purchase of expensive automobiles for Mullah Omar and his loyalists was the first step in that direction. Financial support in the war against the Taliban's opposition, in particular buying off the opposing commanders, proved to be an effective strategy. Osama thus established himself among the Taliban in a position far above that of a mere guest. Using his own financial assets, Osama bin Laden successfully positioned himself among the Taliban.

Abu Walid al Misri is the Egyptian journalist who worked with al Qaeda and the Taliban.[3]

The Taliban leadership consisted of Mullah Mohammad Omar, who lost his right eye while fighting against the Soviets, along with the Taliban Shura Council, which consisted of fifteen people, twelve of whom were severely wounded in the same war and had lost body parts.

Hutaifa Azzam, Abdullah Azzam's son, spent time in Afghanistan in the mid-nineties.[4]

[When bin Laden first arrived in Afghanistan] he wrote a letter to Mullah Omar saying, "I want to come to your areas, but I need a promise from you that you are going to protect me, you will never surrender me." Mullah Omar sent him the answer "You are most welcome. We will never give you up to anyone who wants you."

Osama bin Laden's first declaration that he was at war with the United States was issued in August 23, 1996, three months after his return to Afghanistan. A significant extract follows, laying out bin Laden's case against the West, and the United States in particular, a case that has been quite consistent over time. Conventional wisdom has it that bin Laden adopted the Palestinian issue only recently. Reading this declaration should put that canard to rest.[5]

It should not be hidden from you that the people of Islam had suffered from aggression, iniquity and injustice imposed on them by the Zionist-Crusaders alliance and their collaborators; to the extent that the

Muslims' blood became the cheapest and their wealth as loot in the hands of the enemies. Their blood was spilled in Palestine and Iraq. The horrifying pictures of the massacre of Qana in Lebanon [when Israeli forces struck a UN compound on April 18, 1996, killing one hundred] are still fresh in our memory. Massacres in Tajikistan, Burma, Kashmir, Philippines, Somalia, Eritrea, and Chechnya, and in Bosnia-Herzegovina took place, massacres that send shivers in the body and shake the conscience.

The latest and the greatest of these aggressions, incurred by the Muslims since the death of the Prophet, is the occupation of the land of the two Holy Places (referring to the presence of tens of thousands of U.S. troops in Saudi Arabia). By orders from the USA they also arrested a large number of scholars in the land of the two Holy Places—among them the prominent Sheikh Salman al Awdah and Sheikh Safar al Hawali. Myself and my group, have suffered some of this injustice. We have been pursued in Pakistan, Sudan and Afghanistan, hence this long absence on my part. But by the Grace of Allah, a safe base is now available in the high Hindu Kush mountains in Khurasan (the archaic Islamic name for Afghanistan).

The presence of the USA Crusader military forces on land, sea and air in the states of the Islamic Gulf is the greatest danger threatening the largest oil reserve in the world.

My Muslim Brothers: The money you pay to buy American goods will be transformed into bullets and used against our brothers in Palestine. By buying these goods we are strengthening their economy while our poverty increases. We expect the women of the land of the two Holy Places and other countries to carry out their role in boycotting American goods. The security and the intelligence services of the entire world cannot force a single citizen to buy the goods of his/her enemy. The boycotting of American goods is a very effective weapon for weakening the enemy.

I rejected those who enjoy fireplaces in clubs discussing eternally;
I respect those who carried on, not asking or bothering about the difficulties;
Never letting up from their goals, in spite all hardships of the road;
I feel still the pain of [the loss of] Al Quds in my internal organs; (Al

Quds: Jerusalem, the site of the third holiest place of pilgrimage in Islam, was annexed to Israel in 1967). That loss is like a burning fire in my intestines.

More than 600,000 Iraqi children have died due to lack of food and medicine and as a result of the unjustifiable [UN sanctions during the 1990s] imposed on Iraq and its nation. The children of Iraq are our children. You, the USA, are responsible for the shedding of the blood of these innocent children.

The walls of oppression and humiliation cannot be demolished except in a rain of bullets.

The freeman does not surrender leadership to infidels and sinners.

My Muslim Brothers of the World: Your brothers in Palestine and in the land of the two Holy Places are calling upon your help and asking you to take part in fighting against the enemy—your enemy and their enemy—the Americans and the Israelis.

Abdel Bari Atwan, the editor of *Al Quds al Arabi,* an independent Arabic-language newspaper based in London, met bin Laden three months after he had issued the fatwa declaring war on America.[6]

I decided to meet [bin Laden in November 1996] for many reasons. First, we were a newspaper which was not under the umbrella of Saudi Arabia. Most of the Arab media is controlled by the Saudis. Nobody else could interview him and publish the interview except me. But to be honest, I was hesitant. Because it is very dangerous and also I didn't want to clash directly with the Saudi government because I know this is the arch-enemy of the royal family, and I wanted to stay away from internal Saudi politics at that time, as our newspaper actually was really facing a lot of trouble with the Saudis.

I met Khaled Fauwaz (bin Laden's media contact in London) and he said, are you interested in meeting Osama bin Laden? I was told that Osama bin Laden was fond of my writing, he liked my style and he wanted to meet me personally. I remember the first interview was supposed to be September 1996. So [Khaled Fauwaz] said to me, "You have to go to New Delhi, you take the plane to Jalalabad, and in Jalalabad they will take care of you." I made my inquiries and I wasn't that keen on that.

It was frightening, to be honest. And thank God, [Khaled Fauwaz] phoned me a week before and he said to me "There is no need for travel now, because it is dangerous." I said, "What's dangerous?" He said, "The Taliban have moved into Jalalabad and we don't know what will happen to Osama bin Laden, so wait a bit." Thank God, they actually changed their plans and changed their minds, and I was really relieved, to be honest.

In November [1996] they called me again. They said, now it is safe to go to Jalalabad. I didn't even tell my wife where I am going. I told only one colleague of mine at this newspaper. I told her "I am going to meet Osama bin Laden. This is top secret. If anything happens to me, I have this money, I have this mortgage, I have these bills."

Mohammad Atef [at the time al Qaeda's military commander] was very, very pleased to see me, and he was very happy because I managed to make the trip [to Jalalabad]. And he was really nice, very hospitable, very charming person, and he was very smart, you know—dark skin and green eyes—very beautiful green eyes. I was taken with different people to Tora Bora, the mountain which is looking over Jalalabad. And it was a trip in a pick-up car. It was full of those armed men sitting outside, and there were two seats in the cabin. The first one is for the driver, two people sitting behind him, and the second seat was mine, and then there was another militiaman sitting right beside me. There was snow at that time. It was very cold—freezing. And then to the favorite cave of Osama bin Laden. And actually it was very simple cave, and he was waiting. There were two rooms. The first room was boxes. And then there was some sort of a living room inside with beds. And there were lots of people.

Five minutes after my arrival all of them left the cave with bin Laden. [There were] anti-aircraft guns and rockets. I was left in the cave. I thought the Americans have discovered our place and they are bombing us. And so I started reciting the Koran and thinking, this is the end of me, seriously. And then after twenty minutes they came back and they said, sorry, it was a military maneuver. We do it sometimes. I was really horrified; I was scared to death.

To be honest, it is a mystery whether they are doing it to impress me, whether they are doing it because they thought maybe I could be tracked by American intelligence, or they were routinely doing it. But after half an hour they repeated it again. And then we had dinner. Dinner was really awful; there were about twelve people in that cave. The dinner was rotten cheese, this Egyptian cheese. It's salty cheese, it's really very bad. The peasants eat it in Egypt in particular. And then there was a potato soaked in cottonseed oil. And also there were about five or six fried eggs, and bread, which was really caked with sand. So I think this is their food, typical food. They eat very little, it's bin Laden who actually loves to live such a harsh life with his followers, and that's why his son, Abdallah, left this harsh life and decided to go back to Saudi Arabia.

Abu Jandal is the former bin Laden bodyguard now living in Yemen.[7]

[Bin Laden's] eldest son Abdallah returned to Saudi Arabia [in 1995] after making an arrangement with his uncles and the Saudi ruling family. He wanted to return and settle in Saudi Arabia. Abdallah returned to Saudi Arabia because his views did not agree with his father's. As he saw it, he came from a wealthy family and deserved to live well on the money his family had. This view was completely at odds with his father's. Sheikh Osama avoided mentioning Abdallah's name after this because he had been hurt by him. He wished that his eldest son had remained with him to help him. He respected his son's wishes, however, and allowed him to return to Saudi Arabia.

Hutaifa Azzam, Abdullah Azzam's son.

I met Abdallah [bin Laden] in Dubai when he was coming from Sudan and we spend more than three weeks together. This was in '95. Abdallah was totally different from his father.

Abdel Bari Atwan, the editor of *Al Quds al Arabi* newspaper.

To be honest, the man is likable. He is really nice. You don't see him as somebody who will be the arch-terrorist, who will be the most dangerous man in the world. He doesn't strike you as charismatic. You are with somebody who you feel you knew for maybe ten to fifteen years, you don't feel a stranger when you meet him for the first time. And he doesn't try to impress you. I met a lot of Palestinian leaders. They try to impress you. This man does not try to impress you. Maybe this is his strength. Maybe this is his style. He was extremely natural, very simple, very humble and soft-spoken. You feel he is shy. He doesn't look at you eye to eye. Usually when he talks to you he talks by looking down. His clothes are very, very humble, very simple.

He is not on the defensive, neither on the offensive. And he was a very good listener. You know, he is not like us, we Arabs interrupt the speaker. He waits until you finish your sentence and finish your argument and then he comments with little words. He's not really noisy like us, you know.

It was an important [interview] for them for two reasons. First, because it is in Arabic. Osama bin Laden was pleased to talk to the Arab world and he was pleased to talk to the Saudis and the Arabian Peninsula in particular, and it seemed he wanted media exposure. His major priority is the Arabic audience. He wanted to declare war in his language.

Now he went a step further or maybe more than ten steps further. He wants to say, now I am an international figure; I'm not just a Saudi. I am aggrieved at Americans who are occupying Saudi Arabia who are desecrating the Holy Land. That's the most important message he wanted to say. I didn't expect him to actually declare a war against the United States. I expected him maybe just to concentrate on the Saudi regime, the Saudi royal family, but he surprised me.

Osama bin Laden, in the beginning, never actually presented himself as a religious scholar. He never gave the impression that he has the authority to issue a fatwa. He used to rely on the [fatwas of] other ulema [clerics].

From the intellectual point of view, at that time, he was working very hard in his theological background; you can see in the cave, there were a lot of textbooks about the Koran, about ibn-Taymiyyah (the medieval Muslim scholar who has provided much of the theological ballast for jihadist movements). He was actually influenced by their teaching. And incidentally, on my way to see him, the driver, was playing tapes of Safir al Halawi (the militant Saudi cleric who influenced bin Laden). So he was also influenced by those people, by the new breed of Islamist scholars in Saudi Arabia.

There was something really strange. I took my tape recorder and then, when I asked Mohammad Atef [al Qaeda's military commander], why you don't want me to tape this, he just says, [bin Laden] doesn't want his voice to be recorded. He doesn't want to make mistakes and have a recording and when it is taped it [might] be used against him. I am not a religious man. I am not fundamentalist. And so, for them, they can't trust me. I'm not one of them. So that's why, he told me that he doesn't want to make mistakes on the tape in Arabic, because it's not good for a preacher to make grammatical mistakes in Arabic.

[Bin Laden's] Arabic was actually a classical Arabic. It is very correct Arabic, no grammatical mistakes, full of verses of the Koran, full of *Hadiths* (sayings of the Prophet Muhammad).

I met his two sons. Saad and I think Ali. They were thirteen, fourteen and they were playing Nintendo, in the compound where the family lives in Jalalabad.

[In 1996] I asked him why you are not fighting the Jews, for example—the Israelis. And I said, "You know, you are criticized because of this." He actually did not have an answer for that. It seems he was surprised with my question. In that time, Osama bin Laden also wasn't liked by the Arab nationalists, leftists, who are the majority in the Arab world because he fought Soviet Union, which was the ally of the Arabs.

The PLO (Palestinian Liberation Organization) used to be considered as an atheist organization by Osama bin Laden because they sided with the Soviet Union. He considers [the late PLO leader Yasser] Arafat as a traitor. And a secularist. He hated his guts.

He also didn't like Saddam Hussein. And he considered Saddam Hussein as a man who is a secular, but he didn't actually insult Saddam Hussein the way he insulted Yasser Arafat. He didn't like him and he told me he wanted to kick him out of Iraq, as he considered, the Ba'ath (Iraqi socialist) regime [to be an] atheist regime. He considered Saddam Hussein as an atheist, and he hates an atheist.

We didn't talk about his personal life. We never talked about his wives or something like that because it is a taboo. He took me on a tourist tour in Tora Bora. We walked for about two hours together. We left the cave about 8 o'clock in the morning. It was freezing. And so we went around and the sun started and it was really beautiful and he showed me the houses of some of his people, their mud bricks houses there above the snow. He loved that nature there. He loved the mountain. They were trying to have their own community, grow their foods, and they are marrying each other. It's like an oasis in Afghanistan. You can see their children play together; their families get together, the men together. They have their own food, they bake their bread.

I was told actually he wasn't living in that cave. I was told he chose to meet me in that cave because he loves it; because this cave in particular in Tora Bora, he used to stay during the jihad against the Soviet Union. And he told me he fought a lot of battles in Tora Bora and they managed to win one of the battles in that place, so it is very dear to him. The other thing is he loves the mountain, as he told me. He said, "I really feel secure in the mountains. I really enjoy my life when I'm here. I feel secure in this place."

I asked him, "If you are going to be kicked out of Afghanistan one day the way you were kicked out of Saudi Arabia and Sudan, where will you go?" He said, "You know, Abdel Bari, I will go to Yemen—the mountains of Yemen because it is exactly like Tora Bora. I love the mountains."

He was in perfect health. He never complained about how high it was in the mountains and it was freezing. He had dry mouth most of the time. I noted that he drinks a lot of water and tea.

He told me how he hated Americans and even he wanted to defeat them even in his agriculture project. So he was actually the happiest man on earth when he managed to produce a sunflower, which is, a record in its size, much bigger than the American sunflower. He said, "Even I defeated them in agriculture." He was very proud of his sunflower.

After the fall of the Taliban I toured Tora Bora, where Abdel Bari Atwan had interviewed bin Laden, to get a feel for the place that al Qaeda's leader clearly loves. The caves that dot the hills of Tora Bora are small affairs suitable for shelter from bombardments, but are certainly not the caves of a James Bond villain. The buildings that make up the Tora Bora settlement (more properly known as Milewa) are strung across a series of ridges. When I visited in January 2005 the former al Qaeda settlement was above the snowline, commanding lovely views of the verdant valleys below.

I was guided around the buildings by a local woodcutter. Now all destroyed after the U.S. bombing campaign, they comprised a series of scattered lookout posts, a bakery, and bin Laden's two-bedroom house, all constructed of the baked mud typical of Afghan villages. Incongruously, next to bin Laden's house, was a crude swimming pool, which was also in ruins. (Photos of the site can be found in the photo section.)

In front of bin Laden's house lay a broad field, now scarred by bomb craters, where al Qaeda members cultivated their crops. It all had the feel of a hippie commune that somehow had been airlifted into the Hindu Kush mountains. The overwhelming sensation was one of tranquility and distance from modern civilization. From bin Laden's house all he would have been able to see was his own little feudal fiefdom; the nearest village is out of sight thousands of feet below down a scree-covered slope.

Two hours down a rocky road from Tora Bora, which winds its way past tiny Afghan villages, babbling brooks, and orchards, is the main al Qaeda compound in an area called Hadda, a neighborhood of massive, walled compounds that lies just outside the city of Jalalabad. The Hadda compound is spread over two acres, a complex of some seventy-five rooms, a place that could house hundreds of people. Across the road was another large al Qaeda compound. A group of local boys showed me an entrance to a secret chamber in the compound that extended at least fifty-feet underground. Both buildings had been largely destroyed by U.S. air strikes.

Safiwullah, a fifteen-year-old boy who like many Afghans has only one name, lives in the house next door to bin Laden's compound.

It was very hard to see Osama; you couldn't see him. He came here in 4-wheel drives with blacked out windows. Arab guards patrolled around here at night. They didn't hire locals as guards or cooks. It was a secret place. They checked anybody coming by. Osama is a very nice guy. He's a great holy warrior. Why do they say he's a murderer and a bad guy? Osama is a hero.

The Egyptian-Canadian Khadr family lived with the bin Laden family in Jalalabad. What follows are extracts of Abdurahman Khadr's testimony in the case of Adil Charkaoui, before the Federal Court of Canada, July 13, 2004. Khadr's testimony was made as part of the defense for Charkaoui, who was appealing his detention by Canadian authorities.[8]

My father is from Egypt. He is a citizen of Canada. Our permanent house was in Pakistan from '85 until '96. After '96 our house was in Jalalabad. We got a house in the city and we had a house up north of the city in al Qaeda compound. Osama bin Laden and all the members that are around him all lived in this compound. More or less two hundred and fifty people. We stayed in Jalalabad from mid-1996 until mid-1997. In mid-1997 a commander of the Northern Alliance threatened to attack Jalalabad so the Taliban were concerned about Osama and the compound. So they insisted on Osama that he move his compound from Jalalabad to Kandahar [in southern Afghanistan]. We [then] moved to Kabul where we rented a house and we were staying in that house from 1999 until 2001.

My first trip to Khaldan (training camp in Afghanistan) I think was in mid-'95. I am not sure about the time exactly but I know I was eleven at the point that I first went. And then I went there every year in the summer, in the summer breaks, and I spent two to four months there. As I learned later, it was al Qaeda training camp. They insisted that a person do something with his training, kill an American or trying to go into suicide bombing. So there was a lot of mental training in al Qaeda camps.

In '98 [when I was fourteen] I went to an al Qaeda camp which was Jihad Wel Al Farooq. I was sent to Jihad Wel because my father thought that I was old enough or mature enough to be sent to a bigger camp where there is more mental training and psychological training. I was there for seven days.

Yes [my father was a good friend of Osama bin Laden]. Yes [my father admired Osama bin Laden]. Yes, [Osama bin Laden attended my sister's wedding]. Yes [my father, being in admiration with Mr. bin Laden, therefore approved of Mr. bin Laden's methods and ideologies]. Yes, [if Mr. bin Laden condoned violence, my father condoned violence too]. I described him [my father] before as a member [of al Qaeda] and [to my father] it was a freedom fight [not terrorism]. To him this was a group of the last Muslims surviving to defend Islam. That is what it was to him.

I am against them, because it is violence. It is killing of innocent people. It is not what Islam calls for. Islam for me is a peaceful religion. I am against American troops being in Saudi, I am against it all the way. But I do not deal with it the way Osama does.

[Osama bin Laden is against Western] things like Tabasco [and] ice. Ice is not even American, but it is a luxury of life and he doesn't want his people to get used to that.

[Between 1998 and 2001 when I was aged fourteen to seventeen my father] sat me down with this [religious] scholar and the [military] trainer and they talked about it [serving as a suicide bomber]. We even discussed which clothes I would be wearing, that I would shave my beard, that I would wear a Walkman. And I was like: "No, no. No."

Zaynab Khadr is a sister of Abdurahman Khadr. Terrence McKenna, a correspondent for the Canadian Broadcast Corporation, interviewed Zaynab Khadr in Pakistan for the CBC documentary *Al Qaeda Family*, a profile of the Khadr family and their relationship with bin Laden, which aired on February 22, 2004. Excerpts of the interview follow.[9]

When we lived in Jalalabad, that was the first time that I met them [bin Laden's family]. Actually, it's not that they're not social people [the women in bin Laden's family]. They're very social, but they have lots of restrictions, where they go, when they go, where they come, when they come, who visits to them and how long you can stay in their house and all that. So you can't really have an intimate relationship with them, and you can't be really going and coming because they have to watch many things.

I heard about it [bin Laden interacting with his children]. I never saw it. Men and women don't mix. But as far as I know, it was very important for him to sit with his kids every day at least for two hours in the morning after their morning prayer. They sit and read a book at least. It didn't have to be something religious. He loved poetry very much. So he tried to encourage them to read, memorize, and write poetry. So every once in a while it would be a different book, sometimes it's about poetry, sometimes it's about history or sometimes it's about grammar, language, sometimes a religious book.

He loved playing volleyball and loved horse riding. And he'd do it, I mean amongst people he was not Osama bin Laden. He was just Osama. And kids played around him. Kids would go shake his hand. He played volleyball with them or just horse race with them. He was just a normal person. And [when] they'd go shooting he'd go with them. If he missed his target they'd laugh at him and stuff like that.

He didn't allow [his children] to drink cold water. Probably because he didn't believe in using modern conveniences because he wanted them to be prepared that one day there's no cold water, they'd be able to survive and it wouldn't be so difficult for them. He didn't like to buy American soft drinks, Coke and Pepsi and all that, but his kids sometimes would buy them. And he liked them to live more natural. They had horses and camels. I mean he's a Saudi or more of a Bedouin. They love horses and camels and they had them even in their compound. But one of his kids loved cars so whatever allowance his father was giving him, he got enough money to buy himself a car.

Noman Benotman, the Libyan jihadist, explains the manner in which bin Laden lived in Afghanistan.[10]

You know the theory, if you would like to be a king, treat your servants like one? It's like that [with bin Laden]. Because he is humble he does not consider himself as a dictator, as a king. He's living a normal life, the life of poor people. I saw him many times. He was really living this life. You see his kids—you will never, ever in your life think those kids are bin Laden's kids, [rather] they are people from the poorest family in the world. I saw them. You wouldn't believe it—they're kids running around in old clothes.

He always tells his followers, "you should learn to sacrifice everything, from modern life like electricity, air conditioning, refrigerators, gasoline. If you are living the luxury life, it's very hard for to evacuate and go to the mountains to fight."

And at his camp no one can bring in refrigerators, air conditioning. I have spoken with his people in the camp, and they are laughing. "Okay, I need a refrigerator." And the family, they made fun of [bin Laden] and he just laughed. That gives you the meaning of humble, because he's laughing with them.

Because he's a very democratic guy, he told his wives, "If anyone would like to go back to her family, she is really free to go. It's going to be a very hard life, very tough. But if you want to go home, you can go. I'm not going to prevent you." One of them, she went back to her home [during the period that bin Laden lived in Sudan].

❧

On September 26, 1996, the Taliban swept into Kabul, the capital of Afghanistan. The following day the U.S. State Department spokesman Glyn Davies made a statement that indicated that not much was known about the Taliban, but also suggested a certain lukewarm optimism about their intentions.

We've seen some of the reports that they've moved to impose Islamic law in the areas that they control. But at this stage, we're not reading anything into that. On the face of it, nothing objectionable at this stage. What we haven't had an opportunity to do, of course, is get in touch with the Taliban and discuss with them their intentions.

Similarly, Robin Raphael, the U.S. assistant secretary of state for South Asia, made the following observations at a closed door meeting at the United Nations on November 18, 1996.[11]

The Taliban control more than two-thirds of the country, they are Afghan, and are indigenous, they have demonstrated staying power. The real source of their success has been the willingness of many Afghans, particularly Pashtuns, to tacitly trade unending fighting and chaos for a measure of peace and security, even with severer social restrictions. It is not in the interests of Afghanistan or any of us here that the Taliban be isolated.

Hamid Mir is the Pakistani journalist who was asked by bin Laden to be his biographer.[12]

In November 1996, the American assistant secretary of state, Mrs. Robin Raphael, delivered a speech in support of the Taliban in the United Nations headquarters of New York. So when she delivered a speech in support of the Taliban I wrote a very critical column about Taliban and Robin Raphael, and I said she is the mother of Taliban. So, Taliban were very angry. Some of their officials contacted me and they tried to explain their position and they said we are not working for the Americans. So I asked, "OK, if you are not working for them, you show me evidence and then I will be convinced. So they said, "OK, we can arrange a meeting with Mullah Omar; he is the head of our movement."

I met Mullah Omar in December 1996, first time. I still remember he was sitting on the floor of a mosque, without any carpet and the first thing after shaking hand, [was] *Asslamu Alaikum,* how are you?" He was a very simple man. And the people around him, they were paying lot of respect to him. That was my first meeting with him and it was very unusual that a man who is the head of the Taliban was sitting on a bare floor—no protocol and then he served green tea to me and after green tea I had lunch with him; potatoes, some soup, and some bread that's all, very simple food. And I thought that he is maybe he is trying to impress me that I'm very simple man. I thought maybe he has another lavish office somewhere else.

In that meeting I asked Mullah Omar, "Why is Robin Raphael supporting you?" He asked me, "Who's he?" So I was amazed that the man doesn't know that she's a female and as a journalist it was a big story for me—That the Americans are supporting a movement, but the head of the Taliban is not aware that the lady who delivered a speech in the United Nations for them, is female. So I tried to dig out more facts from Mullah Omar.

And I said, "Okay, if you say that you don't know her and [the Americans are] not supporting you, then why they are delivering speeches in your support in the United Nations." And Mullah Omar said there were three things. One, the Americans are interested in the installation of a gas pipeline project from Turkmenistan (in the former Soviet Union) to Pakistan [through] Afghanistan and the value of the project is five billion dollars. And the American oil company Unocal is interested in the project. But Mullah Omar said that we will not oblige them because we have decided to sign a memorandum of understanding with an Argentinean company whose name is Bridas. And the second thing he said that they want to use us. The Americans want to use us against China. And the third thing he said they want to use us against Iran.

[Mullah Omar] said, "The radio Tehran (in Iran) has created a lot of problems for me. They are quoting your column every second day. Hamid Mir, a famous Pakistani journalist, is saying that Mullah Omar is working for the American CIA. I'm not CIA." In very weak Urdu, he was saying "I'm not CIA. I'm not CIA. Not CIA," repeating it again and again.

In the end Mullah Omar said, "How can I prove that I'm not a CIA agent?" I said, "I don't know. How can you prove?" He said, "Okay, I have a friend who is a great enemy of CIA, who is a great enemy of America and he is my guest in Afghanistan. Do you know him, Osama bin Laden?" I said, "Yes, I have heard his name but why he is important?" He said, "The Sheikh bin Laden is a great enemy of USA and the USA managed his extradition from Sudan and now he is with us. Promise me, that if you meet Sheikh bin Laden that you will write that Mullah Omar is not CIA agent." I said, "Okay, this is my promise."

I was so naive that I contacted the U.S. embassy. I went because I was without any details and the Pakistani media was totally blank about bin Laden. So I went to the U.S. embassy and the librarian was a Pakistani and I said, "Do you know anything about Mr. bin Laden?" and he said, "Please give me in writing what is the spelling." So I gave him "Osama bin Laden." Then he went on the Internet and he gave me two articles. One was from *Time* magazine. I was confused whether I should go for the interview or not because this person is not very important. You see, in March 1997 bin Laden was not a big story.

My first meeting did not create good impressions. I faced lot of problems and especially when they started a body search, and when some of their guards, they put their hands inside my underwear, so there was a big shouting match with them. Maybe I have something with my balls, you see. So I was so pissed that I shouted, "You are gays." They said, "This is our duty." So for fifteen, twenty minutes, I was exchanging hot words with them so in the meantime, [Osama] reached there, he appeared, and he realized the situation and he started saying, "Sorry Mr. Mir. Sorry Mr. Mir." The first words which he said to me [in English] was "Sorry, Mr. Mir."

Then dinner was served to us. Oh, that was, a very lavish dinner, a full-grilled lamb! And some olives, some salads. And I was amazed that they can serve these kind of typical Arab food in Afghanistan in the caves. I noticed that there are some TV sets lying in the cave, lot of books. There were many caves and some of the caves were interconnected with each other.

When I started my interview, he started reading a file which was in his hands. And then he disclosed my bank account numbers, my ID card number, my personal telephone numbers, the amount of money which is in my bank account. So I was confused because I was thinking the man has lot of secrets about my personal life. Then he said, "You are a journalist. I am a freedom fighter. And I hope you will behave like a journalist, you will not behave like an informer or a spy. And if you will behave like a journalist we will maintain our relationship." So he conveyed a message: Don't try play a game with me in a very civilized way.

I forced bin Laden to act [in the photos I took of him]. You see he was very shy. He was not ready to put his gun on the shoulder. I was forcing him. I was treating him like an actor. So, I was saying, "Mr. bin Laden, no, you should smile." And he said, "No I can't do it." So you see that was my first meeting and I was not aware how dangerous he is. In the first meeting he was very soft spoken. He was a very good host. He took a lot of care of us, but there was no depth in his thinking. He was just protesting on one point: Why are U.S. troops present on my soil [in Saudi Arabia], that's all. That was his problem.

He condemned Saddam Hussein in my interview. He gave such kind of abuses that it was very difficult for me to write—socialist Motherfucker—[He said] "The land of the Arab world, the land is like a mother and Saddam Hussein is fucking his mother." He also explained that Saddam Hussein is against us and he discourages Iraqi boys to come to Afghanistan.

I met with Osama bin Laden in 1997. Peter Arnett was the correspondent for CNN and I was the producer of what turn out to be bin Laden's first television interview. At that time bin Laden was regarded only as a financier of Islamic extremism. When his name first publicly surfaced in '96, we started the process of trying to interview him. I had always believed that the first World Trade Center attack in 1993 was not simply the work of a bunch of disaffected Arab cab drivers from Brooklyn, but might have some larger organization behind it, perhaps led by someone like bin Laden. That hunch would turn out to be wrong. Bin Laden had nothing to do with that attack, but the Saudi exile did lead a global terrorist organization, as we would find out when we met with him in Afghanistan.

I traveled to London to meet with his media contact, Khaled al Fauwaz. He was very cagey, worrying, "Are you an agent of the CIA, will you give this guy a fair shake?" I said, "CNN will give anybody a fair shake that we talk to." And I went back to the States. Peter Arnett and I got a call about a month later saying that the trip was on. We then traveled to London; we met our cameraman Peter Jouvenal and two other people who took us to bin Laden. Our chief guide was known to me as Omar (of whom more later).

We traveled to Pakistan, and then across the Hindu Kush into Afghanistan. At the time the Taliban had just banned filming, which obviously posed a problem for our project since we were doing a television interview with bin Laden. We chose not to alert the Taliban that we were coming into the country, didn't get visas, and just went over the border. We arrived in Jalalabad and waited around for several days, receiving a visit or two from some of bin Laden's people, including one shaggy-haired young man who described himself as a media adviser to bin Laden. They told us you can't bring any of your equipment; to do the interview we'll give you our own camera. Obviously this was not a subject that we could debate about with them.

Peter Jouvenal is the cameraman who shot CNN's interview with bin Laden.[13]

I decided when I was sixteen I wanted to be war photographer so I decided that it would be advantageous to spend some time in the military because you're operating in that sort of environment, so that's why I joined the army. And then when I left the army in '79, I was just waiting for a war, a relevant war to come up, or any war. And—lucky for me, but not for Afghanistan—the Soviets invaded Afghanistan. So I thought there was a good opportunity for a freelancer so I got on the bus from Victoria coach station [in London]. I got a bus all the way—different buses but I ended up in Peshawar [Pakistan]. What was important about that particular war; it was a proxy war between two superpowers. If it had been one of these irrelevant wars in Africa I wouldn't have succeeded because no one would have been interested in the pictures, but there was a fantastic appetite for material.

So that's basically why I ended up in Afghanistan. And by the time the

Soviets left in '89 I had done seventy-two trips with the mujahideen across the border.

For me it was just another assignment [interviewing bin Laden]. We had been waiting several days at the hotel and one of Osama's camera-men came and he checked out my gear. He was concerned that there would be a bomb in the camera, which is ironic considering how [Afghan leader Ahmad Shah] Masood was killed [on the 9th of September 2001 by al Qaeda assassins posing as television reporters]. For some reason [he] decided that I couldn't use my camera.

So we got into a van. This was in the evening, it was already dark. And then we were given these black sunglasses with bits of cardboard that had been cut out and we were asked to put those on, which we did. I didn't feel threatened at all because, you know, Osama wouldn't invite someone and then kill them. In those days he wouldn't be doing that sort of thing. So I wasn't really worried at all. I knew we were his guests and therefore the guards would behave themselves.

So we headed off to the Black Mountains [surrounding Jalalabad] and then we were challenged. There was this shout, lights went on, and some people behind boulders obviously waiting for us. They all popped out, pointed their weapons at the vehicle, and we had to get out and then we were warned that if you have a tracking device if it is declared now then nothing would happen to us, but if they were to find something on us later on then there would be serious consequences, which I interpreted as your head's going to get chopped off.

[We arrived in] a very shallow valley, dark, maybe three houses—mud huts. This building we went in I think it was for keeping sheep in the win-ter. It wasn't a proper house for people to live in. There was the hum of a generator because I had asked them beforehand if the interview was going to be conducted at night, I would need lights and therefore we'd need a generator. So we set up the gear and then we sat down and had our kebabs and then Osama turned up. I just remember this rather limp sort of handshake. Not a proper handshake. I remember his hands were cold, like sort of shaking hands with a fish.

Osama bin Laden arrived out of the darkness. I didn't even know what he'd look like. I don't think I'd seen a photo of him. It turned out

that he was six-foot-five, very tall, very thin, and he carried himself in a very low-key kind of way, he wasn't a fire-breathing terrorist, he comported himself like a cleric.

One of the conditions of the interview is that we would submit a lot of questions in advance. Some of the al Qaeda members made it clear that bin Laden was not going to answer questions about his family, his money, or his personal story; he just wanted to get his political message out. And at the end of the day, that's why we were there. We were there to find out why he had declared war against the West, the United States in particular; who in the United States he was directing the war at; what were the reasons for this war.

He told us that he declared war against the United States in particular because of American foreign policies, particularly the fact that U.S. troops in Saudi Arabia seemed to be a permanent military presence in the holy land of Arabia. He also had other reasons that he was declaring war: the sanctions then in place against Iraq, U.S. support for Israel, and the U.S. backing of Egypt and Saudi Arabia, regimes he doesn't consider sufficiently Islamic.

Those set of reasons he's stuck to. He's been pretty consistent about why he's attacking the United States. It's because of American foreign policies. He did not say anything about Madonna, Hollywood, drugs, sex, or any of the kind of cultural issues you might expect him to be concerned with. It's all about what America is doing in his backyard, as he sees it. He sees this as a defensive war responding to a record of humiliation that began after the end of World War I when the Ottoman Empire was carved up by the British and the French. And bin Laden believes that today Muslims are still being humiliated whether it is in Kashmir or Palestine or in Iraq. As far as he's concerned his war is about humiliation and reclaiming Muslim pride.

He was extremely soft spoken. I remember he drank quite a lot of tea. If you didn't know what he was saying, you would have thought he was talking about the weather, but when you read the transcript of his remarks they were full of rage and of fury against the United States.

It was all business, he spent about an hour with us, he did not plan to hang around. After the formal part of the interview was over, he was talking to Peter Arnett, the correspondent, and the subject of Saddam

Hussein came up, and he delivered this quite negative assessment of Saddam. This is in 1997 long before what bin Laden thought of Saddam was a subject of any wider interest.

Interestingly, CNN's story about bin Laden, which aired on May 10, 1997, didn't get a lot of reaction, given the fact that this was the leader of the organization that would attack the United States on 9/11 four years later.

On April 30, 1997, as we were editing our story about bin Laden, I received this fax from Tim Metz of Abernathy MacGregor, a Madison Avenue media relations firm, representing the Binladin Family.[14]

You may attribute the following to a spokesman for the Binladin Family:

The family does not condone the reported activities of Osama Binladin, who has had no contact with, or support from, the family or its businesses since 1994 when his Saudi citizenship was revoked.

Bin Laden's CNN interview was the first time that he told Western reporters he was declaring war on the United States.[15]

We declared jihad against the U.S. government, because the U.S. government is unjust, criminal and tyrannical. It has committed acts that are extremely unjust, hideous, and criminal whether directly or through its support of the Israeli occupation of the Prophet's Night Travel Land (Palestine). And we believe the U.S. is directly responsible for those who were killed in Palestine, Lebanon, and Iraq. Due to its subordination to the Jews the arrogance and haughtiness of the U.S. regime has reached, to the extent that they occupied the qibla of the Muslims (Saudi Arabia) who are more than a billion in the world today.

As for what you asked, whether jihad is directed against U.S. soldiers, the [U.S.] civilians in the land of the Two Holy Places [Saudi Arabia], or against the civilians in America, we have focused our declaration on striking at the soldiers in the country of the Two Holy Places. The country of the Two Holy Places has in our religion a peculiarity of its own over the other Muslim countries. In our religion, it is not permissible for any non-Muslim to stay in our country. Therefore, even though American civilians are not targeted in our plan, they must leave. We do not guarantee their safety.

Peter Arnett: What are your future plans?
bin Laden: You'll see them and hear about them in the media, God willing.

Wadih el Hage, bin Laden's personal secretary in Sudan, testified before a U.S. grand jury on September 24, 1997. He claimed that bin Laden's call for war against the United States surprised some of his former employees.[16]

Abu Ibrahim, [the manager of some of bin Laden's businesses in Sudan] told me, he saw bin Laden in the CNN interview. He said that he mentioned things he should not speak about. I don't know what he meant, but what came to my mind then is that Osama bin Laden said things that should not be said at that time because it doesn't make him look good in front of people who are looking at him as an example.

"Omar," the man who had taken us to interview bin Laden in 1997 was, by his own account, a journalist who covered Islamist struggles and had worked as a medic alongside bin Laden's troops in the war against the Soviets.

In my discussions with Omar in early 1997, which were conducted in French, as he spoke no English and I no Arabic, he explained that he ran an independent journalistic outfit, the Bureau for the Study of Islamic Conflict. He said that he had correspondents in Kashmir, Bosnia, and Pakistan whose reports he used in his publications, and a branch of his bureau had an office in Kabul. He also explained that he had provided humanitarian assistance in Afghanistan from 1987 to 1990, and had lived most of the past fifteen years in the West, marrying a Spaniard, which meant that he had a Spanish passport. This would turn out to be only part of Omar's full story, which would only become public seven years later when the State Department announced a reward for information about him under his real name, Mustafa Setmariam Nasar.

On November 18, 2004, Adam Ereli, a U.S. State Department spokesman, released the following statement:

Secretary of State Colin L. Powell has authorized a $5 million reward offer to encourage individuals to come forward with information regarding Mustafa Setmariam Nasar. Mustafa Setmariam Nasar, also known as Abu Musab al Suri, is an al Qaida member and former trainer at the Derunta and al Ghuraba terrorist camps in Afghanistan where he trained terrorists in poisons and chemicals. Nasar is a Syrian with dual Spanish Nationality.

On January 25, 2005, Abu Musab al Suri released his own statement to jihadist Web sites in response to the U.S. government's offer of the $5 million dollar reward.[17]

I was honored to know Sheikh Osama since 1988, and I was honored to join al Qaeda and to work in it until 1992. I also trained some of its first vanguards, and I taught in its camps and other Arab Afghan camps especially in my area of expertise: explosives engineering, special operations and guerrilla warfare, in which I was highly trained in Iraq and Egypt and Jordan.

I was honored during that period to participate in the Afghan jihad against the Russians and the communists, until we annihilated their life and folded their flags, and we made them an example, as we will do with America with God's help.

I was also honored to migrate to the home of Islam in Afghanistan when it was established, and I was honored to pledge allegiance to the emir of the believers Mujahid Mullah Muhammad Omar, hand in hand, in Muharram 1421 (2000).

Then I worked as a Mujahid with the Taliban defense ministry. And I established the "foreigners camp" (al Ghuraba); I trained in it many Arabs and non-Arabs. Infidels and apostates have tasted the strength of some of my trainees in central Asia, the country of the two Holy Mosques that is unfairly known as "Saudi Arabia" and other countries.

In al Suri's history of jihadist movements *The International Islamic Resistance Call,* he explained that he had facilitated CNN's interview with bin Laden.[18]

I met [bin Laden] in 1997 to arrange an interview, which was broadcast on CNN, as I had established in London the "Centre for Media and

Research" specializing in the Islamic world's conflicts. During that work, we met bin Laden several times.

Vahid Mojdeh is an Afghan who worked in Abdullah Azzam's and bin Laden's Services Office during the eighties in Peshawar. Between 1995 and the fall of the Taliban in 2001, he held several posts in various divisions of the Afghan foreign affairs ministry.[19]

When I met bin Laden again [after an interval of almost a decade] now under the Taliban he was so important. One day at the Foreign Ministry my friend said, "Let's go to bin Laden." He was staying in the Karte Parwan neighborhood of Kabul near the Intercontinental Hotel. It was lunchtime. Among the Arabs around bin Laden there was someone who seemed to be different. One of the Taliban asked him where he was from and he said he was Jamaican. He said he had come with several others and they had spent the past year in Afghanistan. It was then that I found out that bin Laden had influence not only in Islamic countries. We asked the Jamaican, "What is produced in your country?" The answer was "We are all dancers."[20]

After that I had a brief meeting with bin Laden. I asked him about the foreigners who were joining him. Bin Laden said, "Anyone who travels to Afghanistan feels close to their true nature." He was dressed in white clothes and a turban.

Abu Jandal is a Saudi of Yemeni decent who would become bin Laden's chief bodyguard.[21]

I got acquainted with Sheikh Osama and I met him [in 1997] and we stayed together for three days. During those three days, he was waging a kind of a campaign directed at us, in an attempt to convince us of the justification for his call for jihad against America. He told us about the bad state the Arabian Peninsula had reached and sought to convince us of the bad things that happened there as a result of U.S. interference in the region. The details of the story of my first meeting with Sheikh Osama were very beautiful, although more than six years have passed since it took place.

In the evening, when we decided to go to the guest house where we were staying, Sheikh Osama came and said to me: "How are you, Abu-Jandal?" He asked how long it had been since I ate ma'subah al-qarmushi (flour, bananas, and sugar, fried together). Ma'subah is a popular meal in Saudi Arabia. I answered: "Almost more than four years." He said to me: "Then we will eat ma'subah for breakfast at my place tomorrow morning, because I usually have ma'subah for breakfast."

After three days of continual sessions with Sheikh Osama, he called me after the afternoon prayers and said to me: "What is your view, Abu-Jandal, of what you heard?" I said to him: "I will not hide from you, sheikh, that what you said is convincing and that you are putting forward a clear case, but it is clear to me you have [not recruited] anyone from the Arabian Peninsula, whose cause this is." He said to me: "What you say is true. Most of the brothers around me are Egyptians, Algerians, and North Africans. That is why I invite you to join our caravan."

After I spent the month of Ramadan with Sheikh Osama, he decided two or three days after the Eid (the three-day religious holiday marking end of Ramadan) to send me to the camps in the city of Khost for military training. It is true that we had trained in Bosnia and gained some practical experience in Somalia and in Tajikistan, but the keys to action and dotting the *i*'s and crossing the *t*'s were skills acquired in al Qaeda's camps. That is because the period of our training in Bosnia was short and there was no organized military action in Somalia. Training in these camps was on how to use weapons. However, it indirectly included certain educational messages. For instance, all the targets were in U.S. uniform. The instructions were: "Hit the U.S. soldier or officer; blow up the U.S. vehicle." When the target was hit, it would be announced that someone hit the U.S. soldier or target. Thus, the United States and all that was American occupied our mind. Indeed, hitting American targets became a dream of everyone in the organization.

The al Qaeda Organization camps libraries contained many books and military encyclopedias, including the *Encyclopedia of Jihad* in Afghanistan, which explains everything that is connected with the military aspects, beginning with the machine gun and then guerrilla warfare, urban warfare, undercover wars, the wars of security and intelligence, data gathering, tank wars and chemical wars. This encyclopedia was in about twelve volumes with pictures, maps, and charts. It was a comprehensive military education in an Islamic form.

Other than al Qaeda's training camps in Afghanistan, the *Encyclopedia of Jihad* is the organization's most important contribution to instructing jihadists about guerrilla warfare and terrorist tactics. The *Encyclopedia* is a massive work of several thousand pages that contains advice for every imaginable hostile situation, from how to a booby trap a napkin; to how to conduct a drive-by shooting; to how to recognize a rattle snake, or treat a scorpion sting.[22]

Each of the volumes of the *Encyclopedia,* which cover the gamut of subjects from tanks to bomb making to intelligence, are dedicated to bin Laden, "Our beloved brother Abu Abdallah, who fought the jihad in Afghanistan with his soul and his possessions." The encyclopedias draw on a mix of sources that include U.S. Army manuals, early Islamic military history, and the experience the Afghan Arabs gained from fighting the Soviets.

What follows is a training exercise in the *Encyclopedia* aimed at springing Sheik Omar Abdel Rahman from his U.S. prison cell, an al Qaeda preoccupation.

A) TARGET: THE AMERICAN (JEWISH) TRADE ATTACHÉ
   The American Trade Attaché
   Daily Schedule

1) He leaves the residential compound (under heavy guard) to go to work in the embassy, accompanied by a protection vehicle in addition to the personal guard in his car. He occasionally drives the car himself, sometimes there is a driver. He does not have a specific car assigned to him; rather he uses the embassy's official vehicles which are usually armor plated.
2) He returns to the residential compound. The residential compound in which he lives is heavily guarded
3) The embassy is very heavily guarded
4) He does not have a clear, set schedule; he is always moving and traveling (he is an active man), and his appointment schedule is unknown. There are many places he visits and frequents and they are of various types.
5) His break is on Saturday and Sunday, but he does not have a schedule for those days. Sometimes he travels, goes to the club, stays at

home, goes to work, and makes visits. He never moves except in embassy vehicles and with guards.

6) After great, detailed research and analysis, we were able to see an E-mail on the Internet. The bank sends him an account statement monthly. After examining the statements we noted that he spends a certain amount of money from his account at the M restaurant (a first class restaurant, but not well known).

7) After visiting the restaurant's Web site, we found that he reserved a table from time to time.

8) While observing the restaurant we were able to be sure of this information and confirm his identity.

9) It appears that he gathers in the restaurant each time with the manager of the Sheraton Hotel (Brian Kelly), American businessmen and three Saudi businessmen.

10) He is watched over by two guards and transported by embassy cars.

11) The operation group visited the restaurant, ate a meal there, and reserved a special table. They familiarized themselves in depth with the area of operations: the building, the neighboring roads, and the parking lot.

12) The operation group continued to observe the restaurant's Web site to determine the time of the operation.

HOW TO GET TO THE THEATER OF OPERATIONS

a. The van leaves the safe house at seven, carrying one (the driver), two, three and four.

b. The van arrives at the parking lot and enters without problems, parking in the last row. Then four gets out (without weapons) and goes into M restaurant like any regular customer (he had a prior reservation).

c. Four uses the phone to call one and two when the target and his gang arrive.

d. Three goes into the building dressed like a janitor, carrying a trash bin. (There are explosives in the trash bin, and a silenced machine gun.)

e. One and two go to the restaurant wearing repair worker uniforms, appearing to repair the central air, with cases holding machine guns and the harness.

f.   One and two ready the harness and put on clothing for the operation, masks, and stand ready.

EXECUTION

a.   Four calls one and two to begin.
b.   Before that, four prepares the entrance location (the bathroom and window).
c.   Three heads for the gate.
d.   One and two use the harness (thief's knot) and enter the bathroom through the window, then take the harness (to tie up the American later) and two engages the private room (with the silencer-equipped MP-5); at the same time, one enters the room (with a silenced MP-5); they do not engage until they secure the rear.

At the same time, three engages the guard and four heads to the trash bin to pull out his MP-5 then returns quickly to the main room of the restaurant. Immediately after three finishes the guard, he takes the Beretta, quickly enters the room and locks the automatic door to the office and the electronic door to the kitchen. The situation is now as follows:

a.   Control of the private room
b.   Control of the courtyard
c.   Control of the entrance
d.   Control of the restaurant's main area

The workmen and the chef are held in the kitchen.

Four, three and two direct the hostages into the kitchen; one directs the target and his gang into the kitchen. In the kitchen: three guards the door, one watches the target and his gang, and two searches the target and his gang. Four guards the remaining hostages. After this, all of the hostages are searched; the strong young men are put in the closet. The target and his gang are put in one corner, the rest of the hostages in another corner. The hostages are tied up using the harnesses. Those who remain after the harnesses are used are tied up using table cloths and napkins. The same is done to the target and his group; they are, however, given precedence. The new situation is as follows:

e. Two guards the target and his gang
f. Four guards the hostages
g. One walks around inside and inspects the rest of the places
h. Three begins to secure the doors and windows, also closing the blinds

Jobs are distributed as follows after this:

i. One: negotiations
j. Two: patrolling within the restaurant (responsible for security)
k. Three: guarding the target and his gang
l. Four: guard the hostages
m. Negotiations:
    i. The program is:
        • Give the enemy 12 hours to meet demands.
        • Kill one hostage as a beginning (a Christian worker).
        • Kill one of the Christian businessmen every 60 minutes in front of one of the security cameras. Put the bodies in the refrigerator, and set the bomb to blow up 12 hours later.

Demands:

a. A helicopter occupied only by a pilot to land on the building's platform
b. A Boeing 707 ready to go and to run on a long trip, only occupied by a pilot and a co-pilot.

Pulling out:

1. When the helicopter arrives, two leaves through the door and three opens the door, covering him.
2. Two confirms the readiness of the airplane.
3. Two contacts one to move.

4. Three knows how to use the helicopter.
5. One, three and four pull out with the hostages up to the helicopter. Two is the last one up.
6. Two asks the pilot to head to the airport, to the Boeing plane.
7. Upon arrival, four gets out to check the Boeing (ready on the runway).
8. He contacts one, to enter the Boeing.
9. He enters with all of the hostages, and the situation on the plane is as follows:
    a. One inspects the plane
    b. Four is in the cockpit (busy studying the Boeing 707)
    c. Three is on the plane
    d. Two guards the target, the American
10. This takes 20 minutes altogether.
11. The plane takes off. In the air, one tells the captain to go directly to Kandahar.
12. Three verifies the plane's path using a Magellan GPS [Global Positioning System] he has with him.
13. Upon arrival in Kandahar [in southern Afghanistan], we demand the following.
    a. The release of Sheikh Omar Abdel-Rahman and his followers
    b. 20 million dollars
    c. Turn over the war criminal Norman Schwarzkopf [commander of U.S. forces during the first Gulf War]

The entire operation takes no longer than 24 hours.
Do not accept any intermediary other than the Taliban.

What follows is a discussion in the *Encyclopedia* of the properties of RDX, a high explosive useful for terrorist operations.[23]

RDX is considered a very effective, basic cutting explosive, at the same time it is considered an activating explosive used in making fuses, and primers. RDX is shock sensitive, nonflammable when burnt, with an explosive temperature of 197 centigrade and explosive speed of 8387 meters/second, it is humidity proof and its power is 1.6 of TNT power. RDX color is white in its pure state and it is crystalline powder like salt.

RDX is made either by extraction from C4 explosives [or] laboratory preparation.

The *Encyclopedia* then gives detailed instructions about how to manufacture RDX. Ahmed Ressam, who plotted to blow up Los Angeles Airport in December 1999, is a graduate of al Qaeda's Afghan training camps, where he learned how to manufacture his own RDX. He would use that knowledge to build the bombs he was planning to detonate in Los Angeles before he was arrested in Washington State.

Abu Jandal.[24]

I recall that Brother Osama used to explain to us certain strategic military issues and concepts and he used to tell us that the struggle was not only between the al Qaeda organization and the United States, that al Qaeda is merely a nucleus and a tool to wake up and defeat the American offensive against our Islamic world and drag the United States into a large-scale battle which it cannot control. He used to say: "We are working for a big operation; namely, dragging the United States into a confrontation with the entire Islamic world."

As we were concluding our training period there was an attempt to assassinate Sheikh Osama while he was in Jalalabad. However, the Taliban Movement's security apparatus arrested those who implemented the attempt. Mullah Omar sent a helicopter to Sheikh Osama who was in Jalalabad and he asked him to meet with him in Kandahar [in southern Afghanistan]. They met at Kandahar Airport. Mullah Omar told Sheikh Osama bin Laden: "You must come and settle with us in Kandahar because it is our stronghold and main headquarters. It is safer for you than Jalalabad because in Jalalabad you will find people from various religions and ethnic groups and the security there is weak."

Three days later, Sheikh Osama bin Laden returned to Jalalabad and decided to transfer all his wives and the families of the Arab mujahideen by air from Jalalabad to Kandahar. When he arrived in Kandahar, Mullah Omar gave him the choice of either staying at the Electricity Company housing complex, where there are all the services, or to stay at the Kan-

dahar Airport housing complex, which did not have such utilities. He selected the airport complex because he wanted his followers to live an
austere and modest life in this world. There were no utilities in the complex and there was no running water. Sheikh Osama bin Laden used to
say: "We want a simple life."

[Al Qaeda's recruits] were not escaping from their economic conditions but rather from the political conditions [in their own countries] because many of them did not find an opportunity to express their ideas.
Had the Arab states had freedom of opinion and expression, many of
their sons would not have left and joined al Qaeda given that some of
them graduated from the best universities in the world. Some of them
occupied posts with high salaries like Sayf Adel who was an officer in the
Egyptian Special Forces. Abu-Hafs was an [Egyptian] police officer.
Abu-Ubaidah al Banjshiri was also an Egyptian police officer. These individuals left their countries because there was no freedom so they were
forced to express their opinion in this way.

※

**By 1998 Ayman al Zawahiri had decided to align his Egyptian Jihad
group increasingly with al Qaeda. This was opposed by several members of his organization.**

**Noman Benotman is a Libyan jihadist who fought in Afghanistan in
the early nineties and lived in Sudan in the mid-nineties.**

When he came back to get back to Afghanistan, Zawahiri decided to
join bin Laden—his people don't agree with him. And they sent him a
letter from Yemen. There were five of them from the Shura committee
(i.e., the overall council of the Jihad group) and they said, "How come
you join with bin Laden? We can't trust you."

**On February 22, 1998, bin Laden released a statement on behalf of
the World Islamic Front, a joint declaration made by al Qaeda and Zawahiri's Jihad group.**

Abdel Bari Atwan, the editor of _Al Quds al Arabi_ newspaper.

Osama bin Laden issued this fatwa and Khaled Fauwaz (bin Laden's
media rep in London) phoned me and he said, "I want to come to you to

see you." He came with the fatwa and I looked—it's very dangerous. It was really the first time somebody is calling for the killing of the Jews and the Crusaders, which was shocking for me. It was shocking for Khaled Fauwaz, to be fair to him. He said, "I disagree with this. I think there is something wrong happening; I don't know who influenced Osama bin Laden to issue this fatwa. This is unacceptable and I am against it." And he was really angry and furious, and they were very good friends.

Bin Laden's statement of jihad against Jews and Crusaders, World Islamic Front, February 22, 1998.[25]

The Arabian Peninsula has never—since Allah made it flat, created its desert, and encircled it with seas—been stormed by any forces like the Crusader armies spreading in it like locusts, eating its riches and wiping out its plantations. All this is happening at a time in which nations are attacking Muslims like people fighting over a plate of food. No one argues today about three facts that are known to everyone; we will list them, in order to remind everyone:

First, for over seven years [since the introduction of 500,000 U.S. troops following Saddam Hussein's occupation of Kuwait] the United States has been occupying the lands of Islam in the holiest of places, the Arabian Peninsula, plundering its riches, dictating to its rulers, humiliating its people, terrorizing its neighbors, and turning its bases in the Peninsula into a spearhead through which to fight the neighboring Muslim peoples.

If some people have in the past argued about the fact of the occupation, all the people of the Peninsula have now acknowledged it. The best proof of this is the Americans' continuing aggression against the Iraqi people using the Peninsula as a staging post.

Second, despite the great devastation inflicted on the Iraqi people by the Crusader-Zionist alliance, and despite the huge number of those killed, which has exceeded one million, despite all this, the Americans are once against trying to repeat the horrific massacres, as though they are not content with the protracted [United Nations sanctions] after the ferocious [Gulf] war.

Third, if the Americans' aims behind these wars are religious and economic, the aim is also to serve the Jews' petty state and divert attention from its occupation of Jerusalem and murder of Muslims there. The best proof of this is their eagerness to destroy Iraq, the strongest neighboring Arab state, and their endeavor to fragment all the states of the region such as Iraq, Saudi Arabia, Egypt, and Sudan into paper statelets and through their disunion and weakness to guarantee Israel's survival and the continuation of the brutal Crusader occupation of the [Arabian] Peninsula.

All these crimes and sins committed by the Americans are a clear declaration of war on Allah, his messenger, and Muslims. And *ulema* (clerics) have throughout Islamic history unanimously agreed that the jihad is an individual duty if the enemy destroys Muslim countries.

On that basis, and in compliance with Allah's order, we issue the following fatwa to all Muslims:

The ruling to kill the Americans and their allies—civilians and military—is an individual duty for every Muslim who can do it in any country in which it is possible to do it, in order to liberate the al-Aqsa Mosque [in Jerusalem] and the holy mosque [Mecca] from their grip.

Signed by:
Sheikh Osama bin-Muhammed bin Laden
Ayman al Zawahiri, amir of the Jihad Group in Egypt
Abu-Yasir Rifa'i Ahmad Taha, Egyptian Islamic Group
Sheikh Mir Hamzah, secretary of the Jamiat-ul-Ulema-e-Pakistan
Fazlur Rahman, amir of the Jihad Movement in Bangladesh

An excerpt from a CIA memorandum, dated February 23, 1998, released a day after the publication of the World Islamic Front statement, follows.[26]

These fatwas are the first from these groups that explicitly justify attacks on American civilians anywhere in the world. Both groups [bin Laden and a coalition of Islamic groups in London] have hinted in the past that civilians are legitimate targets, but this [is] the first religious ruling sanctifying such attacks.

The announcement of the formation of the "World Islamic Front for Jihad against the Crusaders and Jews" marked an important evolution

in the relationship between Zawahiri and bin Laden, who had first met in Peshawar more than a decade earlier. Bin Laden had long helped finance Zawahiri's jihad group, and now they had set up an umbrella organization for joint operations. Often Zawahiri is seen as the real brains of al Qaeda who provided bin Laden the political/theological arguments underlying the organization's attacks, and while there is certainly some element of truth to this, it was bin Laden who focused Zawahiri's attention away from his Egyptian "near enemy" to attacking the "far enemy," the United States.

Noman Benotman, the Libyan jihadist.

Osama influenced [Egypt's Jihad group] with his idea: Forget about the "near enemy" (i.e., the Egyptian government). Bin Laden said, "The main enemy is the Americans because they dominate the whole area and they're supporting these [Arab] regimes."

Feroz Ali Abbasi is a Ugandan Briton who was captured in Pakistan after the fall of the Taliban. He had trained at an al Qaeda camp in Afghanistan. He was released from Guantánamo Bay in January 2005 and he is now back in the United Kingdom keeping a low profile. The U.S. government says that he met bin Laden on three occasions. Abbasi wrote a 146-page memoir in Guantánamo Bay, excerpts from which follow explaining how bin Laden's views about directly attacking the United States prevailed over those of Zawahiri's Egyptian Jihad organization.[27]

The merger (more like assimilation of [Zawahiri's] Jihad) with al Qaeda happened. Before it was assimilated [Jihad] had the outlook that the biggest enemy of them all was the apostate leader ruling over a Muslim country. This meaning that the brunt of our efforts should be to remove him (by force if necessary) and replace him with a legitimate leader.

Al Qaeda does not contradict al Jihad's outlook. But al Qaeda says nowadays Muslims are ignorant of the fact their Government leaders are apostates. They consider their Government leaders legitimate rulers. Al Qaeda then says if we fight the biggest of the unbelievers—the Big Satan America—the Muslims will rally around us. When they do, we can then, as we fight the big Satan America, teach the Muslims that their leaders are ruling by other than Allah's law, are apostates, and that they are the ones to be fought.

Montasser Zayyat, the Egyptian militant imprisoned with Zawahiri in Cairo in the early eighties, similarly believes that bin Laden strongly influenced Zawahiri.

Osama bin Laden had an appreciable impact on Zawahiri though the conventional wisdom holds the opposite to be the case. Bin Laden advised Zawahiri to stop armed operations in Egypt and to ally with him against their common enemies: the United States and Israel. His advice to Zawahiri came upon their return to Afghanistan [in 1996], when bin Laden ensured the safety of Zawahiri and the [Egyptian] Islamic Jihad members under the banner of the Taliban.[12]

Ahmed Ibrahim al Sayyid al Naggar was a senior member of Jihad, the Egyptian terrorist group headed by Zawahiri. In October 1997, al Naggar was sentenced to death in absentia by a military court in Egypt. The following year, he was arrested by Albanian authorities, working with the CIA, and extradited to Egypt, where he was likely tortured. In the following excerpts of his interrogation records from June 1998, he outlines the organization of the Egyptian Jihad group and states that bin Laden financed its operations.[28]

THE INTERROGATION OF THE ACCUSED:
AHMED IBRAHIM AL SAYYID AL NAGGAR
    Age: 36
    Occupation: Teacher at Haramain Charity Organization in Albania
    Residence: Al Shaikh al Husari Street, Nahia, Giza Province, Egypt
    [Date:] 2 July 1998

The questioning was conducted by Captain Yasir Azzulddin of the State Security Department.
In the middle of 1994, [Naggar] was asked to travel to Sudan where he was received at Khartoum airport and was taken to meet Ayman al Za-

wahiri in one of the capital's houses. He was asked by al Zawahiri to take over the responsibility of the civil organization [in Egypt].

In October [1995], he was asked by the leader, Ayman al Zawahiri, who was in Yemen at the time, to be responsible for [the] organization in Yemen in addition to his responsibility of the civil organization inside Egypt.

In January 1996, he was informed that [there was] a job for him in a charity in Albania. He accepted the offer and left Yemen using a fake passport under the name Ahmed Rajab Mohammed. In Tirana, the capital, he worked for al Haramain Charity Organization.

He [later] received a telephone call that if the situation in Albania worsens, the Saudi Osama bin Laden has expressed his readiness to receive the members of the organization in Afghanistan as his relation with the Taliban government is close. Osama also promised to give $100 to every family monthly.

The Sources of Finance [for the Jihad organization]: support from Osama bin Laden who coordinates with the leader Ayman al Zawahiri personally. [Other sources of financing are] 10 percent of the members' salaries [and] projects such as trading in sugar or trading in South East Asia or rearing of goats in Albania, [and] renovation of an old building in London.

In April 1998 the U.S. government rebuked the Taliban regime as a facilitator of terrorism. The following month bin Laden would, in turn, up the ante and go public with his intention of attacking American targets with an interview on American television and his first, and only, press conference in Afghanistan.[29]

The following are excerpts of a statement issued by bin Laden following the U.S. government's designation of the Taliban as a state that tolerated terrorism.[30]

The Taliban government has long been in need of such a U.S. resolution to clear the charges that it was an agent of the U.S., to prove its firm and independent position, to make its own decisions, and not to be subject to outside pressures even from America. So congratulations to the

Taliban government on the medal of honor presented by America through the decision to charge it with sponsoring terrorism.

Hamid Mir, bin Laden's Pakistani biographer.[31]

I again interviewed him May 16th 1998 close to Kandahar. I spent two days there and in that meeting Ayman al Zawahiri was present. I realized that now Osama bin Laden is not just talking about the presence of U.S. troops in Saudi Arabia. He has a big agenda. He is talking about the theft of the oil from the Middle East. He is talking about the Israel-Palestine problem. He is talking about the Kashmir-India problem. He is talking about the Chechens. And he is trying to become an international leader of the Muslims. The two sons of Sheikh Omar Abdel Rahman (the blind Egyptian cleric imprisoned in the U.S.) were also there.

Most of the time I spent with him was only discussing only one point. I asked him a question, "How can you prove in the light of Islamic teaching that we should kill the Americans? Please convince me." And he was trying his best to convince showing me this book, this fatwa. You see I'm not a religious man. I don't have command of the Islamic law, but I have read the Koran and I said a very simple thing: "The Koran says that the blood of an innocent non-Muslim is equal to the blood of a Muslim. If you are killing an innocent non-Muslim Christian who is an American citizen, if you are killing an innocent non-Muslim Jew, this is the violation of the Koranic teachings. How can you prove that your fatwa is correct?" And in the end he said, "Actually, this is not my fatwa. Actually, the fatwa is issued by some very big Islamic scholars. I'm just following that fatwa."

When he was talking about the political issues he was good. But when he was talking about the religious issues, he was not very convincing. I watched one of his lectures which he delivered to his fighters. I was just there as a silent observer. There were more than three hundred fighters and there was a big board. Bin Laden pasted a map of the Middle East on that board and he was trying to explain: "Why are Americans present in Kuwait? Why are Americans present in Yemen? Why are they present in Saudi Arabia? What are they doing in Bahrain?" And he said, "They are here to plunder our oil wealth." And the fighters were chanting slogans, *"Allahu Akbar! Allahu Akbar!"* God is Great!

When he started quoting from the Islamic Sharia and Islamic books and Koran, that the Koran says to fight against the non-Muslims for the supremacy of the Islamic law, there was no thrill. Because, you see, he cannot prove through the Koran that the killing of Americans is Islam, that the killing of every non-Muslim is Islam. He cannot prove that.

During the interview one of his colleagues said to me that, "Mr. Mir, would you like to write a book [about] Sheikh." Sheikh means Osama bin Laden. I said, "Yes, but the book will be a book. It will not be propaganda." So next morning we exchanged views on that project and I wrote a synopsis and I said I will write my observations, which may be negative, which may be positive, and you will not raise any objection. [Bin Laden] said "OK, I accept your condition but there is a one condition from me that you will not distort the facts; I have three wives. You will not write that I have five wives. I have sixteen children. You will not write that I have 56 children." I said "OK, I will not distort the facts." At that time he was not a famous person and I thought that I will complete this book within three to four months.

I saw bin Laden when he went out hunting birds. I also saw the people around bin Laden play football, good players; bin Laden watched. His son Mohammed was a goalkeeper.

I met his three sons. Mohammed, Ali, Saad [who] is in Iran [now]. [Saad was] sixteen. I had [taken] a picture with Saad sitting with his father and a gun is lying in his lap and I asked bin Laden, "He is a young boy. Why is he carrying a gun?" And he said that this is his own decision. So I asked a question to Saad, "Are you following the footsteps of your father?" and then he answered very confidently, "No. I am following the footsteps of my Prophet." I said, "Okay."

Bin Laden told me that he is going to hold a press conference very soon and he invited me, "You should come to that press conference." And he told me, "I'm inviting many journalists." So I said, "How many journalists?" And then from a file he took a paper and he showed me the list. There were more than 22 people. Your name [Peter Bergen] was there. Peter Arnett was there, and many other people. There was one guy from BBC also.

I said, "Sorry, I will not come there." He said, "Why?" I said, "I think that you are inviting a lot of Pakistani journalists. No doubt I have contacts with the intelligence guys, but I'm not their informer. They will go

back; they will help the intelligence agencies to bomb your compound."
He said, "No, no, no. You will come. You will come." I said, "No, I will not
come." I refused. I never attended that press conference because I was
sure that the place will be bombed. The place was bombed [three
months later in a U.S. cruise missile strike]. And when I met [him the
next] time, bin Laden told me, "You were right." He said, "I admit your
wisdom."

**On May 26, 1998, bin Laden held a press conference to announce
publicly that he had "formed with many other Islamic groups and organizations in the Islamic world a front called the International Islamic
Front to do jihad against the Crusaders and Jews."[32] Also present were
the sons of the Egyptian cleric Omar Abdel Rahman, "the Blind
Sheikh," who distributed small cards containing their father's "will."
Ismail Khan, a Pakistani journalist, attended the press conference.[33]**

I could see a plume of dust coming up not far in the distance. Then I
saw three cars coming, and these hooded guys escorting Osama. Osama
came out of the car and the moment he stepped out, there was shooting,
frenzied shooting, and these guys started firing RPGs, rocket-propelled
grenades, at the mountains. This thing went on for five minutes before
the press conference began.

I mean this thing still boggles my mind—he spoke of some "good
news" in the weeks ahead. Osama [was] sitting in the middle and there
was Dr. Ayman al Zawahiri.

**Bin Laden and Zawahiri both spoke at the press conference, and ap-
peared on a videotape filmed by an al Qaeda cameraman. The tape was
later discovered in Afghanistan by CNN after the fall of the Taliban.**

Bin Laden.[34]

By God's Grace, we have formed, with many other Islamic groups and
organizations in the Islamic world, a front called the "International Islamic Front to do jihad against the Crusaders and the Jews." And one of
the main organizing groups is Dr. al Zawahri's group and he is with us in
this meeting. And we have received requests from some other organiza-

tions that want to join this front. And the matter is moving quickly. So we would like to announce this as good news, by God's Will. We hope this to lift the shame from the face of Muslims.

Zawahiri:[35]

We are working with brother bin Laden. We know him for more than ten years. We fought with him here in Afghanistan. We worked with him in Sudan and many other places.

After the press conference was over, a Pakistani journalist, Rahimul-lah Yusufzai, asked bin Laden some personal questions.[36]

We had a small conversation over a cup of tea and I asked Mr. bin Laden, that your family in Saudi Arabia has disowned you. And his short answer was that blood is thicker than water, which meant that it's not true. And then I asked him about his family and children. He said, "I have lost count because there are so many." And then I asked him about his wealth. And he put his right hand on his heart saying, "I am rich and generous here." So this is a very subtle sense of humor and Mr. bin Laden, despite living in very tough conditions, he has retained some of that wit.

His followers were saying that he is very fond of horse riding. So even in Afghanistan, despite being a hunted man, he still occasionally finds time to do horse riding. His people told me that he also sometimes wants to play soccer. I told them that he's suffering from this pain in his back, it's a permanent pain and he walks with the help of a stick, so how can he play football. But they said, sometimes when he feels better he joins them in playing soccer.

Ismail Khan is a Pakistani journalist who covered al Qaeda's press conference.

The two sons of the blind Egyptian scholar, Sheikh Omar Abdul Rahman, [were also present at the press conference]. It was Zawahiri who introduced us to his younger son, whose name is [Asim] Omar Abdul Rahman. He was distributing these leaflets which contain the will of the

Sheikh Omar Abdul Rahman (who has been imprisoned in the United States on terrorism charges since 1993). He said that the U.S. prison authorities were not treating his father well. And they had not spoken with him in some time. And that he's not allowed to wash his clothes and offer prayers. And he said that [the Americans] were killing him slowly.

It's only a colorful, plastic-laminated card (a photograph of which can be found in the photo section) of Arabic script with a picture of a Muslim cleric praying in a prison cell, but it is a key to understanding why some three thousand Americans lost their lives on the morning of September 11, 2001. The card was distributed to several of the journalists who were attending bin Laden's press conference, which is how I acquired my copy.

The full text of the Arabic on the card, which is reproduced here in full for the first time in English, reads:

My Brothers . . .

If they [The Americans] kill me, which they will certainly do—hold my funeral and send my corpse to my family, but do not let my blood be shed in vain. Rather, extract the most violent revenge, and remember your brother who spoke the truth and died for the will of God . . . The Mujahid Sheikh Omar Abdel al Rahman.

In the name of God the kind and merciful.

THE FATWA OF THE PRISONER SHEIKH DOCTOR OMAR ABDEL RAHMAN

America is in the process of eliminating the *ulema* (clergy) who are speaking the truth. And America has suggested to its clients in Saudi to imprison Sheikh Safar al Hawali and Sheikh Salman al Awdah, and all the others who speak the truth, just as Egypt had done . . .

And the Koran has made a decree upon these Jews and Christians, which we have forgotten or allowed to be forgotten:

Allah said, "If they could, they will continue to kill you until they make you turn away from your religion."

And so all Muslims everywhere.

Cut off all relations with [the Americans, Christians, and Jews], tear them to pieces, destroy their economies, burn their corporations, destroy their peace, sink their ships, shoot down their planes and kill them on air, sea, and land. And kill them wherever you may find them, ambush them, take them hostage, and destroy their observatories. Kill these Infidels. Until they witness your harshness. Fight them, and God will torture them through your hands, and he will disgrace them and make you victorious over them, and the nation of the believers is on the verge of creation, and the rage will go from them.

Your brother Omar Abdel Rahman from inside American prisons.

Hamid Mir, bin Laden's Pakistani biographer.[37]

The language by Sheikh Omar Abdel Rahman in his will is very, very strong. [Up until 1998] bin Laden didn't issue any fatwa or anything against the ordinary Americans. He's against American troops, American government, but Dr. Zawahiri he is against every American, because he is directly affected. His leader [Sheikh Rahman] who is blind is arrested by the American authorities.

If you go through that fatwa, this is the basic ideology of the al Qaeda. They say, "Kill Americans in the air, kill Americans in the borders, kill them everywhere, destroy their companies, everything." So I think what [Sheikh Rahman ruled upon in the fatwa] someone is implementing.

Algerian Ahmad Ressam plotted to blow up Los Angeles International Airport in December 1999. In mid-1998 he was training at the Khaldan training camp in Afghanistan, which has graduated several of al Qaeda's more dangerous alumni. In a subsequent terrorism trial he testified that Sheikh Rahman's fatwa was widely distributed at the training camp he attended.[38]

A fatwa issued by Sheikh Omar Abdel Rahman, a piece of paper with his photograph on it. It said it was a fatwa by Omar Abdel Rahman from prison. It says fight Americans and hit their interest[s] everywhere. A fatwa is something that a learned person would come up with. If there is an issue that people want an opinion on, the religious, learned man would study the issue and pass judgment on whether it was permissible or not.

The significance of Sheikh Rahman's fatwa to al Qaeda has gone unre-marked. Sheikh Rahman's fatwa seems to be the first time that a Muslim cleric had given his religious sanction to attacks on American aviation, shipping, and economic targets. The fatwa, with its exhortations to "bring down their airplanes," "burn their corporations," and "sink their ships," would turn out to be a slowly ticking time bomb that would ex-plode first on October 12, 2000, when a suicide attack blew a hole the size of a small house in the USS *Cole* in Yemen, killing seventeen sailors, and it would explode again with even greater ferocity on 9/11.

To understand the significance of the fatwa you have to understand the spiritual authority that its author, the militant Egyptian cleric Sheikh Rahman, exercises over al Qaeda. Al Qaeda may be led by bin Laden and his deputy Zawahiri, but neither of them have any standing as religious scholars, while Sheikh Rahman has a doctorate in Islamic jurisprudence from al-Azhar University in Cairo, the Harvard of Is-lamic thought. Indeed, Sheikh Rahman has long been the spiritual guide of Egypt's two most violent terrorist groups, members of which now occupy senior leadership positions within al Qaeda.

The special reverence that al Qaeda has for Sheikh Rahman is under-lined by a two-hour propaganda videotape that the group's media divi-sion, known as "the Clouds," released sometime in the spring of 2001. Halfway though the tape, in a segment entitled "Reasons," bin Laden explains why Muslims should wage a holy war against the United States. Over a picture of Sheikh Rahman, bin Laden fulminates: "He is a hostage in an American jail. We hear he is sick and the Americans are treating him badly." At a later point on the tape bin Laden explains: "We consider the American government directly responsible . . . for holding Sheikh Abdel Rahman, whom we consider one of the great scholars of Islam, who is now languishing in jail." Rahman is the only religious fig-ure mentioned in the course of the two-hour videotape.

Indeed, the American incarceration of Sheikh Rahman has been a hot-button issue for al Qaeda for many years. When the Sheikh was ar-rested in New York in 1993 on terrorism charges, al Qaeda members based in Sudan debated whether or not to bomb the U.S. embassy in Saudi Arabia in retaliation, a plan that was rejected because of the risk of injury to civilians, scruples the group would later abandon. When al Qaeda first publicly declared war against the United States in August

1996, bin Laden explained that the "Zionist-Crusaders" had arrested the "holy warrior" Sheikh Rahman. And in 1997 bin Laden told CNN that "Sheikh Omar Abdel Rahman is a Muslim scholar well known all over the Muslim world. He represents the kind of injustice that is adopted by the U.S. A baseless case was fabricated against him even though he is a blind old man . . . The U.S. sentenced him to hundreds of years . . . He is now very badly treated." [39] In September 2000 Al Jazeera television aired a videotape of al Qaeda's leaders in Afghanistan sitting under a banner that read CONVENTION TO SUPPORT HONORABLE OMAR ABDEL RAHMAN. On the tape bin Laden vowed: "We promise to work with all our power to free our brother, Sheikh Omar Abdel Rahman." [40] Off camera, one of the sheikh's sons shouted: "Forward with blood." This was the first time that a member of Sheikh Rahman's family had publicly identified himself to be part of al Qaeda.

The intense interest that al Qaeda has taken in the fate of Sheikh Rahman may come as something of a surprise to most Americans who, if they remember him at all, may dimly recall television pictures of the corpulent cleric when he lived in New York in the early nineties, invariably dressed in flowing robes, wearing a red felt hat denoting his senior clerical status, and dark sunglasses that disguised his blind, opaque eyes. On television Sheikh Rahman came off like a cuddly Middle Eastern Father Christmas who had somehow morphed into Ray Charles. The reality is more sinister: The blind sheikh is the Zelig of Islamist terrorism, repeatedly cropping up as the spiritual inspiration or instigator of the most spectacular terrorist attacks of the past two decades, from the 1981 assassination of Egyptian President Anwar Sadat in Cairo to the 9/11 plot itself.

Sheikh Rahman is important to al Qaeda not only because of the high regard the terrorist organization has for him as a religious scholar, but also because he has long been the spiritual guide of the Egyptian militants who are at the heart of al Qaeda's operation. It is a fact little understood in the West that while bin Laden, a Saudi exile, is the public face of al Qaeda, its key members are Egyptian, and the terrorist organization's ideology and tactics first emerged in Egypt. The ideological godfather of al Qaeda is the Egyptian writer Sayyid Qutb, whose brother Mohammed influenced bin Laden when he was a college student in Saudi Arabia. All three of al Qaeda's successive military commanders have been Egyptian: First Abu Ubadiah al Banjshiri, who died in 1996, then Mohamed Atef, who was killed in the Afghan war in 2001, and now Sayf Adel, a former Egyptian army officer, who is presently in Iran. The lead 9/11 hijacker, Mohammed Atta, was an Egyptian, while one of the key signatories of bin Laden's 1998 declaration of war against the United States, Rifi'a Ahmed Taha, is a leader of Egypt's terrorist Islamic Group.

Rifa'i Taha released the following statement in 2000.[41]

Regarding the case of Omar Abdel Rahman, the Islamic Group's spiritual leader who is detained in a U.S. jail, the policy of talking and making threats is over. We will address the United States in a language that it understands. I believe the time to do so is drawing near.

Sheikh Rahman's fatwa to attack the U.S. economy and American aviation was an important factor in the 9/11 attacks. Al Qaeda's Egyptian leaders wanted to exact revenge on the United States for the imprisonment and "ill treatment" of their spiritual guide. At the same time, Sheikh Rahman gave his followers his spiritual sanction for terrorist attacks. Sheikh Rahman's fatwas are the nearest equivalent that al Qaeda has to an ex cathedra statement by the Pope. As someone with a doctorate in Islamic law—for Islam is a religion of laws much like Orthodox Judaism—Sheikh Rahman was able for the first time in al Qaeda's history to rule that it was legally permissible, and even desirable, to carry out attacks against American planes and corporations, exactly the type of attacks that took place on 9/11. Indeed, up until 9/11 al Qaeda had confined its attacks to American governmental and military targets and had eschewed attacks on American corporations and airliners.

Further, in 1996 a pamphlet was published by supporters of Sheikh Rahman in the U.S. titled *My Testimony to History.* In the pamphlet, which shows a photograph of Sheikh Rahman in a wheelchair in a U.S. prison, the cleric is quoted in similar language to the will that was distributed at the press conference in Afghanistan, saying, "Take revenge on whoever kills me. Do not let my blood be shed in vain."[42]

Of course, it is possible that Sheikh Rahman, who has been incarcerated in American prisons since 1993, did not write the fatwa himself.

However, in the past Sheikh Rahman's incarceration has not prevented him from communicating important messages to his followers through his family or lawyers; for instance, in 1997 he endorsed a ceasefire between the Egyptian government and the terrorist Islamic Group. Then in 2000 Sheikh Rahman publicly withdrew his support from that ceasefire. In his 2001 autobiography, al Zawahiri approvingly noted that "people of the stature of Omar Abdel Rahman . . . oppose the [ceasefire] initiative." [43]

We will simply never know if Rahman did write the fatwa or whether al Qaeda's leaders wrote it and presented it as the cleric's fatwa. In either case, the al Qaeda leadership knew that they needed some theological cover for their future campaign against American civilians, and that only someone of Sheikh Rahman's "stature" could provide that cover.

Abu Walid al Misri was the editor of *Al Imara* (the Emirate) magazine, the Arabic-language magazine of the Taliban, and he also wrote a book about the "Afghan Arabs" serialized in *Al Sharq al Awsat* newspaper in December 2004. An extract follows:[44]

During this period [1996–1998], it was noticeable that bin Laden was maniacally obsessed with the media, especially the international media. Mullah Omar's greatest failure was his inability to shut up al Qaeda's leader. The [Taliban] ministers used to come from Kabul to Jalalabad out of courtesy to bin Laden and sometimes consult him about technical issues in their ministries, especially issues related to agriculture, electricity, and construction. They knew about his experience in these issues, and perhaps they were hoping that he would throw his weight behind the construction of the Afghan "Islamic Emirate," as he had done previously in Sudan. Bin Laden did not stint in his advice, but he was very close to financial bankruptcy. The visits were at the instructions of Mullah Omar, who wanted to convey to bin Laden the message: We will consider you as one of us, but do not address the media. However, bin Laden proved that he was prepared to sacrifice Afghanistan and Mullah Omar rather than stop talking.

Then the U.S. television stations entered the arena, and the media noise around bin Laden escalated to a maximum. In turn, bin Laden, with every atom of his personality, became more enthusiastic about talking. The appeals by Mullah Omar himself and through his prime minister and foreign minister were useless. These cries and appeals poured down during the last two months of 1996. On the surface, bin Laden agreed with them on this, but he proved that he was the only person in Afghanistan who thought that he had the right and the ability to do whatever he wanted. By this, he was able to drive the Islamic march in Afghanistan over the precipice.

Control of bin Laden was not easy. His gentle disposition hides a wild horse that no one can control, nor can he control himself.

Rick Bennett is a Canadian freelance cameraman. In the past decade and a half he has worked mostly for ABC News, covering the first Gulf war in 1990, and the wars in Somalia and Bosnia in the mid-nineties. In the spring of 1998 he received a call about going to Afghanistan. The assignment was to film an interview with bin Laden, working with the ABC News correspondent, John Miller.[45]

I was approached about doing this interview. I talked to two or three of the staff cameramen [at ABC News] who thought it was a bit risky and it obviously was. My thinking was, let's give it a try. I certainly had heard about bin Laden and I went to the ABC research department and I got any reading material I could about his background. I didn't quite appreciate at the time how strong a following he had or how popular he was becoming within the Muslim world.

It was my first time into Afghanistan. It was like being in a different time, a different planet almost. I remember at times just driving through these villages and people living in mud houses. You had to remind yourself what century it was: it was that kind of experience. How poor people were, how they lived, how remote it was and how barren it was.

I guess having been on other trips into places like Somalia and having worked in the Third World I sort of took it in my stride. I wasn't too worried about it. There wasn't really any anxiety at this stage. In some respects maybe that was a bit naive. And certainly as we got closer and were driving up this mountain in the middle of the night, I did think at that stage: What the hell have I got myself into? But early on it was a bit of an adventure, new place, new people. That is why I got into the business after all.

By dusk we ended up at this camp. As we arrived, I remember there was a fenced-off area in the mountain and there were two gun emplacements and there we stayed for a number of days. I was a bit surprised. It seemed more like a military camp than I had thought and was relatively well organized in terms of the structure of the place. We ended up staying there three evenings in the end and they always kept us guessing. We were never told when we would meet him, how we would meet him.

Right around this time we were handed over to this guy who spoke perfect English. When you think about al Qaeda you think these guys are uneducated and easily brainwashed but no, this guy in particular, I felt he was very much his own man, very articulate, very well spoken.

These guys would show up: the elders. They would meet with us. Then go into a separate room and have a discussion. It would go back and forth.

John Miller, the ABC News correspondent.[46]

We are introduced to [al Qaeda's leaders]. Zawahiri is all about the message: "We are so pleased to have you here and you are welcome" in perfect English and [Mohammed] Atef [the military leader] is all about the security. He has got his people rifling through our bags and checking our stuff and he is not very friendly. They take us to a collection of maybe four huts and inside there were flannel blankets laid out on the floor and wall-to-wall carpeting and a couple of pillows, and they said, "This is where you will sleep." They said, "We know that this is not what you are used to, but around here in these camps," Zawahiri says, "this is the Ritz." And he said, "You are not prisoners, you are guests, but we ask that you stay inside." So we stayed there for about two to three days.

Zawahiri—a smart guy, that was my short-range take on him. My long-range take reflecting back on the trip later was that he was running the show and that he was running bin Laden. Zawahiri was to Osama bin Laden what Karl Rove is to the White House. I mean, he crafted the message, he called the tunes. Bin Laden seemed to be the inspirational leader, the front guy, you know the guy that they would put out on camera, but the guy who was working on policy and deciding the direction on reflecting back seemed to be Zawahiri.

He came back the next day and he said, "We would like to know what questions you are going the ask Mr. bin Laden in this interview." I gave him a little Journalism 101 about we don't really go into questions, but then I looked around at the five guys with the AK-47s, and I said, "Look, have you got a pad?" So I wrote out off the top of my head about sixteen questions. Zawahiri's rationale, by the way, was based on solid journalistic grounds: he said, "We are going to use our translator and if he can have the questions in writing, he can write them in Arabic so that when you ask your number one question and he reads his number one they are exactly the same." I wrote out sixteen questions—Did you pay for the bombing of the World Trade Center [in 1993]? Did you know Ramzi Yousef? Did you plan to assassinate Clinton and the Pope? And then a boilerplate one at the end: Is there any message that you have for America?

Rick Bennett.

They ultimately came in and said, "Today we go." It must have been afternoon. We were like, "Go where?" They said tonight we go do the interview. They wouldn't give us much more than that. We were pretty well stripped of all our personal possessions to make certain I guess we didn't have any homing devices, any transmitters. And they brought us into the back of this vehicle.

There were really no roads. It was all riverbeds and off road and was very hard going, bumping all over the place up this mountainside. On three occasions along the way we would be driving along and all of a sudden these guys would just appear behind the bushes carrying AK-47s and grenade launchers. They'd jump out of the bushes and point all their weapons at us which were extremely intimidating as you could imagine. We were told to keep quiet no matter what happens. At one stage they would open a door to the vehicle and hold a gun to your head and a torch to your eyes. I remember thinking at one stage this is just designed to intimidate so stay cool. But it was obviously having the desired effect. I was obviously very freaked out by it, but at this stage there is no going back.

You can't say, "This isn't fun anymore: I've changed my mind." So you forge ahead.

As we came to the summit just before we hit the ridge [at] the top of this mountain, this guy jumps from behind a rock and starts shooting his gun off and from where I was I couldn't tell if he was shooting at us or if he was trying to stop the vehicle.

There was quite an open plateau at the top of this mountain and there were four large gun emplacements at the top of this mountain. And as we arrived, I recall there were two buildings. Both of which were probably forty feet by twenty feet; rectangular-shaped buildings. They took us into one of the buildings and said he would be arriving any time. And I said, "Listen I need my camera, what's going on." They replied, "We have a camera for you." And they gave me this little Panasonic DV camera and I said, "Well that's fine, but I need my lights. How can I light this interview without them?" Then I realized my camera had been brought up in another vehicle. But where it was and how to get access to it was another story. So I set up my lights.

John Miller.

So we get up there and there is kind of a production—there are generators that are going and there are lights that are set up and there is a big tent and a little hut and then there is a big gathering of people in a semicircle—like a hundred. And Zawahiri is there and he says, "I have very good news for you. Mr. bin Laden has agreed to answer each of your questions." And I said, "That's terrific." He said, "There is one other thing, though: for procedure we will not translate his answers." I said, "You know, that can't really work because I won't know what he is saying—how am I going to ask the follow-up questions?" He said, "This will be no problem: There will be no follow-up questions."

I kept thinking if the boys at the White House could get a press policy like this, life would be so easy for them. So that didn't go over too well, but I was also happy that we were going to be able ask him everything that was on my list because some of it was fairly provocative.

I had asked about B-roll [video pictures of an interview subject doing something other than being interviewed] of bin Laden around the camps and Zawahiri said, "This is not like your Sam Donaldson [of ABC News] and the president walking through the Rose Garden. Mr. bin Laden is a very important man." I explained to him, "We are not just going to put bin Laden on for half an hour talking. We need to build a story around elements." He said, "Elements, we will get you elements."

So they had apparently staged what was about to take place based on my request for B-roll. So, bin Laden arrives gets out of an orange SUV and a whole bunch of bodyguards get out around him and everybody starts firing in to the air. This, I guess, is what's Zawahiri meant when he said, "There is always a great celebration when Mr. bin Laden comes." Everybody's shooting and rockets are going up and tracer bullets. I thought it was an interesting way to welcome a guy. I also was looking at this big security phalanx around him, saying how do you secure a guy when everybody's instructions are to open fire? I got what was going on. They were doing this for us. We needed some footage and they needed to put on a show.

Rick Bennett.

I just finished setting up the lights and all of a sudden all hell is breaking loose; it's like World War III is happening outside the door. So I come rushing out and I see forty-five or fifty of his men all firing their automatic weapons up in the air. These heavy weapons gun emplacements they're all firing, there's red tracer fire shooting up into the sky.

John Miller.

So bin Laden is ushered straight past me while this kid is shooting his AK-47 in my ear. I actually pushed the barrel away and he put it right back up, so I am now deaf in one ear at least.

First of all I am shocked, the guy is huge. He is like 6'5". There weren't a whole lot of big guys in the camp, so to see him kind of above the heads of this phalanx of bodyguards, he was like a giraffe. I am introduced to him, we shake hands. It's not like a great handshake. It's kind of like yeah-I've-got-to-shake-your-hand handshake. And he sits down on a kind of a little bench or and he has got a map of the world behind him, which I thought was instructive also. I think they were trying to transmit al

Qaeda is a worldwide organization and that bin Laden is the leader of it and he had his AK-47 with him and he kind of laid it gently against the back wall and he was a little impatient, as were his aides, about how long it will take to set up the lights.

It was hard to form an impression of a guy that you couldn't really converse with, but they were [showing] that he was a spiritual man. He had a kind of calm in him that I did not expect. What I expected was somebody in the mold of the "Blind Sheikh" (the Egyptian cleric, Sheikh Omar Abdel Rahman), a fiery orator who would be pumping his fist and saying a lot of things at the top of his lungs. If you didn't lean in to bin Laden, you couldn't hear him. As he spoke in a very kind of almost high pitched, but very soft voice. He also struck me as a teacher. He looked you right in the eye and he would stay looking in your eye, but then he would kind of drift off us as he was reaching for a thought. His deputies looked up to him as a great leader and a guy that they would follow into anything. There is that charismatic aura or a scent that make people follow him; either you have it or you don't. They spoke of him with godlike reverence and then meeting him and you saw the way they greeted him, the way they sent him off, and the way they talked with great excitement about the Sheikh.

They had a little Panasonic al Qaeda camera there and Rick Bennett said, "I am not shooting it with that." And I am like, "Rick—you know—we've come a long way to do this. Let's go along to get along." And he said, "No. Sometimes in this culture you have to put your foot down and say 'that's it' and you will be surprised how quickly they fold."

Rick Bennett.

So my strategy was at this stage, I need to have my camera. So I made this big scene in front of [bin Laden], the idea being if I make his people look bad in front of him I might get somewhere and sure enough my camera appeared. Just before we were about to sit down and start rolling, Osama insisted that everybody leave because there were too many insects, too many mosquitoes, or whatever in the building. We had to spray for insects. I remember thinking this is not a guy who lives in a cave. The other thing I noticed on first meeting him was he was immaculately dressed. When he first walked into the room he definitely had a presence. I'm six foot two and he towered above me. You could tell his men when they all came in around him they sort of worshipped the ground this man walked on.

Before we started the interview, he insisted everybody clear off because there were far too many flies and mosquitoes in the room. So everybody left and it was this bizarre moment when it was just myself and Osama in this room. And one of the other guys came in and sprayed all this insect repellant. And it was just a bit surreal to be standing in the room with this guy. We didn't really discuss anything. I mean I'm quite certain he speaks English, but he certainly wasn't willing to speak English with us.

When we first met, he shook my hand. He was very gentle, mild-mannered, very soft-spoken, not sort of a raving lunatic or anything, not really what I expected to be honest. The interview started, and John asked his questions in English and Osama answered in Arabic.

John Miller.

[I asked him] "What about the World Trade Center bombing [in 1993]. It's not like fighting the Russians on the field of battle. This is targeting innocents and civilians." And he said, "This is a very strange question coming from an American. Was it not your country that bombed Nagasaki and Hiroshima? Were there not women and children and civilians and noncombatants there? You were the people who invented this terrible game and we as Muslims have to use those same tactics against you." It was a very well-formed argument.

He said, "I predict a black day for America; a day after which American will never be the same and the States will not be united," and he pretty much laid it out that this would be a sustained battle.

And at that point he went in to one of the answers that we ended up playing a lot, which is he had this message for America—and the one that always struck me because it sounded hyperbolic at that time: "I'm declaring war on the United States. I'm going to attack your country." And I thought, "Yeah, you and what army?" If you took those words and you played them on September 12, 2001, as opposed to say September 9, 2001, it went from sounding quite hyperbolic to—he was telling us all along.

Rick Bennett.

So once we finish the interview I break free, I start shooting cutaways and wide shots of the room. During the whole interview Osama had his AK-47 sitting on his lap and I remember doing a shot from the AK up to him. The room was a long rectangular room and had a map of the world behind him. That was the background to the interview. So I kept rolling. Osama got up and I thought this is my opportunity, so I ran outside and turned on the toplight and waited him to emerge into the darkness. So he comes out of the building and I follow him. He has all his men around him. That's when I shot all that footage of him walking, getting into the vehicle. When all this is happening everybody is firing their weapons off, it's complete madness. He gets into the vehicle and he drives off. These guys keep firing their weapons so I shoot video of them all firing their weapons off.

When we first arrived the guys that really intimidated me were these young guys who were in their late teens, early twenties, who had obviously been there for a while, had obviously been under the influence of al Qaeda and would just as soon shoot us dead as deal with us. You could just tell from the look in their eyes that they wanted us dead. These guys really worried me. The young guys would try and intimidate you, run up to you, put a weapon to your ear, and fire off half a dozen rounds to try and take your ear drum out.

Well then they insisted we stay and have a chicken dinner. At this stage I had no appetite. We got what we wanted; it was time to go, so let's get the hell off this mountain. I packed my camera and started walking towards our vehicle to find that Tariq [our fixer-translator] is involved in this huge argument with two of these young guys who had guns. I said, "Tariq, what the hell are you doing, these guys have the guns." He said, "They're insulting me, they're saying I'm a traitor, that I'm with the West. I'm telling them we've been invited by Osama, we're his personal guest. How can they be treating us this way?" At this point I said, "I don't give a shit, they have the guns, we have what we want, let's get the hell out of here."

Obviously there was huge relief once we were actually on our way out and we had actually survived this ordeal. Because there were a couple of times along the way when I wasn't sure that I was going to make it back. At the time I thought it was quite a coup to get the interview, but I didn't quite appreciate the significance because September the 11th hadn't happened.

It was just such a great sense of relief to get back into Pakistan. It's funny, it's all relative. Pakistan seemed like a very normal, safe place after Afghanistan. To get back to the hotel room was a huge relief. I remember getting into the room and calling for room service and getting six liter-and-a-half bottles of water and, having suffered from dehydration before, I knew all the symptoms; dizziness, headache and one of the symptoms is that you're not thirsty. So I took all these six bottles and drank every last drop: it was either that or go to the hospital.

We did an hour special on ABC *Nightline* with Ted Koppel hosting the show. I remember it going to air and him starting out the whole hour saying, "Tonight we are going to introduce you to the man who poses the greatest threat to America and it's a name that nobody has ever even heard of, and his name is Osama bin Laden." [47]

7

Al Qaeda Attacks

On August 7, 1998, two months after bin Laden had announced on ABC News his intention (yet again) to attack American targets, al Qaeda blew up two U.S. embassies in Kenya and Tanzania within nine minutes of each other. The attacks came exactly eight years after President George H. W. Bush announced the introduction of hundreds of thousands of U.S. soldiers into Saudi Arabia, following Saddam Hussein's invasion of Kuwait—bin Laden's particular grievance against the United States.

The embassy attacks signaled that al Qaeda was capable of mounting sophisticated operations thousands of miles from its base in Afghanistan. Following those attacks the U.S. launched ineffectual cruise missile strikes against bin Laden's training camps in eastern Afghanistan, which had the counterproductive effect of increasing the profile of al Qaeda's leader around the Muslim world.

Al Qaeda would then again demonstrate an ability to strike an American target far from its Afghan base two years later in Yemen when suicide attackers almost sank the USS *Cole,* a U.S. destroyer, in October 2000.

Throughout this period, seeking to placate the United States, the Taliban tried to stop bin Laden from giving provocative interviews, and an intense, but concealed, debate developed inside the Taliban about what to do with al Qaeda's leader. Several key Taliban officials, such as the Taliban foreign minister Wakil Muttawakil, wanted to expel bin Laden from Afghanistan, but his most important protector, Taliban leader Mullah Omar, remained adamant that bin Laden would continue to be protected by his regime.

John Miller, the ABC News correspondent, remembers the news of the attacks against the U.S. embassies in Africa.[1]

When bin Laden declared war, I said, "What are we talking about?" He said, "You shall see the results of this fatwa in the next several weeks." And I thought that was interesting. Later, in mid-August, you have the embassy bombings and I'm out on a boat and the phone rings. They said, "Two embassies blew up simultaneously in the early morning hours in East Africa. We're trying to figure out what that's about. What do you think it is—is there a thing between African nations?" And I said, "This is bin Laden. This is the results of the fatwa."

I would later come to learn that somewhere in that mix in that room [with bin Laden during ABC News' interview] was Mohammad al 'Owhali, who had come to bin Laden and said, "I want a mission," and was assigned to the embassy bombings.

Mohammad al 'Owhali was interviewed by FBI agent Stephen Gaudin in Nairobi, Kenya, two weeks after the embassy bombings. The following are extracts from Gaudin's testimony during the embassy bombings' trial in which al 'Owhali was sentenced to life without parole. Al 'Owhali traveled from his native Saudi Arabia to attend al Qaeda camps in Afghanistan in 1996 when he was twenty. He pleaded with bin Laden for a suicide mission.[2]

Al 'Owhali explained to me that during the end of this training he had met with Mr. bin Laden several times, and had expressed to him interest in missions that he would like to do, and Mr. bin Laden told him—take your time. Your mission will come in time.

[Later] he was contacted by Azzam [the al Qaeda member who drove the truck bomb into the American embassy in Nairobi] and Azzam had told him that the mission that you said you might be interested in is going forward.

From there al 'Owhali tells me that he, Azzam, and four others attended what he described as a very specialized training for about a month. Al 'Owhali explained that this was training which dealt with the cell. He explained to me that the cell is made up of four separate sections, the intelligence section, the administration section, the planning and preparation section, and then the execution section.

Khalid [an al Qaeda member who helped plan the embassy attacks] told him that the mission was going to be a martyrdom operation that would result in al 'Owhali's own death, where al 'Owhali would be assisting in driving a truck full of explosives.

Al 'Owhali explained to me that around this time, around the time of the filming of the ABC interview [in] Khost, Afghanistan, of bin Laden that he did meet with bin Laden one more time.

Al 'Owhali explained to me that Osama bin Laden is at the very top of al Qaeda but that he has several senior military leaders directly under him, and that bin Laden provides the political objectives to these military leaders or these senior leaders and that these people would then provide the instructions down lower to the lower chains of command. Al 'Owhali explained that it wouldn't be normal for bin Laden to directly give instructions to someone like Azzam or directly to him. Al 'Owhali explained to me that he was never specifically told that this mission was Osama bin Laden's mission, but he always believed it to be so. Al 'Owhali explained to me that his understanding of the way things work is that Osama bin Laden—it's not likely that he would take direct credit for attacks like this.

Like al 'Owhali, Mohammed Sadiq Odeh was also sentenced to life in prison without parole following his conviction of conspiracy in the U.S. embassy bombings. On August 6, 1998, the day before those bombings, he left Nairobi, Kenya, for Pakistan, making his way to Afghanistan for a meeting with bin Laden. Immigration authorities at the Karachi International Airport, suspicious of his passport, arrested him. FBI agents interviewed him in Nairobi from August 15 through August 28, 1998.[2] Excerpts of their report follow.[3]

Odeh came to Kenya in August 1994. Odeh stated that in November 1994, Abu Hafs [a military commander of al Qaeda] came to visit him in Mombassa. Abu Hafs gave Odeh a fiberglass boat to be used in a wholesale fish business. The arrangement was that the business was for al Qaeda. Odeh was entitled to take money for his need to live and give the rest to employees that were in al Qaeda. Odeh stayed in the fish business for two years. Odeh further stated that he was paid money by al Qaeda on a yearly basis. Odeh last received his yearly advance in November 1997.

[In April 1998,] Mustafa [Fadel, an Egyptian member of al Qaeda] came to visit him in Witu [a small town in Kenya]. Odeh talked to Mustafa about bin Laden declaring war against American people in his last two fatwas. They discussed if al Qaeda was right in doing this; they were concerned if they were ready to face such an enemy. Mustafa stated that the Mujahideen in Sudan were against attacking U.S. targets. They feared that the U.S. was too powerful. Even al Qaeda in Afghanistan was questioning bin Laden but they still wanted to be ready to back up bin Laden's fatwa.

Approximately forty days prior to August 6 [1998], Ahmed the Egyptian [a member of al Qaeda] delivered a message to Odeh that Sheikh Hassan [a leader of the Ogaden tribe] from Somalia wanted to meet bin Laden. There was also a message that bin Laden had new plans and Odeh had to travel [to Afghanistan] to confer with bin Laden. [This] second message was regarding the latest fatwa from bin Laden and how bin Laden got other Islamic terrorist groups to join the front against the American people and because of this they all have to travel to see bin Laden.

Odeh stated that on August 1, 1998, Saleh [the leader of al Qaeda's cell in Kenya] ordered him to be out of Kenya by August 6, 1998. Odeh stated that for all the time he had been a member of al Qaeda, something this urgent had never happened to him before.

Mohammed al 'Owhali was interviewed by FBI agent Stephen Gaudin in Kenya. The following are extracts from Gaudin's testimony during the embassy bombings trial.[4]

[It was] explained to him through Saleh [who ran the Nairobi operation] there were several reasons why the embassy in Nairobi was picked. First, there was a large American presence at the U.S. embassy in Nairobi; that the ambassador of the U.S. embassy was a female and if the bomb resulted in her being killed, it would further the publicity for the bombing. Also, that there were embassy personnel in Nairobi who were responsible for work in the country of Sudan. There were also a number of Christian missionaries at the embassy in Nairobi. And lastly, that it was an easy target. Saleh explains to al 'Owhali that we have to have many attacks outside the United States and this will weaken the U.S. and make way for our ability to strike within the United States.

Al 'Owhali arrived in Nairobi on the Sunday, the 2nd of August. Saleh explained to al 'Owhali that in fact there were going to be two bombings, there was going to be a bombing of the U.S. embassy in Nairobi, Kenya, and the bombing of the U.S. embassy in Dar es Salaam, Tanzania; that both of these were going to occur on the same day, on Friday, August 7th, between 10:30 and 11:00 in the morning. Saleh explained to al 'Owhali that al 'Owhali's role was to assist Azzam in getting the bomb truck to the embassy in Nairobi. Azzam would be the driver, al 'Owhali would be the passenger. Al 'Owhali told me that Saleh had bragged to al 'Owhali that they were able to build this bomb and get everything ready in only ten days.

Al 'Owhali and Azzam are in the bomb vehicle, and on their way. Al 'Owhali described to me that he and Azzam were listening to an audio-cassette of what he described as chanting poems for motivation in preparing to die on the way to the embassy. Upon reaching the rear parking lot of the embassy, Azzam pulls into the embassy and starts to head for the drop bar in the back of the U.S. embassy by the parking lot. Al 'Owhali jumps out of the vehicle and starts to go towards the guard. He ends up pulling out one of those stun grenades in his right hand and approaches the guard and demands that the guard open the drop bar in English. And al 'Owhali explained to me that the guard didn't move fast enough, so he pulls the pin with his left hand and he throws the stun grenade in the direction of the guard and that that caused a loud explosion and the guard ran. Al 'Owhali says at this point Azzam starts shooting directly at the U.S. embassy with a pistol. And al 'Owhali explains between Azzam firing the pistol at the embassy and the loud explosion that was created from when he threw the stun grenade, people started to scatter.

And al 'Owhali explains to me at this point he realized that his mission is complete, that he did exactly what he was instructed to do. His mission was to help Azzam get the truck as close as possible to the embassy and to scatter away the Kenyan people in and around the area. Al 'Owhali told me that, at that point, it was no longer necessary for him to die in the attack. Al 'Owhali explained to me that he was fully prepared to die in carrying out the mission and that that would equate to being a martyr, to reach martyrdom, dying in completion of your mission. But to die after your mission had already been complete, al 'Owhali explains to me, is not martyrdom, it's suicide. He explains to me that he ran towards the building, and as he was running towards the building, Azzam detonated the bomb, causing the explosion.

The August 7 bombings of the U.S. embassies in Kenya and Tanzania killed 212 people. Bin Laden publicly denied any role in the attacks. On August 20, 1998, Zawahiri, speaking with the Pakistani journalist Rahimullah Yusufzai by satellite phone, delivered this statement on bin Laden's behalf.[5]

Bin Laden calls on Muslims to continue jihad against Jews and Americans to liberate their holy places. In the meanwhile, he denies any involvement in the Nairobi and Dar es Salaam bombings.

An hour after Zawahiri finished speaking to Yusufzai, cruise missiles fired by the U.S. Navy rained down on al Qaeda's training camps near Khost in eastern Afghanistan.

Abu Jandal recounts how an impulse decision by bin Laden meant that al Qaeda's leader was hundreds of miles away when the U.S. cruise missile strikes hit his camps.[6]

I was working as a personal bodyguard with Osama bin Laden. The night of the [U.S. cruise missile] strike, I moved with him from Kandahar to Kabul. The next day, they attacked these camps thinking that bin Laden and his guards were in the Khost camps. One night before the bombing, Sheikh Osama bin Laden decided to go to the Khost camps. When we left Kandahar toward Khost, the Americans were able to know our destination through the Afghan cook who was working with us. Later on, we discovered that he was a U.S. intelligence agent.

I remember that when we reached a crossroads between Khost and Kabul, Sheikh Osama bin Laden said: "Where do you think, my friends, we should we go, to Khost or Kabul?" We said we would go to Kabul in order to visit our comrades there. He said: "With God's help, let us go to

Kabul." We arrived in Kabul and the U.S. attack against the Khost camps occurred the next day. It was a concentrated bombardment. Each house was hit by a missile, but they did not destroy the camps completely. They hit the kitchen of the camp, the mosque, and some bathrooms. Six men were killed.

Excerpts from President Clinton's Address to the Nation on August 20, 1998.

Good afternoon. Today I ordered our armed forces to strike at terrorist-related facilities in Afghanistan and Sudan because of the imminent threat they presented to our national security. I want to speak with you about the objective of this action and why it was necessary. Our target was terror, our mission was clear—to strike at the network of radical groups affiliated with and funded by Osama bin Laden, perhaps the preeminent organizer and financier of international terrorism in the world today. The groups associated with him come from diverse places, but share a hatred for democracy, a fanatical glorification of violence and a horrible distortion of their religion to justify the murder of innocents. They have made the United States their adversary precisely because of what we stand for and what we stand against.

With compelling evidence that the bin Laden network of terrorist groups was planning to mount further attacks against Americans and other freedom-loving people, I decided America must act. And so this morning, based on the unanimous recommendation of my national security team, I ordered our armed forces to take action to counter an immediate threat from the bin Laden network.

Earlier today, the United States carried out simultaneous strikes against terrorist facilities and infrastructure in Afghanistan. Our forces targeted one of the most active terrorist bases in the world. It contained key elements of the bin Laden network's infrastructure and has served as a training camp for literally thousands of terrorists from around the globe.

We have reason to believe that a gathering of key terrorist leaders was to take place there today, thus underscoring the urgency of our actions.

Khaled Batarfi, bin Laden's childhood friend in Jeddah, Saudi Arabia.[7]

It was a shock to most people I know, especially his playmates and his schoolmates, that he was the top wanted man in the world. I remember when I was in America, Clinton was talking about bin Laden, about this dangerous man and he was responding by sending Tomahawk rockets to Afghanistan. I couldn't believe it. That was our bin Laden? It's amazing someone you grew up with and you felt he was special, but not that special. He was just an ordinary man with some special merits, to then be the enemy number one of the greatest power in the world, it was like: Wow!

Habib Ahmed was in one of the camps where the U.S. cruise missiles landed. Ahmed claimed he was merely receiving Koranic instruction at the camp. He was interviewed a couple of weeks later in his hospital bed in Peshawar, Pakistan, as he was suffering from burns that he had sustained in the attacks.[8]

My name is Habib Ahmed. I am from Swat (an area in the far north of Pakistan). My age is nineteen years. After evening prayer, we were studying the Koran. When we finished, we went to sleep in camp. At that time we heard a loud noise. We got up. As soon as we left the camp we heard the second loud noise. We saw a missile attacking the same camp. Many people were there. They were crying after they were injured. The Holy Koran was burned. We were very shocked about this. Around three hundred [were in the camp]. [It was the] Khalid bin Walid camp. It was a [cowardly] act; attacking late at night from afar.

It is our duty to support Osama bin Laden who is standing alone in the mountains of Afghanistan. Osama is Muslim and we are Muslims. He is against oppression and we are against oppression. He attacks from a distance whoever attacks him, whether the United States or the British. And we, the Muslims, share his ideas.

The unsuccessful cruise missile strike against bin Laden raised the profile of al Qaeda's leader. Abdel Bari Atwan, the editor of *Al Quds al Arabi* newspaper, recalls this:[9]

It was [20] August 1998. I was in Tunisia holidaying with my family and suddenly the attacks took place. You know my journalistic instincts start to work. I said, "Maybe something will come from al Qaeda." I stopped my vacation and left my family there and then came to my office here [in London]. On my way from the airport to my office, Mohammed Atef [al Qaeda's military commander] called me on my mobile [phone]. And he said, "Osama bin Laden is alive and kicking and nothing happened to him. We have a message to President Clinton. We will take revenge and we will hit them where it hurts. We will teach the Americans a lesson they will never forget."

The effect [of the attacks on al Qaeda] was actually minimal. And it worked for Osama bin Laden because it lifted the embargo that was imposed by Mullah Omar. Mullah Omar actually felt insulted. And so Osama bin Laden felt freer to move in Afghanistan. His profile increased a lot. He's the underdog and he's attacked by the mighty Americans. So this actually elevated him to a higher prestigious position in the eyes and minds of those frustrated people in the Arab and the Muslim world.

An unidentified prisoner held at Guantánamo Bay in an appearance before a U.S. military tribunal.[10]

DETAINEE: I knew Osama bin Laden for a long time. When I met him, he was not famous. This was about fifteen years ago during the war with Russia. When the Russians attacked Afghanistan, Osama bin Laden was like anyone else. After the Gulf War, he became famous. Who made him famous? Do you know who made him famous?

TRIBUNAL PRESIDENT: You tell me.

DETAINEE: I will tell you: America. By the media and television and by magazines. Everybody is talking about Osama bin Laden. Through the media, you made him famous. In the seventies, it was Carlos ["The Jackal," a notorious terrorist]. Today, it is Osama bin Laden.

Sami ul Haq is the head of the Darul Ulom Haqqani, a vast madrassa outside Peshawar, which has graduated several cabinet members of the Taliban. Haq socialized with bin Laden in Peshawar during the eighties. He was interviewed shortly after the U.S. cruise missile strikes on al Qaeda's camps in Afghanistan.[11]

I think America has made Osama a supernatural being. Wherever the terrorism occurs, right away they think of him. I don't think he has such influence, or such control and resources. Osama bin Laden has become a symbol for the whole Islamic world. All those outside powers who are trying to crush Muslims interfering with them; he is the courageous one who raised his voice against them. Yes, he is a hero to us, but it is America itself who first made him a hero.

After the strikes on al Qaeda's camps in Afghanistan I wrote the following two letters to Mohamed Atef, who at the time I believed to be some kind of media adviser to bin Laden. I later learned he was, in fact, al Qaeda's military commander, generally known as Abu Hafs. Abu Hafs was one of the founding members of al Qaeda. Our exchange of faxes and phone calls took place between the Kabul central post office where Atef was located and hotels in Pakistan where I was staying.[12]

To: Dr. Mohammed Atef
From: Peter Bergen, CNN Correspondent
Fax: 81-837-655 [a fax number at the Kabul central post office]

Dear Dr. Atef,

I am a correspondent for CNN. Last year I traveled to Afghanistan, a trip with which Khaled al Fauwaz said you helped. Khaled gave me your fax number and suggested I contact you. I will be in Pakistan for about a week. I would very much like to meet you whenever it is convenient for you. Right now I am in Islamabad staying at the Marriott hotel. I plan to stay here until Friday, when I will travel to Peshawar. I will be staying at the Pearl Continental. You could also try my cell phone, which is 0300-594336. I look forward to hearing from you.

Yours sincerely,

Peter Bergen
CNN Correspondent

On September 12, 1998, Atef called me saying he was in Afghanistan. He suggested meeting at the Intercontinental Hotel in Kabul, and also offered footage of the aftermath of the U.S. cruise missiles strikes on al Qaeda's camps three weeks earlier.

To: Dr. Mohammed Atef
From: Peter Bergen, CNN Correspondent
Fax: 81-837-655
Date: September 14th

Dear Dr. Atef,

Thank you for calling me two days ago. I am interested in meeting you. Last year I was the producer for an interview near Jalalabad for CNN with Osama Bin Ladin. CNN is interested in again talking to Bin Ladin. We will be in Pakistan for another week. Monday you can reach me at the Pearl Continental in Peshawar. Tuesday evening we are going to Islamabad to apply for visas for Afghanistan from the Taliban. We will be staying at the Islamabad Marriott.

Regarding the footage you have of where the U.S. missiles landed near Khost, of course I am interested, but you should be aware that BBC and ABC News have already broadcast those pictures, and I have numerous photos of the site already.

I look forward to hearing from you.

Yours sincerely,

Peter Bergen
CNN Correspondent

On September 16, 1998, I received another phone call from Atef saying that it was "difficult now" for bin Laden to do another interview with CNN.

Abu Jandal, bin Laden's personal bodyguard.[13]

Atef was a serious-minded man, a disciplined man. He was not the gregarious type who could live with the young mujahideen and understand and solve their problems and address their concerns, like Osama bin Laden. Perhaps this was due to his military position in the organization. His work and activities sometimes compelled him to avoid people and keep away from others. He was a first-rate sportsman and he loved

Pushtun, including Omar, should allow a guest or refugee seeker to abuse Afghan Pushtun hospitality. He said that Bin Ladin was like a guest who was shooting at neighbors out of the host's window.

Omar conducted himself in a careful and controlled manner. At no time did he bluster or threaten.

Comment: Omar's contact with a USG [U.S. government] official is rather remarkable, given his reclusive nature and his past avoidance of contact with all things American. It is indicative of the seriousness of how the Taliban view the U.S. strikes and our anger over Bin Ladin. The Taliban, despite implying that we should initiate the contact, are interested in a dialogue with us on Bin Ladin and other issues. This is a long way, however, from the Taliban doing the right thing on Bin Ladin.

The following cable summarizes a frank exchange between Abdul Hakim Mujahid, a Taliban official, and a U.S. diplomat in Pakistan. It appears to be the first time that a U.S. government official was informed of the extent to which senior Taliban officials had turned against bin Laden.

U.S. Department of State
Declassified Cable, Afghanistan Desk
September 13, 1998

Summary: In a September 13 meeting with Taliban official Abdul Hakim Mujahid, DCM [deputy chief of mission at the U.S. embassy in Pakistan] deployed counterterrorism talking points in their entirety. Mujahid replied that the U.S. should exercise "patience" on the Bin Ladin issue. He claimed that Taliban leader Mullah Omar is the key supporter of his continued presence in the country, while 80 percent of Taliban officials oppose it. DCM responded that Bin Ladin has put the Taliban and the U.S. on a collision course; it is time for the Taliban to deal with him and his network. Mujahid said the Taliban have "shortcomings" and the world should not expect too much from them.

In response to U.S. points, Mujahid made the following comments:

a. He said he had checked earlier in the day with Wakil Ahmed [a key Taliban official], and although reports that Usama Bin Ladin had been placed under "house arrest" were inaccurate, the Taliban have warned him once again not to engage in political or press activities. In addition, the Taliban have taken away all of his "instruments of communication."

b. Mujahid added that he had personally urged Wakil Ahmed to ensure that the Taliban fully control Bin Ladin's activities.

c. Very few Afghans are in favor of Bin Ladin's presence in Afghanistan. Eighty percent of the Taliban leadership opposes his presence, including Taliban deputy leader Mullah Rabbani, Wakil Ahmed, and "Acting Minister of Mines" Mullah Jan. Mullah Omar is the major supporter of Bin Ladin.

d. The Taliban are made up of "10 separate groups." They are only united by the desire to defeat "the warlords" and end "chaos." Once this task is completed, and the war is over, the different Taliban groups will fight among themselves, and issues like Bin Ladin and the treatment of women will be dealth with in a positive way.

e. It is quite a complex issue; the Taliban cannot simply push Bin Ladin out because they will then fall under pressure from other Muslims. However, according to Mujahid, the end result will be that Bin Ladin will one day leave Afghanistan.

f. Therefore, the U.S. should be "patient" and "act wisely." The issue of Bin Ladin will be dealt with.

COMMENT

Though his comments during the hour-long conversation were often contradictory and seemed designed to distance his attitudes from the Taliban, Mujahid seemed to hear our message on Bin Ladin. However, it has long been known that Mujahid—a Taliban "Moderate"—was not close to Mullah Omar, who calls the Taliban's shots, and the conversation tended to underscore the limits of Mujahid's influence in Kandahar [the de facto capital of the Taliban]. His remarks were frank and definitely the best give-and-take we have had with any Taliban official on Bin Ladin. Mujahid appeared to believe strongly that Omar is Bin Ladin's main protector and that most of the Taliban leadership do not favor his presence. (Note: It has been well-known that Omar was strongly in favor of Bin Ladin's presence; the attitudes of other Taliban leaders have been less clear.) Given Omar's staying power into the immediate future, Mu-

2. Through Iran to the port of Bandar Abbas. Laying pipelines through Iran gives the Iranians the ability to have a dominant control of this oil, and the Americans totally refuse this.
3. The third route is through Afghanistan to Pakistan (Karachi), and this is the best and the most reliable route, and it has a big profit to Pakistan and America.

In conclusion, the American government is keen on laying the oil and gas pipelines from Turkmenistan through Afghanistan and Pakistan, and this will be under American control in the Gulf and it also goes through the territories of Pakistan which are allied to America. Hence, Iran will be deprived of this and American companies will also get to contract the project which amounts to 5 billion dollars.

In his analysis of the Taliban, Abu Hafs comments on their hospitality and the risks they are facing by sheltering al Qaeda.

The welcoming is total and this is a clear indication about their sincerity especially as the pressures on them are big due to the presence of Arab mujahideen and their refusal to hand over any of [Arab mujahideen] leaders to the governments requesting their extradition day and night.

He also acknowledges the following Taliban weaknesses.

THE DISADVANTAGES OF THE MOVEMENT.
1. A movement of students and scholars who don't have enough administrative or organizational or political expertise.
2. Their economic situation is very weak.

Abu Jandal, bin Laden's chief bodyguard.[23]

Relations between Mullah Omar and the Sheikh [bin Laden] were strengthened and consolidated after the advance of the Afghan commander Ahmad Shah Massoud toward Kabul [after 1996] and after Sheikh Osama bin Laden alerted the Arab mujahideen in Afghanistan to defend Kabul. They played a great role in defending it and in repulsing the Massoud forces, given their good military experience. During that time the blood of the Arabs and Afghans was spilled at the Afghan fronts and this was an important factor in strengthening the relationship and bolstering links between the al Qaeda organization and the Taliban Movement.

As for Ahmad Shah Massoud and his differences with Sheikh Osama, I assure you that these differences were not because of his short-term differences with Taliban, and that they were not new. They were rather old differences between Massoud and bin Laden. These differences started in the first days of jihad in Afghanistan.

The relationship between Mullah Omar and Sheikh Osama bin Laden began as a result of the two sides' agreement in terms of religion and ideology. They agreed on the same enemy; namely, the United States. Mullah Omar used to say that the United States wanted to strike at the Taliban not because of Osama bin Laden, but because it wanted to strike at Afghanistan to drive out the Taliban Government because it was implementing the Islamic sharia law in the country.

The Saudi Government continued its dialogue and sent many delegations to bin Laden and tried to persuade him to retreat from his jihadist policies. This was because of the strong relations between the bin Ladin family and the ruling House of Saud. Sometimes they sent his brothers to him and sometimes they sent his mother. At one time, the Saudi Government sent his mother and his half brother on the maternal side by a special Saudi plane that landed at Kandahar airport. When they arrived there, they tried to convince him. Sheikh Osama said: "This is a principle. I keep it in my heart and I have promised God not to abandon it. Like one of the Companions of the Prophet, who said: 'By God, you will not be able to deviate me from my path even if you have one thousand souls and these souls are given up one by one unto death.' " Yet he was very kind to his mother and he treated her well and used his own methods to convince her. She returned empty-handed.

Khaled Batarfi is bin Laden's childhood friend. He has remained in touch with bin Laden's mother and the children from her second marriage.

For her, it's became worse and worse and worse. Then he went to Afghanistan. At the beginning, he was talking to her, and after that the only channel—the phone—was dead.

He's always been a very obedient son, more than any of his brothers and sisters. I mean, very obedient. He never raises his voice in her face. And he was always smiling, kissing her hands, and he was kissing her feet. It was kind of an I-am-your-slave thing. And always calling her—always. Asking her about the smallest of things: what she was cooking today and what she did, where she went. And that's why she loves him, but she doesn't subscribe to his line of thinking or what he does. So I guess it's tough. She doesn't talk to people much. She doesn't want even my wife—who was close to her—to see her because she doesn't want anybody to see her: she's not in a mood to talk.

Prince Turki al Faisal, the head of Saudi intelligence until 2001.[24]

[In June 1998] King Fahd and Crown Prince Abdullah sent me to meet Mullah Omar to persuade him to hand bin Laden over to the Kingdom. This was because of some of his acts and statements. I asked Mullah Omar to hand him over and he agreed. I was told their interests were with us and not with any individual. Mullah Omar asked me to inform the king and the crown prince that he wanted to set up a joint Saudi-Afghan committee to arrange procedures for the handover. [An adviser to Mullah Omar] came to tell the crown prince that the Kingdom's request for bin Laden had been approved and that a joint committee was being set up to oversee the handover.

I wished I had not gone [again to Afghanistan in September 1998 after the U.S. embassy bombings in Africa]. After previously agreeing to hand the man over, I discovered Mullah Omar had reversed his decision and he was abusive about the [Saudi] Kingdom and its people. Under those circumstances, I had no choice but to break off negotiations. I still remember, however, that as I was leaving, I told Mullah Omar that one day he would regret his decision and that the unfortunate Afghan people would pay the price.

According to bin Laden's chief bodyguard, Abu Jandal, the Saudis were sending not only diplomats to Afghanistan, but also assassins.[25]

The Saudi intelligence sent agents more than once to assassinate Sheikh Osama bin Laden but failed. I participated in the arrest of one such agent who tried to assassinate bin Laden in Afghanistan. The Saudi intelligence sent a young Uzbek man living in Saudi Arabia to Kandahar, promising him two million Saudi riyals (more than $500,000) and Saudi nationality if he succeeded in killing bin Laden. When we arrested him, we asked him: "Did you expect that you would be able to kill Sheikh Osama bin Laden and escape from fourteen guards armed with automatic weapons and with such high level of training?" He was very dazed as though he had just woken up from a coma. He looked like a child. He was only eighteen and had been deceived. He was crying in a very pathetic manner and said: "I made a mistake." Finally, bin Laden said: "Release him." [The assassination attempt] almost coincided with the [U.S. cruise missile] attack against the al Qaeda organization camps [on August 20,] 1998.

Jamal Ismail, a Palestinian journalist who was Al Jazeera's bureau chief in Pakistan, interviewed bin Laden in December 1998, further heightening his media profile and further antagonizing some Taliban officials.[26]

Must have been the 18th December '98, I was sitting in my house. There came a call from somebody in Mullah Omar's office. Abu Hafs the Egyptian, Mohammed Atef, said, "Jamal, I am telling you frankly just reach Kandahar and we will arrange your interview." I said to him that I have my questions for Al Jazeera. I have questions also from a friend of mine [submitted by CNN's Peter Bergen]; who met Osama, and he is requesting these questions. He said; "I have to talk to Osama about it."

We drove nearly two hours forty-five minutes from Kandahar city towards Helmand [province], and then we went from the main road. We saw tents on one of the hills there and some Arab fighters. Some of them were carrying Stinger [American anti-aircraft] missiles. There were three tents. One tent was for prayers, one tent for the interview, and the other was for the bodyguards. There were more than twenty people in these tents, and maybe the same number on the top of the mountains surrounding [the camp].

Mohammed Atef told me, "Jamal, we have one request from you. Don't take any shot of anybody except Osama and Ayman [al Zawahiri], for security reasons." Osama came and I requested him questions [from

Peter Bergen]. He said, "Jamal, I have a commitment not to give any interview or any news item for any Western media. I consider all of them as non-Muslim media and we have to release our stories through Muslims." I said: "If you have this commitment it's okay."

Since '92, before he left to Sudan, it was the first time I had seen him. A lot of changes because after six years you can see a difference. Then he was not holding his machine gun wherever he goes. [Now] he was so committed to his belief in fighting against Americans and the West in general, and more especially against the Israel-Jewish state. We spent four hours with him.

I've seen two of his sons were there, as his bodyguards. One of them was at that time I believe 18 or 19 and the other's 15 or 17; Osman. And the other son, either Omar or Abdel Rahman.

According to Islamic religion and Islamic teaching particularly in jihad, we are not supposed to start killing civilians. Osama said, "If they [the Jews and Christians] are killing our civilians, occupying our lands, raping our sisters and brothers, and they don't spare any one of us, why spare any one of them?"

Excerpts of bin Laden's interview with Al Jazeera's Jamal Ismail, 1998.[27]

Any aggression by America today against Afghanistan should not be seen as mere aggression against Afghanistan itself, but should be seen as an aggression against the one waging Jihad in the name of the Islamic world. Our relationship with the Taliban is very strong and it is an ideological relationship not based on mere political or financial relationships.

We are continuously thankful to God for I enjoy very excellent health. We here in the mountains endure severe cold weather, as well as extreme hot summers. My favorite hobby is horse riding and I can still ride a horse nonstop for 70 kilometers (40 miles).

Jamal Ismail.

That documentary [that I interviewed bin Laden for was broadcast in] June '99. Al Jazeera advertised it for one month: "See only on Al Jazeera a man against a state and a state against a man, [the documentary]

"Destroying al Qaeda." And they were bringing some portion of Osama's interview, that portion where he was accusing the American administration is against Arabs, against Muslims, and supporting Israel, and we have the legitimate right to force them to flee from our Holy Lands and some other portions from Bill Clinton's speeches against Osama bin Laden.

According to AFP (news agency), the streets of Riyadh and other Saudi cities, when al Jazeera started broadcasting this program were deserted. And when it was broadcasted, many articles and comments were published in Arab media. Some of them not supporting him directly, but at least defending his point of view and asking Americans to withdraw from our Holy Land or to finish their support to Israel.

In early July 1999 the patience of the Clinton administration ran out for the Taliban's intransigence on bin Laden. President Clinton signed an executive order that imposed economic sanctions on the Taliban leadership, an excerpt of which follows.[28]

July 6, 1999

THE WHITE HOUSE
Office of the Press Secretary
For Immediate Release   July 6, 1999
EXECUTIVE ORDER
BLOCKING PROPERTY AND PROHIBITING
TRANSACTIONS WITH THE TALIBAN

I, WILLIAM J. CLINTON, President of the United States of America, find that the actions and policies of the Taliban in Afghanistan, in allowing territory under its control in Afghanistan to be used as a safe haven and base of operations for Usama bin Ladin and the Al-Qaida organization who have committed and threaten to continue to commit acts of violence against the United States and its nationals, constitute an unusual and extraordinary threat to the national security and foreign policy of the United States, and hereby declare a national emergency to deal with that threat.

I hereby order:

(a) all property and interests in property of the Taliban; and

(b) all property and interests in property of persons determined by the Secretary of the Treasury, in consultation with the Secretary of State and the Attorney General:

  (i) to be owned or controlled by, or to act for or on behalf of, the Taliban; or

  (ii) to provide financial, material, or technological support for, or services in support of, any of the foregoing,

that are in the United States, that hereafter come within the United States, or that are or hereafter come within the possession or control of United States persons, are blocked.

WILLIAM J. CLINTON
THE WHITE HOUSE,
July 4, 1999

Abu Mousab al Suri is a Syrian affiliated with al Qaeda who is an important ideologue for the jihadist movement. He was the person that I knew as Omar who had taken us to meet bin Laden in 1997 for CNN's interview with al Qaeda's leader. Despite his importance as an al Qaeda theoretician, al Suri's relationship with bin Laden would often prove tempestuous.

Six videotapes, recovered in Afghanistan after the fall of the Taliban dated August 2000, show al Suri in front of a whiteboard addressing a class. The camera is trained throughout on al Suri, who writes on the board as he makes his points.[29]

In the first tape al Suri outlines what his lecture series aims to achieve. First he wants to distribute the videotapes, to teach individuals how to incite jihadist followers by highlighting the "Jewish-Crusader oppression of Muslims." Second he wants to deal with the operational side: for example, how to keep jihadist cells secure and how to create contingency plans if an original operation fails.

The tape then cuts to Suri's first lesson. Suri dwells on the degeneracy of the Western world and says it is a good way to incite Muslims. He dwells on sin, gays, and lesbians.

With a world map behind him Suri says 80 percent of the petroleum is in the Muslim world. He charges the West keeps the price down artificially.

Suri describes how individual Muslims can play a role by attacking targets of opportunity even if they are not on the frontline. "If you hear in Malaysia what is going on in Chechnya, go and knife the Russian attaché to death.

"If a Muslim is in Britain he doesn't need to leave his job or university and go and fight jihad at the front. What he can do is call the press agency and tell them I'm from the global Islamic resistance and claim responsibility for whatever action is being done in the world. If a man living in Sweden spots a Jewish security target, he attacks it."

Suri explains targets should be selected on two criteria. They should cause as much pain as possible to the enemy and they should awaken Muslims as much as possible.

LIST OF TARGETS:
1. Missionary Centers and Cultural Missions because they manufacture enemies [of Islam] and secularism.
2. Companies, mines, engineers and agents of foreign companies, representatives of the Aramco company [in Saudi Arabia] that steal Muslim oil.
3. All forms of diplomatic facilities and consulates.
4. All forms of military facilities, including the homes of families on bases.
5. All forms of foreign security, all Western teachers and doctors are actually in disguise and are spies.
6. All forms of tourism.

Suri then launches into a critique of the hierarchical structures prevalent in al Qaeda in 2000. He drew a diagram indicating how easy it is to round up a cell structure in which many cells are traced back to a leader:

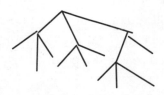

"In the new stage," Suri tells his class, "You should form a brigade. I advise that your brigade doesn't exceed ten members."

In 2003, a Spanish judge, Baltasar Garzon, indicted thirty-five for alleged terrorist activities, including Abu Mousab al Suri, whose real name is Mustafa Setmariam Nasr. Al Suri's training methods in Afghanistan are referred to in Garzon's indictment.[30]

Mustafa Setmariam Nasr, Abu Mousab al Suri is a Syrian citizen, nationalized Spaniard. He became the Emir (leader) of a Syrian group associated with al Qaeda becoming a member of its council or "Shura." Setmariam first met with bin Laden in Afghanistan in 1988. When Setmariam arrived in Afghanistan, he immediately set up a mujahideen training camp for al Qaeda. Setmariam received militants and mujahideen converts from France, Italy and Spain whom he would train at the camp. Once training was completed, these European mujahideen would return to their respective countries. There they would reintegrate into society, while really acting as "sleepers" and would await orders from al Qaeda. When al Qaeda moved to Sudan in 1991, al Suri (Setmariam) stayed in Afghanistan traveling sporadically to Khartoum. He moved to Spain in 1995 and later to the U.K.

Vahid Mojdeh published an insider's account of his time as a Taliban official, *Afghanistan Under Five Years of Taliban Sovereignty*. Extracts from the book, which appeared in the Dari language in late 2001, follow.[31]

It shouldn't be assumed that al Qaeda in Afghanistan was a coherent and flawlessly efficient organization or that every Arab volunteer was one of their affiliates. Osama's spiritual influence was not so great as to gain the absolute obedience of all. Abu Mousab al Suri was also among Osama's opponents. A naturalized British citizen, Abu Mousab had come to Afghanistan from the time of jihad against the Soviet Union. He always advised the Taliban to stop Osama's actions because he was sure that Osama didn't know what he was doing. The dispute between Abu Mousab and Osama reached a point where Abu Mousab said their relationship had ended in an interview with the Al Jazeera television network.

After the fall of the Taliban, *Wall Street Journal* **reporter Alan Cullison purchased a used computer in Kabul, which turned out to be one of al Qaeda's main computers—a computer often used by Ayman al Zawahiri himself. Together with his colleague Andrew Higgins, Cullison deciphered nearly a thousand documents stored on the computer, which were often encrypted or written in code. The results of that investigation were published in the** *Journal* **and later in** *The Atlantic* **magazine. One of the documents on the al Qaeda computer was a letter from Abu Mousab al Suri to Zawahiri, dated July 19, 1999, an excerpt of which follows.[32]**

The strangest thing I have heard so far is Abu Abdallah [bin Laden] saying that he wouldn't listen to the Leader of the Faithful [Mullah Omar] when he asked him to stop giving interviews. I think our brother [bin Laden] has caught the disease of [television] screens, flashes, fans and applause.

Noman Benotman is the Libyan who fought with al Qaeda in Afghanistan.[33]

Before 9/11, [al Suri and bin Laden] hated each other. Al Suri didn't like bin Laden's leadership because, he said, "bin Laden is a dictator," and he even called him "a Pharaoh."

⚜

Vahid Mojdeh, the former Taliban foreign ministry official, describes the increasing radicalization of the Taliban leadership in 2001, evident from its campaign to destroy Afghanistan's cultural heritage.

Omar's order about the destruction of the [Buddhist] statues [in the Kabul museum in the spring of 2001] was absolute but it was meant to be a secret to avoid broader worldwide attention. All hopes of preserving the objects faded away. Taliban officials went to the museum to execute the order. The museum door opened and the group each armed with a stout club of some kind, entered and hammered the statues while uttering the phrase "God is Great."

Mullah Omar's order of the destruction of the Bamiyan statues was announced [on February 24, 2001]. (They are Afghanistan's most well-known monuments, two statues of the Buddha, hundreds of feet high, carved from cliffs in the third and fifth centuries A.D. Despite exhortations from the world community, including many Muslim nations, the Taliban would destroy the Buddhas with artillery and explosives in May 2001.)

Maulana Muttawakil was then foreign affairs minister in Kabul. The morning after the issuance of the order, I visited him in his office and found him depressed. He said that he was informed of Mullah Omar's order the day before and had spoken with him on the phone. Muttawakil was more open-minded than many highly positioned Taliban. Knowing Mullah Omar, Muttawakil was well aware that the order would definitely be carried out and the efforts of the international community to avert his decision were futile. The destruction of the Bamiyan statues inspired feelings of hatred and disgust worldwide towards the Taliban.

Foreign forces in Afghanistan including the Arabs and Central Asian fighters, however, were most satisfied by the destruction of the Bamiyan statues. One of the people defending the Taliban was Sheikh Mahmoud Uqala, a blind Saudi spiritual leader. He was among the most highly honored Arab clerics and considered by some as the successor to Sheikh Mohammad bin Baz [the former Saudi grand mufti]. He is the same person who approved the 9/11 attack as a retaliatory measure taken by Muslims and openly admired the persons who planned it.

Many cassette tapes of Sheik Uqala's lectures were sent to Kandahar praising Mullah Omar for his conduct. [Ugala] also wondered why it took so long to destroy the statues. In response Mullah Omar ordered a hundred cows to be slaughtered and the meat distributed among the needy throughout the country to make up for the delay. That cows had to be slaughtered carried a political meaning. While Buddhists all over the world condemned the destruction of the statues, slaughtering one hundred cows totally enraged the Hindus against the Taliban. It was said that the expense for the animals was paid for by the Al Rashid Trust, an ostensibly charitable organization in Pakistan. I heard from some Arab fighters and Taliban officials that one month after the Bamiyan incident, the number of Arab volunteers joining al Qaeda and the Taliban troops in Afghanistan was ten times that of the previous months.

One of the documents recovered on the computer purchased in Kabul by *Wall Street Journal* reporters after the fall of the Taliban was a letter from bin Laden to Mullah Omar.[34]

I pray to God, after having granted you success in destroying the dead, deaf, and mute false Gods [the Bamiyan statues] that He will grant you success in destroying the living false gods [such as] the United Nations.

Vahid Mojdeh explains that the Taliban regime sustained itself through a campaign of endless war, yet it was also riven by internal disagreements, not least of which was what to do with bin Laden.

The Taliban leadership had no plan but war. Their military commanders enjoyed unlimited power. In the early stages the Taliban treated their war captives in a humane manner and in several cases commanders released them after taking their weapons. Taliban military commanders only reported to Mullah Omar. In addition military commanders never reported their financial activities to any office. Naturally, with such power and authority to wage war, they never desired that peace be established in Afghanistan and as a general rule opposed any peace initiative.

The Taliban were also ruthless torturers, their most commonly used technique was beating people with electric cables.

One of the more interesting Taliban initiatives in the area of diplomacy was the oral order issued by Mullah Omar in 2001 regarding the ways in which diplomatic communiqués with foreign governments were to be handled. Even though the Taliban did not have formal diplomatic relations with most countries, their foreign ministry on the occasions of birthdays or deaths of foreign leaders sent congratulatory notes or messages of condolences to these states. Mullah Omar ordered that no leader of a non-Muslim country should be sent a congratulatory note on his birthday. No nation suffering from natural disasters such as a flood or earthquake should receive a message of solidarity or sympathy since these are acts of God. Further, no non-Muslim foreign leader should receive a message wishing him a long or healthy life.

The Taliban was not free of internal disagreements. The disparity reached a point where Mullah Omar had to encourage these factions to set aside their differences. In his letter of advice he noted that "Due to certain tensions, the future of the struggle is at risk. Each man talks behind the back of the other and the leaders more than the rest." Many of these differences had simply to do with people and differences in tastes, but some were of a more fundamental nature. The most important figure in this regard was Maulana Muttawakil.

After Muttawakil took the job of foreign minister he tried his best to perform differently. But the situation with Osama bin Laden had really tied his hands. He believed that if the Taliban wished to be accepted by the world community, they should not take actions that would antagonize it. For this reason, while he was in Kandahar, he ordered that Osama be placed under surveillance and not be permitted to do whatever he wished. When Muttawakil took charge at the foreign ministry he asked Mullah Omar to restrict Osama's activities more closely. Osama used to say about Muttawakil, "Two entities are against our jihad. One is the US, and the other the Taliban's own foreign affairs ministry."

In 2000, bin Laden's attention turned to Yemen, his ancestral homeland. Al Qaeda would plot to blow up U.S. warships there, while bin Laden would take his fifth bride, a Yemeni.

Abu Jandal, bin Laden's Yemeni bodyguard.[35]

Regarding Sheikh Osama's marriage to his latest wife the Yemeni Amal al Sadah, my mission consisted of taking the dowry from Sheikh Osama and carrying it to the bride's family. The Sheikh gave me $5,000 and told me to deliver it to a certain man in Yemen and that man in his turn took the money to the bride's family. I did not know at that time that the money was a dowry for Sheikh Osama's bride. I found out later. When I decided to return to Afghanistan the brothers asked me to take Sheikh Osama's bride and the male relatives accompanying her with me. I waited for two more months in Yemen for that purpose and finally I could wait no more and I left. The bride and her male relatives followed me a month later. We held a splendid wedding ceremony for the Sheikh in Kandahar in which his wives and children participated. Songs and merriment were mixed with the firing of shots into the air. From what I know she is still with her husband Sheikh Osama in Afghanistan.

On October 7, 2000, two al Qaeda suicide bombers piloted a bomb-laden skiff into the USS *Cole,* a U.S. Navy destroyer refueling in the Yemeni port of Aden. The bomb blew a hole the size of a small house into the hull of the ship, killing seventeen American sailors. That attack came a year after a similar, failed attempt by al Qaeda to blow up the destroyer USS *The Sullivans,* also in Yemen.

Abu Jandal was bin Laden's chief bodyguard at the time of the *Cole* bombing. He explains al Qaeda's rationale for the attack.[36]

Actually there are several reasons: the first is to break U.S. prestige in the sea and raise the morale of the Islamic nation by saying that its sons can deal blows to the enemies of the nation wherever they may be on the land, in the sea, or in the air. It is to say that we can face the enemies even with individual capabilities. Take the Islamic World, which consists of about 71 states. It cannot say no to the United States, but we individuals can do so. They proved to the Islamic World a Muslim ability to break U.S. prestige and hegemony over Muslim shores and sea. This was the main reason for choosing the U.S. destroyer Cole for bombing. Otherwise, there were many ocean liners. But, the choice of the best destroyer in the U.S. Navy was intended to be a slap in the face for the United States. It was to tell the United States that we can deal it a blow whenever and wherever we want.

In November 2002, the United Arab Emirates government arrested Abdal Rahim al Nashiri. Nashiri, al Qaeda's commander in the Arabian Peninsula, had led al Qaeda's attack on the *Cole.* Nashiri, a Saudi, is currently held by the United States at an undisclosed location. Based on its review of U.S. interrogation reports of Nashiri and other al Qaeda members, the 9/11 Commission constructed the following profile of him.[37]

Abdal Rahim al Nashiri—the mastermind of the *Cole* bombing and the eventual head of al Qaeda operations in the Arabian Peninsula—appears to have originally been recruited to his career as a terrorist by bin Laden himself.

Having already participated in the Afghan jihad, Nashiri accompanied a group of some 30 mujahideen in pursuit of jihad in Tajikistan [a country that borders Afghanistan in what was once the Soviet Union]. When serious fighting failed to materialize, the group traveled to Jalalabad and encountered bin Laden, who had recently returned from Sudan [in May of 1996]. Bin Laden addressed them at length, urging the group to join him in a "jihad against the Americans." Although all were urged to swear loyalty to bin Laden, many, including Nashiri, found the notion distasteful and refused. After several days of indoctrination that included a barrage of news clippings and television documentaries, Nashiri left Afghanistan, first returning to his native Saudi Arabia and then visiting his home in Yemen. There, he says, the idea for his first terrorist operation took shape as he noticed many U.S. and other foreign ships plying the waters along the southwest coast of Yemen.

Nashiri returned to Afghanistan, probably in 1997, primarily to check on relatives fighting there and also to learn about the Taliban. He again encountered bin Laden, still recruiting for "the coming battle with the United States." Nashiri pursued a more conventional military jihad, joining the Taliban forces in their fight against Ahmed Massoud's Northern Alliance and shuttling back and forth between the front and Kandahar, where he would see bin Laden and meet with other mujahideen. During this period, Nashiri also led a plot to smuggle four Russian-made anti-tank missiles into Saudi Arabia from Yemen in early 1998.

At some point, Nashiri joined al Qaeda. Nashiri traveled between Yemen and Afghanistan. In late 1998, Nashiri proposed mounting an attack against a U.S. vessel. Bin Laden approved. He directed Nashiri to start the planning and send operatives to Yemen, and he later provided money. Nashiri reported directly to bin Laden, the only other person who, according to Nashiri, knew all the details of the operation. When Nashiri had difficulty finding U.S. naval vessels to attack along the western coast of Yemen, bin Laden reportedly instructed him to case the Port of Aden, on the southern coast, instead. The eventual result was an at-

tempted attack on the USS *The Sullivans* in January 2000 and the suc-
cesful attack, in October 2000, on the USS *Cole*.

Nashiri's success brought him instant status within al Qaeda. He later
was recognized as the chief of al Qaeda operations in and around the
Arabian Peninsula. While Nashiri continued to consult bin Laden on the
planning of subsequent terrorist projects, he retained discretion in se-
lecting operatives and devising attacks. In the two years between the
Cole bombing and Nashiri's capture, he would supervise several more
proposed operations for al Qaeda. The October 6, 2002, bombing of the
French [oil] tanker *Limburg* in the Gulf of Aden also was Nashiri's hand-
iwork. Although bin Laden urged Nashiri to continue plotting strikes
against U.S. interests in the Persian Gulf, Nashiri maintains that he actually delayed one of these projects because of security concerns. Those
concerns, it seems, were well placed, as Nashiri's November 2002 capture in the United Arab Emirates finally ended his career as a terrorist.

Abu Jandal.[38]

Al Qaeda pursues a method or principle that calls for "centralization
of decision and decentralization of execution." The decision was made
centrally, but the method of attack and execution was the duty of field
commanders. For example, the persons who were in Yemen like Abd al
Rahim al Nashiri and others took part in this operation. They planned for
it and God granted them success in its fulfillment after a long watch. The
planning for the Cole operation was carried out by the people [on the
ground]. The idea was formed and the target was set and then it was referred to a higher military control committee in al Qaeda called the Military Affairs Committee, which does not plan, but gives the green light,
the support, and the funds for these operations. But, the planning, execution, and method of attack were all undertaken by field commanders
in the operations field.

**A few weeks after al Qaeda's attack on the *Cole*, I traveled down
Wadi Doan, a hundred-mile-long valley in the Yemeni region of Hadra-
maut, on a road that that was little more than a river bed to reach
Rubat, the bin Laden family ancestral village which is at the very end of**

the wadi. The wadi with its looming cliffs and rocky outcrops reminded me strongly of Afghanistan. Indeed, the trip to Rubat is reminiscent of the trip to Tora Bora from Jalalabad, with the difference that in Wadi Doan you are in a desert region. Working the fields of the wadi were women swathed in black wearing conical hats of straw, figures that seemed to have stepped out of a medieval painting.

The bin Laden village is comfortably tucked into the shade of the wadi cliffs (a photograph of which can be found in the photo section). Rubat's genial mullah, who runs a school out of the old bin Laden family compound, told me, "We are against this holy war. The *Cole* attack does more to harm Yemen's reputation than America's reputation. We feel sorry for the American boys and girls. They are our guests." Khaled al Omeri, a thirty-year-old cousin of bin Laden's who owns a food shop on "Bin Ladin Street," avoided direct questions about his most famous relative, but when asked about his view on jihad he pointed proudly at his three-year-old son saying, "This is my jihad." [39]

A month after the *Cole* bombing Ahmad Zaidan, Al Jazeera's bureau chief in Pakistan, received a summons to speak to al Qaeda's leaders, who privately admitted they were behind the attack.

November, 2000. Somebody called me and said, "We need you to come to Quetta [Pakistan]; we have good things for you." We then reached Kabul [where I met Osama who told me,] "Of course, we have a lot of things which we disagree with Taliban, but they are better than other [Afghan groups]. There is no anarchy, in the country." And then I told him, "Okay, so if you disagree with Taliban with different issues like woman, so why are you not coming out to clarify your position? Because, many Arabs don't like this rigid policy by Taliban." He said, "This is not our concern. Our concern is to fight Americans or to fight the Westerners."

Most of the viewers [of Al Jazeera], they think he is only just talking about religion. No, it's not true. He is using religion to prove his ideas on current affairs or interpret current affairs according to religion.

Osama was sitting and I wanted to go [to the] bathroom. And I go to the bathroom and the bathroom was occupied and I came back. And he gave a hint to his people; said, "Okay check whenever this bathroom is free." And really, after only just a few minutes somebody told me, "Okay, it's free" and [Osama] asked me to go. It was some sort of human touch.

I disagree totally with the people who are saying that he is under the influence of Ayman Zawahiri. Not at all. Osama bin Laden is very confident and you can see from his body language when he is talking. For example, when he's reading in Arabic, he is perfect. I can't maybe prove it, but Osama bin Laden wants to project himself as little bit different from Zawahiri and my feeling is that he is always keeping little bit of distance with Zawahiri.

And if Osama is trusting somebody, he was so much trusting Abu Hafs (the Egyptian military commander of al Qaeda who would be killed in a U.S. airstrike in Afghanistan in November 2001). Abu Hafs joined al Qaeda and became al Qaeda totally. He is very quiet. And you feel that he is planner. Very well organized and smiling all of the time. Reading a lot. Knows what's going on in the world. He was very much futuristic. I still remember when he told me things as if he is reading [the future]. He was telling me in November 2000 after I finish my interview with Osama bin Laden. He said, "I will tell you one thing. We did [the USS] *Cole* [attack] and we wanted United States to react. And if they reacted, they are going to invade Afghanistan and that's what we want. We want them to come to our country, and then we know that they would have bases in Pakistan, in Uzbekistan, Kazakhstan. And they are going to hit Afghanistan from these countries. And then we will start holy war against the Americans, exactly like Soviets."

So then [al Qaeda] called me again on January, the 26th 2001. I was preparing to go to Hajj with my wife. Every year my wife is waiting to go to Hajj (the pilgrimage to Mecca) and the problem is, you know, we are journalists; always something happens. Always something . . . Only six days left for Hajj and my wife said that "I'm sure that we will not go this year." I said, "No, we will go." [Then I got the call from al Qaeda] I was feeling selfish at that time. We drove to Afghanistan, Kandahar. I was thinking that we are going to do an interview with Osama bin Laden.

[Instead] this wedding party took place and it was the wedding party of Osama bin Laden's son, Muhammad, who was marrying Abu Hafs' daughter. And it was really interesting to see how they are making their wedding party. More than four hundred, five hundred people were sitting just like in a row, just like they are praying. Didn't take much time, maybe one hour, and then food, and then serving fruits. Mostly al Qaeda; few Taliban.

Osama bin Laden and Abu Hafs were there. I have a video [camera] with me. Of course, the main thing in [this type of] wedding party, the [bride] was not there! And then Osama bin Laden, usually he is giving like poetry. He doesn't give a speech. He tried his level best to make some poetry and he failed. He gives his poetry and the people say, "Allah Akhbar!" (God is Great!) encouraging him on.

Then we finish the wedding party and he said, "Okay, come with me." And we went into his room in his house. And we sat there and started to talk and he said, "Ahmad, I don't think my delivery was good." He's very much caring about public relations. Very much caring how he would appear on the TV. And he said "I didn't like it. I'm going to deliver it again." And he did it [again] and then he was comparing. He said, "No, no. The first one was better." The poem [he delivered was] against America, of course. And he was very much praising [the USS] *Cole* [attack].

Osama bin Laden's poem celebrating the attack on the USS *Cole*.[40]

A destroyer: even the brave fear its might.
It inspires horror in the harbor and in the open sea
She sails into the waves
Flanked by arrogance, haughtiness and false power.
To her doom she moves slowly
A dinghy awaits her, riding the waves.

(The reference to the dinghy is to the skiff that the al Qaeda suicide attackers used to blow a forty-foot hole in the Cole.)

Ahmad Zaidan.

[Osama's] brother Hassan was there. He is very nice person. You know, this family is very articulate. And then bin Laden [said] that, "My mother is here and my brother is here. I am very much feeling guilty. If there is no [United Nation's] embargo on Taliban, I could bring a special plane for her to take her from here [directly] to Saudi Arabia." He was a little bit upset [saying], "I'm not so kind to my mother."

Osama's son Usman bin Laden delivered a speech honoring his father at his brother's wedding. It was recorded on videotape, excerpts of which follow.[41]

How can any one blame my father or hold him accountable if he endeavored to instill in one and all a feeling and desire to stand against the might of the *Kuffar* (the infidels)? My father raised a voice and urged the Muslims to unite against the infidels. My mother taught and instilled in me an unending everlasting feeling that I should always be motivated to fight and die for the glory of Islam. I stand for a jihad against *Kuffar* today, and shall so do till eternity. Jihad is in my mind, heart and blood veins. No fear, nor intimidation can ever take this feeling out of my mind and body.

8

The Charismatic Leader

The attack on the USS *Cole* confirmed bin Laden's position at the helm of the global Islamist jihad. Bin Laden's reputation was an important factor in drawing aspiring jihadists to Afghanistan, many of them from Western countries, who had heard about the Saudi militant through radical preachers, Web sites, or simply on television. Indeed, something of a bin Laden cult was taking shape in the period between the U.S. cruise missile strikes in Afghanistan in the summer of 1998 and the 9/11 attacks. That cult helped fuel an unprecedented volume of recruits to al Qaeda's camps. It also attracted various militant Islamist groups into affiliate relationships with al Qaeda.

Though bin Laden was careful to take security precautions that limited his accessibility, many aspiring jihadists heard him come to speak in al Qaeda's camps. This made a personal audience with al Qaeda's leader that much more sought after. And for those who sought to undertake a mission on behalf of al Qaeda, some form of meeting with, and final approval of planned ventures by, bin Laden was de rigueur. Bin Laden's modus operandi, though, was to leave much of the operational planning to trusted lieutenants, such as Abu Hafs and Sayf al Adel. He was a figure who, for the most part, stood above the fray, interceding only occasionally in the everyday running of al Qaeda.

Abdessater Dahmane, a Tunisian who had settled in Belgium, assassinated the Northern Alliance leader Ahmed Shah Massoud on the 9th of September 2001, after being personally recruited to do so by bin Laden. Dahmane traveled to Afghanistan in 2000 after being inspired by seeing bin Laden appear on a television news item in Belgium. His wife, Malika Malik, remembered the moment vividly, as she explained in a self-published book about her husband's experiences in Afghanistan, written in French and called *Soldiers of Light*.[1]

One day Osama bin Laden appeared on the news: "Look at that face, don't you think that it is beautiful?" my husband said to me. "You are very handsome too," I told my husband. "I love him" said Abdessatar. "Me too, I love him," I replied. When Abdessater was speaking of the beauty of Osama bin Laden he was alluding to the light of faith illuminating his face. At that moment, but only that moment I confused Osama and my husband in my head. Because the love I feel for my husband is one of a loving wife, but that of Osama as a great brother in Islam. I don't believe for a minute that he ordered the 9/11 attacks.

What serenity I saw in both their expressions! I turned my eyes to the face of my husband and towards that of the Islamic leader, whose expression was fixing on the camera to call out for combat against the aggressors of the poor and the unarmed, the Muslim community and a frisson went through me and I felt a presentiment that God only knows.

Something had just put a shadow over the happiness of Abdessatar: he was scared of dying without having made the supreme effort on the path of God: Jihad. And he had the impression that it was to himself in particular that Osama was delivering a message.

In a series of interviews in Yemen with Khaled al Hammadi, a correspondent for the *Al Quds al Arabi* newspaper, Abu Jandal provides an insider's account of al Qaeda. Those interviews appeared in the *Al Quds* newspaper in August 2004. Abu Jandal described his first meeting when he was personally recruited by bin Laden in 1997 as "beautiful." In this extract he describes how he was chosen to be bin Laden's chief bodyguard in 1998, and how he then acted as a troubleshooter for bin Laden, insulating his leader from internal disputes in al Qaeda.[2]

I was chosen to be bin Laden's personal bodyguard after I completed all my training courses. There was a specific incident after which I was chosen. We were sitting in a gathering in Kandahar and a man belonging to the Takfiri stream (the ultra hard-line Islamist group that had earlier tried to assassinate bin Laden in Sudan) arrived. He was called Abu al Sha'tha the Sudanese. Right there in the gathering he began to speak offensively and rudely to Sheikh Osama. Because I moved around the city a lot I recognized the man as a member of the Takfiri group.

When Abu al Sha'tha then drew close to Sheikh Osama, I spoke out:

"Sheikh Abu-Abdallah (bin Laden), allow me to sit next to you." He replied: "No, there is no need." I repeated my request and insisted on it because I was afraid for his safety and feared that the man might do him harm. I loved Sheikh Osama deeply and, indeed, after a while I stopped calling him Sheikh and started calling him "Uncle." Finally after a lot of entreaties on my part, bin Laden said: "Come and sit behind this door that is next to me."

I went behind the door and kept looking out for any sudden movement from that Sudanese fearing that he might assault him or even try to assassinate him. Sheikh Osama meanwhile kept his hand on his pistol while talking with the man. Finally the Sudanese man did something strange and stretched out his hand towards Sheikh Osama. Without thinking I threw myself on the man and sat on top of him until he could no longer move. He screamed for help and said: "I did not do anything." I told him to keep quiet or I would remove his head from his body. Sheikh Osama laughed and said: "Abu-Jandal, let the man be." Afterward he told me to take the man out of the house and lead him away.

After that day Sheikh Osama gave me a pistol and made me his personal bodyguard. The pistol had only two bullets for me to kill Sheikh Osama with in case we were surrounded or he was about to fall into the enemy's hands so that he would not be caught alive. I was the only member of his bodyguard who was given this authority [to kill Osama] and I was to use this pistol. I took care to keep the two bullets in good condition and cleaned them every night, while telling myself: "These are Sheikh Osama's bullets. I pray to God not to let me use them."

According to our security arrangements, if enemy forces surrounded Sheikh Osama and there was no possibility that he would escape, I was to kill him before they could catch him alive. For six months, the period during which I was personal bodyguard, I constantly stood behind his back and accompanied him round the clock. He refused to be captured alive, he would become a martyr, not a captive, and his blood would become a beacon that arouses the zeal and determination of his followers. I remember that he used to say: "Martyrdom rather than captivity." This was his frank view.

My basic duty was to defend Sheikh Osama. Sometimes, however, he sent me as his representative to some al Qaeda outposts and camps. I was regarded as his representative during debates. He sometimes instructed me to visit some military outposts to talk to people about certain issues that troubled them. I sometimes examined those issues and their causes and presented my view to Sheik Osama to make a decision.

Actually there were rivalries among al Qaeda members depending on their countries of origin. The Egyptians used to boast about being Egyptian. The Saudis, Yemenis, Sudanese, and Arab Maghreb citizens used to do the same thing sometimes. This troubled Sheikh Osama and he used to send me to them to help eliminate these regional rivalries because the enemies of God, those who have sickness in their hearts, and informants would exploit these ignorant attitudes and try to sow divisions and disagreements among al Qaeda members.

I regarded myself as someone properly educated by Sheikh Osama. I regarded him as a father. I believed that if we wished to confront our strong enemy or confront the broad front that the United States wielded against us, we needed unity among ourselves and eliminate regional rivalries. The sheikh himself did not personally intervene in these issues and I frequently intervened to solve these problems in my own way, even without telling the sheikh because I used to regard myself as being one with Osama bin Laden, one with the al Qaeda organization, and one with the Islamic nation.

Would-be al Qaeda recruits often had to go through vetting procedures before they gained prized access to bin Laden. Shadi Abdalla, a Jordanian of Palestinian descent, briefly became bin Laden's bodyguard in Afghanistan in 2000. The following are summaries and direct quotations from Shadi Abdalla's interrogation by German police after his arrest in 2002. His interrogation provides an illuminating account of how he reached bin Laden's inner circle, his experience of al Qaeda's training camps, and a firsthand glimpse of bin Laden's appeal to al Qaeda recruits as he bragged about major planned attacks against the United States.[3]

Shadi Abdalla moved to Krefeld, Germany, in July 1999. On December 14, 1999, Abdalla travelled in a group of five persons from the Krefeld mosque from Germany to Saudi Arabia, and later to Pakistan and Afghanistan. In Mecca, he met a man by the name of Abdallah al Maki alias Abdallah al Hallabi, who recommended that he go to

Afghanistan, where the "true Islam" was taught. Al Maki, who—Abdalla later discovered—is a son-in-law of Osama bin Laden, gave Abdalla the telephone number of a contact in Karachi, Pakistan. This contact guided Shadi Abdalla to a "Taliban center" in Quetta and arranged for him to be smuggled across the border of Afghanistan into Kandahar.

In Kandahar, Shadi Abdalla stayed in an al Qaeda guesthouse, the so-called Arabic house, for about one week. That is where he met Mohamed Atef alias Abu Hafs, Osama bin Laden's deputy, as well as Saif Al-Adel Makkawi alias Sayf al Adel, Abu Hafs' deputy. Both interviewed him regarding his abilities and about his political and religious attitude. Abu Hafs suggested Abdalla learn "fighting" before deepening his knowledge of the religion.

In early 2000 Shadi Abdalla began military basic training at camp "Al Farouq" near the airport in the city of Kandahar, known as the "airport camp." While in the training camp, he was sworn into participating in the "Jihad." He was taught the basic ideological extremist attitude of "al Qaeda." Shadi Abdalla ended his training prematurely after approximately twenty days due to a head injury he suffered while at the camp. He was admitted to a hospital and treated for this head injury and upon release returned to the "Arabic house." During his subsequent two-week stay at Osama bin Laden's headquarters at the airport in Kandahar, he met Ramzi Binalshibh [the 9/11 planner].

Abdalla enjoyed a special position of trust within the leadership-circle of the camp because Binalshibh had recommended him and Osama bin Laden's son-in-law, al Maki, had sent him there. (Bin Laden's daughter married al Maki when she was fifteen.) Al Maki acts as bin Laden's body guard, and, secondly, it is his job to win people for bin Laden's cause. This he does very skilfully by at first putting the question of Jihad into the background but later on making an open appeal. He is, in addition, a well-versed martial artist. For example, he boxes well and knows how to use knives. Also, he is a good shot. All of bin Laden's guards are skilled in weapons.

Shadi Adalla's direct remarks to German interrogators follow.

I had gotten from bin Laden's son-in-law a phone number, which I was supposed to call in Pakistan. I reached a person named Hamza. I stayed with him about 48 hours and he then took me to Quetta. That is a city in the region bordering on Afghanistan. I entered a large house there, a Taliban centre. The actual purpose of this house is to receive injured Taliban fighters, but it also has three rooms which are intended as guest rooms for Arabs.

In the first few days, I was questioned a lot by [Ramzi] Binalshibh. His special status within al Qaeda was documented by the fact that he wore a head covering that was reserved in Afghanistan for secret leadership-level persons. When I met him for the first time in Afghanistan, there were very few persons in the guesthouse in Kandahar, Afghanistan. At that time (Binalshibh) wore no "veil." Later, in 2000, when many new recruits came to Kandahar, he usually wore this veil because he could not rule out the fact that there could perhaps be spies and traitors among them.

When I was asked if I wanted to become a bodyguard for bin Laden, it was because of a shortage of personnel. After all, other young men asked to do this job. I was watched over and checked over in my activities. I was allowed into bin Laden's vicinity when he was on the move. Then, I always had to walk behind him. We had one task and one task only: to protect bin Laden. Those bodyguards who had been on the job for some time, were also entrusted with other tasks. From all this, it was obvious that we were not trusted 100 percent.

There are two ways of becoming a member of al Qaeda. One can take a so-called little oath or a big oath. The first one is taken in the presence of Osama bin Laden. In essence one promises him to keep the secrets and to obey him. One simultaneously shakes hands with him. The other possibility, i.e., the big oath, contains the same promise, but in the presence of Mullah Omar [the Taliban leader].

The [training] camp had the shape of a big oval. The buildings were made from light construction material, only the kitchen and the officers' building were from stone. The mosque consisted of straw; the sanitary facilities were made from tin. The Afghans put up the buildings for money. We also bought daily necessities like food from them. Russian arms, rifles as well as small firearms, were also bought from the Afghans. The training sites for each of the training components, e.g., house-to-house warfare, lay around the camp. There was also a part that was separated from the camp. It was for bin Laden's stays. Al Qaeda financed everything.

Newcomers to the training camps were lodged in special guesthouses. They had to hand in all their belongings (bank cards, passports, etc.). In conversations the instructors try to find out if the newcomers are sincere. There was much fear of spies.

After the basic training it was possible to receive special training in an area of special talent and/or interest. The final decision rested with Abu Hafs (bin Laden's deputy). Possible areas included: tactical training in mountain, urban or desert warfare; anti-aircraft combat on rocket grenade launchers; fighting against armoured targets, i.e., tanks; terrorist attacks and assassinations. Special training for poisons was offered at camp "Abu Khabab." All special trainings took place in separate camps to which only persons enrolled in the training had entrance.

The training units usually consisted of six to ten people at most. Each unit had a name. The trainees slept in tents of six to ten people. There were also a few cases where only two people were in a tent. Each tent had a supervisor who was responsible. This person had to inform the others when an instructor was coming. He had to report, e.g., when someone was sick. He was responsible for discipline in the tent.

The first subject in which we were trained was the use of firearms. The second subject included correct behaviour in outside terrain: camouflage, forms of movement, deception. In the third subject they taught us how to orient ourselves outside. The fourth and last subject was the use of explosives. The arms training lasted three weeks; all other subjects involved a week of training each.

During my training I did hear the instructor frequently talk about the U.S. as an occupying power in Saudi Arabia. This was meant to incite the trainees against the U.S. At the Kandahar airport I saw a large map of the Arab world. It also showed the location of bases and ships of Western forces, e.g., of the British, the French and the Americans. This included the whole Gulf region, the Middle East and Turkey. They also showed propaganda movies about Chechnya, Bosnia, Saudi Arabia, Palestine, Afghanistan, Indonesia and Somalia. One time they showed a movie about the USS *Cole*.

After the training sessions we had meetings at night with the instructors in which we talked about mistakes and misbehaviour of the trainees. Punishment was marshalled on the spot. It was a very frequent and pop-

ular punishment to let people climb the mountains in complete darkness. The punished had to give signs with a flashlight or shouts to show
they had in fact complied with the punishment. In particularly severe
cases we had to fill big containers with water and carry it on our backs on
the way up. The containers were very heavy. A relatively frequent punishment was they would order you to take off your shoes. You then had to
walk in the hot sand at noontime.

Many young men broke off [from the training] or would have liked to.
This was generally not a problem if someone important had sent them. It
was different with those who had come by themselves or did not belong
to any faction. These people would even be tortured. This happened also
during the training period. Popular torture methods were beating with
cables, strangulation until almost death, tearing out of fingernails, and
food and sleep denial. I can remember someone who died while I was
there because he had been strangled for too long. In Kandahar, there
were two cells which had ropes hanging from the ceiling. People would
be tied to these ropes by their arms. In addition there was a tiny cell
without windows that was always dark. Many people were put in there so
that they wouldn't have any space and no air to breathe. They would go
literally crazy.

Bin Laden met high-ranking foreign guests in some sort of guesthouse
that was outside the area he used as private living quarters. Whenever
bin Laden drove anywhere—which didn't happen often—he used a
black pick-up truck. He was very secretive about his trips. He'd just show
up surprisingly. Bodyguards would clear the route before bin Laden
would pass through it. Bin Laden was generally not greeted with much
fanfare since his trips were secret; only when a propaganda film or something similar was being produced did the organization fire rockets, etc.,
to impress the press.

While on tour with bin Laden I noted several disagreements between
the boss and his men, e.g., over potential targets in the U.S. I also witnessed the detention of several people as spies. Those were usually critics of bin Laden.

I want to say that bin Laden is a very charismatic person who could
persuade people simply by his way of talking. One could say that he
"seduced" many young men. In our conversations he asked me if I was

ready for the "jihad." He said that our common path must be the sacrifice for Islam. This was the right path. I responded that I wasn't ready for that yet. I would have to deepen my religion first.

[Bin Laden] constantly talked about [attacks against the U.S.] I know that from others. However he didn't name specific targets as far as I know. It was said that he wanted to break the back of the United States. I don't know what exactly he meant by that.

Abu Jandal describes living with bin Laden. He explains that the simple manner in which bin Laden lived was inspirational to his followers.[4]

My wife used to live with me in a special compound for the families of the mujahideen, at Kandahar airport [in southern Afghanistan]. As for the families of the mujahideen who lived in Kabul, they used to rent small houses, just like other Afghans. Indeed, the Arab mujahideen in Kandahar and Kabul used to share with the Afghans their numerous occasions, their weddings, and their sad occasions. We lived a normal social life, but in a society that was alien to us in language, environment, and way of life.

[Bin Laden] used to go the wilderness outside Kandahar with all his wives and little children. He would ride with us in his private car and his family would ride in a bus. His grown sons would follow us on horseback although the distance was about one hour by car. He would then sit with his wives and we used to take the car far from that place so that he would not see us and we would not see him. We would communicate by radio. In that place he would teach his wives how to use firearms. They would play together and do some simple physical exercises. He used to lead a normal family life.

He was a fine horseman who loved horses. He did not ride daily, however, but he had a lot of experience with horses. He knew about pedigree and could tell a horse's likely lineage by simply looking at it. Perhaps his early wealthy life and his contacts with the Saudi ruling family taught him that because the ruling family members love horses and racing. Other members of the bin Laden family also loved horses. Sheikh Osama, moreover, loved horses from a purely religious perspective because the Prophet, may God's prayers and peace be with him, used to say: "There is goodness in horses until the Day of Judgment." Bin Laden sometimes arranged horse races among the organization's members. Once he came and asked me: "Can you ride a horse, Abu-Jandal?" I said: "I can drive anything but I cannot ride a horse." He said "What a shame" and instructed me to take lessons but I evaded the training and did not finish the course.

So we never really felt afraid as long as we were with that man. We ate with him, walked with him. Our love for Sheikh Osama springs from the fact that we went hungry together and were filled together. We wept and rejoiced with him. We were joined by a common destiny. We lived a full life with him. The man was very simple in all his dealings and in everything in his life. He was consistently very generous with others. No one ever came to ask for financial assistance and was rebuffed. An Arab brother who wished to travel abroad came and explained his difficult circumstances to him. Sheikh Osama went into the house, came out with whatever money his family had, which was around $100, and gave it to the man. I was aware of the Sheikh's financial situation and said: "Abu-Abdallah, why did you not leave a part of that money for us. Those who are staying here are more deserving than those who are leaving." He replied: "Our situation is not hard. God will send us money." For five days after this incident we had nothing to eat except pomegranates that grew around his house although they were not yet ripe. We ate raw pomegranates with bread, three times a day. I believe that God raised Osama bin Laden to a high status because despite his great wealth, he was very modest, and attached only to what rewards God would give him.

He treated his family and children in the same way. He brought his children up in a simple way of life to teach them self-reliance in everything. I remember that when we were staying at the Kandahar Airport post, his son Saad came and said: "Father, I wish to get married." Osama said: "This does not concern me. Rely on yourself." The son said: "What should I do?" Sheikh Osama replied: "Take this plot of land and this budget. Till the land and from the revenue that you get, save money and get married." And the son tilled the land and raised crops. His father merely gave him advice on how to do it. Thus he relied on himself and got enough money to get married. Sheikh Osama used to give to each of his sons a plot of agricultural land and a budget to cultivate it. Bin Laden accustomed his sons to shoulder responsibility and rely on themselves, not on their father's millions. I used to hear him telling his sons: "Sons, your father's millions about which you hear are not for your father to use. This money is for the Muslims and I hold it as a trust for the cause of God. Not one riyal [the equivalent of thirty cents] of it is for you. Each of you is a man. Let him rely on himself."

I spent most of my time with him because I was his personal bodyguard. When his family moved with him from one place to another, when he visited Kabul, for example, the group of bodyguards which consisted of fourteen to sixteen men traveled with him. His family, which consisted of his wives and children, used to ride in a bus accompanied by a vehicle full of guards.

His three wives lived in one house that had only one floor. They lived in perfect harmony. Sheikh Osama was firm in managing his household's affairs just as he was firm in handling matters outside his home. We never heard about any conflict among the wives. One comes from a Syrian family, like his mother. Two are Saudis. His last wife whom he married after divorcing Um Ali [the mother of Ali] is a Yemeni. His first wife Um Abdallah [the mother of Abdallah] is a Syrian. The other wives he married after he embarked on a life of jihad. I know that his wife Um Khalid [the mother of Khalid] is of the al Sharif family and was the sister of one of his jihadist comrades.

I left Afghanistan for the final time shortly after his Yemeni wife arrived. I heard later that she had given birth to a daughter. After my final departure from Afghanistan, which occurred two months prior to the bombing of the U.S. destroyer *Cole* in Aden in [October] 2000, I heard that all his wives stayed with him in Afghanistan except for his first wife Um Abdallah, who left before the incidents.

I remember that his male children who were with him in Kandahar up to the time I left the country were nine. If we add Abdallah and Ali, the number of his male children would rise to eleven from all his wives except the last one, the Yemeni wife. As to daughters, there is no possibility of knowing the number.

Those volunteering for al Qaeda missions often sought out contact with bin Laden. The following interrogations of al Qaeda operatives reveal that what they remember most is time spent with their leader, rather than detailed discussions of their planned attacks. This planning tended to be managed by bin Laden's top aides.

Nizar Trabelsi is a Tunisian who became a professional soccer player in Germany. In his late twenties he drifted into drug addiction and then turned to Islam, subsequently traveling to Afghanistan in 2000 where he became an ardent bin Laden disciple. Trabelsi was arrested in Brussels on September 13, 2001, and was interrogated by Belgian police officers. He told them that al Qaeda had tasked him with the bombing of a NATO base in Belgium.[5]

This meeting [with bin Laden] dates back, more or less, to some weeks after the attack against the USS *Cole* (on October 12, 2000). At night this person [Abu Zubaydah, an al Qaeda recruiter] came to me and he took me to a villa in the Jalalabad vicinity [in eastern Afghanistan]. I arrived in a room where many people were gathered. I shook the hand of the many people who were present and I sat down. Right then I realized that Osama bin Laden was attending. After eating, Abu Zubaydah took me to Osama bin Laden. It seemed he had already gotten news about me. Abu Zubaydah explained to bin Laden that I was a soccer player and I had recently converted to Islam. He also said that I came to Afghanistan to stay here with my wife and help the local people. Osama bin Laden told me that if I needed something I could ask him.

After two or three weeks I again tried to contact bin Laden through the man who looked after his villa. I addressed this man and the following day I had an answer: I could get to Kabul on Saturday to take the plane leaving at 8:45 bound for Kandahar. When I reached Kandahar, someone was waiting for me at the airport. He attended my first meeting with Osama bin Laden. That man took me to a house called Dar Es Salaam, where only people invited by bin Laden are allowed to enter. This villa was an hour and half from the airport. I had a shower and I ate something. The person who picked me up told me that Osama bin Laden was not there, but he could probably arrive during the night. During the night the man who waited for me at the airport and picked me up, took me to another villa where I met with bin Laden. He was happy [to see me].

I was so impressed when I saw him that I didn't dare to speak to him. He asked me questions about my family and realizing that I felt uneasy he tried to cheer me up. I stayed there three days and I was always with Osama bin Laden. I was his guest. During this time we chatted about many aspects of life.

During my stay I met with Abu Hafs, the Egyptian, and with Doctor Ayman Zawahiri. During my first stay in Kandahar I didn't dare to explain bin Laden the problems I dealt with, being so deeply impressed by this figure. This was the reason why I stayed there only three days.

My second stay lasted nine days. I took the plane on Saturday and I came back on the Sunday of the following week. I told him all the troubles I suffered during my life. I spoke of my father and mother. In the end Osama bin Laden told me that I could consider him as my father. This is the reason why I'm very fond of him. He told me that I could stay with him and that he could help me.

During this stay I was in contact with the information agency run by bin Laden. I went to the agency and a man gave me a videocassette and two CDs. Watching a videocassette I saw images showing the pains suffered by Muslims in various parts of the world. There were images from Bosnia, Chechnya, Palestine and also Indonesia. In particular I saw a Christian who had taken out the heart of a Muslim and had eaten it. Also there was a woman who was raped by seven men. My wife watched the videocassette many times. She said that she saw a sequence where a little baby of four months in Palestine was killed: she was shot in her abdomen while she was in her mother's arms on a bus.

At the end of this week I came back to Jalalabad. I watched the videocassette I brought from Kandahar many times. I was deeply struck by these images and I was convinced to increase my commitment towards the [Afghan] people I loved. Their poverty was for me comparable to the poverty of the people I watched in the videocassette.

My troubles in Jalalabad continued. There were two people who gave me troubles. One of these men was much too interested in my financial means. His questions bothered me and then I decided to go back to Osama bin Laden in Kandahar. This happened a week or two after my return to Jalalabad. I met again with bin Laden and I asked him if I could do something for Islam. He told me that I didn't have to worry. He tried to brighten up the atmosphere.

While I was in Kandahar a discussion was under way about the possibility of destroying the Buddhist statues in Bamian. (The two statues of the Buddha, each more than a hundred feet high, were carved from cliffs in the third and fifth centuries A.D. They were once one of Afghanistan's most famous tourist attractions. The Taliban destroyed the Buddhas with artillery and explosives in May 2001.)

A day or so after my arrival in Kandahar Osama bin Laden suggested to me to accompany him to [Bamian in central Afghanistan]. We went there by helicopter. We stayed there a half day. We climbed the mountain and we participated in wrecking one of the statues, hitting it with our feet on its head. I remember that the [Taliban] explosives hadn't completely destroyed the statue and the Taliban launched a missile at the statue making a hole in Buddha's head.

When I got back home I resumed my activity and I watched the videocassette [of atrocities against Muslims] brought from Kandahar. After watching the videocassette I lost control of my emotions and I came back to Osama bin Laden in Kandahar. I stayed in a villa where bin Laden was. Afterward I left for a training camp close to the neighbourhood of Kandahar airport. When I arrived a rally against the Americans was under way. During the rally a video where Osama bin Laden and Ayman Zawahiri shook hands was recorded. Bin Laden announced that what happened to the USS *Cole* is nothing compared to what the Americans are in for next. During the rally [in July 2001] an alliance between Ayman Zawahiri and bin Laden was made against the Americans and the Jews. Before this alliance bin Laden and Zawahiri formed two separate groups. After the rally I came back to Kandahar where I stayed and I talked to Abu Hafs [al Qaeda's military commander].

I explained him my feelings after watching the videocassette and I spoke of my resentment towards the Americans. I expressed my wish to talk to Osama bin Laden, but he replied that I had to make a clear speech towards him. Then I said to Abu Hafs that I was ready to commit an attack. This meant for me a suicide attack, the offer of my life. As I was in a bad mood and I wanted to act in the fastest possible way, I didn't wait for Abu Hafs' answer and I went directly to bin Laden. I explained to [bin Laden] what I said to Abu Hafs and he expressed his reservations about my project. He suggested that I should wait because the list of [people wanting to be] martyrs was full.

The following day I talked again to bin Laden and I insisted a lot with him. He gave me his authorization to talk directly to Abu Hafs. In a certain way he was giving Abu Hafs an order. This meant that bin Laden had accepted that my name was to be added to the martyrs' list for the next attacks. Afterward I talked to Abu Hafs who told me that it was all right and I had only to wait. In the meantime someone informed me that my wife had problems. As she was pregnant, I decided to allow her to go back to Europe. I sold our house and my wife went back to Europe.

I spent three or four weeks in that villa [in Kandahar] where I was trained in the use of explosives. A certain number of targets were suggested to me, including what later became my target: an American base in Belgium. It was a NATO base in Kleine Brogel. The attack should have been carried out by three people beyond me: two of them, a Saudi and a Yemeni, were in the same villa in Kandahar with me. My assignment was to carry out the attack and to buy the ingredients to make the bomb.

I was given a list of chemical products to buy and I learned their names by heart. I took the Swissair flight Karachi-to-Zurich. Then I took a train to Brussels. One or two weeks after my arrival in Brussels I called a Saudi who was in Holland to check if the Saudi and the Yemeni guys who were trained with me had arrived. Yes was the answer.

I bought acetone, sulphur and nitrate. I tried also to buy hydrazine, without success. The hydrazine was later provided by the Saudi guy living in Holland. I surveyed the area [of the attack] to become familiar with it. The chosen place for the attack, Kleine Brogel [the NATO base], was suggested by the Saudi guy. No date was indicated for the attack. We only had to inform [al Qaeda] when the bomb was ready.

In 2003 Trabelsi was sentenced to ten years by a Belgian court for his plot to blow up the NATO base.

What follows are excerpts from the interrogation of a Canadian al Qaeda recruit, Mohammed Monsour Jabarah, by Canada's Security Intelligence Service in 2002. Jabarah was to attack the U.S. and Israeli embassies in the Philippines in late 2001. Similar targets were cased in Singapore. This plot was ultimately disrupted after documents and videos, relating to the Singapore operation, were found in Afghanistan during U.S. military operations. Jabarah fled to Thailand, Qatar, and then Oman.[6] He was arrested there in March 2002 and was delivered to Canadian and then U.S. authorities, with whom he has cooperated.[7]

Jabarah met with OBL [bin Laden] circa July 2001 in an effort to convince OBL of his potential as an AQ [al Qaeda] operative by highlighting his excellent English skills, his clean Canadian passport and his high standing in his AQ training courses. OBL was apparently impressed and told Jabarah to meet with Mohammed the Pakistani ["MP"], who would give Jabarah instructions and funds for an operation. Mohammed the Pakistani was identified by the source as Khalid Sheikh Mohamed [the 9/11 operational commander].

Jabarah travelled to Karachi, Pakistan, in mid-August 2001 to meet MP. MP provided advice and lessons on how to handle life in a city and how to prepare himself for AQ missions. This was necessary as he would need to be reacquainted with life outside Afghanistan. MP told Jabarah that Jabarah's job would be to provide money for a suicide operation in the Philippines. Jabarah would be the go-between for the local SE [Southeast] Asian operatives and AQ.

Jabarah was not asked to be a driver or a suicide bomber for an operation as there were hundreds of others in Afghanistan eagerly ready to fill that role. He was considered a more valuable entity given his abilities, language capability and his clean Canadian passport. After one week, Jabarah met a Malaysian man named Hambali at Hambali's apartment in Karachi. Hambali began giving details regarding the planned operations in the Philippines, including targets such as the American and Israeli embassies.

Next day, MP told Jabarah to make sure you leave before Tuesday, meaning that Jabarah had to ensure that he left Pakistan by September 11, 2001. According to the source, Jabarah understood this meant a big operation would happen on 11 September 2001, though he did not know where or what this would entail. The source advised that Jabarah now believes MP was one of the masterminds behind the 9/11 attack. M[P] gave Jabarah $10,000 for expenses.

Jabarah left [for] Hong Kong on 10 September 2001 and stayed there for three days. When Jabarah was in the hotel in Hong Kong, he began to question whether or not he could really handle the task at hand. He felt, however, that as OBL had personally chosen him out of all the men in Afghanistan, he simply couldn't refuse the operation. In the end, Jabarah decided to go ahead with the plans.

NOW

"Information derived from Mohammed Mansour Jabarah," U.S. Department of Justice, Federal Bureau of Investigation, August 21, 2002.[8]

Jabarah stated that there were code words used by al Qaeda. The code words were generally established by the individual cells. Some of the code words they used in Asia were:

Murkel = Malaysia
Soup = Singapore
Terminal = Indonesia
Hotel = Philippines
Book = Passport
American = White Meat

Feroz Ali Abbasi is a Ugandan Briton who was captured in Pakistan after the fall of the Taliban. He had trained at an al Qaeda camp in Afghanistan during 2000 and 2001. Imprisoned at Guantánamo Bay (and released in 2005), Abbasi wrote a 146-page prison memoir explaining how he was sounded out for a operation against the United States in the period before 9/11 not by bin Laden but by his key aides, Abu Hafs and Sayf Adel. They were interested in Abbasi because of a mistaken assumption that because he came from Britain, he had a non-Muslim name that would allow him to travel in the West without attracting attention.[9]

Abu Hafs and Sayf Adel were present in the room. The second and third highest in the command of al Qaeda. The interview went as follows:

Abu Hafs: "What is your real name"
Abbasi: "Why do you want to know that?"
Abu Hafs: "Do not worry. Everything you say here is confidential. What is your name?"
Abbasi: "Feroz Ali Abbasi."
Abu Hafs: "Where are you from?"
Abbasi: "I'm from Uganda."
Abu Hafs: It was at this point that he pushed his turban off his head

slightly and scratched. "Would you like to take any actions against the Americans and the Jews?

Abbasi: I replied, "Yes, I would like to take action against the American and Israeli forces because Jihad (military struggle against an aggressor) is an obligation on my person.

Abu Hafs: "Do you know of any involvement of the Jews in Uganda's affairs?

Abbasi: This question threw me right off. "No."

Abu Hafs: "Okay, we'll see about getting you some special training".

[They] had made the assumption that I had Christian name. I think I'm also right to speculate that Abu Hafs was actually looking for [this as a] most important condition to whatever he was devising. I did not get to hear about the scheme from Abu Hafs because they could not let me be party to such secrets if I could not be part of them. My name is wholly Islamic. And I think Abu Hafs had been thrown off when he had asked me what my name was expecting a Christian name.

According to the U.S. government, Feroz Abbasi heard bin Laden speak several times in al Qaeda training camps.[10] However, Abbasi did not have a personal audience with bin Laden, so for him al Qaeda's leader emerges as a somewhat remote figure in his memoirs. As far as Abbasi was concerned:

Abu Hafs was the brains behind al Qaeda, Osama bin Laden was just there for show.

Others with limited contact with al Qaeda's leader were more impressed. Mohammed Abdullah Warsame is a legal permanent U.S. resident and Canadian citizen who attended al Qaeda training camps in Afghanistan in 2000. The following is from the affidavit the FBI filed before a grand jury hearing his case in 2005.[11]

By the defendant's admission, in or about early 2000, he became interested in the "utopian" Muslim society that had been created in Afghanistan. Warsame maintained to the interviewing agents that he had not intended to travel to Afghanistan to attend a training camp but admitted that, soon after arriving in Kabul, Afghanistan, he in fact did attend an al Qaeda training camp

When asked how he knew that bin Laden was the Emir of the camp, the defendant stated that he saw him on several occasions, that he attended lectures given by bin Laden and that Warsame [the defendant] sat next to bin Laden [on the floor] at a meal. The defendant stated that bin Laden was very inspirational.

A jihadist recruit with a somewhat remote view of bin Laden was John Walker Lindh, the "American Taliban." Lindh was born in Washington, D.C., in February 1981, where he spent his childhood before his family moved to Marin County, California. When he was sixteen, he converted to Islam, which ultimately led him to travel to Yemen to study Arabic and then to Pakistan. In June 2001, he joined the Taliban and trained at the al Qaeda training camp al Farouq for seven weeks where he met bin Laden. Lindh was part of a Taliban force seized by the Northern Alliance in late November 2001, following the 9/11 attacks and the start of U.S. military operations. Below are excerpts from FBI reports of its interviews with Lindh in early December 2001. In these reports Lindh recalls meeting bin Laden and training in Afghanistan.

FBI report, "Interview of John Philip Walker Lindh," December 9–10, 2001.[12]

Lindh advised that Usama bin Laden (UBL) visited the camp [al Farouq] on three to five occasions and was usually accompanied by one or two of his sons. Lindh believes UBL's first visit was after having been in the camp for three weeks. UBL would give lectures on the local situation, political issues, old Afghan/Soviet battles, etc. Lindh, along with four others, met UBL for approximately five minutes in a private setting. UBL made small talk and thanked them all for taking part in the Jihad.

Lindh described UBL as being approximately 6'4", well built, sits down a lot, drinks a lot of water, tires easily, sometimes stops talking and excuses himself, mild mannered, and a quiet speaker. UBL traveled in at least two Toyota Landcruisers (believes white) in the company of at least six guards. Lindh believes the guards looked like they were from Saudi Arabia or Yemen, based on their features.

Within the first several weeks of the training, early June 2001, Lindh

stated that he believes the [camp's] Emir, Abdul Quddods, if not, another instructor told the trainees that UBL sent 50 people to carry out 20
"Amniat Istish Hadia" (suicide operations). The talk, amongst the group,
was that UBL had planned attacks against the U.S. and/or Israel.

Lindh, along with approximately 20 other foreigners (Brits, Australians, Africans, Filipinos) were called one by one to a meeting with
Abu Mohammad al Misri, Egyptian, the general manager of all camps.
Al Misri asked Lindh if he was interested in taking part in operations
against the United States and Israel. Lindh advised he declined and told
al Misri that he wanted to go to the front line and fight [against the
Northern Alliance]. At some point during the training, Lindh said he had
been offered to swear allegiance to UBL/al Qaeda. Lindh stated that he
declined; however, he swore allegiance to jihad.

**While most of those in al Qaeda's training camps had limited per-
sonal interaction with bin Laden, some visitors, who claim they were
not affiliated with al Qaeda, were granted relatively easy access to him.
Fouad al Rabia is a Kuwaiti held in Guantánamo who is married with
four children. Al Rabia is, by his own account, a businessman and relief
worker who was visiting Afghanistan in June of 2001 where he had a
purely social visit with bin Laden. Al Rabia says he was chosen by the
Kuwaiti government to run the Peshawar office of an Islamic relief
agency.**

**Al Rabia's testimony before a U.S. military tribunal in Guantánamo
starts as he leaves Kuwait with a Muslim scholar named Abu Muldah
who believes that bin Laden might be the key to leading the way to
the Mahdi, a savior figure in Islam; a person who is absolutely guided
by God.[13]**

As we were traveling from Kuwait, I realized the purpose of Abu
Muldah's trip to Afghanistan differed from mine. I was there to see the
refugees and to assist with their situation. Abu Muldah said there was a
missionary man that told him there was a ruler, bin Laden. Abu Muldah
said maybe bin Laden is al Abu Asaa [someone who will pave the way for
the return of the Mahdi]. Abu Muldah said he had to find out if this were
true. If this were not true, the word had to get out to the people so they
would not follow a false prophecy. I asked Abu Muldah how he was plan-

ning to see this person. I asked if we were going to climb mountains or go out in the middle of the night. Abu Muldah said no, and he was told that bin Laden is living inside a residence in Kandahar. Many people visit bin Laden there just like any normal person. Abu Muldah assured me we were not sneaking about to do anything illegal. I said fine. I am going to Afghanistan for my purpose.

To us in Kuwait before this, bin Laden was an eccentric millionaire who became a revolutionary. This was way before September [11] happened, and way before we realized what bin Laden was capable of doing. [Bin Laden's] house was in Kandahar, and everything looked peaceful there. We went inside. There were no guards and we were not searched. Bin Laden was sitting in an open room and he greeted us. We sat down. Abu Muldah talked and I listened.

Abu Muldah asked this person, bin Laden, where he was from; so on and so on. Then Abu Muldah asked bin Laden his opinion about killing civilians. I think Abu Muldah was referring to the bombing in Africa [of the two U.S. embassies in 1998]. Bin Laden replied, he did not order the bombing but he was not shocked by it. Bin Laden cited words from Arabic stating I do not order massacres, but I do not object if I see them. So, this did not sit well with Abu Muldah; al Abu Asaa is not supposed to be killing people, he was supposed to be preaching to them and guiding them, to [the Mahdi]. The conversation ended about late afternoon.

A young man named Abu Suliyman came and showed bin Laden the hand warmer [that Al Rabia had brought from Kuwait]. Abu Suliyman said that in Kuwait the item was used as an incense burner, but it is actually a hand warmer. It could be useful for people in the mountains. [Bin Laden] looked at me and said we would rather have three hundred pairs of woolen underwear instead of hand warmers.

Abu Muldah asked bin Laden straightforward what he wanted. Bin Laden said he wanted the Americans out of the Gulf. Then, I asked "How about Kuwait? Last time we had Saddam enter Kuwait [in 1990 before the first Gulf War] because there was no one there to protect us." Bin Laden said, "Look at the big picture," meaning it was okay for Saddam to enter Kuwait again.

It is our custom if someone invites you to their home, then before you leave the town, you have to go back and say farewell. So we went back to the house, but bin Laden was not there. So, Abu Muldah and I went into a room where a videotape was played of bin Laden's interviews with CNN, Al Jazeera, and other news agencies.

Nafia Noureddine was born in Morocco in 1967. In 1991 he left Morocco for Afghanistan, where he founded the Moroccan Islamic Combat Group. Noureddine's negotiations with al Qaeda's leaders are emblematic of the kinds of deals that they cut with smaller groups animated by a specific national grievance.[14]

At the beginning of 2001 I met with Osama bin Laden and Ayman Zawahiri. During the meeting I made a speech on the concepts of "Jamaa Islamiya Moukatila Maghrebia" [the Moroccan Islamic Combat Group] and I talked about the targets and the principles of the group. I asked al Qaeda's leader to support the group both materially and militarily. Osama bin Laden said that the group's members could have paramilitary training in al Qaeda's camps, inviting me to contact Abu Hafs [al Qaeda's military commander].

Two days after the meeting with bin Laden we had a meeting with Abu Hafs. [We were] promised the assistance of al Qaeda to train mujahideen and the men of the Moroccan Islamic Combat Group, and [were] handed over the sum of 3,000 dollars by way of support from al Qaeda to the group.

In September 2003 a tribunal in Morocco convicted Noureddine of "criminal association for the preparation of attacks aimed at destabilizing the public order and fabrication of documents," and sentenced him to twenty years.

⚜

Egyptian Mahmodu Abdelkader Es Sayed (aka Abu Saleh) was sentenced in absentia in Egypt for ten years for his role in the 1997 killings of fifty-eight foreign tourists in Luxor, Egypt. In the spring of 1998 Es Sayed arrived in Rome and requested political asylum. In late 1998 he moved to Milan, where he set up a mosque and was put under surveillance by DIGOS, an antiterrorist unit of the Italian police. On July 10, 2001, Italian law enforcement raided Es Sayed's apartment (he was not captured, having already fled Italy) where a letter was found dated May

14, 2001, with instructions for how militants could reach Kandahar, Afghanistan. On December 31, 2001, the Arabic daily *Al Hayat* confirmed that Es Sayed had been killed in Afghanistan.

What follows are edited transcripts of tape recordings made before the 9/11 attacks by Italian law enforcement of Es Sayed's discussions with his circle of like-minded jihadists. It is illustrative of a strong, almost mystical, desire amongst jihadists to travel to meet bin Laden.[15]

Conversation intercepted December 7, 2000, at 12.04 pm with a microphone planted in a Citroen ZX 16V, a car with the number plate 4-G9887, registered and used by Es Sayed.

Abu Saleh is Mahmodu Abdelkader Es Sayed, an Egyptian militant who forged documents for al Qaeda.
Nabil is Benattia Nabil, a Tunisian
Adel is Ben Soltane Adel, a Tunisian

Nabil—Today we've seen a sensational thing. I've seen four decapitated heads of Russians. (Probably a reference to videotapes widely circulated in militant circles, featuring jihadists fighting the Russians in Chechnya.)
Abu Saleh—What, decapitated or cut?
Nabil—Cut . . . (they laugh) as goats. It's a party . . .
Adel—Sheikh, if one wants to go and fight, why you don't let him go?
Abu Saleh—The important thing is that you dream of it. It's to cultivate your faith. When the moment arrives you'll never know if you will be a martyr here, in Algeria, in Tunisia, in America or in Central Asia.
Adel—I want to eliminate those pigs, those swine, I hate them.—It's necessary to leave. If only I could see the emir.
Abu Saleh—What emir?
Adel—The emir Abdallah [Osama bin Laden].
Abu Saleh—There's a long way to go, but take it into your head that all the paths are dangerous.
Adel—I'm ready to take them, it's better than staying here [in Milan].
Abu Saleh—You don't understand. To see the emir you've many ways to ride and many groups to pass. As for my past experience, before

getting a meeting with him, I had to swear with different groups, I was transferred in different training camps.

Nabil—What was your impression?

Abu Saleh—It's a sensation. I can't explain, pray with me.

Adel—This is what we ask, sheikh.

Nabil—Our places are in the mountains [of Afghanistan] and every person wishes this. He who doesn't think this way is a donkey that doesn't understand anything, because this is the way one can ride to face God.

The contents of the following conversation thirteen months before the 9/11 attacks are important because of references to a plot aimed at attacking the U.S. using airplanes.

Transcript of a conversation intercepted on August 12, 2000, hour 10.16 a.m., with a microphone planted in a Citroen ZX 16V, car with the number plate 4-G9887, registered and used by Es Sayed:

Abu Saleh is Mahmodu Abdelkader Es Sayed, the Egyptian militant who forged documents for al Qaeda.

Abdessalam is Ali Ali Abdulrahman Abdulsalam, a Yemeni who entered Italy holding a diplomatic passport.

Abu Saleh: How was your trip?

Abdessalam: Well, I'm studying airplanes.

Abu Saleh: What?

Abdessalam: I'm studying airplanes.

Abu Saleh: [Airplanes] of a Yemeni company or another?

Abdessalam: I hope, if God will wish, to bring you a window or a piece of an airplane the next time we will be together.

Abdessalam: But the surprise strike will come from the other country.

Abu Saleh: Yes.

Abdessalam: This will be one of those strikes that will never be forgotten.

Abu Saleh: Yes.

Abdessalam: It will wreak such a great havoc that they will never know how to put things in order. This is a terrifying thing. This is a thing that spreads from north to south, from east to west. The person who engineered this program is a madman from a mental hospital, a madman but a genius; he is obsessed with this program. He will leave all dumbfounded.

We will marry the Americans, so they will study the faith and the Koran. Remember, in the future listen to the news and remember these words. We can fight any power using airplanes, they can't even stop us with heavy arms, we have only to hit them, hit them in the dark, day and night, the important thing is to reach the goal. The danger is in the airports.

Abu Saleh: Rain, rain.

Abdessalam: Yes! There are clouds in the sky, in international territory, in that country the fire has been lit and is awaiting only the wind.

9

The 9/11 Plot

The 9/11 plot amply demonstrates the central importance that bin Laden plays in al Qaeda. While bin Laden did not involve himself in the details of the 9/11 operation, he was its ultimate commander. In 2002, when the Al Jazeera reporter Yosri Fouda interviewed Khaled Sheikh Mohammed and Ramzi bin al Shibh, who together had coordinated the 9/11 attacks, bin al Shibh told Fouda that he had traveled to Pakistan from Hamburg in late August 2001 to ensure that bin Laden was apprised of the timing of the attacks five days before they happened. Bin Laden's supervisory role in the attacks on Washington, D.C., and New York is amplified in the 9/11 Commission Report, which explains that in 1999 bin Laden appointed the Egyptian Mohammed Atta to be the lead hijacker. The report concludes, "It is clear, then, that bin Laden and Atef [his military commander] were very much in charge of the operation."[1]

Osama bin Laden discussed the 9/11 plot in a private meeting with a Saudi supporter that was recorded on videotape by al Qaeda sometime in November 2001. The tape was recovered in Jalalabad by U.S. forces after the fall of the Taliban. What follows are excerpts from that tape.[2]

We calculated in advance the number of casualties from the enemy, who would be killed based on the position of the tower. We calculated that the floors that would be hit would be three or four floors. I was the most optimistic of them all due to my experience in this field [of construction. I] was thinking that the fire from the gas in the plane would melt the iron structure of the building and collapse the area where the plane hit and all the floors above it only. This is all that we had hoped for.

[Members of al Qaeda in Afghanistan] were overjoyed when the first plane hit the building, so I said to them: "Be patient." The difference between the first and the second plane hitting the towers was twenty minutes. And the difference between the first plane and the plane that hit the Pentagon was one hour. We had notification since the previous Thursday that the event would take place that day. We had finished our work that day and had the radio on. It was 5:30 p.m. our time. Immediately, we heard the news that a plane had hit the World Trade Center. After a little while, they announced that another plane had hit the World Trade Center. The brothers who heard the news were overjoyed.

Sulayman Abu Ghaith, al Qaeda's spokesman, recalls sitting with bin Laden as the events of 9/11 unfolded on television.[3]

I was sitting with the Sheikh [bin Laden] in a room. Then I left to go to another room where there was a TV set. The TV broadcasted the big event. The scene was showing an Egyptian family sitting in their living room, they exploded with joy. Do you know when there is a soccer game and your team wins, it was the same expression of joy. There was a subtitle that read: "In revenge for the children of al Aksa' [the Palestinians], Osama bin Laden executes an operation against America." So I went back to the Sheikh [bin Laden] who was sitting in a room with fifty or sixty people. I tried to tell him about what I saw, but he made a gesture with his hands, meaning: "I know, I know."

In the summer of 2001 Jamal Ismail was working as a television correspondent in Pakistan with Abu Dhabi television. He remembers that a competing network announced some big news from al Qaeda's leaders.[4]

In late June [2001] Bakr Atyani, the bureau chief of MBC (Middle East Broadcasting Corporation) saw bin Laden in Afghanistan with Ayman al Zawahiri and Abu Hafs. Some aides of bin Laden informed him unofficially that "We have a big gift for the Intifada. We are going to strike against American interests more than the *Cole.*" The news was realized through MBC on the 23rd of June [2001]. The Taliban government denied this story and forced Abu Hafs to deny it immediately. After that report Mullah Omar asked bin Laden "do not do anything on Afghan soil without informing us."

Bakr Atyani, the former Middle East Broadcasting Company (MBC) bureau chief in Pakistan.[5]

[Al Qaeda] contacted me. MBC; it's an important channel in the Middle East, so maybe this is the reason. They took me to their place around Kandahar. You couldn't really figure out or identify where are you, especially as it was desert.

[Osama] was there with Ayman al Zawahiri and Abu Hafs—Mohammad Atef. [Osama] was very easy when he received me. Bin Laden said that he had had prepared a *mensaf* [Arabian rice and meat dish] in my honor because I was his guest. When I started eating I was embarrassed because the rice started falling through my fingers. Bin Laden looked at me and asked his assistant to go and fetch a knife and fork.

I said, "Now I need to do my job. Please can you bring [the] camera and then we can do the interview." Then they said, "We'll bring the camera but there's no interview."

Bin Laden said [to me] that he may not be able to speak directly in front of the camera because he promised the Taliban that he would not give any press statements. Osama said, "You are here because there is some material which we are going to give to you [footage of al Qaeda training and a celebration of the attack on the USS *Cole*] and some news. This is what we can give you now. When we were in front of the camera [bin Laden] didn't talk.

Abu Hafs [said,] "In the next few weeks we will carry out a big surprise and we will strike or attack American and Israeli interests." And that was the news [they were giving me] that day. I asked [Osama,] "Would you please confirm that." He smiled. That was [when the camera was not] recording. I believe that was the main reason [they had brought me there]. Well for me it was big news, really.

Abu Hafs, I realized that he is an important person. [The fact] that he was sitting with Osama. [Abu Hafs] is a very sharp person; you can see that from his eyes, very sharp. He asked me specific questions about myself and about my channel. And I recall one statement he said, "We are expecting an American strike, yes, but we are ready to evacuate our bases within 30 minutes."

When they brought their camera, Osama asked [Zawahiri] to come and sit near to him. So he came. Then [Osama] asked Abu Hafs. Abu

Hafs refused and said, "I don't want to be in front of camera." But it was very clear that when the three were sitting in the same place that they were having a good understanding. I believe that Abu Hafs was more close to Osama than Ayman.

I think really no one took [al Qaeda's threats] seriously. I remember when I was interviewed by the *Washington Post* [July 8, 2001, edition], their correspondent was Pamela Constable and she asked me after the interview, "Do you really believe that they are going to do it?" and I told her, "Really Pam, I believe, they're going to do it really, because it sounds serious."

Vahid Mojdeh is the former official in the Taliban foreign ministry.[6]

The journalist [from MBC], upon leaving Afghanistan, reported this incident with much flare and created a huge international brouhaha. This incident helped escalate tensions between Osama and [Taliban Foreign Minister] Muttawakil to new heights. Muttawakil said that from this point on the world would blame us for any attacks conducted against American targets anywhere.

This incident created more tension inside the Taliban. Muttawakil was of the thinking that the Taliban took Osama and his followers as guests, but now they want to destroy [Afghanistan].

An al Qaeda member revealed that in early 2001, their leaders issued an order to obtain a list of volunteers for suicide missions. In Kandahar, Kabul and east Afghanistan alone, 122 were found. If those in north Afghanistan had registered, the list would have been much longer. Al Qaeda members spoke openly about the martyrs of their suicide operations and made no effort to conceal it. Long before the 9/11 attacks al Qaeda talked in their gatherings of large-scale suicide missions against the U.S.

Abu Walid al Misri was the editor of Al Imara (The Emirate) magazine, the Arabic-language magazine of the Taliban. He also wrote a book about the "Afghan Arabs," serialized in the *Al Asharq al Awsat* newspaper in December 2004. An extract follows.[7]

Bin Laden's extremism reached the point where he believed that the United States was much weaker than some of those around him thought.

He stated this at several meetings and as evidence he referred to what happened to the United States in Beirut when the bombing of the Marines headquarters led them to flee from Lebanon [in 1983]. Some young Saudi followers confirmed to bin Laden his delusions from the gist of the experiences they had gained from their visits to the United States, namely, that the country was falling and could bear only few strikes. Relying on what apparently he liked to hear and what he had repeatedly asserted, they stressed to him that the United States could not bear two or three strong strikes. This view was basically wrong and dangerous.

According to Hamid Mir, bin Laden's Pakistani biographer, there was a widespread belief both inside the Taliban and among other Afghan leaders in the six months before the 9/11 attacks that the United States might invade Afghanistan.[8]

I met [Afghan leader Gulbuddin Hekmatyar] in Tehran in April 2001. He openly supported bin Laden: "Osama bin Laden is a great man and I support his ideology and I support his objectives. I know Osama bin Laden from many years. He is a good friend of mine and he is a real Mujahid," and he also predicted that Taliban government will fall this year. America will attack Afghanistan this year. He said that in April 2001, he was telling me that the Americans will attack Afghanistan, Taliban government will fall, and then we'll continue our jihad against the Americans.

It was 2nd or 3rd August 2001. Maybe forty days [before 9/11] in Kabul. I started reporting the information which I took from a senior official in Taliban defense ministry that we believe Americans are going to invade Afghanistan and they will do this before 15 October 2001, and justification for this would be either one of two options, Taliban got control of Afghanistan, or a big major attack against American interests either inside America or elsewhere in the world.

British cameraman Peter Jouvenal was using a twenty-three-year-old Afghan, "Ahmed," as a gofer in Kabul and Peshawar in 2001. At the same time Ahmed was also running errands for bin Laden. In the spring of 2001 Ahmed wanted to tell U.S. officials that al Qaeda was planning

to hijack jets in the United States to secure the release from U.S. prison of al Qaeda's spiritual guru, the Egyptian "Blind Sheikh" Omar Abdel Rahman. Ahmed approached Jouvenal to help him.[9]

I had been using Ahmed because he speaks very good English and Arabic and he is very good on computers. In those days Taliban were in control of Kabul. If I needed to see someone to talk to them about their story, I would send Ahmed. And so I was using him like a courier. I would have known him from about '99. And then one day he comes to me and he said, "Would you help me get to a foreign country? It's too dangerous for me here." And he started to tell me how he had been working for Osama as a courier; meeting people in Pakistan and taking them across the border, taking messages around for Osama, buying his food, taking messages to the Internet and logging on and receiving, printing, sending. He used to do his shopping for food. He said that bin Laden was into noodles and feta cheese. So he used to get him his feta for breakfast. And noodles to have in the evenings.

Ahmed needed an income. There was nothing else for a young kid in Kabul. So that's how he started getting involved. He looked a bit Arabic and he got on quite well with them speaking Arabic and that's how he ended up in Osama's circle.

Ahmed, told me most Arabs and Afghans respect Osama [because] if they knew he was coming to a house, they would always make a special effort to make it comfortable in a room. And he would always sleep somewhere else on the floor with his gun. He wouldn't want any refineries and basically roughed it all the time. And they were all very impressed by that.

Now, somewhere on the line Ahmed tied up with the CIA. And al Qaeda was trying to find him and they had met his family. When someone gets involved with al Qaeda, they actually come and meet your family members and they know where they live and stuff like that. So they were trying to find him.

In the Easter of 2001 [Ahmed] said that [al Qaeda was] planning to hijack an aircraft in the States, but he said that it was linked to try to get the blind sheikh [Omar Abdel Rahman] released. They were going to hijack an aircraft and then demand that the blind sheikh [be released].

Then the fun starts because I thought that maybe the FBI was a competent organization. One of the [FBI agents] was Lebanese, the other one was a New Yorker. And they said that they want me to go [with Ahmed] to Thailand. So I said, "What about a visa?" Ahmed said, "Oh, [the FBI agents] said its okay. They've sorted it all out." And I thought, well, this is the FBI, they are the big boys on the block. And so we get to the check-in counter. I handed over Ahmed's passport and ticket and they say, "Where is your visa?" We go back to the hotel: there is this message on my machine: "Don't tell anybody. We really fucked up," in the New York accent.

So [later Ahmed] goes off to Bangkok [the capitol], and spends three weeks hanging out waiting for these dickheads [the FBI] to come back. Fairly soon after, 9/11 happens and [Ahmed and his] whole family go off to the States. So obviously they [the FBI] become a bit more serious after 9/11.

This is the highly classified memo that President Bush received on August 6, 2001, about al Qaeda's determination to attack the United States, which was released during the course of the 9/11 Commission inquiries. The president was briefed about the memo at his ranch in Crawford, Texas, where he was taking a four-week vacation. The memo further underlines the centrality of Sheikh Omar Abdel Rahman to al Qaeda.

BIN LADIN DETERMINED TO STRIKE IN US
Clandestine, foreign government and media reports indicate Bin Ladin since 1997 has wanted to conduct terrorist attacks in the US. Bin Ladin implied in US television interviews in 1997 and 1998 that his followers would follow the example of World Trade Center bomber Ramzi Yousef and "bring the fighting to America."

After US missile strikes on his base in Afghanistan in 1998, Bin Ladin told followers he wanted to retaliate in Washington, according to a————service.

An Egyptian Islamic Jihad (EIJ) operative told an————service at the same time that Bin Ladin was planning to exploit the operative's access to the US to mount a terrorist strike.

The millennium plotting in Canada in 1999 may have been part of Bin Ladin's first serious attempt to implement a terrorist strike in the US. Convicted plotter Ahmed Ressam has told the FBI that he conceived the idea to attack Los Angeles International Airport himself, but that Bin Ladin lieutenant Abu Zubaydah encouraged him and helped facilitate the operation. Ressam also said that in 1998 Abu Zubaydah was planning his own US attack.

Ressam says Bin Ladin was aware of the Los Angeles operation.

Although Bin Ladin has not succeeded, his attacks against the US Embassies in Kenya and Tanzania in 1998 demonstrate that he prepares operations years in advance and is not deterred by setbacks. Bin Ladin associates surveilled our Embassies in Nairobi and Dar es Salaam as early as 1993, and some members of the Nairobi cell planning the bombings were arrested and deported in 1997.

Al-Qa'ida members—including some who are US citizens—have resided in or traveled to the US for years, and the group apparently maintains a support structure that could aid attacks. Two al-Qa'ida members found guilty in the conspiracy to bomb our Embassies in East Africa were US citizens, and a senior EIJ member lived in California in the mid-1990s.

A clandestine source said in 1998 that a Bin Ladin cell in New York was recruiting Muslim-American youth for attacks.

We have not been able to corroborate some of the more sensational threat reporting, such as that from a——————service in 1998 saying that Bin Ladin wanted to hijack a US aircraft to gain the release of "Blind Shaykh" 'Umar 'Abd al-Rahman and other US-held extremists.

Nevertheless, FBI information since that time indicates patterns of suspicious activity in this country consistent with preparations for hijackings or other types of attacks, including recent surveillance of federal buildings in New York.

The FBI is conducting approximately 70 full field investigations throughout the US that it considers Bin Ladin–related. CIA and the FBI are investigating a call to our Embassy in the UAE in May saying that a group of Bin Ladin supporters was in the US planning attacks with explosives.

In mid-August 2001, I was alerted to a two-hour al Qaeda videotape circulating on clandestine chat rooms on the Internet. I found the tape to be of great interest, as it was a professionally produced documentary that laid out all of al Qaeda's views and goals. The tape was the first

production of al Qaeda's video production arm; *Al Sahab (The Clouds)."* A brief description of the tape follows.[10]

Bin Laden dressed all in white, reads a poem recalling Saladin's victory over the Crusaders in the Middle Ages: "Saladin, his sword dripping with the blood of the Unbelievers."

Bin Laden: "Jews are free in al Quds (Jerusalem) to rape weak Muslim women and to imprison those young cubs who stand up to them. All the Arab presidents and kings betrayed the Muslim nation. It is better to seek out death, than to wait for it."

Film of Israeli soldiers striking out at Palestinian women, and of a young Palestinian boy who is shot, played over and over again.

Anguished narrator: "The Jews broke their word; we've been suffering for fifty years."

Shots of Israeli soldiers pushing Palestinian women, youths being shot at, bodies being dragged away.

Bin Laden punching the air for emphasis: "The blood of Muslims is the cheapest of all blood."

Abu Hafs (al Qaeda's military commander): "The scum of the earth, Jews and Israelis, have invaded our holy places."

Bin Laden: "We speak of the American government, but it is in reality an Israeli government, because if we look into the most sensitive departments of the government, whether it is the Pentagon or the State Department or the CIA, you find that it is the Jews who have the first word inside the American government. Consequently they use America to execute their plans throughout the world."

This last comment from bin Laden is quite illuminating. I was always puzzled by the fact that bin Laden, who had declared war on the "Crusaders and the Jews" in 1998, had hitherto not attacked Israeli or Jewish targets. After the 9/11 attacks I came to realize that for bin Laden, and his rabidly anti-Semitic colleagues, the Pentagon *was* a Jewish target.

I also found al Qaeda's new videotape alarming, as it seemed to presage a major al Qaeda attack. I emailed the following letter to John Burns, generally regarded as the *New York Times'* finest foreign correspondent. The 9/11 attacks were only three weeks away.[11]

August 17th 2001

John,

I think there is a major story to be told wrapping around the new bin Laden videotape and the various threats against US facilities in past months which can paint both a compelling picture of the bin Laden organization today, and responsibly suggest that an al Qaeda attack is in the works.

Let me try and lay it out for you. As you know there were very strong indications of attacks on U.S. targets in Yemen in June. Also in June two men were picked up in New Delhi, who said they were planning to blow up the busy visa section of the US embassy. There were also indications that they planned to blow up the American embassy in Bangladesh.

On July 18th the State Department issued a statement that the USG has "strong indications that individuals may be planning imminent terrorist actions against US interests in the Arabian Peninsula."

Clearly al Qaeda was and is planning something.

Now comes the two-hour bin Laden recruitment-propaganda tape, brief snippets of which were shown on CNN and Reuters ran a story about it when it surfaced in Kuwait in late June [2001]. But no one has looked at the entire tape, or if they have, they did not bother to sit down and translate the whole thing. The tape is in a Real Player format which can be played on Windows.

Also no one has thought to put the videotape in the context of al Qaeda's modus operandi which is to subtly indicate a plot is in the works before it takes place. We saw this in May 1998 when bin Laden held a press conference in Afghanistan where he talked of "good news in coming weeks" and a few days later told ABC News that he predicted a "black day" for America. Nine weeks later the embassies in Africa were bombed.

The Taliban later banned bin Laden from talking to journalists. Now bin Laden observes the letter, but not the spirit of the ban, by making himself available to his media arm who distributes his videotaped statements to Arabic media outlets around the world, which are then in turn picked up by Western media.

A few months before the Cole bombing [in Yemen], as you know, a tape appeared which is notable for two things: bin Laden is wearing the jambiya Yemeni dagger, which he had never previously worn in any of the dozens of photos that exist of him, and his deputy Ayman al Zawahiri specifically called for attacks on American forces in Yemen. This tape is of more than passing interest to U.S. investigators, and again shows how al Qaeda subtly signals its next move.

Now the videotape I have in hand is circulating around the Middle East, which has all sorts of juicy stuff on it detailed below, not least of which is that on the tape bin Laden makes a set of statements taking credit for a number of anti-American actions, his most explicit and wide-ranging to date.

The skillfully edited two-hour long recruitment/propaganda tape is a useful distillation of bin Laden views and al Qaeda's tactics. On the tape, bin Laden and his advisers make impassioned speeches about Muslims being attacked in Chechnya, Kashmir, Iraq, Israel, Lebanon, Indonesia and Egypt; speeches which are laid over graphic footage of Muslims being killed, beaten and imprisoned. The videotape devotes ten to fifteen minutes to images of Palestinians under attack by Israeli soldiers. There is also an important clue as to when the tape was possibly edited together as it shows [Israeli Prime Minister Ariel] Sharon, which implies the tape was put together in March [2001], or sometime thereafter, as Barak [Sharon's predecessor] resigned at the end of February.

For bin Laden, however, the greatest insult to Muslims is the continued presence of Americans in the holy land of Arabia. Bin Laden says: "These Americans brought women and Jewish women who can go anywhere in our holy land" adding "the Arab rulers worship the God of the White House." These statements are made over images of the Saudi royal family members meeting American leaders such as Colin Powell.

Bin Laden says that Muslims must seek revenge for these insults: "If you don't fight you will be punished by God." The Saudi exile says the solution to these problems is that Muslims should travel to Afghanistan, and receive training about how to do jihad. The tape then shows hundreds of bin Laden's masked followers training at his al Farooq camp in eastern Afghanistan, holding up black flags and chanting in Arabic "fight evil." Bin Laden's fighters shoot off anti-aircraft guns and RPGs, hold up their Korans and their Kalashnikovs, run across obstacle courses, dive into pools of water, blow up buildings and shoot at images of President Clinton. Bin Laden himself looses off some rounds from an automatic rifle. Chillingly, the tape also shows dozens of young boys, most of whom appear to be around ten, dressed in military camouflage uniforms, chanting for jihad while tackling the same obstacle courses seen earlier on the tape.

Towards the end of the tape, bin Laden implies more action against the United States: "The victory of Islam is coming. And the victory of Yemen [against the USS *Cole*] will continue . . ." The entire video is now available in a DVD format and is also circulating in clandestine chat rooms on the Internet, according to those familiar with bin Laden's organization. According to a Saudi dissident: "My information is that these threats on the videotape are genuine, that bin Laden's followers are making real preparations against more than one American target . . ."

I would love to collaborate on this story with you if you felt it made sense. And perhaps I am overestimating what I think is a really important story.

Look forward to talking to you. Best, Peter

John Burns subsequently wrote a prescient story headlined ON VIDEOTAPE BIN LADEN CHARTS VIOLENT FUTURE, which was posted to the *New York Times* Web site on September 9, 2001, but because of an editing dispute, the newspaper did not run a version of Burns's story until a day *after* the 9/11 attacks. In an Orwellian rewriting of history, the *Times* took Burns's pre-9/11 story off its Web site, an episode an editor later conceded to be "a bad screw-up." Excerpts of Burns's story follow.

The image on the grainy videotape is mesmerizing: a tall, slim, middle-aged Arab man, with the bushy beard, white robes and draped white head cloth of a devout Muslim, standing before a gathering somewhere in Afghanistan. He is reading an Arabic poem, apparently his own, on papers that riffle in a breeze.

In the verses, read at the wedding in Afghanistan of his oldest son earlier this year, Mr. bin Laden declares his purpose—killing Americans and Jews—more starkly than ever. Proudly, he salutes the suicide bombing of the American destroyer *Cole* in the Yemeni port of Aden last October in which 17 American sailors died, and promises more attacks.

Mr. bin Laden uses the tape to spell out a continuing nightmare for his principal enemies, the United States and Israel. He promises an intensified holy war that includes aid to Palestinians fighting Israel—an important shift in emphasis, according to intelligence analysts. In recent years, through a series of violent attacks, Mr. bin Laden's main focus has been on driving American forces from the Arabian peninsula.

He also outlines plans for an expansion of his terrorist training operations in Afghanistan, saying that the Taliban, the Islamic militant movement that has sheltered him since 1996, have built an ideal, purified Islamic state that provides the perfect base for a worldwide holy war against "infidels."

The same day that the *Times* chose to hold Burns's story Ahmad Shah Massoud, the Afghan commander who represented the only obstacle to the Taliban taking over the whole of Afghanistan, was assassinated by two al Qaeda members posing as television reporters.

Former Taliban official Vahid Mojdeh recounts how Massoud's killers insinuated themselves into Afghanistan.[12]

[Taliban Foreign Minister] Muttawakil was planning to close down Markaz al Elaam, an al Qaeda network that fronted itself by printing propaganda for the Taliban. Here, magazines in Arabic, Urdu, Pashto, English and Dari were printed. One day some cardboard boxes containing computer equipment arrived at the offices of Markaz al Elaam [in Kandahar]. The equipment had been shipped from Pakistan. The next day three people came to the center. One of them was Abu Hani, another was named Abed, and the third was introduced as Karim. These two last ones had recently arrived in Kandahar and claimed to live in Belgium.

They collected from amongst the boxes a big box, which had been marked and had a video camera in it and claimed that it was theirs. Once the box was opened the Taliban members present at the room were surprised to see a very old camera in it, which made Abed and Karim very anxious. The Taliban took notice of Abed and Karim's nervousness. Three days later the same three people came to the center saying they had an appointment with [Foreign Minister] Muttawakil. When the interview with Muttawakil was over, the translator asked to receive a copy of the interview video. They agreed, but this video never arrived.

It seemed that these three people had intentionally arranged the interview with Muttawakil, and taken the camera with them, to quench any curiosity raised the previous day. This showed extreme cautiousness on their part. Abed and Karim later went to Kabul and from there to northern Afghanistan, where they were able to assassinate Ahmad Shah Massoud.

Malika Malik, the Belgian wife of Abdessatar Dahmane, one of Massoud's assassins, wrote a self-published book in French about her husband's experiences in Afghanistan called *Soldiers of Light*. It recounts the story of how a Western woman and her Tunisian husband traveled from Belgium to Afghanistan, beguiled by bin Laden's message and his charismatic appeal. Excerpts of *Soldiers of Light* follow." [13]

The story of my husband and myself is one of a religious Muslim couple to which history threw up an unexpected act: my husband killed the famous Massoud, the "Lion of Panjshir" who had faced down the Russian army. But what pushed us to leave the comfort of a European country to go and share life with the Afghan people under the Taliban regime?

On the 9th of September 2001, a Sunday, an audacious 39-year-old Tunisian transformed himself into a kamikaze along with an accomplice who was 28. In the manner of the Palestinians, they exploded a bomb hidden in the belt of the younger of the two, but there was also a second bomb hidden in the camera, which appeared to be recording an interview with the chief opposition to the Taliban Commander Massoud, but in reality was going to kill the "Lion of Panjshir." One of the two small kamikazes died on the spot, and the other was taken down by bullets. It was the latter that was designated by the media the instigator of the crime. He was a criminal for some, but he was a hero for the oppressed people of the Third World who took hope that they could now be listened to and treated with a bit more respect and not just be manipulated according to the interests of the powerful of the planet. This hero was my husband, Abdessatar.

And so passed the days [while I was living in Jalalabad, Afghanistan] until the 12th of September [2001]. When I crossed the street a Pakistani woman addressed me in Arabic. I hardly understand the few words she says that make my heart freeze. I went to the mosque to the brother that my husband had entrusted me to. "What has happened to Abdessatar, this woman says he is dead?" He lowers his head. He doesn't want to talk about it in the street. A few minutes later he comes to my house and from behind the door he says, "Yes, it's true, Abdessatar is dead." We both could not stop crying. Apparently everybody knew that my husband was dead, but the agreement was not to tell me because my husband had recorded an audiocassette for me in which he announced his death to me himself. He had not wanted me to find out from somebody else. At that time I descended into deep depression. When the threat of a war by the Americans was announced, I didn't care if all the bombs in the world were to fall on me.

They did not leave me alone during this period. Ironically it was the time when the Afghans were celebrating the death of Massoud and dozens of Afghan women and non-Afghans came to congratulate me on what my husband had done. I eventually received this cassette that my husband had left for me to say a final goodbye, a final I love you. I hoped to find the reason for his action but there is none. I won't reveal the contents of the tape. Abdessatar would have wanted our last words to be between him and me. He told me he would love me to the end of my days.

The brother [who came to drop the audiotape] handed an envelope to me and said "This is Osama bin Laden that is sending this to you and here is $500 that he is giving you to reimburse the debt of your husband." I thanked him, but I did not understand why I had received an envelope from Osama bin Laden.

Malika Malik expanded in an interview on what she had written in her book.[14]

It wasn't a great amount [of money from bin Laden]. It was to repay a small debt. The money was not for me. We Muslims cannot die and leave debts. So when we make a will, we write the debts that we owe. When the person dies and it is found that they have debts, then their debts must be repaid. My husband had had a debt of $500 to somebody for several years. Apparently Osama knew this and this was a service he was rendering. If I had a debt I would have to let the person closest to me know in case I were to die. We can't have debts. It's very important.

I didn't meet the family of Osama bin Laden. But he [Osama] was there in Jalalabad. He was at a base. People spoke a lot about him. In every family the first born was called Osama. He was loved because he was combating injustice. He wanted to liberate the Islamic lands. That was the opinion of everyone. He was rich, he had money and he put his money at the service of his community and to spend it on others. That is worthy of being respected and loved. It's not everybody who does this. It's normal that we love him and he is a hero for us, a big brother, and the one who is calling out for Islamic resistance against occupation.

[My husband] Abdessatar never spoke to me about his meeting with Osama. I know only what people told me afterwards. They told me that he had met Osama. And that he gave him allegiance, that he put himself under bin Laden's orders.

Youssef al Aayyiri took control of al Qaeda's operations in the Gulf region in late 2002. He was on the Saudi government's most-wanted list and was killed in Riyadh in May 2003. *Voice of Jihad,* an al Qaeda magazine in Saudi Arabia, printed his biography. This excerpt deals with al Qaeda's role in and reaction to Massoud's assassination.[15]

Afterwards, the greatest event in Afghan history occurred—the assassination of the despicable commander, Ahmed Shah Massoud, and there was no describing Sheikh al Aayyiri's joy. I remember asking him, "What happened?" And he replied by saying that Sheikh Osama asked the brothers: "Who will take it upon himself to deal with Ahmed [Shah] Massoud for me, because he harmed Allah and His sons?" A few brothers volunteered to assassinate Massoud and be rewarded by Allah, and you heard the good news.

Feroz Ali Abbasi is the Ugandan Briton who was captured in Pakistan after the fall of the Taliban. An excerpt of his prison memoir follows.[16]

The significant event was the death of Massoud. We got wind from the brothers then listened to the radio. Massoud had been taken out by a martyrdom operation—the Arab mujahideen were responsible. When this happened I thought that at last the Taliban were going to take the whole of Afghanistan. Massoud was crucial to the Northern Alliance. He was a highly skilled General.

I was so touched by the event that I went to Sayf al Adel [al Qaeda's number two military commander] in his office. I was nervous but wanted to put my request in. I said to him "I heard about Massoud being killed by a martyrdom operation. I would like to do something like that (e.g., martyrdom operation against a military target)." He said, "Did you like the operation against Massoud?" I said, "Yes."

Abdullah Anas is an Algerian who fought alongside Massoud for eight years during the jihad against the communists.[17]

I swear to Allah. Massoud is the clearest, the purest mujahid inside Afghanistan. The purest Islamists are not extremists, but Massoud is an Islamist, a very deep Islamist, but not an extremist.

Jamal Khashoggi is a Saudi journalist who covered both bin Laden and Massoud during the Afghan war against the communists.[18]

[Massoud was] very pragmatic. And maybe Massoud is the future of the Islamic movement. Pragmatic Muslims can make success, but rigid Muslims do not succeed because they will just keep on fighting left, right, and center.

I met Massoud in Kabul in the first week after he captured Kabul [in 1992]. And I fell in love with him just like everybody else. He was truly an astonishing guy. I wish that Osama met Massoud. Maybe if Osama met Massoud it could have changed the course of history.

Khalid Sheikh Mohammed, the key operational planner of the 9/11 attacks, spent his childhood and adolescence in Kuwait. He joined the Muslim Brotherhood at age sixteen and, after attending college in the United States, traveled to Pakistan and then Afghanistan for jihad against the Soviets. In 1996, he met bin Laden in Tora Bora, Afghanistan, long after their first encounter during the Afghan jihad. It was

then that Sheikh Mohammed "presented a proposal for an operation that would involve training pilots who would crash planes into buildings in the United States."[19] On March 1, 2003, Khalid Sheikh Mohammed was arrested in Rawalpindi, Pakistan, near Islamabad, and was subsequently transferred to U.S. custody. He remains held at an undisclosed location. Excerpts of the 9/11 Commission's profile of Khalid Sheikh Mohammed, or KSM, follow.[20]

KSM continued to travel among the worldwide jihadist community after [Ramzi] Yousef's arrest [in 1995], visiting the Sudan, Yemen, Malaysia, and Brazil in 1995. No clear evidence connects him to terrorist activities in those locations. In January 1996, well aware that U.S. authorities were chasing him, he fled to Afghanistan.

Just as KSM was reestablishing himself in Afghanistan in mid-1996, bin Laden and his colleagues were also completing their migration from Sudan. Through Atef, KSM arranged a meeting with bin Laden in Tora Bora, a mountainous redoubt from the Afghan war days. At the meeting, KSM presented the al Qaeda leader with a menu of ideas for terrorist operations. According to KSM, this meeting was the first time he had seen bin Laden since 1989. Although they had fought together in 1987, bin Laden and KSM did not yet enjoy an especially close working relationship. Indeed, KSM has acknowledged that bin Laden likely agreed to meet with him because of the renown of his nephew, Yousef, [who masterminded the first attack on the Trade Center in 1993].

At the meeting, KSM briefed bin Laden and Atef on the first World Trade Center bombing. KSM also presented a proposal for an operation that would involve training pilots who would crash planes into buildings in the United States. This proposal eventually would become the 9/11 operation. KSM knew that the successful staging of such an attack would require personnel, money, and logistical support that only an extensive and well-funded organization like al Qaeda could provide. He thought the operation might appeal to bin Laden, who had a long record of denouncing the United States.

From KSM's perspective, bin Laden was in the process of consolidating his new position in Afghanistan while hearing out others' ideas, and had not yet settled on an agenda for future anti-U.S. operations. At the meeting, bin Laden listened to KSM's ideas without much comment, but did ask KSM formally to join al Qaeda and move his family to Afghanistan.

KSM declined. He preferred to remain independent and retain the option of working with other mujahideen groups still operating in Afghanistan. According to KSM, the 1998 bombings of the U.S. embassies in Nairobi and Dar es Salaam marked a watershed in the evolution of the 9/11 plot. KSM claims these bombings convinced him that bin Laden was truly committed to attacking the United States. He continued to make himself useful, collecting news articles and helping other al Qaeda members with their outdated computer equipment. Bin Laden, apparently at Atef's urging, finally decided to give KSM the green light for the 9/11 operation sometime in late 1998 or early 1999.

KSM then accepted bin Laden's standing invitation to move to Kandahar and work directly with al Qaeda. In addition to supervising the planning and preparations for the 9/11 operation, KSM worked with and eventually led al Qaeda's media committee. But KSM states he refused to swear a formal oath of allegiance to bin Laden, thereby retaining a last vestige of his cherished autonomy.

At this point, late 1998 to early 1999, planning for the 9/11 operation began in earnest. Yet while the 9/11 project occupied the bulk of KSM's attention, he continued to consider other possibilities for terrorist attacks. During the summer of 2001, KSM approached bin Laden with the idea of recruiting a Saudi Arabian air force pilot to commandeer a Saudi fighter jet and attack the Israeli city of Eilat. Bin Laden reportedly liked this proposal, but he instructed KSM to concentrate on the 9/11 operation first.

KSM appears to have been popular among the al Qaeda rank and file. He was reportedly regarded as an effective leader, especially after the 9/11 attacks. Co-workers describe him as an intelligent, efficient, and even-tempered manager who approached his projects with a single-minded dedication that he expected his colleagues to share.

Yosri Fouda, Al Jazeera's chief investigative reporter, never met with bin Laden, but he is the only reporter to have interviewed Khalid Sheikh Mohammed and Ramzi Binalshibh, the operational planners of the 9/11 attacks. Fouda met them both in the spring of 2002, in Karachi, Pakistan, where they laid out the details of the 9/11 plot. Much of what

**they volunteered to Fouda was later confirmed by the 9/11 Commission
Report.**[21]

I walk upstairs. I make my way upstairs with my intermediary, who
drove me from outside Karachi. I counted four floors as I was walking
upstairs. I hear a doorbell ringing. And then he started taking my blind-
folds off. I open my eyes. It took me a while to get used to the place. I
counted four rooms including the kitchen. And, in one of the rooms inside, there was another guy sitting on the floor surrounded by laptops
and mobile phones. By then, I started to get the idea, but I was not absolutely sure. Khalid Sheikh Mohammed asked me, "Have you recognized us yet?" I said, "You look familiar." I knew by then who they were.

They told me the whole story. Khalid said that between two-and-a-half
years and three years before the zero hour [9/11], they held some meetings within [al Qaeda's] military committee and discussed planning and
executing an operation against some American targets on American soil.
They sent some reconnaissance units into the United States to study some
recommended targets on the ground. He threw a heavyweight punch at
me at the very beginning when he said that they did consider striking at a
couple of nuclear facilities. And he said that later they decided to take it off
the list because they were not sure if they could control the operation.

They said having studied the targets on the ground, that the White
House was initially on the list, but they decided that it be taken off the
list for navigation reasons. Apparently it was difficult to hit it from the air,
according to them. And it was later replaced by another spectacular target, Capitol Hill.

Khalid Sheikh Mohammed is a very shrewd man. He knows very well
what he's after, very much aware of security. And he is very much an operational man rather than a man of religion. For instance, when it was
time for prayers, in Islam usually the eldest would lead the rest in the
prayer, and although Ramzi [Binalshibh] was younger than Khalid, he is
about eight years his junior, he was leading us in the prayers. That tells
you that Ramzi is really a man of religion, and he struck me as such.
Khalid is not. Khalid is very much a man of operations, a man of action,
he is very restless. Yes, he is a Muslim, and he prays, and he is the son of
a preacher in Kuwait, but he didn't strike me as a man of religion.

Nobody knows exactly the timing when Khalid Sheikh Mohammed

decided to ally with bin Laden. But it would seem to me that it was around the time of '96, '97 that Khalid found in bin Laden some sort of a mentor, a religious umbrella under which he could express his operational skills. When the so-called Bojinka operation [to bring down a dozen U.S. airliners in Asia] failed, Khalid Sheikh Mohammed looked around, and the year after, in 1996, bin Laden moved to Afghanistan. Bin Laden needed someone like [Khalid Sheikh Mohammed]. Bin Laden is the symbol of al Qaeda, the Sheikh, the ultimate boss of al Qaeda. Khalid Sheikh Mohammed is the guy who gets things going. He has a very long, solid experience in this.

In 1995, Khalid Sheikh Mohammed tried to execute a spectacular operation, a mini-9/11 at the time, with a dozen American airliners in [Asia] and crashing them. It failed, but the dream of Khalid Sheikh Mohammed never faded. He's very much an operational man, in short. He likes being on top of a certain operation, directing people here and there, thinking of targets and stuff. It's in a sense also a game. He puts it in a religious context. When I arrived first to that safe house in Karachi, I said, "They say that you are terrorists." Khalid said, "Yes, they are right; we are terrorists. We like to terrorize disbelievers."

It doesn't surprise me [that Khalid Sheikh Mohammed organized 9/11]. It's not exactly bin Laden's territory. He's not very fond of details, looking at details. He's the enigma; he's the chairman of the company, so to speak. He is the symbol of the organization. He would still need people like Khalid Sheikh Mohammed to be advising him on certain operations, and Khalid Sheikh Mohammed would, in turn, need people to execute things.

What follows are excerpts from Fouda's documentary, The Road to September 11th, which was broadcast on Al Jazeera on the first anniversary of the attacks. Khaled Sheikh Mohammed and Binalshibh's subsequent statements to U.S. interrogators, which are reflected in the 9/11 Commission Report, track closely with what they said in Fouda's documentary.[22]

Ramzi Binalshibh:

As for your questions about coordination [of the 9/11 attacks], it is simply a process of interconnecting various cells, establishing a line of contact between these cells and the General Command in Afghanistan as well as following up on work priorities of these cells until all phases of preparation are complete—up to the moment of execution.

I spoke with brother Ziad [Jarah one of the pilots in the 9/11 attacks] and asked him: "How do you feel?" He said: "My heart is at ease, and I feel that the operation will, inshallah (God willing), be carried out."

[In late January 2001] what the [9/11 pilots] now needed were more flying hours, more training on simulators of large commercial planes such as Boeing 747 and 767 as well as studying the security precautions in all airports. One of the times, brothers Marwan and Ziad [two of the 9/11 pilots] were tailed by security officers throughout their reconnaissance flight, from New York to California, but God was with them.

[The lead hijacker, Mohammed Atta,] used to assure us that we shall one day meet. He always said: "Do not be saddened. We shall soon meet in paradise by the will of God." I told him that if he was to see the Prophet Mohammed, peace be upon him, and reach the highest place in heaven, he should convey our salaam (greetings) to him.

Khalid Sheikh Mohammed:

[The so-called muscle hijackers who were not the pilots] knew they were in for a martyrdom operation. But, to prevent any leakage of information, they were not informed of many details. We told them that brother Abu Abdul Rahman [the lead hijacker, Mohammed Atta,] would provide them with details at a later stage.

Ramzi Binalshibh:

[Shortly before the 9/11 attacks Mohammed Atta] told me in an Egyptian dialect: "A friend of mine gave me a puzzle I am unable to solve, and I want you to help me out." I said to him: "Is this time for puzzles, Mohammed?" He said: "Yes, I know, but you are my friend and no one else but you can help me." He said, "Two sticks, a dash, and a cake with a stick down. What is it?" I said: "You wake me up to tell me this puzzle?!" As it turns out, sticks is the number 11, a dash is dash, and a cake with a stick down is the number 9. And that was September 11th." (Outside the United States, the date September 11 is written 11-9 rather than 9/11.)

These were very apprehensive moments. You are going into an unconventional battle against the most powerful force on earth. You are facing them on their land, among their forces, and soldiers, you fight with a small group of 19 [hijackers].

This is not just a single hijacking operation, but four. It was crucial that all were executed simultaneously, and that all the brothers are on the flights at the same time. And it is crucial to consider the first 15 minutes as the golden opportunity to take control of the aircraft and steer it toward its target.

[The day of the attack,] all camps and residential compounds [in Afghanistan] were put on high alert. Brothers were dispersed. The message was great news for Sheikh Abu Abdallah (bin Laden), may God protect him.

[When they found out], the brothers shouted "Allah-u-Akbar! Thanks to God!" and cried. Everyone thought that this was the only operation (the attack on the first World Trade Center tower). We said to them: "Wait, wait." Suddenly our brother Marwan [the pilot] was violently ramming the plane into the Trade Center in an unbelievable manner! We were watching live and praying: "God . . . aim . . . aim . . . aim. . . ."

Immediately after the Al Jazeera documentary aired, Ramzi Binalshibh was arrested in Karachi, Pakistan, on September 11, 2002, and was then transferred to U.S. custody.

The U.S. Department of Justice provided summaries of the interrogations of Ramzi Binalshibh to German prosecutors in May 2005 for a terrorism case in Hamburg. These summaries show that it was a chance encounter on a train in Germany in 1999 that led the key 9/11 plotters to travel not to Chechnya to perform jihad as they had originally planned, but rather to Afghanistan, where they would fatefully meet with al Qaeda's top leaders, including bin Laden, and from there they would start down the road to implementing the 9/11 attacks two years later. Excerpts of what the Department of Justice provided to the Hamburg court follow.[23]

The following comments come entirely from Ramzi Binalshibh and may have been meant to influence as well as to inform. Binalshibh may also have been intentionally withholding information and employing counterinterrogation techniques.

Binalshibh stated that his initial contact with Mohamed Ould Slahi, also known as Abu Musab al Mauritania, occured in late October or early November 1999 by telephone. Binalshibh had been given Abu Musab's name and telephone number by a man name Khalid al Masri, whom Binalshibh met while traveling via train in Germany with Marwan al Shehhi and [Ziad] Jarrah [two of the 9/11 pilots]. Binalshibh reported that the meeting on the train was entirely by chance, and that Khalid probably approached them because they were bearded and had Gulf Arab appearances.

Abu Musab gave Binalshibh a date and told him to travel to Duisburg, Germany, for a personal meeting, which Binalshibh, Ziad, and Marwan did about two or three days later. Binalshibh said the train ride from Hamburg to Duisburg was about three or four hours, and Abu Musab met them at the train station. After hearing about their desire to travel to Chechnya, Abu Musab discussed the difficulties of traveling to that country and of the dangers individuals faced in traveling by way of Georgia [a country abutting Chechnya]. According to Abu Musab, many travelers were arrested and held at will by the local authorities in Georgia. Binalshibh stated that, at this point, Abu Musab began to convince the group that it would be in their best interest to travel to Afghanistan. According to Binalshibh, Abu Musab told them that the best route to Chechnya was via Afghanistan, where they would get the necessary training for the Jihad and have a chance to meet other jihadists who had been to Chechnya. Abu Musab indicated that it would eventually be possible for the group to travel onward to Chechnya.

Binalshibh said they were initially suspicious of Abu Musab, but came to trust him as the meeting progressed. Abu Musab told them that the first step was to get Pakistani visas, as Pakistan would serve as their point of entry for onward travel to Afghanistan. He instructed them to apply for the visas using their authentic passports and to return in a specific period of time. Binalshibh was unsure how much time passed between the first and second meetings, but estimated it was approximately two or three weeks.

Binalshibh said that, although Mohammed Atta [the lead hijacker] did not attend the meetings, he also decided to go to Afghanistan. They each applied for and acquired a 30-day Pakistani visa. Atta got his visa in

Berlin; Marwan went to the United Arab Emirates to get his visa; and Binalshibh and Ziad acquired their visas in Frankfurt, Germany.

In approximately November 1999, once the group had obtained their visas, they called Abu Musab, who instructed them to travel, again to Duisburg. Abu Musab was waiting for the group upon their arrival at the train station and brought them to this house. Once he confirmed that they had received their Pakistani visas, he instructed them to travel to Karachi, Pakistan, and from there to Quetta [Pakistan]. Binalshibh clarified that the group made the trip to Afghanistan between mid-November 1999 and December 1999.

Ali Hamza Ahmad Sulayman al Bahlul, a Yemeni, is accused of serving in al Qaeda's media office and as bin Laden's bodyguard at the time of the 9/11 attacks. Excerpts from his Guantánamo charge sheet describe what was allegedly happening in al Qaeda's camps around the time of 9/11.[24]

After being placed on alert by Osama bin Laden in the weeks just before the attacks of September 11, 2001, al Bahlul assisted Osama bin Laden and other al Qaida members in mobilizing and moving from Qandahar [the city of Kandahar in southern Afghanistan].

On September 11, 2001, Osama bin Laden tasked al Bahlul to set up a satellite connection so that bin Laden and other al Qaida members could see news reports. Despite his efforts, al Bahlul was unable to obtain a satellite connection because of mountainous terrain.

In the weeks immediately following the attacks of September 11, 2001, Osama bin Laden tasked al Bahlul to obtain media reports concerning the September 11th attacks and to gather data concerning the economic damage caused by these attacks.

Both prior to and after the attacks of September 11, 2001, al Bahlul served as a bodyguard and provided protection to Osama bin Laden. From late 2000 until November 2001, al Bahlul routinely traveled in a caravan of vehicles with Osama bin Laden. While traveling, al Bahlul was armed and wore an explosives-laden belt so that he could provide Osama bin Laden with physical security and protection.

Feroz Ali Abbasi describes his surprise that there was no American action against bin Laden, given that it was common knowledge around al Qaeda's camps that an attack against the United States was imminent.[25]

Bin Laden was in a country that was favorable to him and his people. He was always surrounded by people and although he took precautions (like bodyguards), strangers, people he did not know, could actually come close enough on occasions to shake his hand. It's BS that Osama bin Laden hid in super-tech caves all over Afghanistan. Where are the caves! There are none! Where were America's, in fact the world's special agents on the ground in Afghanistan? They must have been there but yet they did not catch wind that Osama bin Laden was planning an attack on an American target. This information being so commonly known amongst everybody in the training camps. What was stopping them [the Americans] from assassinating bin Laden? Was it the fact that, that because Osama bin Laden was surrounded by his own people that would have meant sacrificing, yes sacrificing, one American life for thousands?

Abu Musab al Suri is the Syrian jihadist who had sometimes clashed with bin Laden.[26]

In September 2001, bin Laden told his followers that it was time to leave [Afghanistan] and go back to Yemen. As rumors, astonishment and hope of this change spread among the Arab Afghans, the 11th of September explosions occurred.

Sayf Adel, al Qaeda's present military commander.[27]

The Goals of the New York Strike: Since its establishment and independence from the British crown and for more than two centuries of human history, the United States has gone on the rampage everywhere in the world. It was intimidating and assaulting people. It was seizing the resources of nations. Some people might be surprised if we tell them that the United States was preparing its armada to occupy Algeria in 1817. Mujahidin and Arab sailors in the Mediterranean—whom the West labeled as [the Barbary] pirates—confronted and defeated the

U.S. fleet. The battles between the U.S. and Islamic parties lasted for more than three months.

Our main objective, therefore, was to deal a strike to the head of the snake at home to smash its arrogance. This objective was partially achieved, thank God. Had the other strikes succeeded the way the strike against the Twin Towers did, the world would have felt the sudden change. Our ultimate objective of these painful strikes against the head of the serpent was to prompt it to come out of its hole. This would make it easier for us to deal consecutive blows to undermine it and tear it apart. It would foster our credibility in front of our nation and the beleaguered people of the world. A person will react randomly when he receives painful strikes on his head from an undisclosed enemy. Such strikes will force the person to carry out random acts and provoke him to make serious and sometimes fatal mistakes. This was what actually happened.

The first reaction was the invasion of Afghanistan and the second was the invasion of Iraq. The mistakes might happen over and again and there might be other random reactions. Such reactions prompted the Americans and their allies to deal powerful strikes to the head and other important parts of the body of our nation, which has been in hibernation for almost two centuries. God willing, these strikes will help the nation to wake from its slumber.

Abdul Aziz al Omari, a Saudi from Asir Province, together with Mohammed Atta and three other terrorists, boarded American Airlines Flight 11 at Boston's Logan International Airport on the morning of September 11. At 8:45 a.m., American Flight 11 crashed into the North Tower of the World Trade Center. The following are excerpts of al Omari's videotaped "will," which was broadcast by Al Jazeera on September 10, 2002.

I am writing this will and do not know where I should begin. Ideas are accumulating in my mind. This is a message to all the infidels and to America. The message is: "Leave the Arabian Peninsula defeated and stop supporting the coward Jews in Palestine." We will continue to seek your death and humiliation so long as the book of God and the teachings of Prophet Muhammad are in our hands.

I would like to particularly mention mujahid leader Sheikh Osama bin Laden, may God protect him from the plots of the plotters, the envy of the envious ones and the rancor of the rancorous ones. May God add these deeds to his balance of good deeds.

Mohammed Atta, the lead hijacker, left a copy of his own "will" in some baggage that was recovered at Boston's Logan Airport after the 9/11 attacks. An excerpt follows.[28]

Those who wash my body must be good Muslims. He who washes my body around my genitals should wear gloves so that I am not touched there. (Of course, Atta's body was atomized in the 9/11 attacks. There was no body to wash or bury.)

No one should cry for me, scream or tear his clothes and beat his face—those are foolish gestures.

Neither pregnant women nor unclean people should say goodbye to me—I reject that. Women must not be present at my funeral or go to my grave at any later date.

This was the exchange between ABC News correspondent John Miller, who had interviewed bin Laden in Afghanistan in May 1998, and ABC News anchor Peter Jennings at 10:29 a.m. on September 11, 2001.

MILLER: The north tower seems to be coming down.

JENNINGS: Oh, my God.

MILLER: The second—the second tower.

JENNINGS: (*A very long pause.*) It's hard to put it into words, and maybe one doesn't need to. Both Trade Towers, where thousands of people work, on this day, Tuesday, have now been attacked and destroyed with thousands of people either in them or in the immediate area adjacent to them.

10

The Fall of the Taliban
and the Flight to Tora Bora

Bin Laden disastrously misjudged the American response to the 9/11 attacks, which he believed would be one of two strategies: an eventual retreat from the Middle East along the lines of the U.S. pullout from Somalia in 1993, or a full-scale American ground invasion of Afghanistan similar to the Soviet invasion of 1979, which would then allow the Taliban and al Qaeda to fight a classic guerrilla war. Neither of these two scenarios happened. The U.S. campaign against the Taliban was conducted with massive U.S. airpower, tens of thousands of Northern Alliance forces, and no more than three hundred U.S. Special Forces soldiers on the ground. And al Qaeda, which means "the base" in Arabic, subsequently lost the best base it ever had. 9/11 may have been a tactical victory for al Qaeda, but it was a strategic disaster for the organization.

Osama bin Laden.[1]

America is a great power possessed of tremendous military might and a wide-ranging economy, but all this is built upon an unstable foundation which can be targeted, with special attention to its obvious weak spots. A small group of young Islamic [fighters] managed to provide people with proof of the fact that it is possible to wage war upon and fight against a so-called great power. They managed to protect their religion better than the governments and peoples of the fifty-odd countries of the Muslim world, because they used Jihad as a means to defend their faith.

Jamal Ismail, Abu Dhabi television's correspondent in Pakistan in 2001.[2]

Next day morning [after 9/11] I received the message from Osama. He did not claim responsibility. Someone came from Afghanistan, he said to me, "Jamal, I came last night in a hurry from Afghanistan." I said "Okay, just give me one moment. Let me write whatever you are saying." He read it and I edited it and typed it on the computer. I dispatched it through fax and read it on telephone for Abu Dhabi television. In that message Osama did not claim responsibility. He said, "We believe what happened in Washington and elsewhere against Americans, it was punishment from Almighty Allah and they were good people who have done it. We agree with them." And Osama never praised anyone who is non-Muslim. From this I determined he knows something and he's confident of their identity; they have links.

When the second plane hit the Trade Center, I knew it was al Qaeda. No other group had both the intention and capability of attacking the United States. I was sure that there was going to be a major al Qaeda attack against American targets sometime that summer, but I could not conceive that it would be in the United States itself. But as the second plane hit I remembered that one of bin Laden's men, Ihab Ali, had trained in the U.S. as a pilot in the nineties and bin Laden himself had arranged for the purchase of a jet in Arizona in 1993.

Jamal Khashoggi is the Saudi journalist who covered bin Laden in the mid-1980s.[3]

I was in my office in *Arab News* in Jeddah [Saudi Arabia]. I was thinking of Osama at that time. I was thinking of him—no doubt about it. Two days later I wrote an article about 9/11 and I said, "May God help us. The Americans will come out from their wounds, but we will have a problem to last us some time." And I think I'm right.

Paulo José de Almeida Santos, a Portuguese convert to Islam, was an early al Qaeda recruit who met bin Laden on a number of occasions in Pakistan in 1990 and 1991.[4]

The Koran and Islam expressly forbid the death of women, children and old people. What leaves a rather bitter taste in my mouth was that planes were used, on which there were innocent people and perhaps even children. I believe it was a strategic mistake to attack the towers of the World Trade Center. If they had attacked Langley, it might have been more intelligent. Langley is the CIA base. It would be a legitimate act of war. In the Towers, people of many, many nationalities died, many of them neutral.

When we were in Afghanistan [in the 1990 period], our objective was to create an Islamic State, a caliphate [a Muslim community modeled on the first days of Islam]. This objective has, in recent years, changed. At present, the objective seems to me to be to wage war on the United States. I do not believe that we have the possibility of [successfully] going to war against the United States. As regard the Towers, I continue to believe it was a mistake. But if it had been the Pentagon or Langley, I could give my support.

Brian Fyfield-Shayler, bin Laden's former English teacher in Saudi Arabia.[5]

When his face and those very soulful eyes again appeared as the backdrop of the news commentaries on September 11th, I will say that there is something amiss here because the student I knew was not a fanatic at that age, so something has happened between the time I knew him and the time of these hideous events. So that was my motivation in going public: to say that instead of just screaming, "Oh, what a monster this is, what an appalling person and how terrible these fanatics and fundamentalists and so on are," I should say, hold on: there is a flesh and blood person behind all this. There is a very pleasant, charming, ordinary, not exceptional student. What is it that turned him from that into the person with the views he has today? And, of course, I thought it might have been his experiences in Afghanistan.

Bakr Atyani, the MBC bureau chief in Pakistan, had been told by al Qaeda's leaders ten weeks before that a big attack against American interests was in the works.[6]

I believed that al Qaeda was behind 9/11 but on the 11th of September and even one week after that in the Muslim world, you could not say that al Qaeda did that. Otherwise you would be classified as someone who is working against the Muslims. Everybody was talking about Mossad (Israeli intelligence).

Musad Omar is a Yemeni held at Guantánamo Bay. Omar claims to have gone to Afghanistan "to observe the situation" under the Taliban after being recruited to do so by an acquaintance in Yemen. In extracts from his testimony before a U.S. military tribunal at Guantánamo, he recalls what it was like to be in al Qaeda's camps around the time of the 9/11 attacks.[7]

It was the first day of the events of 9/11. The people at the [Farouq military training] camp said, "If anyone wanted to leave, we were free to leave. There might be problems and there might be bombings; so if you don't want any problems, just go. If you want to stay, then you can stay." I did not want any problems, so I left because my objective was not to fight.

I only saw bin Laden once at that training camp [al Farouq]. Bin Laden was visiting the training camp and I saw bin Laden from about thirty, to forty, to fifty meters away. The second time I saw bin Laden was in Khost (eastern Afghanistan). Bin Laden would pass through all the villages to see the people. It was one month before Kabul fell (on November 12, 2001).

I left the training camp on a regular truck from al Farouq to Kandahar. It was about a two- or three-hour ride. Then I completed the trip from Kandahar to Kabul on a civilian bus. Twenty-five of my friends were in the same group. They were not Taliban. We didn't go through official roads. We went through the mountains. [I was with] a group of Arabs, Afghans, Pakistanis and other people. [We traveled] from Khost to a place called Zurmat. After that, a place right on the border, a small village. That is how I got to Pakistan.

Question from Tribunal Member: Were any of [the people who helped you] fighters?

Omar: No, no, no. The people were just helpers. They were people who lived there. People who lived in one place would take us to the next place and go back home.

Tribunal Member: Why would these people help you?

Omar: They were Muslims.

On September 21, 2001, the Voice of America radio network interviewed Mullah Omar. Following pressure from the U.S. State Department, the interview was not aired. An excerpt follows.[8]

Interviewer: So you won't give Osama bin Laden up?

Mullah Omar: No. We cannot do that. If we did, it means we are not Muslims; that Islam is finished. If we were afraid of attack, we could have surrendered him the last time we were threatened and attacked. So America can hit us again.

Abu Walid al Misri is an Egyptian who had access to both the inner circles of al Qaeda and the Taliban.[9]

Mullah Omar pronounced with his well-known openness: "I will not hand over a Muslim to an infidel." There is no doubt that this sentence conclusively decided the fate of the relationship between the United States and the Taliban. Moreover, it was the sentence that decided that war was inevitable.

Rahimullah Yusufzai is one of Pakistan's leading journalists. He has interviewed both bin Laden and Mullah Omar.[10]

I met Mullah Omar many times. Both before and after 9/11 he told me: "I will never deliver bin Laden. I believe God will help us." He said he knew what would happen as a result. Others like Muttawakil, the [Taliban] foreign minister, said that Mullah Omar did not understand the affairs of the world.

Mullah Omar told me: "I know I can't fight the Americans, but if God helps me I will survive. I don't want to go down in history as someone who betrayed his guest. I am willing to give my life, my regime; since we have given him refuge, I cannot throw him out now."

Mullah Omar was a strong believer in dreams. He asked me, "Have you been to the White House?" I told him, "Yes, I was there once." Mullah Omar said, "My brother had a dream that there was a white house in flames. I don't know how to interpret this."

The following are excerpts of bin Laden's interview with the Pakistani newspaper *Ummat* published on September 28, 2001. Bin Laden states that U.S. government efforts to seize his financial resources fol-lowing the 9/11 attacks are futile.[11]

God opens up ways for those who work for Him. Freezing of accounts will not make any difference for al Qaeda or other jihad groups. Al Qaeda has more than three alternative financial systems, which are all separate and totally independent from each other.

One of the documents recovered on the computer purchased in Kabul by *Wall Street Journal* reporters after the fall of the Taliban was a letter from bin Laden to Mullah Omar dated October 3, 2001, four days be-fore the U.S. bombing campaign against the Taliban started. In the let-ter bin Laden states that the United States is on the verge of implosion. An edited excerpt follows.[12]

Newspapers mentioned that a recent survey showed that seven out of every ten Americans suffered psychological problems following the at-tacks on New York and Washington.

A U.S. campaign against Afghanistan will cause great long-term eco-nomic burdens [on the United States] which will force America, to resort to the former Soviet Union's only option: withdrawal from Afghanistan, disintegration, and contraction.

Faraj Ismail, an Egyptian journalist who works for *Majallah* maga-zine, covered the Afghan jihad in the nineties and the war against the Taliban in the fall of 2001.[13]

The first time I met Mullah Omar was in the war against the Russians; he was a friendly young man with only one eye. More religious than the others, he had studied at a religious institute in Kandahar. He speaks un-derstandable Arabic. He also attended Abdullah Azzam's lectures during the '80s.

I interviewed Mullah Omar on 7 October 2001 in Kandahar. That night the U.S. bombing began and I went back to Pakistan. I was very ex-cited about the interview: Mullah Omar was not convinced that bin Laden was behind the 9/11 attacks. He said, "I have control over Afghanistan. I'm sure he didn't do it." Mullah Omar really didn't know what was going on in the world. Television and newspapers were prohibited by the Taliban.

Majallah magazine published Mullah Omar's interview with Faraj Ismail on October 14, 2001. An excerpt follows indicating that Mullah Omar, like many in the Muslim world at the time, had bought into the absurd conspiracy theory that the 9/11 attacks were a Zionist plot.[14]

Mullah Omar: Neither Osama nor the Taliban has the resources to implement the recent incidents against the United States. I believe the perpetrators were from inside the United States itself.

Ismail: How?

Omar: For example, the investigation has not taken into account the absence on the same day of the incident of 4,000 Jews who worked in the World Trade Centre Twin Towers in New York.

As the U.S. bombing campaign against the Taliban began on October 7, 2001, bin Laden made a surprise appearance on TV networks around the world in a videotape, which had likely been shot some time earlier. It was the first time he had been seen since the 9/11 attacks.[15]

I bear witness that there is no God but Allah and that Muhammad is his messenger.

There is America, hit by God in one of its softest spots. Its greatest buildings were destroyed, thank God for that.

There is America, full of fear from its north to its south, from its west to its east. Thank God for that. What America tastes now, is something insignificant compared to what we have tasted for scores of years. Our nation [the Islamic world] has tasted this humiliation and this degradation for more than eighty years.

When God blessed one of the groups of Islam [on 9/11] they destroyed America. I pray to God to elevate their status and bless them.

To America, I say only a few words to it and its people. I swear by God, who has elevated the skies without pillars, neither America nor the people who live in it will dream of security before we live it in Palestine, and not before all the infidel armies leave the land of Muhammad, peace be upon him.

Hamid Mir, bin Laden's Pakistani biographer.[16]

On the night of 7th of October, after the launching of American attacks on Afghanistan, Osama bin Laden released a videotape statement
through our Arab TV channel, and in that statement he praised the attacks. He said God gave courage to some Muslims who attacked the
United States of America and those Muslims will go to heaven. So you
can find a big contradiction in the opinion of Osama bin Laden on the
terrorist attacks and in the general opinion in Islamic countries. All the
prominent Islamic clerics and Islamic religious leaders condemned the
attacks. They declared that the attacks are un-Islamic. But Osama bin
Laden praised those attacks. This is a big contradiction and it proved that
he is not a religious scholar. He is fighting the United States of America
because he hates America. Whatever the reasons—Palestine—the presence of American troops in Saudi Arabia. But I don't think that his religious ideas are correct.

[Bin Laden] watches TV, CNN, BBC. I have seen with my own eyes
Osama bin Laden watching CNN. I'll tell you a very interesting thing.
When I met him after 9/11, [bin Laden] said, "I was watching you on the
Larry King show a few days ago and you told Larry King that when
Osama bin Laden talks on religion he is not convincing, but when he
talks on politics he is very much convincing, so today I will convince you
on some religious issues." So I said, "Okay, you watch Larry King show?"
He said, "Yes, I am fighting a big war and I have to monitor the activities
of my enemy through these TV channels." And an interesting thing is
that in those days the Taliban government was intact and Mullah Omar
imposed a ban all over Afghanistan that nobody can watch TV and bin
Laden was violating the orders of Mullah Omar.

The book written by Mr. Yossef Bodansky [*Bin Laden: The Man Who
Declared War on America,* published in 1999] was lying in front of [bin
Laden]. So during the interview, the book was not mentioned. After the
interview, I mentioned, I said, "Mr. bin Laden, you are reading these
kind of books these days?" So he laughed and said, "Yes, it is very interesting book. If you read this book, you can find out many jokes in this
book. And I think Mr. Yossef Bodansky is a great friend of mine. He is
misguiding Americans about me. And if the Americans have this kind of
information about me, then I am the happiest person on this earth."

I was not ready to say that bin Laden is involved in the [9/11] attacks. You see, I was questioning the accusation that he is involved. When I visited Afghanistan, I spent some days there, I was totally changed because I saw the pictures of Atta [the lead hijacker] hanging in the [al Qaeda] hideouts. Privately they admitted everything. They said, they [who attacked on 9/11] are our brothers, but they said that, "When the Americans kill Muslims in Sudan, they don't admit that we are responsible. When the Israelis kill Palestinians, they don't admit that we are responsible for the attacks. When the Indians kill Kashmiris, they don't admit that we have killed them. So now this is our turn. We have killed them and we are not going to admit that."

My tape recorder was on and one very important al Qaeda leader he turned off my tape recorder and said, "Yes, I did it. Okay. Now play your tape recorder." I played the tape recorder and he said, "No, I'm not responsible."

[Bin Laden] told me, "I became father of a girl after 9/11 and I gave her the name of Safia." I said, "Why Safia?" And he said, "I gave her the name of Safia who killed a Jew spy in the days of Holy Prophet Muhammad, so that's why." I said, "What is the age of your daughter?" He said, "Just one month. She will kill enemies of Islam like Safia of the Prophet's time," he said to me about his little daughter. So you are visualizing a one-month-old girl as Safia who should kill a lot of Jews . . . this is the mind-set.

Khaled Batarfi, bin Laden's childhood friend, has remained in touch with bin Laden's mother.[17]

After 9/11 she talked about how she followed the news desperately looking for any clues of his well-being, and how when there was conflicting stories about his capture or his injury, she would feel sick.

There was a time when they said he was sick and has this kidney problem. From what I understood from his family, that he has something. He needs to drink water to reduce the salt in his body because he was affected by the yellow gas that the Russians used in chemical warfare [against him during the eighties]. He has to drink a lot of water.

There has been considerable speculation about the state of bin Laden's health and numerous reports that he suffers from life-

threatening kidney disease. This is nonsense. While bin Laden suffers from low blood pressure and he sustained a foot wound in the war against the Soviets and a shoulder wound at the battle of Tora Bora, it appears that he will not die of natural causes any time soon, as the following accounts suggest.

Abu Jandal became bin Laden's chief bodyguard in 1998.[18]

During my close association with him I never noticed that he suffered from any illness except some acute inflammation of his vocal cords. This was caused by a chemical weapons attack that affected his throat during his jihad against the Soviet forces. This did not affect him much except whenever he spoke for a long time with those around him, he needed to drink a lot of water. So whenever he gave an interview to a journalist he used to spend a whole day after that communicating only by gestures to preserve his ability to speak. Apart from this the man was fit and in good health. I remember that he even used to ride in horse races with the young men for distances of up to 70 kilometers [40 miles] without stopping. If he had suffered from an illness, he would not have been able to do that.

Ahmad Zaidan of Al Jazeera interviewed bin Laden eight months before 9/11.[19]

[On Osama's health] I didn't see anything abnormal. I sat with him for two, three hours. There was nothing.

Bakr Atyani of the Middle East Broadcasting Corporation met bin Laden three months before 9/11.

I believed that [Osama] was putting on weight, he's in good health and I don't believe that he was having any kidney problems; I don't believe it, from his face, his health.

Dr. Amer Aziz, a prominent Pakistani surgeon and Taliban sympathizer, encountered bin Laden after the 9/11 attacks while he was trav-

eling in Afghanistan in November 2001. He had previously met with al Qaeda's leader in 1999 when he treated him for an injury that he had sustained falling from a horse.[20]

When I saw him last he was in excellent health. He was walking. He was healthy. I didn't see any evidence of kidney disease. I didn't see any evidence of dialysis.

☸

The following interview between Al Jazeera correspondent Taysir Alouni and bin Laden took place in October 2001, the only television interview that al Qaeda's leader has done since the 9/11 attacks. CNN aired the interview on February 5, 2002, after Al Jazeera chose not to air its interview for a number of reasons that have never made much sense, such as that it wasn't "newsworthy." Key excerpts follow.[21]

Alouni: Dear viewers, welcome to this much-anticipated interview with the leader of the al Qaeda organization, Sheikh Osama bin Laden. Sheikh, the question that's on the mind of many people around the world: America claims that it has convincing evidence of your collusion in the events in New York and Washington. What's your answer?

bin Laden: If inciting people to do that is terrorism, and if killing those who kill our sons is terrorism, then let history be witness that we are terrorists. Just as they're killing us, we have to kill them so that there will be a balance of terror. This is the first time the balance of terror has been close between the two parties, between Muslims and Americans, in the modern age. The battle has moved to inside America. We will work to continue this battle, God permitting, until victory or until we meet God before that occurs.

Q: How about the killing of innocent civilians?

bin Laden: The killing of innocent civilians, as America and some intellectuals claim, is really very strange talk. When we kill their innocents, the entire world from east to west screams at us. Who said that our blood is not blood, but theirs is? Who made this pronouncement? Who has been getting killed in our countries for decades? More than one million children died in Iraq and others are still dying. Why do we not hear someone screaming or condemning, or even someone's words of conso-

lation or condolence? We kill civilian infidels in exchange for those of our
children they kill. This is permissible in law and intellectually. The men
that God helped [on September 11] did not intend to kill babies; they intended to destroy the strongest military power in the world, to attack the
Pentagon that houses more than 64,000 employees, a military center
that houses the military intelligence.

Q: How about the Twin Towers?

bin Laden: The Towers are an economic power and not a children's
school. Those that were there are men that supported the biggest economic power in the world.

Q: What do you think of the so-called Clash of Civilizations? You always keep repeating *crusaders* and words like that all the time. Does that
mean you support the Clash of Civilizations?

bin Laden: No doubt about that. The Jews and the Americans made
up this call for peace in the world. The peace they're calling for is a big
fairy tale. They're just drugging the Muslims as they lead them to slaughter. And the slaughter is still going on. If we defend ourselves, they call us
terrorists.

**On October 19, 2001, twelve days after the U.S. bombing against the
Taliban had begun, *The News,* a Pakistani daily, interviewed Jalaluddin
Haqqani, the Taliban's military commander, and a close ally of bin
Laden's for more than a decade and a half.**[22]

We will retreat to the mountains and begin a long guerrilla war to reclaim our pure land from the infidels and free our country again like we
did against the Soviets. We are eagerly awaiting the American troops to
land on our soil. The Americans are creatures of comfort. We have so far
held to our defenses. There is no retreat anywhere. The military strikes
have failed to inflict any serious or crippling damage. Mullah Omar,
Osama bin Laden and all other commanders are safe and sound and carrying out their duties. I can't [tell you when I last met bin Laden]. However, let me state clearly that bin Laden is not only safe and sound, he is
also in good spirits.

**Kabul fell to the Northern Alliance on November 12, 2001. Peter
Jouvenal, who filmed bin Laden's interview with CNN in 1997 and had**

covered Afghanistan intensively since 1980, was probably the first Westerner to set foot in Kabul as it fell. Jouvenal was working with the well-known BBC correspondent John Simpson (whom bin Laden had once threatened with death during the siege of Jalalabad in 1989).[23]

I decided it might be nice to be nearer the front line; people had given me plans about the ground offensive. The first day they broke through at 11 o'clock [at night]. I was not with the lead [group,] but behind it. I bumped into some friends I knew from the Jihad. All of them now were generals and senior commanders who just tend to sit on top of roofs and watch the battle go on. So they pointed me in the right direction. We were the lead element. We walked down the road and there were more and more people coming out of Kabul. So that made great TV and John [Simpson] did his piece. When someone asked him who was liberating Kabul, and because the Northern Alliance was up the road, he made this flippant remark that the BBC was liberating Kabul.

The people were overjoyed to be relieved of such a suppressive regime. When the Taliban initially came I think they were good, but they became a lot of crooks. For a lot of Afghans the main thing was there was just no business. The economy was zero, it was going nowhere. You weren't free, you couldn't fly kites, play music, you had to go and pray at prayer time, you were restricted by the length of your beard, you couldn't wear Western clothes. I had one friend who was stopped at Kabul airport with a bottle of shaving lotion and it was taken off him by the Taliban. He asked, "Why are you taking my shaving lotion? They said, "Because you don't shave." He was going out of the country, he wasn't coming into the country.

The problem about the Taliban they were a lot of ignorant uneducated people. They became more and more brutal. So people were really fed up. I worked in Kabul during the time of the Taliban. I wasn't around during the Second World War living in Paris, but I got a feel of what it might be like with the Gestapo trying to find the French resistance and trying to control the city. It was very suppressive, very quiet, and I had to grow a beard just to blend in. So that all suddenly went.

I went to the first [al Qaeda] address and they said the Arabs had moved from that building across the street to another building. So I went to that building. There was a chart on the wall how you could promote yourself in al Qaeda by doing these courses and moving up the ranks. Ahmed [the Afghan friend of Jouvenal's who had worked with al Qaeda] said that one of the houses was bin Laden's wife's house. He didn't say which wife. From the outside it was pretty bland and run down, but most buildings in Afghanistan were run down in those days anyway. I found the owner who actually lived next door; luckily a very nice chap who let me in. He had no idea the bin Laden family had been living there. He said a Yemeni family were living there.

I used to live in Kabul before. I thought why not get a house again. John Simpson suggested that people might like to stay [in the bin Laden house]. My first idea wasn't to make a hotel, it was really to make a house for myself.

The landlord was very happy because the Osamas had been paying $150 a month, but they left owing three months rent. As far as the landlord was concerned it was Yemenis who rented it. There were women there and he didn't really engage in conversation with them. They were very unfriendly to anybody who was too interested. The gardener was not allowed to work there at all, who's now again working for me.

I went to the second place. It used to be the Saudi Embassy before. So I went in to the basement of that building. It was very interesting. They had all these seats all around the walls so they could face in. And there was all this stuff all on the floor—clothing, paperwork, drugs, you know aspirin and stuff like that, a few syringes but no narcotics, it's forbidden. Obviously this had been used as a center for Arabs coming into fight fairly soon after 9/11. When the Americans were building up the operation to go into Afghanistan, I think quite a lot of Arabs came in to Afghanistan to support the Taliban. Some of them brought these ridiculously big suitcases as if they were going on holiday. And a tie would be put on it with a number and then they would put all their personal effects in it. Then they would get into their gear and off they would go.

The Afghans had got into that building and ransacked it and taken all the good clothes so there was just munitions, passports, box cutters, which I had never seen before in my life. I was a bit more aware of them after 9/11, but a few of those were around as well. I filmed all this and John did a piece to camera walking through all this debris. It was quite strange because there was electricity in the building and a sauna. It wasn't being used.

All these [al Qaeda] houses were really basic, pretty dirty, not even painted. There was these gray blankets on the ground as carpets, mattresses around the wall. There was always a musty smell. There was always a pile of dried bread somewhere in the corner because they never chuck bread away because it's a sin. So they were in there for the hardship. The harder the better. A bit like Lawrence of Arabia. They wanted to test themselves. I think it was out more out conviction, not out of necessity. They could have bought a tin of paint; it doesn't take much to smarten up a place. They came there to do the Jihad, not to live in luxury.

Vahid Mojdeh, the former Taliban foreign ministry official, recalls the fall of the Taliban.[24]

In a gathering a few days before the start of the American air attack on Afghanistan, Mullah Omar said to a group of his companions, "You may consider me weak or scared, but I have to send my family to Pakistan." Up until this point, the Taliban thought that even if Mullah Omar lacks other good qualities, at least he was both pious and courageous. But now he was showing the first lapse into weakness.

Despite the fact the Pakistan government had turned its back on the Taliban; thousands of people from [Pakistan's] tribal areas were willing to join the jihad against the Americans in Afghanistan. These people, thought, as the Taliban did, that they would be engaging American troops in a land war, face to face. When America's heavy aerial bombardment started, the Taliban fighters maintained their ranks for several weeks against it.

After those weeks passed the situation in the north became critical and many of the Pakistani volunteers freshly arrived in Afghanistan were sent to Mazar-i-Sharif (in northern Afghanistan), even though they had no knowledge of the lay of the land. Mullah Omar's hope was that by sending these troops to the north, the problem would subside.

In Kandahar the conviction was that the resistance would continue, but slowly the intense bombardment made the situation very difficult for Mullah Omar. He was forced to spend his nights in open spaces or places where he had not been seen spotted at before. Even though Mullah Omar was officially in charge of the military, in fact he had no contact with the front because he was afraid his location would be pinpointed and bombed. But the Taliban leaders would take no orders from anyone except Mullah Omar. Mullah Nouri, the Northern Zone commander, would scream in one such call, "We are under aerial bombardment, the lines at Mazar-i-Sharif are being attacked from the ground, and inside the city there is an uprising forming. Mullah Omar must tell me what to do."

The Taliban feared the anger of the populace more than anything. They had never tried to gain popular support and were fully aware that people would avenge all the torture and hardship they had suffered at their hands at the first opportunity. This is a destiny common to all tyrannical regimes upon defeat.

In Kandahar, Mullah Omar had resorted to fortune-telling and dream-interpretation to aid him in his decisions. He told his commanders to continue fighting, because America would soon be destroyed. But the destruction of America kept all waiting while the destruction of Kandahar became a reality. Mullah Omar finally gave up dreaming and decided to abandon Kandahar. He reached this conclusion after the American planes destroyed all the forces he had sent to retake Uruzgan Province [Mullah Omar's home province].

Feroz Ali Abbasi is the Ugandan Briton who was captured in Pakistan after the fall of the Taliban.[25]

After September 11 most of the English-speaking brothers remained in the Guest House [in Kandahar]. I became more and more frustrated with just sitting around weaponless and defenseless expecting imminent attack. Sayf al Adel [al Qaeda's number two military commander] gave all of us three options, "You can either go to Kabul, or remain in Kandahar with the mountain group or the Airport group. The airport group was the most dangerous. Which one do you want?" Everybody including me went for the most dangerous—the Airport group. Camp Obaidah [where we would be located] was a short distance away from [the Airport].

I was in civilian clothes and weaponless. I decided to do some scavenging looking through the camp for anything that will increase my chance of survival in the coming fight. I changed out of my civilian clothes into military threads. I was about the only one who did this. The premise behind the mujahadeen wearing civil clothes, one actually told me this, was he could try to play that he is a civilian if things got too heated. The rest of the time before the bombing I went scavenging to increase my arsenal of weapons.

Allied planes came on Sunday night [7th of October]. I had been expecting them to bomb on the Tuesday coming because I had heard nearly a month ago that a fax had been sent to Osama Bin Laden from [an individual] in America who had a fax line with Osama Bin Laden. I had known this since [basic training] when Osama Bin Laden had come to talk in the Mosque and mentioned [the] warning that America was going to bomb in one months' time.

Even funnier is how the Americans broadcasted to the media the fact that the they had told the Northern Alliance to ground its planes. Telegraphing that they were coming. Maybe just in case Osama Bin Laden hadn't quite packed and left yet.

Anyway the bombing started and I spent the rest of the time at the Airport running around like a mad man out in the middle of nowhere trying to dodge missiles which seemed to ever come closer.

Possibly on the 17th of Ramadan [December 3, 2001] the opposition Pashtun forces attempted to take over the Airport area. There was a gun fight that went on into the night. Possibly on the 19th of Ramadan the Pashtun forces made another attack and this time gained ground significantly upon us. We were pushed back to another line of cover. Most of Afghanistan had fallen (only Kandahar and Tora Bora and possibly another Taliban stronghold in the north that was under siege were in the mujuhideen hands). Maybe thoughts of "run today to fight another day" were creeping into the mujahideen's minds.

I was following what Mullah Omar had said, which was translated/relayed to me, "All the mujahideen are to retreat back to Kandahar. From here we either spread out and retake Afghanistan or we die here." I had taken it literally, Death or Victory.

The group that had adopted me were staying in a dry river bed. I was teamed with one Yemeni guy who had all but given up listening to my baby Arabic and was enthralled by looking out for an American helicopter. [But] one morning I woke up at dawn and none of them were there. They had all fled.

An unidentified Guantánamo Bay detainee before a U.S. military tribunal.[26]

As the Recorder read the Unclassified Summary to the Tribunal, the Detainee stated each point was correct.

Whatever evidence was brought against me, I admit to. I've been telling the same story and I'm not lying about it. I helped out bin Laden.

My word is what I said. I am going to tell the truth. I helped [redacted] and I have been with Osama [bin Laden]. I agree to the evidence. I did this for money. For five years, I have been a member of the Taliban and when the Americans came, [redacted] was giving money to finance attacks on Americans. We were told by the Arabs, who had all the money, that they were planning an attack on the United States with twenty pilots. This is the first story. I was working for money.

The second story is [redacted] was with me. We went to Jalalabad. Bin Laden was in Jalalabad and we took him up to the Pakistan border. It's a way that nobody knows, it's a secret. We left [bin Laden and his family] at the Pakistani border and we came back. They [bin Laden and his family] disappeared. This is the story of al Qaeda that I took part in.

Question by a Tribunal Member:
Q: Do you consider the United States an enemy?
A: I worked for money. Other people would tell me Americans were bad, but I never thought about Americans. I just did it for the money.

Fouad al Rabia is a 45-year-old Kuwaiti held in Guantánamo who had met bin Laden in June 2001. Four months later he was back in Afghanistan as the United States was launching its attack on the Taliban. Al Rabia says he intended only a short visit to Afghanistan, but got sucked in by the war. He provides a vivid account of al Qaeda's retreat to the mountains of Tora Bora in eastern Afghanistan near the city of Jalalabad.[27]

During that time, no one would rent a house to an Arab for fear of being shot or bombed. They would let us stay at their house for a couple of days as a courtesy. So, we were moving from one house to the other every few days, looking for a way to get out. We were then told we had to go to the north to Jalalabad. There was supposed to be a way out from there. So we went to Jalalabad looking for the way out. Now the country is falling. No one believed the country would fall so quickly—within one week. So you can imagine the chaos that was going on there.

The vehicles [leaving Jalalabad] were full of people who were like luggage thrown on top of each other. We went to a house on the edge of Jalalabad that belonged to a person called Abdul Ghoudous. He turned out to be a very big man in al Qaeda. We took everything in the house with us, and we left because Jalalabad fell. There was no more control. Simply being out on the street was an invitation to be killed. We walked from there to the baseline edge of the mountains. Those mountains were the border mountains known as the Tora Bora Mountains. This was an escape route to get out of the country, because it is the border between Pakistan and Afghanistan. That was the only way to get out. Up in the mountains, there was bombing night and day. All the way up the mountain, I could hear children; I could hear men; I could see small children walking around. The mountains were filled with civilians fleeing the area. I reached the top of the mountain.

Then Abdul Ghoudous gave the order that everybody go because we feared snow was coming. The roads would be blocked.

Dr. Mohamed Asif Qazizanda is the deputy governor of Naranghar province in which Tora Bora is located. Dr. Qazizanda, a veterinarian by training, spent years fighting the Soviets in Tora Bora, and would encounter bin Laden on several occasions during the jihad against the communists between 1989 and 1991, observing "at that time he was very well respected." His historical perspective about Tora Bora explains why bin Laden retreated there.[28]

I was the deputy commander in Tora Bora from 1980 to 1983 when I was in my early 20s. We made machine gun emplacements and installed antiaircraft guns. It was difficult for the Russians to attack us because of the caves and shelters built into the mountains. Tora Bora had easy access to Pakistan because there were paths by foot to Parachinar (a "parrot's beak" of Pakistani territory that juts into Afghanistan).

I witnessed many offensives by the Soviets against Tora Bora. At one time 2,000 Russian and 2,000 Afghan communist soldiers mounted an offensive against Tora Bora, supported by 50 Russian helicopters and MIG jets. We shot down two of the helicopters with machine guans and captured a soldier from the Ukraine. During the jihad against the Soviets we had a force of 120 to 130 people stationed in Tora Bora.

There are two reasons the Arabs fled to Tora Bora after 9/11. First, it was difficult for the Americans to attack; and there was a way to escape Tora Bora into Pakistan.

Commander Mohammed Musa is an Afghan militia leader who commanded frontline troops at the battle of Tora Bora. Musa is the brother-in-law of Hazarat Ali, who was one of the overall commanders of the battle. When I interviewed him in the summer of 2003, Musa told me that he had met bin Laden in 1991, without providing any further details. A decade later he would be leading soldiers into battle to dislodge al Qaeda's leader from his Tora Bora hideout.

When we moved from Jalalabad to Tora Bora I had six hundred men with me. When we started the attack, for one week we couldn't make any advance. They were on the mountains sending rockets at us. It was very hard fighting with them. They were hiding in their posts and we were in the open. They had rockets, submachine guns. Al Qaeda fought very hard with us. When we captured them, they committed suicide with grenades. I saw three of them do that myself. Over our radios they were telling us, "You must not fight with us. We don't want to fight against you. You are Muslims." The very hardest fighters were the Chechens, who were resistant to the end.

[On December 12, 2001,] Haji Zaman (another Afghan commander) told me about a ceasefire with the Arabs. Al Qaeda wanted to escape from a particular village; Ghalanjali village in the mountains. Al Qaeda said, "We want to surrender to the United Nations. We want a cease-fire." Zaman said, "We'll accept a cease-fire at 4 p.m. in the afternoon." That night al Qaeda and the Taliban all escaped to Pakistan. We only captured thirteen people who escaped. We did not want the cease-fire to happen. It was Haji Zaman who agreed to it.

[U.S. forces] were not involved in the fighting. They had some guys with us to coordinate the bombing. There were six American soldiers with us, U.S. Specials Forces they coordinated the air strikes. The American bombardment was very effective; very precise bombing of al Qaeda's positions. Very useful in that way.

My personal view is if the Americans had blocked the way out to Pakistan, al Qaeda would not have a had a way to escape. The Americans were my guest here, but they didn't know about fighting; how to do it.

At the end of the battle the Americans gave me four or five Datsun four-wheel drive vehicles. Four of my men died and eight were injured.

Peter Jouvenal, the former British army officer turned combat cameraman, covered the Tora Bora battle for ABC News.

America's special forces are very good generally, but the mistake they made [at Tora Bora] was they relied on Afghans for information. And so it was pretty easy for Osama to slip out. It's no criticism of the special forces. I think there weren't enough of them on the ground. I only actually saw around twelve special forces guys.

The Americans had a very successful war with a very small number of SF (special forces) guys and I don't think psychologically they were ready to commit so many troops to the ground. Maybe there was too much of an emphasis put on the SF, who did a brilliant job—they got rid of the [Taliban] regime. But this is a fox you are after, so you have to put a lot of boots on the ground.

The question of whether the United States missed an opportunity to capture or kill bin Laden during the battle of Tora Bora in eastern Afghanistan in December 2001 became an issue in the razor-close 2004 U.S. presidential campaign. During the September 30, 2004, presidential debate, Democratic contender Senator John Kerry said of capturing bin Laden, "He escaped in the mountains of Tora Bora. We had him surrounded."[29] Writing in *The New York Times* two weeks later, General Tommy Franks, a Bush supporter and the overall commander of the Tora Bora operation, wrote, "We don't know to this day whether Mr. bin Laden was at Tora Bora."[30] At a town hall meeting in Ohio on October 19, Vice President Dick Cheney said Kerry's critique of the Tora Bora campaign was "absolute garbage."[31]

President Bush himself weighed in on the question of bin Laden's Tora Bora presence, or lack thereof, at a campaign rally a week before

the election, saying: ["It's part of Kerry's] pattern of saying anything it takes to get elected. Like when he charged that our military failed to get Osama bin Laden at Tora Bora, even though our top military commander, General Tommy Franks, said, 'The Senator's understanding of events does not square with reality,' and intelligence reports place bin Laden in any of several different countries at the time." [32]

However, according to a widely reported background briefing by Pentagon officials in mid-December 2001, there was "reasonable certainty" that bin Laden was indeed at Tora Bora, a judgment based on intercepted radio transmissions. [33] Indeed, General Tommy Franks recounted in his autobiography, *American Soldier,* that in Texas in December 2001 he briefed President Bush, saying, "Unconfirmed reports that Osama has been seen in the White Mountains, sir. The Tora Bora area." [34] In June 2003 I met with several senior U.S. counterterrorism officials, who explained, "We are confident that he [bin Laden] was at Tora Bora and disappeared with a small group." Also Gary Berntsen, the CIA official in charge of the Tora Bora operation for the agency, has publicly said that bin Laden was in the Tora Bora area during the battle. [35]

The following accounts further establish that bin Laden was at Tora Bora.

Peter Jouvenal.

I was told by some Afghan friends of mine that Osama was in Tora Bora. This is a day or so before the Northern Alliance took Kabul [on November 12, 2001]. The information [originally] came from bin Laden's [Afghan] driver.

[Later] I organized a vehicle to take me and we went up to Tora Bora. I did some interviews with Arabs captured [in Tora Bora by a local Afghan commander]. They had been captured at night and they were really exhausted, they were kept in a little house under guard and they let me in and they were all asleep. They were just crashed out. One was black. Must have been from Sudan or something like that. And these chaps, four of them wearing Pakistani winter clothing, snotty noses, they'd obviously caught colds up in the mountains. They weren't used to cold weather. They had long-johns on. They had been living off this Nestlé baby food. I found tins of this Nestlé baby food up in the mountains. Yoghurt and honey and stuff. They must have had the runs all the time. So my first concern was that these men were going to wake up and I was clean shaven with a moustache, so they're going to wake up and think the American army is here.

I have a picture of Peter [Bergen] and myself with Osama bin Laden together [from CNN's 1997 interview]. I knew that it would be useful one day.

It was very dark and I had to get one of these gas lamps and move it around to see them. They were all crashed out. They'd been captured that night. This must have been 9 o'clock that morning. They hadn't slept for two days. So I woke one of them up. I didn't want to wake all four up because they might attack me though I did have one Afghan in the room with me. So I woke one of them up, the Arab-looking one. He was a bit startled. So I showed the picture of Peter Bergen, [Osama] and myself and explained who I was. [I asked him, "Have you seen bin Laden—is he around?" And after seeing the picture he relaxed a bit and spoke good English. He said they'd seen bin Laden a few days before but had no information on where he was now.

Abu Jaafar al Kuwaiti was an eyewitness to the U.S. air strikes on Tora Bora in early December 2001. Bin Laden is believed to have fled the area and escaped around December 10. Excerpts of Abu Jaafar's account—which was posted to al Qaeda's main Web site on the first anniversary of 9/11—follow.[36]

November 14, 2001. Mujahid Sheikh Osama bin Laden and his special group arrived to the area 9,000 feet above sea level in the Tora Bora mountains with its extreme terrain and cold weather. We were with him. This position had more than fifteen trenches to protect the mujahideen from the insane American strikes that started five days before. The trenches were built by our hands and effort and by our brothers, the Afghan mujahideen. But because we needed a large number of trenches, Brother Faris and Abdul Ghoudus requested the assistance of the nearby tribes to help them continue this effort. The men of the tribes kept coming to us. Then we witnessed the increase in flights of drones (U.S. Predator drones) that did not leave the area night or day.

[On December 9] at a late hour of the night, we were awakened to the sound of massive and terrorizing explosions very near to us. It was the place where the trench of Sheikh Osama bin Laden was. The night passed was very long and very worrisome [as we waited] for what the morning would bring [to] see what this barbaric raid had done.

[In the morning,] we received the horrifying news!! The trench of Sheikh Osama had been destroyed; the trench where Sheikh used to come out every day to check the mujahideen situation and follow the news of the battle. [But] God kept Osama bin Laden alive because he left the bunker only two nights [before] to an area only two hundred meters away.

Abdellah Tabarak, a Moroccan who was bin Laden's driver, was detained by both Pakistani and U.S. authorities in December 2001 and was later sent from Guantánamo to his native Morocco in August 2004 to face trial.[37]

Following the U.S. bombing of Afghanistan, I left Kandahar in the company of bin Laden, Ayman al Zawahiri, and a number of guards in the direction of Kabul through Jalalabad and afterward we returned to Kabul once again. After its fall, we returned once again to Jalalabad. During the month of Ramadan in the same year, we entered Tora Bora where we stayed for twenty days. From there, Ayman al Zawahiri fled accompanied by Uthman, the son of Osama bin Laden. Afterwards, bin Laden fled with his son Muhammad accompanied by Afghan guards while I fled with a group made up mainly of Yemenis and Saudis in the direction of Pakistan. We were arrested by the Pakistani authorities at a border checkpoint and they handed us over to the U.S. authorities who deported us to the Guantánamo detention camp in Cuba.

Osama bin Laden himself recounted his experiences at Tora Bora on an audiotape that aired on Al Jazeera on February 11, 2003.[38]

Now, I am going to tell you a part of that great battle [of Tora Bora] so that I [will] prove to you how cowardly [the Americans] are. We were only three hundred fighters. We had already dug one hundred trenches spread out in a space that didn't exceed one square mile.

On the morning of the 17th of Ramadan [December 3, 2001], very heavy bombing started, especially after the American leadership made sure that some of the leaders of al Qaeda were in Tora Bora, including myself and the Mujahid brother, Dr. Ayman al Zawahiri. The bombing became around the clock.

Not a second would pass without a fighter plane passing over our heads day and night. American forces were bombing us by smart bombs that weigh thousands of pounds and bombs that penetrate caves and other kinds of bombs [that] enter into caves. The fighter bombers like B-52s, each one of them, goes over our heads for two hours and in every time it drops between twenty and thirty bombs.

[That was] in addition to the forces [of the Northern Alliance] whom they pushed to attack us for a continuous month. We fought back against all their attacks. And we defeated them every time. In spite of all that, American forces did not dare to go into our posts. What sign is more than that of their cowardice?

With all its forces that were fighting against a small group of mujahideen, 300 Mujahideen in the trenches, inside one square mile, in minus 10 degree of temperature. The result of the battle was that we lost 6 percent of our force [eighteen men].

A visibly aged bin Laden spoke on a videotape that aired on December 27, 2001, his choice of words seeming to confirm his recent brush with death at Tora Bora. Bin Laden, who is left-handed, did not move his entire left side in the 34-minute audiotape, strongly suggesting he had a sustained a serious injury during the battle.[39]

I am just a poor slave of God. If I live or die, the war will continue.

Abdel Bari Atwan spent two days interviewing bin Laden in Tora Bora in 1996.[40]

I wasn't surprised [Osama was in Tora Bora]. I expected him to be there. I was in the Gulf region and I met somebody from al Qaeda and he told me that Osama bin Laden was injured during the Tora Bora bombing, and he was operated on his left shoulder. And then when I saw his first videotape immediately after Tora Bora, I said, something is wrong with his left shoulder, his left shoulder was very stiff and he couldn't move his left hand. And many people from al Qaeda actually were extremely furious I said that [publicly] because they don't want him to be reported as injured.

Why did the United States military—the most powerful armed force in history—not seal off the Tora Bora region, instead relying only on a handful of U.S. special forces on the ground? Historians will no doubt be debating that question for many years, but part of the answer is that the U.S. military was a victim of its own success. Scores of U.S. special forces soldiers calling in air strikes, in combination with thousands of Afghans on the ground, destroyed the Taliban army in a few weeks of fighting, a textbook case of unconventional warfare.

However, this approach was a failure at Tora Bora where large numbers of Americans on the ground were needed to throw up an effective cordon around al Qaeda's leaders. An implicit recognition of this fact can be seen in how the Pentagon approached Operation Anaconda in central Afghanistan three months after Tora Bora. In the Anaconda operation, the very name of which suggests an effective cordon, as many as a thousand U.S. soldiers were deployed into an area near Gardez in eastern Afghanistan to do battle with hundreds of Taliban and al Qaeda soldiers.

Apologists for the U.S. military failure at Tora Bora will no doubt provide some reasons why this was the case, including a lack of airlift capabilities from the U.S. airbase known as K2 in neighboring Uzbekistan. However, such explanations are hard to square with the fact that scores of journalists managed to find their way to Tora Bora, a battle covered on live television by the world's leading news organizations. If Fox News and CNN could arrange for their crews to cover Tora Bora, it is puzzling that the U.S. military could not put more boots on the ground to entrap the hardcore of al Qaeda. Sadly, there were more American journalists at the battle of Tora Bora than there were U.S. soldiers. In sum, the Tora Bora battle was a missed opportunity to bring bin Laden to justice.

11

Al Qaeda's Quest for Weapons of Mass Destruction

Osama bin Laden in 1999.[1]

Acquiring nuclear and chemical weapons is a religious duty.

Bin Laden could not have been more explicit about al Qaeda's policy on weapons of mass destruction (WMD) in the statement he made two years before the 9/11 attacks. Beginning in the early nineties al Qaeda members made efforts to acquire nuclear materials while the group was based in Sudan. When al Qaeda later relocated to Afghanistan, bin Laden started meeting with former senior nuclear scientists from Pakistan and may have attempted to purchase nuclear materials from the former Soviet Union. At the same time members of al Qaeda also started experimenting with crude chemical weapons, and began to educate themselves about biological weapons.

From its earliest days some members of al Qaeda dreamed of inflicting mass casualty attacks with WMD. Paulo José de Almeida Santos is a Portuguese member of al Qaeda who joined the group in 1990. After an eight-year jail term in an Italian prison for attempting to kill the king of Afghanistan in Rome in 1991, Santos settled down somewhere in East Africa, where he was interviewed by José Pedro Castanheira of the Portuguese magazine *Expresso* in April 2002. In that interview he said that al Qaeda's leaders initially had a somewhat negative attitude to the use of WMDs.[2]

I drew up a terrible, diabolical plan to kill Israelis. Something like using mercury to poison the waters, which would poison the harvests and the cereals. Horrific! Now the thought of those diabolical plans sends shivers down my spine. It was rejected [by al Qaeda's leadership].

I spent a few days in a medical library in Pakistan studying synthetic poisons, which could be used on the skin and which rapidly enter the blood vessels (like many creams do). The idea was to create a poison which by simple contact with a person's skin could kill in a matter of minutes or hours. In Peshawar there were a number of people we knew to be western spies. I made a suggestion: "Why don't we catch a spy, an American, a European or whatever, take him home with us and carry out experiments on him?"

Al Qaeda said that in the first place it was necessary to ask the theological opinion of a sheikh (religious authority). We went to see a sheikh, who, when he heard the proposal, almost kicked me. He was furious: "You want to do such tests on human beings? Do you think we are Nazis!?" They then said: "Experiment on animals." We did an experiment on a rabbit, but it didn't work. The best animals for experimenting on are supposed to be pigs because they have the same metabolism as humans. But where do you find a pig [in Muslim Pakistan]?

Jamal al Fadl is a member of al Qaeda who testified for the prosecution in the New York trial of four men implicated in the attacks on the U.S. embassies in Africa in 1998. In the mid-1990s al Fadl lived in Sudan, where he witnessed al Qaeda's attempts to acquire uranium.[3]

I remember Abu Fadhl al Makkee (a bin Laden aide related to Osama by marriage) call me and he told me we hear somebody in Khartoum, he got uranium, and we need you to go and study that, is that true or not. We went to another office in Jambouria Street in Khartoum. [The seller of the uranium] told me, "Are you serious? You want uranium?" I tell him "Yes. I know people, they very serious, and they want to buy it. They need the information about uranium, they want to know which quality, which country make it, and after that we going to talk with you about the price." He say, "I going to give you this information, and we need $1,500,000. We need the money outside of Sudan." And he say this is for the uranium, but he need commission for himself.

I went to Ikhlak Company in Baraka building in Khartoum City, and I told [al Qaeda member Abu Rida al Suri] about the whole information and he say, "Tell him we have our machine, electric machine, we going to check the uranium, but first we want information. We want to see the cylinder and we need information about the quality."

And after few minutes they bring a big bag and they open it, and [it is a] cylinder like this tall [indicating two to three feet tall]. A lot [is] written in the cylinder. The information was like engraved. I remember it say, "South Africa" and serial number. It's all in English.

However, the deal for the uranium seemed never to have gone through.

Mamdouh Mahmud Salim, a founding member of al Qaeda, also allegedly led its efforts to acquire uranium in the early 1990s. In September 1998, after his arrest in Germany, an FBI special agent filed a complaint, charging Salim with one count of conspiracy to commit murder and one count of conspiracy to use weapons of mass destruction. Excerpts of the complaint follow.[4]

In late 1993, after bin Laden had issued private fatwah to al Qaeda members and associates indicating that the United States was an enemy that needed to be attacked, members of al Qaeda made efforts to procure enriched uranium for the purpose of developing nuclear weapons. In particular, a document relating to a proposed purchase of uranium was routed to Salim for his review and after reviewing the document, he indicated that the project to purchase uranium should proceed.

On May 14, 1998, bin Laden issued a statement following the Indian government's nuclear tests three days earlier at a remote desert test site less than one hundred miles from the Pakistan border.[5]

The world was awakened last Tuesday by the sound of three underground Indian nuclear explosions, accompanied by explosive statements from the Hindu government in India. The leaders of the Islamic world were struck by political blindness and failed to see this danger. We call upon the Muslim nation in general, and Pakistan and its army in particular, to prepare for the Jihad imposed by Allah and terrorize the enemy by preparing the force necessary thereto. This should include a nuclear force to raise fears among all enemies led by the Zionist Christian Alliance to overthrow the Islamic world, and the Hindu enemy occupier of Muslim Kashmir.

Dr. Sultan Bashir-ud-din Mahmood, a recently retired senior Pakistani nuclear scientist sympathetic to the Taliban, met with bin Laden and Mullah Omar in Kandahar in 2000 and 2001. He says his contacts with bin Laden were entirely innocent. Nuclear proliferation experts and the U.S. government believe these meetings concerned al Qaeda's quest for nuclear and radiological weapons. Dr. Mahmood gave a rare interview to the Pakistani newspaper *The News*, extracts of which follow.[6]

I have never been in contact with the al Qaeda terrorists, but I met Mullah Omar, members of his council of ministers as well as Osama bin Laden only to seek their cooperation in pursuing the goals of my [charitable] organization Ummah Tameer-e-Nau (UTN). I met Osama to seek $3m for manpower and land development projects in Afghanistan, but he refused any help saying all my accounts are frozen. I feel bad the way everybody played up my meeting with Osama in [the] context of the transfer of nuclear technology. I never thought the meeting would lead to so many complications.

The following are excerpts of a written statement by the U.S. treasury secretary Paul O'Neill upon the designation of Umma Tameer-e-Nau (UTN) as a terrorist organization. UTN was ostensibly established as a charity by several Pakistani nuclear scientists including Dr. Mahmood.[7]

Today, we are blocking the assets of a terrorist organization, UTN, and three of its directors, because they finance terrorism. UTN and its directors provided more than money to al Qaida, they provided knowledge of nuclear, chemical and biological weapons. UTN's founder [Mahmood] was the former chief designer and director of an atomic reactor in Pakistan. He was joined in UTN by a number of other prominent Pakistani scientists, retired military officers, and industrialists. On a number of occasions, UTN delegations traveled to Afghanistan, where UTN directors met with Usama bin Laden and al-Qaida leaders and discussed nuclear, chemical, and biological weapons. Even after September 11th, UTN representatives sought to provide bin Laden and Taliban with still more devastating weapons of mass destruction.

After the fall of the Taliban, CNN acquired some two hundred videotapes from what appears to have been al Qaeda's main video library. On some of the tapes al Qaeda members experiment on dogs with chemical weapons, probably cyanide gas. Those experiments were likely carried out in the Darunta training camp outside of Jalalabad, a camp run by an Egyptian with the wonderful alias of "Abu Khabab," who headed al Qaeda's WMD program. What follows is a description of one of the filmed experiments.[8]

A dog is in a cage in a room. There is a pressure cooker nearby. There is a rope tied around the dog's neck that goes outside of the cage.

A white gas is introduced into the cage. A man with an Egyptian accent can be heard saying: "Start counting the time."

The dog starts barking and moaning. The dog is nervous and tries to break loose from the rope. The dog kicks hard and his tail is moving. Finally, the dog moves no more.

Abu Khabab, al Qaeda's WMD chief, singled out Uzbekistan—a country on Afghanistan's northern border that was formerly part of the Soviet Union—as a possible source of materials for his chemical weapons program. This is an extract from an order he wrote on April 2, 2001, in a document recovered near Jalalabad.[9]

Obtain the liquid and nonliquid chemicals as soon as possible from Uzbekistan because we need them. Take all necessary precautions to ensure the correct delivery of the materials and the lives of our men. Try and recruit Uzbek army individuals who are experienced in this sphere. Procure necessary face masks, protective clothing and protective footwear. Execute this order without delay.

Abu Walid al Misri was the editor of *Al Imara* (the Emirate) magazine, the Arabic-language magazine of the Taliban.[10]

The dreams of the hardline wing in al Qaeda, which sometimes appeared in the form of demands, dealt with the need and importance of possessing weapons of mass destruction and storing some of them on American territory to be used in a fast and direct response to any American aggression against Afghanistan.

The conclusion reached was that al Qaeda must possess weapons for defence, based on what can be obtained or supplied in the nuclear, biological, or chemical fields, so that in a crisis, if the other side used weapons of mass destruction, it will not escape a deadly punishment.

Another group believed that these type of weapons, if bin Laden could obtain them, would be tactical [in nature only] by virtue of their primitiveness and weak destructive capability. However, they will continue to call them "weapons of mass destruction" to create fear. They are primitive weapons with tactical and not strategic capabilities. In other words, using them will give the mujahideen credibility, prestige, and psychological influence.

The people close to bin Laden believed that these destructive weapons would greatly enhance the combat capability and psychological influence of the al-Qaeda fighters. The most important questions were: if such weapons could be obtained, will they be used against the enemy on Muslim territory or against the enemy on his own territory? Will the enemy forces be targeted by these weapons (if they were obtained), or will the civilians in their country also be targeted? There were different interpretations and views in this respect, and then more questions were asked. Which of these weapons will be more appropriate for the current situation of the mujahideen: the nuclear, chemical, or biological? Should the information regarding the ways of obtaining such weapons remain secret, or should it be disseminated among the mujahideen groups in all the areas?

Others raised questions about the possibility of mixing the weapon of suicide action (the only remaining deterrent weapon in the hands of the Muslims) and those weapons [of mass destruction]. They noted that the security measures by the enemy have greatly reduced the effect of suicide operations, and the introduction of these weapons could greatly enhance the value of suicide operations and their effect on the enemy.

As to the WMD proposals, bin Laden did not approve them in the first place and that was obvious from his repeated theory that the United

States could not bear two or three strikes from him. But he refused to voice publicly his rejection of the idea, probably because of his extreme politeness with those around him. Another reason was that his right-hand man in al Qaeda, Abu Hafs, led the hawks' wing and strongly supported the acquisition of new resources, especially WMD. But he did not make up his mind about the strategy of using these weapons, postponing this until they were actually acquired. Abu Hafs took charge of the WMD issue and acted with his known stubbornness and determination.

One of the documents stored on the al Qaeda computer recovered by the *Wall Street Journal* after the fall of the Taliban was a letter from Ayman al Zawahiri to Abu Hafs, dated April 15, 1999, an excerpt of which follows.[11]

The enemy [the West] started thinking about these [chemical and biological] weapons before World War I. Despite their extreme danger, we only became aware of them when the enemy drew our attention to them by repeatedly expressing concerns that they can be produced simply with easily available materials.

The irony of Zawahiri's comment about al Qaeda's growing interest in chemical and biological weapons is worth considering. It was Western concerns about the proliferation of chemical and biological weapons that drew al Qaeda's attention to these weapons in the first place.

Abu Walid al Misri.[12]

The Taliban authorities in Kabul had in their possession a considerable quantity of radioactive materials seized from smugglers who came from the countries [of the former Soviet Union] especially Tajikistan, and other shipments that were left behind by the Soviets in Afghanistan, some of which were for medical use and some for some unknown use. The Taliban officials in Kabul threw up a heavy curtain of secrecy about their nuclear secrets and always preferred to open their hearts to the Pakistanis. They did not trust the Arabs most of the time. The Pakistanis paid small sums of money but obtained much more than their value in the form of radioactive materials that they alone knew their worth and which probably helped them in their nuclear program that came to the surface several years later. The Taliban officials allowed the Arabs to examine what was left of these materials.

In September 1997, five months after we interviewed bin Laden together, Peter Jouvenal, the veteran British cameraman who has reported on Afghanistan since 1980, told me that he had heard about a group of Afghans selling nuclear materials from the former Soviet Union. They approached an Afghan friend of Jouvenal's, who had in turn told him about the offer of nuclear materials.

The material came in five containers inscribed with Russian writing. The sellers of the material claimed that they have sold other weapons-grade material to Iranian buyers for as little as $2,000. The sellers were based in Mazar-e-Sharif in northern Afghanistan, near the border with the former Soviet Union. Common sense would suggest that this was an ideal location to sell nuclear materials from the Central Asian republics of the former Soviet Union.

Peter Jouvenal faxed me information about the markings that appeared on one of the boxes of the radioactive materials the Afghans were selling.

U 235 150 g (a notation indicating uranium)
PU 239 50 g (a notation indicating plutonium)
MO-9999 r OCT 1988
CCCP (a notation indicating the Soviet Union)

Peter Jouvenal.[13]

Since the collapse of the Soviet Union there have always been rumors about nuclear products or bits of plutonium floating through Afghanistan. Looking back in perspective I actually think that most of them are an elaborate con trick by people in Russia who persuaded Afghans to buy nuclear material. It could be radioactive waste from an X-ray machine. So there was all this whispering about plutonium and uranium and what have you for sale. I personally think it was an elaborate scam.

[The information about the nuclear materials came from an Afghan friend.] He was sick. I think he looked at this stuff with a friend in Mazar-e-Sharif. I think we had given him instructions to run a watch over the stuff and see if the watch stopped. All these things he did and then he was sick and his friend was sick the next day. He said his eyebrows started falling out. I always presumed that it was some sort of radioactive waste, maybe it came from an X-ray machine in a hospital.

After consulting with a nuclear physicist, we concluded that the "nuclear" materials were, in fact, nothing of the kind, but were likely some form of radioactive waste. However, this waste can be useful for terrorists wanting to detonate a radiological weapon, or a "dirty" bomb, which marries conventional explosives to widely available radioactive materials such as waste from industrial processes or hospitals. While such bombs would kill relatively few people, they would cause widespread disruption if exploded in an urban area because of both the resulting panicked reaction of the populace and the fact that teams of specialists would have to be sent in to decontaminate the affected areas over long periods of time.

Abu Khabab, al Qaeda's WMD chief, in a letter recovered in Afghanistan after the fall of the Taliban, spelled out the possible uses of radioactive materials by al Qaeda.[14]

As you instructed us you will find attached a summary of the discharges from a traditional nuclear reactor, amongst which are radioactive elements that could be used for military ends. One can use them to contaminate an area or to halt the advance of the enemy. It is possible to get more information from our Pakistani friends who have great experience in this sphere.

Following are excerpts from a memorandum outlining the American Defense Department's rationale for continuing to hold U.S. citizen Jose Padilla as an enemy combatant. Padilla, a former small-time criminal from Florida, met with both Abu Zubaydah, who recruited for al Qaeda, and Khalid Sheikh Mohammed, the operational planner of 9/11, in Pakistan in early 2002 supposedly to discuss a radiological attack on the United States. Padilla was arrested at Chicago O'Hare airport on May 8, 2002.[15]

Padilla admits that after crossing into Pakistan, he met Abu Zubaydah again at a guesthouse in Lahore, Pakistan. After staying there for one month, Padilla, his future Accomplice and several others traveled to Faisalabad, where Abu Zubaydah again joined them. Padilla states that he and his Accomplice approached Abu Zubaydah with an operation in which they would travel to the United States to detonate a nuclear bomb they learned to make on the Internet. Padilla claims that Abu Zubaydah was skeptical of the idea, but nonetheless told them that he would send them to Karachi to present the idea to Khalid Sheikh Muhammed ("KSM"). KSM was at the time al Qaeda's leading operational planner and organizer. Abu Zubaydah arranged for Padilla and his Accomplice to make the proposal to KSM.

Padilla's admissions are corroborated by senior al Qaeda detainee #1, who states that Abu Zubaydah claimed to have thought the nuclear bomb idea was not feasible from the beginning, but thought explosives wrapped in uranium (i.e., a 'dirty bomb') was much more feasible. According to this detainee, Abu Zubaydah warned Padilla and his Accomplice that the dirty bomb plot was not as easy to do as they thought, but they seemed convinced they could do it without getting caught. This detainee states that Abu Zubaydah thought that Padilla and his Accomplice seemed knowledgeable in explosives, had received explosives training, and were jihadis, but that he did not remember them from the camps, did not think the two were members of al Qaeda, and did not think Padilla was willing to do a martyrdom operation.

This senior al Qaeda detainee has stated further that Abu Zubaydah intended to use Padilla and his Accomplice in his own future operations, but sent them to KSM instead due to their impatience. Abu Zubaydah wrote a reference letter to KSM concerning Padilla and his Accomplice. Abu Zubaydah provided money for both men to travel to Karachi to meet KSM to present the plan. Abu Zubaydah advised KSM of the dirty bomb project and that he did not think it practical, but asked KSM to evaluate the proposal. Abu Zubaydah added that KSM could use them in his operations in the United States if he so wished. Abu Zubaydah sent Padilla and the accomplice to KSM in Karachi in mid-March 2002.

Suleiman Abu Ghaith, a Kuwaiti who served as al Qaeda's official spokesman, wrote a three-part essay titled, "In the Shadow of the

Lances," which appeared on Al Neda (The Call), the organization's Web site, in June 2002. Abu Ghaith lays out an extraordinary case for al Qaeda having the "right" to kill and maim millions of Americans using weapons of mass destruction, excerpts of which follow.[16]

Why were millions of people astounded by what happened to America on September 11? Did the world think that anything else would happen? What happened to America is something natural, an expected event for a country that uses terror, arrogant policy, and suppression against the nations and the peoples, and imposes a single method, thought, and way of life, as if the people of the entire world are clerks in its government offices and employed by its commercial companies and institutions.

For fifty years in Palestine, the Jews—with the blessing and support of the Americans—carried out abominations of murder, suppression, abuse, and exile. The Jews exiled nearly 5 million Palestinians and killed nearly 260,000. They wounded nearly 180,000, and crippled nearly 160,000. Due to the American bombings and siege of Iraq (a reference to the UN sanctions placed on Iraq after the first Gulf War), more than 1,200,000 Muslims were killed in the past decade.

According to the numbers, we still are at the beginning of the way. The Americans have still not tasted from our hands what we have tasted from theirs. The [number of] killed in the World Trade Center and the Pentagon are but a tiny part of the exchange for those killed in Palestine, Somalia, Sudan, the Philippines, Bosnia, Kashmir, Chechnya, and Afghanistan.

We have not reached parity with them. We have the right to kill four million Americans—two million of them children—and to exile twice as many and wound and cripple hundreds of thousands. Furthermore, it is our right to fight them with chemical and biological weapons, so as to afflict them with the fatal maladies that have afflicted the Muslims because of the [Americans'] chemical and biological weapons. America knows only the language of force. America is kept at bay by blood alone.

Abu Musab al Suri, a Syrian al Qaeda member and longtime bin Laden confidant, released this statement to jihadist Web sites on January 25, 2005.[17]

I feel sorry because there were no weapons of mass destruction in the planes that attacked New York and Washington on 9/11. We might have been relieved of the biggest number possible of voters who elected Bush for a second term!

The last option remains the destruction of America by strategic operations through nuclear, chemical, and germ weapons of mass destruction, if the mujahideen were able to get them, in cooperation with those who possess them, or through purchasing them, or through manufacturing and using primitive atomic bombs, called "dirty bombs" [radiological weapons].

Hamid Mir, bin Laden's Pakistani biographer, interviewed bin Laden after the 9/11 attacks.[18]

I interviewed him in '98. In that interview I put in this question that according to some reports, you have weapons of mass destruction and you are trying to acquire some nuclear weapons. At that time, he ignored my question, he said, "Next question." So I repeated my question again on the 8th of November, 2001. And he responded then, "We have nuclear deterrence and this is for our defense."

After the interview, we were having breakfast and when breakfast was finished, he brought some tea for us. And during the tea, I was interested to get some more information on this nuclear weapon issue. So I engaged Dr. Ayman al Zawahiri in a conversation and I asked, "It is difficult to believe that you have a nuclear weapon. How can you purchase these kinds of weapons?" He said, "Mr. Hamid Mir it is not difficult. If you have thirty million dollars, you can have these kind of [nuclear] suitcase bombs from the black market of central Asia. It's not difficult."

[Bin Laden talked about] chemical and nuclear weapons. He never used the word biological because I asked this question about anthrax: "Some people think that you are behind the anthrax attacks in America." [There was a series of post-9/11 attacks involving anthrax-laced letters in Florida, Washington, and New York that killed five.] He laughed, and said, "We don't have any link with these attacks. Next question."

Osama bin Laden's statement to Hamid Mir on November 8, 2001.[19]

I wish to declare that if America used chemical or nuclear weapons against us, then we may reply with chemical and nuclear weapons. We have the weapons as a deterrent.

After his capture by U.S. soldiers in Afghanistan in late November 2001, the "American Taliban," John Walker Lindh, told his interrogators that the scuttlebutt around the training camps was that there would be another wave of attacks following 9/11 that would involve WMD. An excerpt follows of the Department of Defense's "Interview of John Walker Lindh" on December 1, 2001.[20]

The second attack was to take place immediately before or at the beginning of Ramadan [December 2001]. The second phase of attacks could involve the use of unspecified biological agents, possible attacks on natural gas resources, or nuclear weapons facilities in the United States [field comment—source was making assumptions and conjectures based on talk among his colleagues]. The second phase was supposed to make the United States forget about the first phase. The third phase was supposed to finish the United States and was to take place within the next six months [field comment—source was making assumptions and conjectures based on talk among his colleagues].

One of the less-appreciated positive outcomes of the American war in Afghanistan in the winter of 2001 is that it ended al Qaeda's fledgling WMD program. As a result, it is highly improbable that bin Laden would have acquired or assembled even the crudest of nuclear weapons. However, it's certainly the case that al Qaeda experimented with chemical weapons, and made a series of efforts to acquire nuclear materials; efforts that seem to have come to naught. Nuclear proliferation experts dismiss as myths the existence of Russian so-called suitcase nukes, so Ayman al Zawahiri's apparent claim to Hamid Mir that al Qaeda had purchased such bombs was simple bravado on his part. Nonetheless, whatever the merits or demerits of the U.S. government's case that Jose Padilla was planning a "dirty" bomb attack in the U.S., it is certainly possible that al Qaeda, or its affiliates, could launch a radiological attack sometime in the future. In fact, it is somewhat surprising such an attack has not happened already, as the technical know-how to build a radiological weapon is not much more than a graduate-level physics degree.

12

How al Qaeda Took Root
in Iraq and the Story of
Abu Musab al Zarqawi

The United States' war in Iraq has energized al Qaeda, its affiliated groups, and like-minded jihadists around the world. What has happened in Iraq is what bin Laden could not have hoped for in his wildest dreams: The United States invaded an oil-rich Muslim nation in the heart of the Middle East, the very type of imperial adventure that bin Laden has long predicted is the "Crusaders'" long-term goal in the region. The American invasion deposed the secular, socialist Saddam, whom bin Laden had long despised, ignited Sunni and Shia fundamentalist fervor in Iraq, and provoked a classic "defensive" jihad that has galvanized jihad-minded Muslims around the world.

This is not an arcane matter of Islamic theology, but a key reason that Americans are dying in significant numbers in Iraq today. The Koran has two sets of justifications for holy war: one concerns a "defensive" jihad, when a Muslim land is under attack by non-Muslims, while another set of justifications concerns grounds for an "offensive" jihad, which countenances unprovoked attacks on infidels. Generally, Muslims consider the defensive justifications for jihad to be the most legitimate grounds for war. It was, for instance, a "defensive" jihad that Muslim clerics invoked against the Soviet occupation of Afghanistan during the 1980s.

To the extent that Sunni Muslims—the vast majority of Muslims—have a Vatican, it is the ancient Al Azhar University in Cairo, the preeminent center of Muslim thought. Before the Iraq war, Al Azhar released a fatwa, a ruling on Islamic law, to the effect that if "Crusader" forces attacked Iraq, it was an obligation for every Muslim to fight occupation forces.[1] The clerics of Al Azhar were not alone in this view. The prominent Lebanese cleric and Hezbollah leader, Sheikh Fadlallah, also called on Muslims to fight American forces in Iraq.[2] This is in sharp contrast to what these clerics ruled following the 9/11 attacks. Sheikh Fadlallah issued a fatwa condemning the attackers, as did the chief cleric of Al Azhar University.[3] And so while leading Muslim clerics condemned the 9/11 attacks, they also have condoned fighting against the American occupation of Iraq.

Some, including President Bush, have suggested that it is better to fight the terrorists on the streets of Baghdad than on those of Boston. This comforting notion is based on the dubious premise that there is a finite number of terrorists who can all be attracted to one place where they can then be killed. The reality is that the Iraq war has greatly expanded the pool of terrorists, reflected in the surge of "significant" attacks since the war began. The year 2003 saw the highest incidence of such acts in two decades. And, astonishingly, the number of significant attacks then tripled in 2004.[4] Given these numbers, it is curious that Secretary of Defense Donald Rumsfeld famously complained that "we lack metrics to know if we are winning or losing the global war on terror."[5] Exponentially rising terrorism figures is one metric that seems relevant.

President Bush has repeatedly said that Iraq is "the central front of the war on terror." This is perhaps the only proposition that the president and al Qaeda's leader can agree on. The following statements from bin Laden demonstrate that he, too, sees Iraq as central to his war.

On October 18, 2003, Al Jazeera released a "Message to the Iraqi People" from bin Laden. Al Qaeda's leader reveled in the difficulties U.S. forces were encountering in Iraq.[6]

Thank you for your jihad and may God help you. Be glad of the good news: America is mired in the swamps of the Tigris and Euphrates. Bush is easy prey. Here he is now in an embarrassing situation and here is America today being ruined before the eyes of the whole world. Oh youth of Islam everywhere, especially in (Iraq's) neighbouring countries, jihad is your duty. As God is my witness, if I had the opportunity to join you, I would not delay.

In an audiotape released on May 6, 2004, bin Laden offered a reward for the assassination of Ambassador L. Paul "Jerry" Bremer and other high-ranking U.S. officials stationed in Iraq.[7]

America has announced major awards to anyone who kills those combating in the name of God (i.e., al Qaeda's leaders). We in the al Qaeda network are committed to an award in the amount of ten kilos of gold to anyone who kills the occupier Bremer, or his deputy, or the American Forces Commander, or his deputy in Iraq.

In a statement posted to the Internet December 16, 2004, bin Laden emphasized the importance of disrupting Iraq's vital oil industry.[8]

Targeting America in Iraq in terms of economy and losses in life is a golden and unique opportunity. Do not waste the opportunity only to regret it later. One of the most important reasons that led our enemies to control our land is the theft of our oil. Do everything you can to stop the biggest plundering operation in history. Be active and prevent them from reaching the oil, and mount your operations accordingly, particularly in Iraq and the Gulf.

This chapter charts the rise of al Qaeda's role in the Iraqi insurgency and the relationship between bin Laden and the most feared insurgent commander in Iraq, the Jordanian Abu Musab al Zarqawi. Zarqawi has had an on-again-off-again relationship with al Qaeda going back to the early 1990s when he first fought in Afghanistan. He set up a training camp in western Afghanistan in 1999 for his Tawhid (Unity of God) group; an organization that was initially somewhat competitive with al Qaeda for recruits and resources. However, as the Iraq war entered its second year in 2004, Zarqawi publicly declared his allegiance to bin Laden and changed the name of his organization to al Qaeda in the Land of the Two Rivers (i.e., Iraq). Now Zarqawi is bin Laden's man on the ground in Iraq, a development that has gratified al Qaeda's leaders.

Hutaifa Azzam, the son of Abdullah Azzam, remembers Zarqawi from the time when they fought in Afghanistan against the communists in the early 1990s.[9]

I met Zarqawi in 1990–1991 in Khost [in eastern Afghanistan]. He was an ordinary guy, a guy who returned to his God after he made a lot of sins. In Jordan he was a street guy—a lot of beating people with knives; around thirty-seven cases [against him] here in Jordan. He was drinking and he finally decided to return back to Allah. He came to Afghanistan and he was a good guy. He was very brave.

He came back to Jordan in 1993 and he was sent to jail for fifteen years, and in 1999, the King gave an amnesty, and he was released in 1999. After that, he went back to Afghanistan again; doesn't join al Qaeda or bin Laden. He went to Herat on the border of Iran. He made his own training camp.

I can tell you that he is brave heart. He is not even a brave heart, he is a dead heart because he's very, very, very famous fighter. And he doesn't know what is the meaning of frightened or to be afraid. He can fight an army alone; even if everyone left him, he's ready to fight.

Sayf Adel has been the military commander of al Qaeda since 2002. Like Hutaifa Azzam, he first met Zarqawi in Afghanistan in the early 1990s. Adel gives a detailed account of the evolving relationship between al Qaeda and Zarqawi in _Al Zarqawi: The Second al Qaeda Generation,_ a book by Fuad Hussein, a Jordanian journalist. The Arabic-language, London-based daily _Al Quds al Arabi_ started serializing the book in May 2005.[10]

I received reports that a group of Jordanians arrived in Kandahar [in 1999]. I was busy with my work outside the region. I returned to Kandahar two weeks after Abu Musab's [al Zarqawi's] arrival and I went to meet him at the guesthouse that provided accommodation for newcomers. In a nutshell, Abu Musab was a hardliner when it came to his disagreements with other fraternal brothers.

I was scheduled to meet with both Sheikh bin Laden and Sheikh al Zawahiri. We had a planned agenda to discuss after which I suggested that we talk about Abu Musab. Abu Musab was a sturdy man who was not really very good at words. He expressed himself spontaneously and briefly. He would not compromise any of his beliefs. He was uncompromising, but he had a clear objective, which he strived to achieve—the reestablishment of Islam in society. He did not have details regarding how to achieve this objective except for comprehending the faith thoroughly, and initiating jihad. One of the topics we discussed was that we were not seeking full allegiance from Abu Musab or his companions. Rather, we wanted coordination and cooperation to achieve our joint objectives.

The main idea of the [resulting] project was based on the importance of finding an area in Afghanistan where a simple camp would be established for daily training. Abu Musab would oversee the camp and bring in fraternal brothers from Jordan, Palestine, Syria, Lebanon, Iraq, and Turkey to forge a presence for us in these important areas. The second point that we discussed with some fraternal experts was the importance that such an area would be remote from our headquarters and would be located on the western border of Afghanistan adjacent to Iran. Iran became a safe passage for the fraternal brothers after the Pakistani authorities began to tighten the noose around our movement. It was very difficult for Arabs to arrive in Afghanistan through Pakistan. It was easy, on the other hand, for the brothers to take the Turkey to Iran to Afghanistan route. Herat was a suitable Afghan city near to the Iranian border and it was somewhat remote from us.

The days passed quickly and the date of our monthly meeting arrived. Abu Musab came carrying good news. The number in the camp amounted to 42 men, women, and children including the families of Abu Musab and his two companions. Three new Syrian families arrived including one that came from Europe. Abu Musab was optimistic that they were establishing a mini Islamic society. He said that fraternal Jordanian and Palestinian brothers would arrive in Herat soon. He said the Iran-Afghanistan route was safe to travel. This issue prompted us to think of building good relations with some virtuous people in Iran to coordinate regarding issues of mutual interest. Coordination with the Iranians was later achieved with sincere individuals who were hostile to the Americans and the Israelis. It was not made with the Iranian government.

During this time, I noticed that Abu Musab became more polished. When we first met he was not the one who would begin a conversation. His ideas and interests in political news were limited. Now, however, he was the one who would start a conversation. He was interested in every issue. He would utilize public relations that might lead his project to success. I noticed that he became more influential when he spoke to someone. He spoke more in standard Arabic, whereas before he used to speak in his normal [Jordanian] dialect. All these issues indicated that he would become a distinguished leader. The fraternal brothers of various nationalities who converged on Herat to join him received training. These included Syrians, Jordanians, Palestinians, and some Lebanese and Iraqis. Abu Musab was able to build relations with the Kurdish Ansar al-Islam and began to establish bases in northern Iraq [in an area outside of Saddam Hussein's control].

The U.S. strike [against Afghanistan] began at the end of 2001. Abu Musab returned to Herat to be close to his fraternal brothers and group. We did not have a clear or defined plan for confrontation. The young men of al Qaeda, Taliban, and Abu Musab's group had no other alternative, but to withdraw quickly and join us in eastern Afghanistan. They left in a 135-vehicle convoy that carried them, their fraternal Arab brothers of al Qaeda in the region, and the remnants of the fraternal Taliban brothers. At the beginning, we decided to defend Kandahar regardless of the consequences. We began to secure the wives and children of the fraternal Arab brothers by sending them to Pakistan. We began to make preparations for confrontation.

One day, there was a meeting with some of the important fraternal brothers including Abu Musab. One fraternal brother used his Thuraya satellite phone. A few minutes after the man used his telephone I left the site of the meeting with three other fraternal brothers. Ten minutes after our departure, a U.S. plane bombed the house where we held the meeting. Abu Musab and some fraternal brothers were still there. The bombardment resulted in the collapse of the ceiling of the home. No one was killed but some of the fraternal brothers sustained injuries, including Abu Musab, who suffered from broken ribs. He had bruises as a result of the collapse of the ceiling.

The [U.S.] assault began on Kandahar. The leadership made a new decision to withdraw to the mountains and evacuate the wounded to safe places. Abu Musab was requested to leave for Pakistan since he was wounded. He refused, however, and insisted on joining us to take part in the battle.

Everyone who dares to harm this giant elephant—the United States—will be punished. Punishment is total extermination. This was one of the major challenges that faced us at the outset. Thus, the leadership made an audacious decision to dismantle the [Taliban] emirate and integrate into the Afghan society once again. This move will enable it to return in seven years, in harmony with a well-examined plan that will defeat the Americans and their supporters.

We began to converge on Iran one after the other. The fraternal brothers in the Peninsula of the Arabs, Kuwait, and the United Arab Emirates who where outside Afghanistan, had already arrived. They possessed abundant funds. We began to rent apartments for the fraternal brothers and some of their families. The fraternal brothers of the group of Gulbuddin Hekmatyar [the hard-line Islamist leader in Afghanistan, long allied to al Qaeda] offered us satisfactory help in this field. They provided us with apartments and some farms that they owned.

Shadi Abdalla, a Jordanian of Palestinian origin, was affiliated with the al Tawhid terrorist group, which was led by Zarqawi. He was arrested by German police in April 2002. In his interrogations by German law enforcement, Abdalla describes the founding of al Tawhid, its presence in the United Kingdom, and the role of Abu Qatada, its spiritual leader. (Abdalla also worked briefly as a bodyguard for bin Laden.)

Abdalla also explains that Zarqawi, at least up until early 2002, was focused on a campaign of terrorism in Jordan and against Israeli and Jewish targets, not against the United States, which was the essential ideological difference between al Tawhid and al Qaeda. What follows are summaries of Shadi Abdalla's interrogations by German investigators and direct quotations from those interrogations.[11]

Al Zarqawi (a.k.a. Muhannad) leads a terrorist organization consisting of Jordanian-Palestinians called the "Group of Muhannad Abu Musab Al Zarqawi" or "al Tahwid." Shadi also explained that the name component "al Zarqawi" indicates Zarqawi's origin from the Jordanian town of Zarka. The center of the organization is Herat [in western Afghanistan]. Their headquarters is there, too, which is a training camp. Muhannad stayed in Kabul, not at the headquarters. He lived with his family in a private home.

One can't tell that Muhannad (Zarqawi) is the leader of an organization. This is different than in the case of bin Laden who is always accompanied by his bodyguards. Muhannad moves around quite normally in the streets.

[You become a member of Zarqawi's group] through a handshake with the leader in which one takes an oath of loyalty and obedience. This is common in all organizations. If you are a member of an organization, anything that happens to the organization affects you. You have to carry out orders and you must not betray the organization. One becomes a member of the organization by promising to one's superior, "I promise before God that I will work with you and do whatever pleases Allah and the Prophet Mohammed." One gives this promise after the criteria have been checked, i.e., when it is clear that one is Palestinian and Muslim, and one comes from Jordan, and a guarantor has vouched for you. One has also committed oneself to following the Sharia faithfully. In addition, one has to reject a worldly order like what exists in Jordan at the moment.

There are many members [of al Tahwid], not only in Afghanistan but also in Great Britain. People from Western countries enjoyed special prestige in the organization because they could move freely between countries. The goals of the organization are attacks on Jewish, Israeli and Jordanian facilities, in particular on Israeli targets in Jordan and the Jordanian army. Concrete plans were developed only immediately before their execution. The attacks are supposed to be carried out with explosives or arms. Al Tawhid ("ALT") is mainly present in two European countries: Germany and the U.K.

The root of the catastrophe from al Qaeda's perspective is the United States, from al Tahwid's perspective it's Israel. The main targets of both organizations are therefore primarily American in the case of al Qaeda, for al Tahwid they are Israeli or Jewish. Al Qaeda recruits its members from all Arab countries. But there are parallel organizations that recruit only from their own countries. An example is al Tahwid which recruits its members only from Jordan. These organizations pursue only goals that have something to do with their home countries. Examples would be organizations consisting of people from Syria, Algeria or Tunisia. Bin Laden pursues the goal of uniting all organizations and of focusing on the common enemy; the United States.

I know that an attack was planned against a significant tourist destination in Jordan [around the time of the Millennium], a mountain on which the prophet Moses is thought to have stood to show the Jews the Holy

Land (Mount Nebo, Jordan). This is a destination for tourists, in particular Jews. (This plot was broken up by Jordanian intelligence.)

Currently, Jewish and Israeli facilities all over the world, and suitable targets in the United States, France, Great Britain and Germany, are all targets. In early 2002 the members of al Tahwid began discussing attacks on Jewish facilities in Germany. The group was very upset about the latest developments in the Israeli-Palestinian conflict. No concrete plans were developed.

I never joined [al Tahwid]. I didn't take an oath of loyalty. My intimate relationship to [Zarqawi] was based on my acquaintance with Abu Ali (an al Tahwid leader). Zarqawi frequently asked me to take the oath but I kept postponing under the pretext that first I would like to get to know better him and the religion. My position (within the organization) was so strong that I could afford to postpone the oath. I was very important for the organization because I had a residence permit for Germany.

I only talked to certain people on the phone under Abu Ali's orders and asked these people to give money. Some of this money was collected in mosques. It comes from rich businessmen who are very religious. We tell these people that the money is used for religious purposes. They don't know in most cases that the money goes to al Qaeda or other organizations.

For the religious legitimation of an attack this was primarily the responsibility of Abu Qatada, not of Muhannad (an alias for Zarqawi). There is a person above Muhannad in England called Abu Qatada.

The interrogation of Shadi Abdallah clarifies an important point: Zarqawi's longtime spiritual mentor is Abu Qatada, a Jordanian cleric who settled in London in 1993. After the July 7, 2005, bombings in London that killed fifty-six people, the British government set in motion a plan to deport Abu Qatada to his native Jordan.

The centerpiece of the Bush administration's case for going to war in Iraq was Secretary of State Colin Powell's presentation to the U.N. Security Council on February 5, 2003. One section of Powell's speech tried to make the case for an emerging alliance between Saddam Hussein and al Qaeda in the person of Zarqawi.[12]

What I want to bring to your attention today is the potentially much more sinister nexus between Iraq and the al Qaeda terrorist network, a nexus that combines classic terrorist organizations and modern methods of murder. Iraq today harbors a deadly terrorist network headed by Abu Musab al Zarqawi, an associate and collaborator of Osama bin Laden and his al Qaeda lieutenants.

However, much of what German intelligence agencies had discovered from their informant Shadi Abdalla and other sources in 2002 indicated that Zarqawi and al Qaeda were as much as in competition as in cooperation. What follows are summaries from a German Bureau of Criminal Investigations (BKA) report on Zarqawi.[13]

Thus, according to Shadi Abdalla, there was a demarcation between al Qaeda and the ideology pursued by al Zarqawi. There is respect as fellow Muslims, but different objectives are followed. The objectives of al Zarqawi are attacks against the officers of the military, the police, and the secret service, the fall of the Jordanian government, and the establishment of an Islamic state, as well as attacks against the Jews and Jewish interests. From the point of view of Zarqawi the Jews represent the "Root of All Evil." But from the point of view of al Qaeda, it is the U.S. Moreover, Zarqawi mentioned to Abdalla that the possibility of a merger conflicted with the religious orientation of Abu Hafs al Mauretani (the Mauritania) who was responsible within al Qaeda for religious or Islamic matters, which contradicted the teachings practiced by Zarqawi. This opinion at that time is said to have led to other groups, such as that of Zarqawi, not joining al Qaeda.

Even in the interrogations of al Qaeda leaders there are no indications of Zarqawi's membership in al Qaeda. Thus, Abu Zubaydah (an al Qaeda recruiter), in one of his interrogations, speaks instead about the "Group of al Zarqawi."

After the 9/11 terrorist attacks, the BKA began to tape telephone conversations between suspected terrorists in Germany and Zarqawi in Afghanistan and Iran. The BKA, the German equivalent of the FBI, taped forty-one conversations between October 19, 2001, and April 7, 2002. Most conversations took place between Zarqawi and Abu Ali, his

closest subordinate in Germany. Others were among Zarqawi's follow-ers in Germany, or between his German and Jordanian followers. This intelligence report was compiled by the BKA in April 2002 and provides an interesting snapshot of Zarqawi's organization as it made the transi-tion from its base in Afghanistan to Iran after 9/11. (Sometime in 2002 Zarqawi would then move to Iraq.)[14]

ZARQAWI'S PERSONAL DATA.
- Mobile phone in Iran: 0098-9135153994.
- Fax number in Iran: 0098-218757638.
- Satellite phone: 0087-0762724528 and 0087-0762944549
- Email address: alzabh@yahoo.com

ZARQAWI'S NAMES AND ALIASES
- The speakers tried to cover up the identity of Zarqawi by using a host of different names for him.
- When addressing him directly they called him "Habib" or "Muhan-nad." When talking to others about him they would also call him "Al Zarqawi" or "Abu Musab." Occasionally they would refer to him as "al Gareeb," "Abu Hossein" or "Eisen." Once someone called him "Ezzarija."
- In some cases one speaker would have to use several names before his interlocutor realized he talked about Zarqawi. The many different names created some confusion.

CODE WORDS
- "university" = prison; "hospital" = imprisonment
- (possibly): "pigs" = Americans; "butterflies" = helicopters
- "Girl" or "(female) dancer" = forged passport;
- "journal" = passport; "band aid" = visa (possibly)
- (probably) "firm" = terrorist organization
- "to be sick" = under observation by the police

COMMUNICATION
- In Afghanistan Zarqawi used satellite telephones. From Iran he used the landline of his friend Rashid Haroun (telephone number 0098-9112311436).

Reorganization of al Tawhid (the Jordanian terrorist organization)

- In early 2002 Zarqawi indicated he wanted to reorganize al Tahwid. The BKA assumes that the previous structure had been destroyed by the war in Afghanistan and that Zarqawi wanted to seize the opportunity to build up a new organization under his leadership.
- During that time the whole terrorist network was in a state of shift. The training camps in Afghanistan had to be abandoned, and the terrorists had to regroup themselves in neighboring countries, particularly Iran and Pakistan.
- Communication with friends and colleagues in foreign countries becomes increasingly difficult because the security services were tightening their control and most telephone lines are under surveillance.
- A few conversations between some of Zarqawi's German followers suggest that the reorganization was unlikely to happen at Zarqawi's then-residence, Iran, because the authorities did not support his political activities.

Sayf Adel, al Qaeda's military commander, describes how Zarqawi left Iran for Iraq in 2002 as the United States was gearing up for the invasion of Iraq.[15]

Abu Musab [Zarqawi] and his Jordanian and Palestinian comrades opted to go to Iraq. Following a long debate, their skin color and Jordanian dialect would enable them to integrate into the Iraqi society easily. Our expectations of the situation indicated that the Americans would inevitably make a mistake and invade Iraq sooner or later. Such an invasion would aim at overthrowing the regime. Therefore, we should play an important role in the resistance.

Contrary to what the Americans frequently reiterated, al Qaeda did not have any relationship with Saddam Hussein or his regime. We had to draw up a plan to enter Iraq through the north that was not under the control of [Saddam's] regime. We would then spread south to the areas of our fraternal Sunni brothers. The fraternal brothers of the Ansar al Islam [a Kurdish jihadist group based in northern Iraq] expressed their willingness to offer assistance to help us achieve this goal. The goal was to go to Sunni areas in central Iraq and begin to prepare for confrontations to face the U.S. invasion and defeat the Americans.

The German BKA traced Zarqawi's progress from Iran to northern Iraq in early or mid-2002 to an area outside of the control of Saddam Hussein's regime. There Zarqawi made contact with the Islamist terrorist group Ansar al Islam; he made a deal with its leader to begin a campaign against U.S. targets in Iraq following the impending U.S. ground invasion.[16]

After the military intervention of the U.S.-led armed forces at the end of 2001 in Afghanistan, al Qaeda members are said to have traveled from Afghanistan via Iran into the territory of Ansar al Islam in northern Iraq. There were said to be a group of 20–25 Jordanians and Syrians among them, who were said to have been led by Zarqawi.

A close collaboration between Zarqawi and Ansar al Islam was also substantiated by the statements of the Jordanian citizen Ahmad al Riyati. According to al Riyati, a meeting between Mullah Krekar [the leader of Ansar al Islam] and al Zarqawi took place probably in mid-2002 in Iraq. During this meeting, both are said to have agreed to equip a group of about fifteen persons with weapons and explosive charges in order to carry out attacks against foreigners and American targets in Jordan.

In early 2004, U.S. intelligence intercepted a letter from Zarqawi to bin Laden in which he advises bin Laden on the situation in Iraq and proposes a strategy for carrying forward the jihad. At its core, Zarqawi suggests unleashing a civil war between Sunnis and Shia, something bin Laden has historically rejected in seeking to restore a unified caliphate, and also because senior al Qaeda leaders are living under some form of arrest in largely Shia Iran. The Coalition Provisional Authority published the translated letter in February 2004, excerpts of which follow.[17]

To the men on the mountain tops [i.e., bin Laden and Zawahiri], to the hawks of glory, peace and the mercy and blessings of God be upon you.

Even if our bodies are far apart, the distance between our hearts is close.

I send you an account [of] Iraq.

After study and examination, we can narrow our enemy down to four groups.

1. The Americans: These, as you know, are the most cowardly of God's creatures. They are an easy quarry, praise be to God. We ask God to enable us to kill and capture them to sow panic among those behind them and to trade them for our detained brothers.

2. The Kurds: These are a lump [in the throat] and a thorn whose time to be clipped has yet to come. They are last on the list, even though we are making efforts to harm some of their symbolic figures, God willing.

3. Soldiers, Police, and Agents: These are the eyes, ears, and hands of the occupier, through which he sees, hears, and delivers violent blows. God willing, we are determined to target them strongly in the coming period before the situation is consolidated.

4. The Shi'a: These in our opinion are the key to change. I mean that targeting and hitting them in [their] religious, political, and military depth will provoke them to show the Sunnis the hidden rancor working in their breasts. If we succeed in dragging them into the arena of sectarian war, it will become possible to awaken the inattentive Sunnis as they feel imminent danger.

[Osama bin Laden and Ayman al Zawahiri] You, gracious brothers, are the leaders, guides, and symbolic figures of jihad and battle. We do not see ourselves as fit to challenge you, and we have never striven to achieve glory for ourselves. All that we hope is that we will be the spearhead, the enabling vanguard, and the bridge on which the [Islamic] nation crosses over to the victory that is promised and the tomorrow to which we aspire. This is our vision. If you are convinced of the idea of fighting the sects of apostasy [the Shia], we will be your readied soldiers, working under your banner, complying with your orders, and indeed swearing fealty to you publicly and in the news media. If things appear otherwise to you, we are brothers, and the disagreement will not spoil [our] friendship. Awaiting your response, may God preserve you.

Hutaifa Azzam, the son of Abdullah Azzam, has known Zarqawi well for more than a decade. He insists that the relationship between

Zarqawi and bin Laden became strong only after the U.S. occupation of Iraq in 2003.

[Zarqawi had] no relations with Osama until he left to Iraq. His relation with Osama started one year [ago in 2004] through the Internet.

An unlikely supporter of this view is Secretary of Defense Donald Rumsfeld, who spoke at a meeting at the Council on Foreign Relations in New York on October 4, 2004.[18]

In the case of al Qaeda, my impression is most of the senior people have actually sworn an oath to Osama bin Laden, and to my knowledge, even as of this late date, I don't believe Zarqawi, the principal leader of the network in Iraq, has sworn an oath.

A couple of weeks after Rumsfeld's comment, on October 17, 2004, Zarqawi issued an online statement in the name of his Tahwid group pledging allegiance to bin Laden.[19] **Zarqawi adopted a new name for his group, "al Qaeda in Iraq." And so nearly two years after Bush officials had first argued that Zarqawi was part of al Qaeda, the Jordanian terrorist finally got around to swearing loyalty to bin Laden.**

[Let it be known that] al Tawhid pledges both its leaders and its soldiers to the mujahid commander, Sheikh Osama bin Laden (in word and in deed) and to jihad for the sake of God until there is no more discord [among the ranks of Islam] and all of the religion turns toward God.

By God, O sheikh of the mujahideen, if you bid us plunge into the ocean, we would follow you. If you ordered it so, we would obey. If you forbade us something, we would abide by your wishes. For what a fine commander you are to the armies of Islam, against the inveterate infidels and apostates!

A bin Laden audiotape that aired on Al Jazeera on December 27, 2004, welcomed Zarqawi into al Qaeda.[20]

I believe that the dignified brother Abu Musab al Zarqawi, and the groups affiliated with him are good and from the group that fights ac-

cording to the orders of God. We were pleased with their daring operations against the Americans. We in the al Qaeda organisation warmly
welcome their union with us. It should be known that the *mujahid*
brother Abu Musab al Zarqawi is the *amir* of the al Qaeda organisation in
the Land of the Two Rivers [i.e., Iraq]. The brothers in the group there
should heed his orders and obey him in all that which is good.

**Zarqawi followed up his pledge of allegiance to bin Laden with a let-
ter in May 2005. The letter asks deferentially for orders from al Qaeda's
leader.**[21]

From a soldier standing in the line of fire, from Abu Musab al Zarqawi
to his great prince, Osama bin Laden, May God grant him with his blessings and give him the best of his divine generosity. Our prince, we ask to
God to keep you safe and give you a longer life, make you a thorn in the
side of the enemies and to make you a martyr at the end. We are waiting
for your directions and orders.

**What follows is an edited version of a letter that Ayman al Zawahiri
sent to an associate of Zarqawi's in July 2005. The letter, which was intercepted by U.S. forces in Iraq and made public in mid-October 2005,
provides a fascinating glimpse of Zawahiri unplugged; bemoaning the
mistakes that al Qaeda has made by not connecting to the "masses," and
urging Zarqawi not to make this same mistake with his campaign
against the Shia and his habit of beheading his victims.**

Dear brother, God Almighty knows how much I miss meeting with
you, how much I long to join you in your historic battle against the
greatest of criminals and apostates in the heart of the Islamic world,
the field where epic and major battles in the history of Islam were
fought. I think that if I could find a way to you, I would not delay a day,
God willing.

My dear brother, we are following your news, despite the difficulty
and hardship. We received your last published message sent to Sheikh
Osama bin Laden, God save him (a possible reference to Zarqawi's October 2004 pledge of allegiance to bin Laden). Likewise, I made sure in my

last speech—that Al Jazeera broadcast Saturday, 18 June 2005—to mention you, send you greetings, and show support and thanks for the heroic acts you are performing in defense of Islam and the Muslims

I want to reassure you about our situation. The summer started hot with operations escalating in Afghanistan. The real danger comes from the agent Pakistani army that is carrying out operations in the tribal areas looking for mujahideen.

So we must think for a long time about our next steps and how we want to attain it, and it is my humble opinion that the Jihad in Iraq requires several incremental goals:

The first stage: Expel the Americans from Iraq.
The second stage: Establish an Islamic authority or emirate, then develop it and support it until it achieves the level of a caliphate—over as much territory as you can to spread its power in Iraq, i.e., in Sunni areas.
The third stage: Extend the jihad wave to the secular countries neighboring Iraq.
The fourth stage: It may coincide with what came before: the clash with Israel, because Israel was established only to challenge any new Islamic entity.

If we look at the two short-term goals, which are removing the Americans and establishing an Islamic emirate in Iraq then we will see that the strongest weapon which the mujahideen enjoy—after the help and granting of success by God—is popular support from the Muslim masses in Iraq, and the surrounding Muslim countries. The Muslim masses— for many reasons, and this is not the place to discuss it—do not rally except against an outside occupying enemy, especially if the enemy is firstly Jewish, and secondly American. Therefore, the mujahed movement must avoid any action that the masses do not understand or approve.

We don't want to repeat the mistake of the Taliban, who restricted participation in governance to the religious students and the people of Kandahar alone. They did not have any representation for the Afghan people in their ruling regime, so the result was that the Afghan people disengaged themselves from them. Even devout ones took the stance of the spectator and, when the invasion came, the (Taliban) emirate collapsed in days, because the people were either passive or hostile.

Therefore, I stress again to you and to all your brothers the need to direct the political action equally with the military action, by the alliance, cooperation and gathering of all leaders of opinion and influence in the Iraqi arena. I can't define for you a specific means of action. You are more knowledgeable about the field conditions. But you and your brothers must strive to have around you circles of support, assistance, and cooperation, and through them, to advance until you become a consensus, entity, organization, or association that represents all the honorable people in Iraq. I repeat the warning against separating from the masses, whatever the danger.

For that reason, many of your Muslim admirers amongst the common folk are wondering about your attacks on the Shia. The sharpness of this questioning increases when the attacks are on one of their mosques. My opinion is that this matter won't be acceptable to the Muslim populace however much you have tried to explain it, and aversion to this will continue.

Among the things which the feelings of the Muslim populace who love and support you will never find palatable are the scenes of slaughtering the hostages. You shouldn't be deceived by the praise of some of the zealous young men and their description of you as the sheik of the slaughterers, etc. I say to you that we are in a battle, and that more than half of this battle is taking place in the battlefield of the media.

I have a definite desire to travel to you but I do not know whether that is possible from the standpoint of traveling and getting settled, so please let me know.

As for my personal condition, I am in good health, blessings and wellness thanks to God and His grace. I am only lacking your pious prayers, in which I beg you not to forget me. God Almighty has blessed me with a daughter whom I have named (Nawwar), and Nawwar means: the timid female gazelle and the woman who is free from suspicion.

Your loving brother

Abu Muhammad [Ayman al Zawahiri]
Saturday, 09 July, 2005.

Unless we plan to occupy Iraq indefinitely, there remains the question of what the "foreign fighters" led by the Jordanian Zarqawi will do when the war ends. It would be nice if they returned to their respective countries to rejoin civilian life. Judging from the "blowback" generated by veterans of the Afghan war against the Soviets, these fighters will more likely swap business cards, gain impressive battle skills and bragging rights, and become the new shock troops of the international jihadist movement.

Several factors could make blowback from the Iraq war even more dangerous than the fallout from Afghanistan. Foreign fighters started to arrive in Iraq even before Saddam Hussein's regime fell. They have conducted most of the suicide bombings—including some that have delivered strategic successes such as the withdrawal of most international aid organizations and the United Nations—and the Jordanian Zarqawi is perhaps the most effective insurgent commander in the field. They are more battle-hardened than the Afghan Arabs, who fought demoralized Soviet Army conscripts. Foreign fighters in Iraq today are testing themselves against arguably the best army in history, acquiring skills in their battles against coalition forces that will be far more useful for future terrorist operations than those their counterparts learned during the 1980s. Mastering how to make improvised explosive devices or how to conduct suicide operations is more relevant to urban terrorism than the conventional guerrilla tactics that were used against the Red Army in Afghanistan. U.S. military commanders say that techniques perfected in Iraq are already spreading to the war in Afghanistan.

Finally, foreign involvement in the Iraqi conflict will likely lead Iraqi nationals to become international terrorists. The Afghans were glad to have Arab money but were culturally, religiously, and psychologically removed from the Afghan Arabs; they neither joined al Qaeda nor identified with its radical theology. Iraqis, however, are closer culturally to the foreign fighters, and some will volunteer to continue other jihads even after the United States departs their country.

13

Bin Laden on the Run

Scott McClellan, the White House spokesman, on October 5, 2005.[1]

We continue to pursue bin Laden. We will bring him to justice. He is someone who has been on the run. We have made great success in dismantling and disrupting the leadership of al Qaeda. And some three-quarters of the top leadership of al Qaeda has been brought to justice in one way or another. But this is a broader movement than any one person.

What follows are some of bin Laden's key statements that he has made while on the run. They reflect an initial pessimism after the fall of the Taliban and the battle of Tora Bora, but over the years, bin Laden's tone becomes more forceful and self-assured. He even has made an attempt to appear statesmanlike from 2004 onwards, offering "truces" with nations that pull out of the coalition in Iraq and, just before the U.S. presidential election, speaking directly to American voters. In recent years bin Laden has increasingly adopted the role of the Elder Statesman of Jihad.

On December 14, 2001, around the time of his escape from Tora Bora, Osama bin Laden wrote his will, which strikes an introspective, dispirited note. The following excerpts first appeared in Al Majallah magazine in October 2002.2

Allah commended to us that when death approaches any of us that we make a bequest to parents and next of kin and to Muslims as a whole. If every Muslim asks himself why has our nation reached this state of humiliation and defeat, then his obvious answer is because it rushed madly for the comforts of life and discarded the Book of Allah. The Jews and

Christians have tempted us with the comforts of life and its cheap pleasures and invaded us with their materialistic values before invading us with their armies while we stood like women doing nothing because the love of death in the cause of Allah has deserted the hearts.

The principal cause of our nation's ordeal is its fear from dying in the cause of Allah. O youth of the nation. Crave death and life will be given to you. My last advice to all the mujahidin wherever they are: Recover your breath and forget for the time being the fight against the Jews and Crusaders. Devote yourselves to purging your ranks of agents and the weak and the bad clerics who are refraining from jihad and who have let the nation down.

Your brother Abu-Abdallah Osama bin Muhammed bin Laden, Friday, 28 Ramadan 1422 Hegira, corresponding to 14 December 2001.

Bin Laden signed his will the day after the Night of Power, which falls on the 27th of Ramadan. As mentioned in Chapter 3, this is a day of special importance for Muslims when it is particularly auspicious to die, as the gates of heaven are open. Death was clearly weighing on bin Laden's mind during this period.

On December 27, 2001 Al Jazeera aired bin Laden's first videotaped statement after his escape from Tora Bora. Bin Laden explained that the emphasis should now not be on the role of himself and his followers (al Qaeda the organization) but the awakening of Muslims (al Qaeda the ideology).[3]

The latest events have proved important truths. It has become clear that the West in general and America in particular have an unspeakable hatred for Islam. Terrorism against America deserves to be praised because it was a response to injustice, aimed at forcing America to stop its support for Israel, which kills our people. We say that the end of the United States is imminent, whether bin Laden or his followers are alive or dead, for the awakening of the Muslim umma (nation) has occured.

Hamzah bin Laden is one of bin Laden's sons. In a poem posted on al Qaeda's main Web site, "Islamic Studies and Research," sometime in

June 2002, Hamzah addressed himself to his father about the difficulties of life on the run.[4]

Oh father! Where is the escape and when will we have a home? Oh father! I see spheres of danger everywhere I look. How come our home has vanished without a trace? Why is it that we only see barriers along our path? Oh father! Why have they showered us with bombs like rain, having no mercy for a child?

Oh father! What has happened for us to be chased by danger? Immortality is our destiny should God Almighty desire victory for us. Tell me father something useful about what I see.

Osama bin Laden replied to his son with his own poem.

Oh son! Suffice to say that I am full of grief and sighs. What can I say if we are living in a world of laziness and discontent? What can I say to a world that is blind in both sight and perception? Pardon me my son, but I can only see a very steep path ahead. A decade has gone by in vagrancy and travel, and here we are in our tragedy. Security has gone, but danger remains. It is a world of crimes in which children are slaughtered like cows. For how long will real men be in short supply? Action must somehow be done to ward off harm. I have sworn by God Almighty to fight the infidel.

Despite being on the run, bin Laden and his number two, Ayman al Zawahiri, have been able to continue to influence jihadist militants around the world by releasing a series of audio and videotapes that have been widely disseminated. There is a strong correlation between al Qaeda's leaders calling for attacks and their later execution.[5] **Shortly after bin Laden called for renewed assaults against the west in October 2002, a disco was bombed in Bali, Indonesia, killing two hundred, mostly Western tourists, and a suicide attack was launched at a French oil tanker steaming off the coast of Yemen. In September 2003, al Zawahiri condemned Pakistan's President Pervez Musharraf for supporting the campaign against al Qaeda; Musharraf narrowly survived two assassination attempts three months later.**[6] **In October 2003, bin Laden**

called for attacks against members of the coalition in Iraq.[7] Terrorists subsequently bombed a British consulate in Turkey and commuters on their way to work in both Madrid and London.

Ahmad Zaidan, Al Jazeera's Pakistan bureau chief, received a mysterious videotape on November 12, 2002, a month after the Bali attacks.[8]

It was at 10:00 somebody called me and he said that, "Okay, I have something for you. There's something urgent for you. Come to the place." And I drive to that place and parked my car, and all of a sudden somebody approached me. It was night, of course. And he said, "Okay. This is yours. Take." I said, "What is it?" He said, "This is the bin Laden tape." I told him, "Okay. Wait, hold on for a minute. I want to ask. . . ." And he disappeared and of course, I couldn't be patient. I put it in the tape and the tape was Osama bin Laden, no doubt. Of course, it was the most important scoop for me, really. He was alive.

The bin Laden videotape was broadcast on Al Jazeera on November 12, 2002. It was his first videotaped statement in almost a year. This is an edited version.

What has happened since the conquests of New York and Washington up until now, like the operations on Germans in Tunisia [an attack on April 11, 2002, on a synagogue that killed seventeen], on the French in Karachi in [May 2002 that killed twelve], on Australians and Britons in the explosions in Bali [on October 12, 2002, that killed two hundred], as well as the recent hostage-taking in Moscow [in October 2002 that killed 129 hostages and 41 terrorists] and other operations here and there were nothing but the response of Muslims eager to defend their religion and respond to the order of God and their Prophet.

Do your governments not know that the clique in the White House is made up of the greatest murderers of the century? Rumsfeld is the butcher of Vietnam who has killed more than two million people. [Rumsfeld was the secretary of defense as the Vietnam War was winding down]. Cheney and Powell have murdered and destroyed in Baghdad more than did Houlagou [a 13th-century Mongolian warlord who conquered the city].

Why did your governments ally themselves with America to attack us in Afghanistan, and I cite in particular Great Britain, France, Italy, Canada, Germany and Australia? Australia was warned about its participation [in the war] in Afghanistan, but it ignored this warning until it was awakened by the echoes of explosions in Bali. Its government subsequently pretended, falsely, that its citizens were not targeted.

If you suffer to see your [people] killed and those of your allies in Tunisia, Karachi, Bali, remember our [people] killed among the children of Palestine, in Iraq. Remember our dead in Afghanistan. As you look at your dead in Moscow, also recall ours in Chechnya.

For how long will fear, massacres, destruction, exile, orphanhood and widowhood be our lot, while security, stability and joy remain your domain alone? It is high time that equality be established to this effect as you assassinate, so will you be [assassinated], and as you bomb so will you likewise be.

Excerpts from a bin Laden statement that was released on February 16, 2003. It's clear from this that the Sykes-Picot agreement of 1916, which set the stage for the carving up of the Ottoman empire between the French and the British following the end of World War I, plays the same role for bin Laden that the 1919 Treaty of Versailles did for Adolf Hitler: a humiliating "stab-in-the back" that must be avenged and reversed.[9]

We still suffer from the injuries inflicted by the Crusaders' wars on the Islamic world in the last century and by the Sykes-Picot agreement between Britain and France which divided the Muslim world into fragments. And now we find ourselves confronted once more with the spirit of the Sykes-Picot agreement [under another name]: the Bush-Blair agreement, which is conducted under the same banner and for the same purpose—the banner is that of the cross, the purpose is the destruction and plunder of [Muslims.]

On April 14, 2004, a month after the multiple bombings commuter trains in Madrid that killed 191, bin Laden offered a "truce" to European nations participating in the coalition in Iraq. Excerpts follow.[10]

[Think about] what happened on September 11 and March 11 [2004, the bombings in Madrid.] I offer a truce to [Europe]. This first truce can be renewed upon expiry and the establishment of a new government agreed upon by both parties. And the announcement of the truce starts with the withdrawal of the last soldier from our land [a reference to Afghanistan and Iraq] and the door is open for three months from the date of the announcement of this statement. Whoever rejects this truce and wants war, we are [war's] sons and whoever wants this truce, here we bring it.

⚜

One of the most significant developments after 9/11 was bin Laden's willingness to approve a terror campaign against the Saudi regime. This was the culmination of bin Laden's journey from his initial reluctance to oppose the Saudi royal family in the late 1980s to becoming an implacable enemy of the Saudi government.

Excerpts of Statement by Osama bin Laden, December 16, 2004, posted to al Qal'ah (the Fortress) Web site.[11]

The government of Riyadh (the capital of Saudi Arabia) has entered into an international alliance with the infidel Crusaders led by Bush against Islam and its people. This is a short message to the Riyadh rulers and decision-makers—there is a contract between the ruler and his subjects entailing rights and obligations on both parties. One of its main features is that the ruler protects his people. But the truth is otherwise. You have oppressed the people without their agreement. The people have woken from their slumber and realized the extent of the tyranny and corruption that you exercise. You might also keep in mind the fate of the Shah of Iran and the fate of Ceausescu in Romania (dictators who were overthrown by popular revolutions).

Abdulaziz al Muqrin, also as known as Abu Hajjer, assumed command of al Qaeda's operations in Saudi Arabia in March 2004. Al Muqrin's cell was involved in attacks on residential compounds in the cities of Riyadh and Khobar in 2003 and 2004 in which fifty-one were killed. He is also believed to be responsible for the killings of Simon

Cumbers, a BBC cameraman, and two Americans, Robert Jacobs and Paul Johnson. Al Muqrin was killed [in Riyadh] on June 18, 2004.

In October 2003, al Qaeda in the Arabian Peninsula launched an Internet magazine, *Voice of Jihad.* In the first and second issues, al Muqrin gave an interview with *Voice of Jihad,* excerpts of which follow.[12] In his interview, Muqrin references an initial disagreement within al Qaeda about launching attacks in Saudi Arabia itself. After the 9/11 attacks and the U.S. invasion of Afghanistan, bin Laden and other al Qaeda leaders are believed to have encouraged local cells to get their operations under way.[13] On May 12, 2003, al Qaeda struck three residential compounds in Riyadh, killing thirty-five and wounding two hundred.

Today, Allah be praised, I am [in Saudi Arabia] at the front that we sought to purify and liberate from the defilement of the treacherous rulers and, even before them, from the defilement of the American Crusaders and their allies. I swore to purify the Arabian Peninsula from the polytheists. We were born in this land and we will fight in it against the Crusaders and against the Jews until we expel them or until we taste [martyrdom].

I received many offers from sheikhs [to go to Iraq]. Unfortunately, what they wanted was to get us out of the Arabian Peninsula. True, Iraq is a front, and, Allah be praised, we are investing efforts in it. It is a front that we want to utilize for fighting the Americans, like the other fronts [of Jihad]. To all those who suggested that I [go to Iraq] I say, "Forget it." You must think also about the conflict with these infidels in [Saudi Arabia].

[On operations in Saudi Arabia,] Jihad members and lovers of Mujahideen were split: There were those who said we must attack the invading forces that defile the land of the two holy places. There were others who said we had to preserve the security of this base and this country [i.e., Saudi Arabia], from which we recruit armies, from which we get [financial] backing. It is true that we must use this country [Saudi Arabia] because it is the primary source of funds for most Jihad movements, and it has some degree of security and freedom of movement. However, we must strike a balance between this and the American invasion of the Islamic world and its [strangling of] the Jihad movement.

We tell them [those opposed to the bombings in Saudi Arabia]: If only you were to see the prisons filled with mujahideen youth and pro-Jihad preachers. You must do something; you must fight the enemies of Allah, the Crusaders and the Jews, and become a bone in their throats and hearts.

As it launched its terror campaign in Saudi Arabia in 2003 al Qaeda also started publishing a newsletter, the *Al Batar Military Camp Publication,* directed at Saudi jihadists, indicating al Qaeda's new resolve to mount operations in the Saudi kingdom. The following edition, from 2003, laid out useful information for al Qaeda members in Saudi Arabia. Sayf al Adel, al Qaeda's present military commander, explains how to choose and operate a safe house.[14]

The safe-house is a place used for undercover operations and security purposes.

How to choose the safe-house
1. Far from official security type places
2. Far from areas with crime and drugs
3. Avoid crowded areas, or the downtown
4. A place that blends into its surroundings
5. A place that is difficult to have constant surveillance
6. Many exits available, preferably secret
7. Used for only one purpose, as a safe-house

How the safe-house should be used
1. Used for secret activities, but publicly, a good cover story must be used.
2. Original owner you are renting from should not know the reason you are renting.
3. The house should reflect its occupants so as not to attract attention (i.e. rich people in a rich looking house).
4. Do regular check-ups to make sure the safe-house is secure.
5. The house should have sufficient medical supplies, food, and other supplies to minimize the need to leave the safe-house.
6. Support only one operation at a time.
7. Have a map of the house with all the doors and exits, and hide it well.
8. Evacuate immediately if you have any doubts for your security.

The Saudi strategy to eliminate al Qaeda in the Kingdom has been an aggressive military and intelligence effort to capture or kill terrorists such as Abdalaziz Muqrin, who personally executed American helicopter-maintenance specialist Paul Johnson in June 2004. Two days after a video of Johnson's beheading surfaced on the Internet, security forces killed Muqrin. According to Saudi officials, since 2003 more than ninety other militants have been killed and eight hundred detained.[15]

For the moment, al Qaeda in Saudi Arabia appears to be damaged, capable of mounting only sporadic and ineffectual attacks. However, the hard-core Saudi jihadists are now fighting in Iraq. Several studies have found that more than half of the suicide operations in Iraq are conducted by Saudis, and so, for the moment, the Saudi militants are distracted. Whenever the Iraq war finally winds down, those militants will likely launch another deadly campaign of terror inside the Saudi kingdom.[16]

Since the 9/11 attacks, bin Laden and his chief deputy, Ayman al Zawahiri, have released more than thirty audio and videotapes, an average of one tape every six weeks. Tracing back the chain of custody of these tapes is the one guaranteed method of finding the location of al Qaeda's leaders. However, despite the fact that most of these tapes have generally been released first to Al Jazeera television, U.S. intelligence services (which are funded to the tune of at least 30 billion dollars a year) are seemingly incapable of tracing the chain of custody of the tapes, an abject failure of intelligence gathering.

The release of a bin Laden videotape just before the U.S. presidential election was no exception to this pattern. Ahmad Zaidan, Al Jazeera's Pakistan bureau chief, who had received a similar bin Laden tape two years earlier following the terrorist attacks in Bali, Indonesia, received a mysterious videotape at his Islamabad office five days before the U.S. election on November 2, 2004. CNN's Barbara Starr reported that the day the bin Laden tape was released, Pentagon officials were not surprised that bin Laden would issue such a statement around the time of the U.S. presidential election, yet there is nothing to indicate that American intelligence agencies were staking out the most obvious recipient of such a tape: Al Jazeera's bureau in Pakistan.[17]

The bin Laden videotape played on Al Jazeera, and television networks around the world, on October 29, 2004. On the tape, in a Halloween parody of an Oval Office address, bin Laden speaks directly to the American people from behind a desk, dressed formally in gold robes. The interview is well lit, suggesting a well-prepared production, and we see bin Laden without a gun at his side, a rare sight. On the tape, bin Laden for the first time makes an unequivocal public admission of his own involvement in the 9/11 plot and he responds directly to President Bush's frequent claim that al Qaeda is attacking the United States because of its freedoms rather than its foreign policy.[18]

You the American people, I talk to you today about the best way to avoid another catastrophe and about war, its reasons and its consequences. And in that regard, I say to you that security is an important pillar of human life, and that free people do not compromise their security. Contrary to what Bush says and claims, that we hate [your] freedom— [So] why did we not attack Sweden?[19]

I wonder about you [the American people]. Although we are [now] the fourth year after 9/11, Bush is still exercising confusion and misleading you and not telling you the true reason [why you are being attacked]. Therefore, the motivations are still there for what happened to be repeated.

We agreed with the leader of the [9/11 hijackers], Mohammed Atta, to perform all attacks within twenty minutes before Bush and his administration were aware of what was going on.

And I tell you, God only knows, that we never had the intention to destroy the [Twin] Towers, but after injustice was so much and we saw the coalition between Americans and the Israelis against our people in Palestine and Lebanon, it occurred to my mind that we deal with the Towers.

Your security is not in the hands of Kerry or Bush or al Qaeda. Your security is in your own hands. Each state that will not mess with our security will find security themselves.

Ahmad Zaidan, Al Jazeera's Pakistan bureau chief.

Osama was looking like he is giving a lecture in Georgetown University. Now he is playing a very good public relations and media game.

Noman Benotman, the Libyan who fought with al Qaeda in Afghanistan during the early nineties, is critical of bin Laden's message on the videotape.[20]

So if you are electing George W. Bush as President, you have to pay—That's the bottom line, it's a very naïve this argument. It's not logical. There are eight million Muslims in America—so they are legitimate targets also?

Jamal Khalifa, bin Laden's brother-in-law and onetime close friend.[21]

Osama is doing these things, which it's not logical, not Islamic, and not even strategic. I'm very sorry. I love him. I really love him, but really he is doing very big mistakes. He is really destroying the image of Islam.

The attacks in London on July 7, 2005, in which four British suicide bombers killed fifty-two are emblematic of the continued influence enjoyed by bin Laden and Zawahiri among jihadists around the world. On a videotape made by al Qaeda's media arm, known as *al Sahab* (the Clouds), which was released on September 1, 2005, the leader of the London terrorist cell, Mohammed Siddique Khan, explains that he was operating on behalf of bin Laden. Khan likely made contact with al Qaeda when he took time off from his job as a teacher in the city of Leeds in northern England to visit Pakistan in November 2004. Khan speaks on the videotape in the broad Yorkshire accent of his native Leeds, and appears without his three fellow British suicide bombers, suggesting that the tape was made on his visit to Pakistan in late 2004. Excerpts of his statement follow.[22]

Praise be to Allah, blessings and prayers upon His Prophet. I'm going to keep this short and to the point because it's all been said before by far more eloquent people than me, and our words have no impact upon you, therefore I'm going to talk to you in a language that you understand. Our words are dead until we give them life with our blood. I, and thousands like me, have forsaken everything for what we believe. Your democratically elected governments continuously perpetuate atrocities against my people all over the world, and your support of them makes you directly responsible, just as I am directly responsible for protecting and avenging my Muslim brothers and sisters. Until we feel security, you will be our targets, and until you stop the bombing, gassing, imprisonment, and torture of my people, we will not stop this fight. We are at war, and I am a soldier. Now you too will taste the reality of this situation. Raise me amongst those whom I love, today's heroes, like our beloved Sheikh Osama bin Laden, Dr. Ayman al Zawahiri, and Abu Musab al Zarqawi, and all the other brothers and sisters who are fighting in Allah's cause.

On the same videotape on which Khan appeared, Zawahiri explains that the London bombings were revenge for Britain's participation in the war in Iraq, and came as a result of ignoring bin Laden's 2004 offer of a "truce" with those European nations participating in the coalition in Iraq, an offer that expired on July 15, 2004, almost exactly a year before the London attacks took place.

I speak to you today about the blessed London raid. Rejoice, oh peoples of the Crusader coalition, in the calamities brought upon you and which, Allah willing, will be brought upon you by the policies of Bush, Blair, and those who follow them. Oh peoples of the Crusader coalition, we have warned you, but it appears that you want us to make you taste the horrors of death. So taste some of what you made us taste. Didn't the Lion of Islam, the mujahid Sheikh Osama bin Laden, may Allah protect him, offer you a truce, so you would leave the lands of Islam?

Abdel Bari Atwan interviewed bin Laden in 1996 for *Al Quds al Arabi* newspaper. He reflects on why it has been so hard to find al Qaeda's leader.[23]

[The U.S.] didn't find Osama bin Laden for one reason: Osama bin Laden is a humble man. He can live on a little food. He can live without any luxury, and he is like millions who are in that part of the world in Afghanistan or Pakistan. And also he is loved by the people who move around or among them, wherever they are, whether inside Pakistan or Afghanistan. And I don't believe they will surrender him. He's adored by the people around him. For them, he is not a leader. He is everything. He's the father; he's the brother; he is a leader; he is the imam. He is a good example: a man who sacrificed all his wealth to come and live with them, among them, and to fight for their causes. He is different and he [is] not corrupt and so he represents the pioneers of Muslim early Islamic history—The Prophet Muhammad's companions.

"Where is bin Laden?" is an often-asked question. It is, however, to some degree an unanswerable question, except to say that he is likely in the border region between Afghanistan and Pakistan. However, the Pakistan-Afghan border stretches 1,500 miles, roughly the distance from Washington, D.C., to Denver. It is lightly guarded and even undefined in some places; clandestine travel in the region is therefore relatively easy. The two Pakistani provinces that abut Afghanistan are Baluchistan, a vast, inhospitable expanse of broiling deserts, and the North West Frontier Province, a flinty, mountainous region punctuated by the fortresses of tribal chiefs. Pashtun tribes, who constitute one of the largest tribal groups in the world, are a major presence in both provinces. They subscribe to *Pashtunwali,* the law of the Pashtuns, which places an enormous premium on hospitality and on the giving of refuge to anybody who seeks it, an obvious boon to fugitive members of al Qaeda.

There is also a possibility that bin Laden may be hiding out in an area that is somewhat urbanized. His most recent videotape that appeared just before the U.S. presidential election of 2004 was a professional production in which he appeared well groomed and well informed about current events, not what you would expect from someone trapped in a remote cave in the tribal border region. Indeed, since 9/11, none of the key al Qaeda operatives captured in Pakistan have been found in the country's tribal areas; instead, they have been run to ground in the cities of Karachi, Peshawar, Quetta, Faisalabad, Gujrat, and Rawalpindi. That suggests that bin Laden might also have found refuge in some kind of urban area, perhaps inside the tribal region, where there are a number of small towns along the Afghan-Pakistan border. But the short answer to the question about where bin Laden might be can be summarized as: Who knows.

14

Bin Laden's Legacy

President George W. Bush delivered a keynote speech about the war on terrorism on October 6, 2005, at the National Endowment for Democracy in Washington, D.C. In that speech the President mentioned bin Laden by name several times, something the President rarely does. An excerpt follows.

The murderous ideology of the Islamic radicals is the great challenge of our new century. Yet, in many ways, this fight resembles the struggle against communism in the last century. Like the ideology of communism, Islamic radicalism is elitist, led by a self-appointed vanguard that presumes to speak for the Muslim masses. Bin Laden says his own role is to tell Muslims, quote, "What is good for them and what is not." And what this man who grew up in wealth and privilege considers good for poor Muslims is that they become killers and suicide bombers. He assures them that this is the road to paradise—though he never offers to go along for the ride.

Like the ideology of communism, our new enemy teaches that innocent individuals can be sacrificed to serve a political vision. And this explains their cold-blooded contempt for human life.

It may take years, but eventually bin Laden will be captured or killed. So what are the implications of either of those outcomes? If bin Laden is captured alive, where, for instance, should he be put on trial? As his crimes have spanned many countries, a case could be made that he should be tried by a specially convened international tribunal. The treatment meted out to Saddam Hussein after his capture in Iraq in December 2003 provides a useful template for the capture of bin Laden, should he be taken alive. The pictures beamed around the world of Saddam submitting himself to a doctor's search for head lice did more to

puncture the Iraqi dictator's mystique than anything else. Similar pictures would do much to deflate bin Laden's mythic persona. Of course, capturing bin Laden alive is unlikely. On several occasions bin Laden has said that he's prepared to die in his holy war—statements that should be taken at face value.

In the short term, bin Laden's death would likely trigger violent anti-American attacks around the globe, while in the medium term his death would be a serious blow to al Qaeda, the formal organization, as bin Laden's charisma and organizational skills have played a critical role in its success. However, bin Laden does have eleven sons, some of whom might choose to take a role in their father's organization. Already Saad bin Laden, who is in his mid-twenties, has played a significant role in al Qaeda.

In the longer term, bin Laden's "martyrdom" would likely give a boost to the power of his ideas. Sayyid Qutb was a relatively obscure writer before his execution by the Egyptian government in 1966. After his death, Qutb's writings, which called for offensive holy wars against the enemies of Islam, became enormously influential.[1] The same process will likely happen with the death of bin Laden, but to a much larger degree, as bin Laden's prestige and fame far eclipse Qutb's. And so, in death, bin Laden's ideas will likely attain a measure of lasting currency.

Following are excerpts from bin Laden's "will," written on December 14, 2001, and which appeared October 2002 in *Al Majallah* magazine.[2]

Allah bears witness that the love of jihad and death in the cause of Allah has dominated my life and the verses of the sword permeated every cell in my heart, "and fight the pagans all together as they fight you all together." How many times did I wake up to find myself reciting this holy verse!

O women kinfolk! Do not ever use cosmetics or imitate the whores and mannish women of the West.

O [my] wives! You were, after Allah, the best support and the best help; from the first day you knew that the road was full of thorns and mines. You left the comforts of your relatives and chose to share the hardships next to me.

As to my children, forgive me because I have given you only a little of my time since I answered the jihad call. I have chosen a road fraught with dangers and for this sake suffered from hardships, embitterment, betrayal, and treachery. I advise you not to work with al Qaeda and the Front (The Islamic Front for Fighting the Crusaders and the Jews).

Jamal Khalifa, bin Laden's brother-in-law.[3]

Omar, the son of Osama, [aged] maybe 24, 25, was in Afghanistan for 9/11. [Before 9/11] his father was telling him that something big was going to happen: Very big. Then he came here [to Saudi Arabia]. He was really angry with his father. He was angry with the situation. He said what are they are thinking when they destroy these two towers? He said it was really silly thinking.

[Now Omar] is trying to educate himself and work because Osama did not educate his children. He did not send them to schools. He wanted to educate them by the very old traditional way. To let them memorize the Koran and after that the Hadith (sayings of the Prophet) and poetry. So Omar, he was really feeling sorry. He saw the difference between himself and the others in the family. They are all graduated [from college].

Hutaifa Azzam, the son of Abdullah Azzam.[4]

[Bin Laden's sons] Abdallah and Omar are in Saudi Arabia. Abdel Rahman is in Syria with his mother [bin Laden's first wife] in Damascus. And the rest are in Afghanistan.

Omar came back after the war in Afghanistan. He is against his father. I met him [two years after 9/11] and we spent four days together in Hajj (pilgrimage in Mecca) in the same tent together.

I told him, "What do you think about September 11?" He said, "It's craziness. He said that those guys are dummies. They have destroyed everything, and for nothing. What did we get from September 11?" He said, "It's just because of those crazy Egyptians" and he was abusing his father.

Abdel Bari Atwan interviewed bin Laden in 1996.[5]

There will be different interpretation evaluations of Osama bin Laden. Some people will consider him a heroic phenomenon, a mighty little David who challenged the might of Goliath, who is the Americans. Other people will say he was disastrous. 11 September managed to actually drag the Americans into the region and occupy Iraq. I believe Osama bin Laden is the one who actually opened the American eyes to their mistake to support rotten, corrupt dictatorships [in the Arab world]. Before, they were happy to deal with these rotten dictatorships. They were happy to keep the region as it is. But after 11 September, the Americans awakened to the fact that they are siding with these regimes which create a huge frustration and radicalism and are actually fueling Islamic fundamentalism against the West.

Abu Jandal, formerly bin Laden's chief bodyguard.[6]

Al Qaeda became an ideology. What effected this transformation from an armed group into an ideology is the United States: All Muslims around the world came to view the source of their tragedy as one, namely the United States. It was the source of all their problems, interfering in all internal Muslim affairs from the Far East to the Far West. They became convinced that the only effective way to stop the United States' interference is the Qaeda way, i.e., by direct attacks and armed confrontations. [Now] every element of al Qaeda is self-activated. Whoever finds a chance to attack just goes ahead. The decision is theirs. This is regardless of whether they pledged allegiance to Sheikh Osama bin Laden or not.

In the case of his death, I think he will be a symbol for all those who follow him, especially in the case of his assassination. He will be an idol for all those who believe in his ideas. He will be a great inspiration for them to follow in his footsteps. His death will be a great force for stirring up everybody's emotions and enthusiasm to follow him on the path of martyrdom.

In case of his arrest, the situation might be a bit different. It might lead to a strong psychological defeat for the group's members and many Muslims.

Khalid Khawaja is the former Pakistani air force officer who fought with bin Laden in Afghanistan in 1987.[7]

He will never be captured. He's not Saddam Hussein. He's Osama. Osama loves death. Bin Laden has played his role. Osama has woken up the sleeping bin Ladens.

Jamal Ismail, a Palestinian journalist based in Pakistan, first met bin Laden in 1984 and has encountered him many times since.[8]

If bin Laden is killed, there is no charismatic personality to replace him. Ayman al Zawahiri is an intellectual, not a leader, and his leadership is anyway challenged by other Egyptians. No one can challenge bin Laden's leadership.

The death of bin Laden will be a thousand times bigger for the jihadist movement than the death [in 1966] of [the Egyptian jihadist ideologue Sayyid] Qutb because of the new information technology.

Montasser al Zayyat is the Egyptian lawyer who first met Ayman al Zawahiri while they were both jailed following the assassination of President Anwar Sadat of Egypt in 1981. In 2002, al Zayyat wrote *The Road to al Qaeda,* a critical biography of Zawahiri, excerpts of which follow.[9]

The point of disagreement among Islamists, and especially between Zawahiri and me, is how best to deal with the world's superpower. Bin Laden's desire to take revenge heedless of the American and international response, and its effect on the future of the Islamic movements in the world, has given the Americans and other government the power to destroy the Islamists before our eyes. Not all Islamists in Afghanistan are connected to al Qaeda or bin Laden, and some even disagreed with the man and the ideas of his group.

Bin Laden and Zawahiri's behavior was met with a lot of criticism from many Islamists in Egypt and abroad. Some of them contacted me and were very critical of the consequences of the [9/11] attacks and the lack of clarity as to whether they [al Qaeda's leaders] were behind them or not. A lot of Islamists, including the hawks as well as those supporting the use of peaceful means, opposed Zawahiri's attempts to link Egyptian Islamists to bin Laden. The hawkish Islamists thought that the American war on Afghanistan shattered any hope that Islamists living outside of Egypt would return to resume their struggle against the Egyptian government. In the post–September 11 world, no countries can afford to be accused of harboring the enemies of the United States.

Rahimullah Yusufzai, one of Pakistan's leading journalists, interviewed bin Laden twice in the late 1990s.[10]

I think that Mr. bin Laden sees himself as a man who would sacrifice his life for his beliefs. He would like to go down fighting; he would like to become a martyr. He won't surrender. I think that he would not allow himself to be captured and to be produced in some court in New York and that is why I have this belief that he will fight until the end. I believe that he will be a much more popular man for many Muslims once he becomes a martyr because Mr. bin Laden as a dead man would be even more potent than when he is alive.

Abu Musab al Suri, long an associate of bin Laden's, released his book *The International Islamic Resistance Call* **in December 2004. By implication, al Suri makes clear that the jihadist movement has been severely damaged by the 9/11 attacks.**[11]

The status of the Islamic people has changed after the incidents of 9/11. We are in a stage where the American and Europeans, and their friends the Jews, have taken the lead role. Some important matters resulting from September 11, which have negatively affected the Muslims:

America destroyed the Islamic Emirate in Afghanistan, which became the refuge for the mujahideen. They killed hundreds of mujahideen who defended the Emirate. Then America captured more than six hundred jihadists from different Arab countries and Pakistan and jailed them. The Jihad movement rose to glory in the 1960s, and continued through the '70s and '80s, and resulted in the rise of the Islamic Emirate of Afghanistan, but was destroyed after 9/11.

The reign of Clinton ended with the election of Bush, son of the first Bush who began the Crusader war against the Muslims under his reign.

This brought the rise of the extremist Christians and the movement known as "The Neo-Cons." They began shamelessly promoting their ideas, beliefs, and plans. And they announced that America is the inheritor of the Roman Empire and is going to take its place in history and the future. And America took justification from its war on terror to wipe out the Islamic reawakening.

Saad al Fagih, formerly a surgeon in Saudi Arabia, runs a Saudi opposition group based in London.[12]

I think that [al Qaeda's] influence is immense now in the Muslim and Arab world. What the [U.S.] leaders have done [after the 9/11 attacks] is actually to implement that bin Laden wanted. That is to wage a cosmic campaign against Muslims.

Noman Benotman is the Libyan who fought with al Qaeda in Afghanistan in the early nineties.[13]

9/11 destroyed 95 percent of the existing organization. The United States of America is involved directly in this war. The organization doesn't exist anymore.

I think bin Laden now is driven by his tactics, not strategy—the tactics have taken over the strategy. It's always about just kill, shoot, destroy, bomb, in Afghanistan, in Iraq, now it's in America, in Europe. You can't talk to these people. It's killing, shooting, sacrificing.

My point of view is bin Laden himself and his group will achieve nothing. They will fail to achieve what they are asking for and bin Laden, his credibility, it's decreasing not increasing. What has been increasing is this kind of new tactic—the suicide attacks.

In the '70s and '80s and even the '90s all these jihadi groups they failed to overthrow the governments. I told them myself that. I told Zawahiri, "We failed. All the jihadi movements failed because we cannot recruit the people." It's as simple as that. That is the rules of the war, especially guerrilla warfare. I think the godfather for all these things is Mao Zedong. That's the theory. It's very complete, it's Mao. We failed to recruit the people.

Zawahiri in his autobiographical *Knights under the Prophet's Banner,* published in December 2001, recognizes that al Qaeda has not engaged the affection of the masses.[14]

The jihad movement must come closer to the masses. We must win the people's confidence, respect, and affection. The people will not love us unless they felt that we love them, care about them, and are ready to defend them.

The Muslim nation will not participate unless the slogans of the mujahideen are understood by the masses of the Muslim nation. The one slogan that has been well understood by the [Muslim] nation and to which it has been responding for the past fifty years is the call for the jihad against Israel. The fact that must be acknowledged is that the issue of Palestine is the cause that has been firing up the feelings of the Muslim nation from Morocco to Indonesia for the past fifty years. In addition, it is a rallying point for all the Arabs, be they believers or non-believers.

In addition to this slogan, the Muslim nation has responded favorably to the call for the jihad against the Americans.

It is a battle of ideologies, a struggle for survival, and a war with no truce. More importantly, this is a goal that could take several generations to achieve. The Crusaders in Palestine and Syria left after two centuries of continued jihad [in the Middle Ages]. The French occupied Algeria for more than a century [before they departed in 1962].

In the United States, bin Laden is commonly seen as an avatar of "Islamofascism," or simply as an evil criminal. Of course, while bin Laden is indeed the intellectual author of many crimes, he is a more complex figure than these caricatures would suggest. In my view, bin Laden is an intelligent political actor who is fighting a deeply felt religious war against the West.

Bin Laden, like others before him, has adopted terrorism as a rational choice to bring certain political goals nearer, and as a shortcut to transforming the political landscape. After World War II, Israel's future prime minister Menachem Begin and his Irgun organization, for intants around the Muslim world, including in places such as Chechnya and Kashmir, areas of conflict that the U.S. government had previously tended to view as legitimate nationalist struggles.

As we have learned to our cost in recent years, much "secret" information is simply wrong, while information that is public—for instance, bin Laden's repeated calls for attacks against the United States in the years before 2001—is too often discounted. One of the lessons of September 11 is that we should pay careful attention to what the jihadists are actually saying. And what they are saying about September 11 is that the attacks may have been a tactical victory, but they were a strategic disaster because of the loss of Afghanistan as a base, and the U.S.-led campaign to detain members of jihadist movements around the world.

That's why Islamist militants are happy that the Bush administration ordered the invasion of Iraq. Without the Iraq War, their movement, under assault externally and fragmented internally, would have imploded a year or so after September 11. For the moment bin Laden is buoyed up by American reverses in Iraq and the fact that the key insurgent leader in Iraq, Abu Musab al Zarqawi, has acknowledged al Qaeda's primacy at the head of the jihadist movement. But bin Laden's larger project, inciting a Clash of Civilizations between the West and the Muslim world—which he believes the forces of Islam will inevitably win in the long term—has been a failure.

Zawahiri complained in his 2001 biography, *Knights under the Prophet's Banner,* that the masses have not embraced al Qaeda. (This is despite the fact that bin Laden enjoys a large degree of personal popularity in the Muslim world for his stance against the United States.) In a passage quoted in this chapter Zawahiri explains, "The jihad movement must come closer to the masses. We must win the people's confidence, respect, and affection." But that is not going to be possible when the average Muslim knows that killing civilians is explicitly prohibited by the Koran, and al Qaeda presents no positive vision of the world it wants to create other than vague references to restoring the Caliphate.

Al Qaeda is against a lot of things: U.S. foreign policy in the Middle East; Israel; India's role in Kashmir and Russia's war in Chechnya, to name a few, but it has articulated no vision of the world it aims to create. Taliban-controlled Afghanistan is the type of utopian society that al Qaeda seems to want to impose on the rest of the Islamic world. This is not a winning vision of the future for the vast majority of Muslims around the globe. Meanwhile, bin Laden and other leaders of al Qaeda seemed to have painted themselves into a corner where their only strategy is to call for more violence. As the Libyan jihadist Noman Benotman perceptively observes in this chapter, this is an example of tactics taking over strategy. And if I were to write an epitaph for Osama bin Laden, it would be that he was a man whose violent tactics became his only strategy.

Osama bin Laden from the will that he wrote in December 2001.[17]

Praise be to Allah and peace be upon the Master of the Messengers, his family, and his companions. We ask for His forgiveness, seek His guidance, and seek refuge from Him for our sins and evil actions. We pray to Allah, praise and glory be to Him, to accept us with the martyrs and the virtuous ones among His worshippers and to make us die Muslims.

Appendix A
Where Are They Now?

Abbasi, Feroz Ali: After he was released from Guantánamo Bay in January 2005, he moved back to the United Kingdom.

Adel, Sayf al: The military commander of al Qaeda, he is currently under some form of house arrest in Iran.

Anas, Abdullah: A founder of the Algerian Islamic Salvation Front (FIS) who served on its executive committee until 1966. Living in London.

Atef, Mohammad (Abu Hafs): Killed by a U.S. air strike in Afghanistan in November 2001.

Atwan, Abdel Bari: Editor of *Al Quds al Arabi* newspaper and a frequent guest on Arabic- and English-language TV channels.

Awdah, Sheikh Salman al: Released from Saudi prison in 1999. In November 2004 al Awdah signed a fatwa (along with twenty-five other clerics), against the U.S. occupation in Iraq.

Azzam, Hutaifa: Living in Jordan, where he is completing his Ph.D. in Arabic literature at the University of Jordan. He also trades in cars, phones, and nuts.

Banjshiri, Abu Ubaidah al: Died in a ferry accident on Lake Victoria, Kenya, in 1996.

Batarfi, Khaled: Living in Jeddah, Saudi Arabia, where he is the managing editor of the conservative *Al Madinah* newspaper. He also writes a weekly column for the English-language *Arab News*.

Bentoman, Noman: Settled in London, where he runs the Libya Human and Political Development Forum, an organization that aims to overthrow the Libyan dictator Muammar Gadhafi.

bin Laden, Osama: At large.

Bin Ladin, Bakr Mohammed: Continues to run the family construction business.

Binalshibh, Ramzi: Captured in September 2002 in Karachi, Pakistan, and now in U.S. custody at an undisclosed location.

Deraz, Essam: Retired and living in Cairo.

Fadl, Jamal al: Living in the United States in the witness protection program.

Faisal, Prince Turki al: Resigned as head of Saudi intelligence ten days before 9/11. In 2002 he was appointed Saudi ambassador to the U.K. In September 2005 he took up a new position as Saudi ambassador to the United States.

Fauwaz, Khaled al: Arrested in London in 1998 after a U.S. extradition request alleging he had a role in the U.S. embassy bombings in Africa the same year. Is currently detained in the U.K. and is fighting the extradition request.

Fouda, Yosri: Al Jazeera's chief investigative reporter and London bureau chief.

Fyfield-Shayler, Brian: Retired and living in Devon, in southern England.

Ghanem, Alia: Living in Jeddah, Saudi Arabia, in the same neighborhood where bin Laden grew up.

Haqqani, Jalaluddin: The military leader of the Taliban. At large in Afghanistan or possibly Pakistan.

Hawali, Sheikh Safar al: Released from Saudi prison in 1999. Presently serves as secretary general of the Global Anti-Aggression Campaign, an anti-American organization established in response to the American-led invasion of Iraq.

Hekmatyar, Gulbuddin: After the Taliban took Kabul in 1996, he fled to Iran, where he later helped al Qaeda members reorganize after the U.S. offensive in Afghanistan. His current whereabouts are unknown, but he is likely to be in Afghanistan.

Ismail, Faraj: Correspondent for *Al Majallah* magazine in Cairo.

Ismail, Jamal: Runs a television production company in Islamabad, Pakistan.

Jandal, Abu: Lives in the Yemeni capital, Sanaa, and is subject to some government restrictions on his movements. In 2004–2005 he gave an extensive series of interviews to *Al Quds al Arabi* newspaper.

Jouvenal, Peter: Lives in Kabul, where he runs Gandamack Lodge, the best guesthouse in town, which was previously the home of one of bin Laden's wives until three months before 9/11.

Julaidan, Wael: Left Pakistan in 1994 and returned to Saudi Arabia, where he worked in the family real estate business. Played an important role in Saudi aid efforts to the Bosnians in the mid- to late-1990s. The U.S. Treasury Department froze his assets in September 2002, and the U.N. designated him a financier of terrorism, which he strenuously denies.

Khalifa, Jamal: Helps his brother run a well-regarded fish restaurant, the Sultana, outside Jeddah, and organizes motivational seminars.

Khashoggi, Jamal: Became deputy chief editor of *Arab News* and, following 9/11, media adviser to Prince Turki al Faisal, who was then the Saudi ambassador to the United Kingdom and who is the present ambassador to the United States.

Khawaja, Khalid: Living in Islamabad. He advocates for Pakistanis held at Guantánamo Bay and is affiliated with the Islamist political party of Imran Khan; he is the famed cricket player turned politician.

Kherchtou, L'Houssaine: In the U.S. witness protection program.

Malik, Malika: Is living in Switzerland. She is not allowed to travel outside the country.

Massoud, Ahmad Shah: Assassinated on September 9, 2001, by two of bin Laden's men.

Miller, John: In September 2005, Miller began work at FBI headquarters in Washington, D.C., as assistant director for public affairs. Before that he served for two years as the head of the Los Angeles Police Department's counterterrorism division.

Mir, Hamid: The Islamabad bureau chief of the private channel Geo TV in Pakistan. He also hosts a popular weekly show on Pakistani politics. He has yet to publish his biography of bin Laden.

Misri, Abu Walid al: Probably in Iran keeping a low profile.

Mohamed, Ali: Arrested in 1998; he is a U.S. government witness under a plea bargain agreement.

Mohammed, Khaled Sheikh: In U.S. custody at an undisclosed location.

Mojdeh, Vahid: Spokesman for the Afghan Supreme Court.

Muttawakil, Wakil Ahmed: Surrendered to U.S. military authorities at Kandahar airbase in 2002. He was set free in 2004. In May 2005 he called for Taliban elements to hold talks with Hamid Karzai's government.

Omar, Mullah Mohammed: After the fall of the Taliban he went into hiding and is believed to be somewhere in Afghanistan, possibly in Uruzgan, his home province.

Qatada, Abu: Under house arrest in London; he is contesting British attempts to deport him to his native Jordan.

Rahman, Sheikh Omar Abdel: Imprisoned in the United States since 1993.

Ridi, Essam al: Was living in Texas after the 9/11 attacks. Present whereabouts unknown.

Rushdi, Osama: Moved from Pakistan to the Netherlands in 1993, and then to Birmingham in the United Kingdom in 2003. He is active in groups opposed to Hosni Mubarak's government in Egypt.

Sanoussi, Ibrahim al: Living in Khartoum, Sudan.

Surayhi, Abd-Rabbuh al: Released by the Saudi government in November 2001 after serving six years in jail.

Suri, Abu Musab al: Arrested in Pakistan in November 2005.

Turabi, Hassan al: Lost out to Sudan's President Omar Bashir in a power struggle in 1999. He was placed under house arrest between 2001 and 2003 and imprisoned between 2004 and 2005. He was released in July 2005 and is living in Sudan.

Yousef, Ramzi: Arrested in Pakistan in 1995 and imprisoned in the "Supermax" prison in Florence, Colorado.

Yusufzai, Rahimullah: The bureau chief of *The News* newspaper in Peshawar, Pakistan.

Zaidan, Ahmad: The bureau chief of Al Jazeera television in Islamabad.

Zarqawi, Abu Musab al: At large in Iraq.

Zawahiri, Ayman al: Currently in Afghanistan or Pakistan, he has released a series of videotapes on behalf of al Qaeda, such as one taking credit for the July 7, 2005, London bombings.

Zayyat, Montasser al: Continues to practice law in Cairo.

Appendix B

Osama bin Laden's Immediate Family

The Bin Ladin family is secretive and Saudi Arabia is a closed society, so the information offered here is not as reliable as it would be for an analogous major business family in the United States. As mentioned in the introduction, there are differences between the Western and Islamic calendar, sometimes dates can be off by a year or more. Additionally, fundamentalists in Saudi Arabia don't celebrate birthdays, so someone's age can sometimes be a matter of guesswork. With those caveats, what follows is some information about Osama bin Laden's family.

MOHAMMED BIN LADIN, FATHER (1908–1967)
Mohammed was the great-grandson of Salim Bin Ladin, grandson of Abud Bin Ladin, and son of Awad Bin Ladin. Mohammed was born in 1908 in the village of Rubat, Hadramaut, now a southeastern province of Yemen. Upon arrival in Saudi Arabia in 1930, Mohammed worked as a porter for pilgrims in Jeddah before turning his construction company, the Saudi Binladin Group (SBG), into one of the top companies in the region. In 1951, he picked up the contract for the road running from Jeddah to Medina, which a British company (Thomas Ward of Sheffield) had asked to be released from as a result of having underestimated the difficulties of the terrain.[1] Mohammed Bin Ladin would go on to found the Binladin Organization Marble Factory and establish himself as the largest contractor in Saudi Arabia. Mohammed also built the road from Jeddah to Taif, the summer retreat of King Abdel Aziz. Mohammed Bin Ladin died in a plane crash in Saudi Arabia in the summer of 1967 at age fifty-nine.[2] In all, he married an estimated twenty wives and fathered at least twenty-five sons and twenty-nine daughters.[3]

ALIA GHANEM, MOTHER

Alia Ghanem is the Syrian-born mother of Osama bin Laden, the only child born to her and her first husband, Mohammed, in 1957. Alia Ghanem comes from Latikia, a coastal resort town in Syria, which the Saudi Binladin Group helped to develop. She and Mohammed divorced after the birth of Osama, and she subsequently married Mohammed al Attas, who comes from an old Jeddah merchant family. She had three sons and a daughter with Attas. After his mother remarried, a young Osama moved into the Musharifa neighborhood of Jeddah, where his mother still lives today.[4]

OSAMA BIN LADEN'S BROTHERS

Mohammed Bin Ladin is said to have had at least twenty-five sons. Those are Salem, Ali, Bakr, Tariq, Hassan, Mahrous, Tabet, Khalid, Yeslam, Abdul Aziz, Ghalib, Isa, Ahmed, Omar, Muhammad, Abdullah, Osama, Haidar, Hamza, Ibrahim, Yahia, Yasser, Khalil, Ibrahim, and Tareg.[5] Below are short biographies of some of the more significant brothers of Osama bin Laden.

Salem, the eldest son of the patriarch Mohammed, was born circa 1945 in Jeddah, Saudi Arabia. He was sent to school in the United Kingdom, where he attended the prestigious Millfield boarding school. On the death of his father in 1967, Salem returned to Saudi Arabia to take his place as the head of the family, a position which was initially contested by Mohammed's second son by another wife, Ali.[6] After the death of his father, the SBG was put in a trust by the Saudi government and was run by Mohammed Baharith, a well-regarded manager. Salem took control of SBG around 1973 and focused on reinvigorating the company.[7] In the early 1970s, SBG was awarded the 400-mile Jizan-Jeddah road contract.[8] Salem died on May 29, 1988, in a plane crash in San Antonio, Texas.[9]

Ali is the second son of Mohammed Bin Ladin from a different mother than Salem. He was educated in Jeddah, Saudi Arabia. He left Saudi Arabia in 1974 and now lives in Paris.

Bakr Bin Ladin was born in 1946 in Mecca and is currently chairman of SBG and head of the Bin Ladin family.[10] Bakr graduated in 1972 from the University of Miami in Florida.[11] He also attended Harvard Law School.[12] He is described as stern, dour, but polite.[13] In the 1970s and

1980s, Bakr is said to have worked closely with his full brother Salem in the running of SBG.[14] In 1988, after Salem's death, he took over the running of SBG. In April 1994, he publicly disowned Osama at the same time that the Saudi government stripped him of his citizenship. He is married to Haifa, a Syrian.[15]

Omar Bin Ladin graduated from the University of Miami in 1974.[16] As of 2001, he is the president of SBG. He is said to be a devout, conservative man.[17]

Hassan Bin Ladin serves as the vice president of SBG and lives in Jeddah.

Yeslam Bin Ladin was born circa 1950.[18] He lives in Geneva, Switzerland, and has Swiss nationality. He was sent to school in Beirut at age six, and then studied in Sweden and England.[19] In 1974 he married Carmen. The couple initiated divorce proceedings in 1988. From 1974 to 1976, he attended the University of Southern California and built up commercial contacts in America. Returning to Jeddah in 1976, he played an important role in designing the financial structure of SBG.[20] He also set up his own companies in Jeddah and Switzerland in the 1980s, including the Geneva-based Saudi Investment Company (Sico). In 2004, Yeslam launched a new perfume venture "Yeslam."[21] According to his ex-wife, Carmen, by the 1980s his wealth had reached a figure of $300 million.[22]

Yahia Bin Ladin was born in 1955. Yahia is another one of the older generation of brothers. He became vice chairman of SBG in 2001. He has interests in construction, telecommunications, and publishing in Saudi Arabia. Yahia also owns shares in Hybridion, a biomedical company in Cambridge, Massachusetts.[23]

Abdullah Bin Ladin, one of the youngest sons of Mohammed bin Laden, was born circa 1967.[24] He has a Harvard law degree and was living in Boston at the time of the 9/11 attacks. The last time Abdullah saw Osama was at Salem's funeral in 1988.[25]

Osama bin Laden's Sisters

Given the intense privacy surrounding the family in Saudi Arabia (especially when it comes to women), the list of daughters is incomplete. Mohammed Bin Ladin is reported to have had twenty-nine daughters, including Aisha, Sheika, Regaih, Fawzia, Taiba, Najia, Randa, and Rafah.

Osama bin Laden's Wives

First Wife; Najwa Ghanem (Um Abdallah, mother of Abdallah). Bin Laden married Najwa circa 1974 at the age of seventeen in the resort of Latikia, Syria. Najwa is his first cousin, the daughter of his mother's brother. Carmen Bin Ladin, who knew her in the 1970s, describes Najwa as "meek, submissive, highly religious and constantly pregnant." She traveled with Osama to Sudan and Afghanistan. According to Abu Jandal, one of Osama's bodyguards, she left Afghanistan before September 11 and did not return.[26] Hataifa Azzam says that she now lives in Damascus with one of her sons, Abdel Rahman.[27]

Um Ali (mother of Ali). She is from the Sharif family, according to bin Laden's brother-in-law Jamal Khalifa.[28] While living with her husband in Sudan Um, Ali asked for a divorce, saying she could no longer live his life of hardship. Osama acceded to his wife's wishes.[29] She returned to Saudi Arabia with Ali, her son, and a daughter.

Um Khalid (mother of Khalid). She is the sister of one of bin Laden's jihadist comrades, who offered her hand in marriage to Osama. Highly educated, she has a doctoral degree in Islamic sharia. She reportedly stayed with Osama in Afghanistan.[30]

Um Hamza (mother of Hamza). She comes from the Sabar family, according to Jamal Khalifa. She has a degree in Arabic language. She also stayed with Osama in Afghanistan.

Amal al Saddah (youngest wife). Amal was a seventeen-year-old Yemeni when Osama married her in 2000. Bin Laden's bodyguard Abu Jandal carried a dowry of five thousand dollars to Amal's family in Yemen and made arrangements for her to travel to Afghanistan. A wedding in which Osama's children and other wives participated was held in Kandahar.[31] She bore Osama a daughter who traveled with her out of Afghanistan when the U.S. campaign started in late 2001, probably the daughter born to Osama after 9/11 named Safia. Some accounts put Amal al Saddah back in her native Yemen today.

Osama bin Laden's children

Abu Jandal, bin Laden's former bodyguard, says that as of 2000 Osama had eleven sons, nine of which were in Afghanistan. Abdallah and Ali were not living in Afghanistan at that time.[32]

Abdallah is the eldest son from Osama's first wife, Najwa. Born in the late 1970s. He left Osama in the Sudan to return to Saudi Arabia in 1995, as he did not like the austere life there.[33] In October 2001, Abdallah, who prefers to be called Abdallah Ladin, told the London Press Association what he thought of his father's chances of survival: "America and Britain will never track down my father. He has vanished into the landscape."[34]

Abdul Rahman is another son from Osama's first wife, Najwa. He is reportedly residing in Damascus with his mother.[35]

Omar is in his mid-20s, born circa 1982–1983 and, like his full brother Abdallah, now lives in Saudi Arabia.[36]

Muhammed married the daughter of Abu Hafs al Masri in Kandahar in January 2001.

Khalid and Hamza are two other sons about which not much is known.

Saad is the son of Najwa Ghanem (Osama's first wife). He is in his mid-20s and living in Iran under some form of house arrest. Although there is a dispute about the extent of Saad's operational influence in al Qaeda, most agree he is a player. He is computer literate and fluent in English.[37]

Ali was born circa 1982. Abdel Bari Atwan, the Palestinian editor of *Al Quds al Arabi* newspaper says he met both Saad and Ali, who were playing Nintendo in Jalalabad in November 1996, at ages thirteen and fourteen.[38]

Osman was acting as a bodyguard for his father when Jamal Ismail interviewed bin Laden for Al Jazeera in 1998.[39]

Uthman is said to have escaped from Tora Bora with Ayman al Zawahiri, according to Abdellah Tabarak, bin Laden's driver.[40]

Appendix C
The Bin Ladin Family Businesses

The following information on the Saudi Binladin Group was derived from its Web site in the summer of 2001 before it was taken down around the time of the 9/11 attacks.

BINLADIN GROUP INTERNATIONAL

Executive Board

Eng. Bakr M. Binladin	Chairman
Eng. Yahia M. Binladin	Vice Chairman
Eng. Omar M. Binladin	President
Hasan M. Binladin	Vice President
Abu Bakr S. al Hamed	Managing Director

Public Buildings & Airports Division

Ahmed M. Binladin	Managing Director

Special Buildings Division

Henry H. M. Sarkissian	Managing Director

Power & Industrial Projects Division

Mu'taz Sawwaf	Managing Director

Architectural & Interior Design Division

Eng. Abu Bakr Bin Ali Al Akhdar	Managing Director

Petroleum, Chemicals & Mining Division

Safiq M. Binladin	Board Member
Hagop Boyadjian	Board Member
Tahsin Jarrah	Board Member

PROJECTS UNDERTAKEN BY BINLADIN GROUP INTERNATIONAL
IN THE LATE 1990S:

Cairo International Airport [Egypt]: The widening and renovation of existing runways and introduction of new taxiways. The provision of a new airport runway lighting system.

Cairo, Al-Rehab Project, Phase 1 [Egypt]: This consists of 28 villas of six types and 249 residential buildings of five types. Phase 1 of the development of this new suburb of the city of Cairo will also include schools, and municipal and retail buildings.

Kuala Lumpur International Airport [Malaysia]: The construction of Aprons & Cross Taxiways, East and West, along with service roads, drainage, and service ducts.

Putra Mosque [Malaysia]: The design and construction of the Putra Mosque, including all facilities, at Putrjaya, Selangor, Darul Ehsan. The project includes . . . ingress roads and landscaping. The Mosque shall form the highlight of a new "city within a city," including government offices, commercial, and residential developments close to Kuala Lumpur.

Amman Grand Hyatt Hotel [Jordan]. A five-star, 313-room city center hotel. It served the needs of visiting business travelers and tourists and provided a mixture of first-class retail food and beverage, conference, and recreational facilities to complement the guest accommodation and management offices of the Hyatt International.

Al Faisaliah Center: SBG is also responsible for building the Al Faisaliah Center in downtown Riyadh [the Saudi capital]. The Center is the second-tallest building in the country. SBG has been selected to build the prestigious Al Faisaliah Center on behalf of the King Faisal Foundation with completion April 1, 2000.

IRIDIUM Project: SBG also acted as a partner in the IRIDIUM Project, launched by Motorola in the mid-nineties. This project involved the launch and management of a network of satellites to provide worldwide telecommunications capabilities for a wide range of devices, including cell phones, pagers, and pay phones.

THE SAUDI BINLADIN GROUP WEB SITE ALSO LISTED THE
COMPANY'S U.S. HEADQUARTERS IN ROCKVILLE, MARYLAND.

SBG International Offices
United States of America
51 Monroe Street, Suite 1700
Rockville, MD 20850

Notes

INTRODUCTION

1. President George W. Bush, press conference, Washington, D.C., March 13, 2002.
2. "A Year After Iraq War: Mistrust of America in Europe Ever Higher, Muslim Anger Persists," The Pew Global Attitudes Project, March 16, 2004.
3. "Views of a Changing World 2003: War with Iraq Further Divides Global Publics," The Pew Global Attitudes Project, June 3, 2003.
4. Khaled Nasr, "Bin Laden's Wife Interviewed on Life with Him, His Mental State Before 11th of September," *Al Majallah*, March 10, 2002.
5. Osama bin Laden, "Letter to America," *The Guardian*, November 24, 2002.

CHAPTER 1

1. Osama bin Laden, interview by Jamal Ismail on December 22, 1998, later aired on Al Jazeera in a documentary titled, "Osama bin Laden: the Destruction of the Base," June 10, 1999.
2. Brian Fyfield-Shayler, phone interview by Paul Cruickshank, Devon, England, June 2005.
3. It is generally considered acceptable in Islam for a man to marry up to four wives, as long as they are treated equitably. The Quran [4:3] notes, "If ye fear that ye shall not be able to deal justly with the orphans, Marry women of your choice, Two or three or four; but if ye fear that ye shall not be able to deal justly (with them), then only one, or (a captive) that your right hands possess, that will be more suitable, to prevent you from doing injustice."
4. Saudi Binladin Group (SBG) Web site documents, http://binladen.com/history.htm (no longer operational), October 30, 2000.
5. Essam Deraz, interviews by author, Cairo, Egypt, January 2000 and May 2005.
6. Hutaifa Azzam, interview by author, Amman, Jordan, September 13, 2005.
7. Hamid Mir, interview by author, Islamabad, Pakistan, March 2005.
8. *"Allah commands you regarding your children. For the male a share equivalent to that of the two females."* (Quran 4:11).
9. Christina Akerblad, phone interview by Paul Cruickshank, Tallberg, Sweden, August 24, 2005.
10. Khaled Batarfi, interviews by author, Jeddah, Saudi Arabia, September 5 and 9, 2005.
11. Carmen bin Ladin. *Inside the Kingdom: My Life in Saudi Arabia* (New York: Warner Books, July 2004), pp. 38–9.
12. Jamal Khalifa, interviews by author, Jeddah, Saudi Arabia, September 6 and 9, 2005. Jamal Khalifa was arrested in 1994 in California en route to the Philippines. According to contemporaneous news accounts, in his possession were terrorist training manuals in Arabic and a contact list with the phone numbers of persons involved in terrorism, including Ramzi Yousef. The Philippine government later would provide evidence to the U.S. government alleging Khalifa was involved in terrorism. Khalifa was extradited to Jordan in 1995 to face charges of involvement in a series of theater bombings. He was ac-

quitted. Khalifa also ran the International Islamic Relief Organization (IIRO) office in the Philippines. The IIRO has been accused of being a financial front for terrorist operations around the world, and Khalifa himself has been accused of providing financing for terrorist groups in the Philippines, including Abu Sayyaf and the Moro Islamic Liberation Front. Khalifa now lives in Saudi Arabia (where he was arrested briefly after 9/11), a free man who insists he has been the victim of a smear campaign. The U.S. government has not designated Khalifa as a financial supporter of terrorism and there appear to be no jurisdictions where he is under indictment.

13. Sayyid Qutb was born in 1906 in Egypt. He spent his early years as an author, public teacher, and literary critic, and also worked for the Egyptian Ministry of Education beginning in the late 1930s. From 1948 to 1951, Qutb studied at the Colorado State Teachers College (now the University of Northern Colorado), where he received his Master's degree. His experiences in the United States would shape his negative opinions of the West.

14. Ayman al Zawahiri. *Knights under the Prophet's Banner,* extracts published by *Al Sharq al Awsat,* December 2001.

15. Sayed Qutb. *Milestones* (Mumbai: Bilal Books, 1998), p. 62.

16. Yesiam Bin Ladin, interview by *Al Arabiya* television, May 28, 2005.

17. Carmen Bin Ladin, op. cit., pp. 70–1.

18. Jamal Khashoggi, interview by author, London, United Kingdom, June 13, 2005.

19. The account provided by Khaled Batarfi that Osama bin Laden traveled to the United States to treat his young son is uncorroborated.

20. Osama bin Laden, audio recording, posted to the jihadist Web site Al-Qai'ah [The Fortress] located at www.qal3ah.net (no longer operational) on December 16, 2004, (translated by the U.S. government).

CHAPTER 2

1. Osama bin Laden, interview with CNN (produced by author), aired May 10, 1997.

2. United Nations High Commission on Refugees Fact Sheet, "Return to Afghanistan," October 11, 2005.

3. Hutaifa Azzam, interview by author, Amman, Jordan, September 13, 2005.

4. Jamal Ismail, interview by author, Islamabad, Pakistan, March 2005.

5. Abdullah Azzam, *Defense of Muslim Lands, The Most Important Personal Duty,* published in booklet form by Modern Mission Library, Amman, 1984.

6. Jamal Khalifa, interviews by author, Jeddah, Saudi Arabia, September 6 and 9, 2005.

7. Abdullah Anas, interviews by author, London, United Kingdom, June 15, 17, and 20, 2005.

8. Wael Julaidan, interview by author, Jeddah, Saudi Arabia, September 11, 2005. Wael Julaidan has been designated by the U.S. Treasury Department as a terrorist financier (see U.S. Treasury Department Office of Foreign Assets Control Specially Designated Nationals list, updated October 21, 2005). The U.S. and Saudi governments also both submitted Wael Julaidan's name to the United Nations for worldwide asset-freezing on September 6, 2000. He is currently living in Saudi Arabia, and denies any involvement in terrorist activities.

9. Asne Seierstad, *The Bookseller of Kabul* (London: Little, Brown, October 2003).

10. Abu Walid al Misri, excerpts from *Afghan Arabs,* published by *Al Sharq al Awsat,* December 2004.

11. Basil Muhammed. *Al Ansar Al Arab fi Afghanistan* ("The Arab Volunteers in Afghanistan"), (The Committee for Islamic Benevolence Publications, 1991), pp. 85–86.

12. Faraj Ismail, interview by author, Cairo, Egypt, June 2005.

13. Vahid Mojdeh, interview by author, Kabul, Afghanistan, January 2005.
14. Jamal Khashoggi, interview by author, London, United Kingdom, June 13, 2005.
15. USA v. Usama bin Laden, Testimony of Essam al Ridi, February 14, 2001.
16. USA v. Usama bin Laden, Testimony of Jamal al Fadl, February 6, 7, 13, and 20, 2001.
17. Khaled Batarfi, interviews by author, Jeddah, Saudi Arabia, September 5 and 9, 2005.

CHAPTER 3

1. Mark Urban, War in Afghanistan (London: Macmillan, 1988), p. 244.
2. As Ahmed Rashid notes in his book Taliban: Islam, Oil and the Great Game in Central Asia (London: J. B. Tauris Publishers), several thousand Arabs likely circulated through Afghanistan during the course of the war against the Soviets (p.132). However, at any given moment, my findings indicate that no more than several hundred Arabs were fighting on the ground.
3. Jamal Khalifa, interviews by author, Jeddah, Saudi Arabia. September 6 and 9, 2005.
4. Basil Muhammed. Al Ansar Al Arab fi Afghanistan ("The Arab Volunteers in Afghanistan"), (The Committee for Islamic Benevolence Publications, 1991,) p. 307.
5. Hasin al Banyan, "Interview with Hassan Abd Rabbuh al Surayhi (the Arab Afghan Veteran)," Al Sharq al Awsat, November 25, 2001. Al Surayhi trained and fought with the mujahideen in Afghanistan and witnessed an early meeting of al Qaeda in Peshawar, Pakistan in 1989. He is the former imam at the Ibn Baz Mosque in Mecca and served six years in prison in Riyadh, Saudi Arabia, before receiving a royal pardon in 2001.
6. Jamal Ismail, interview by author, Islamabad, Pakistan, March 2005.
7. Edward Giardet, interview by author, Kabul, Afghanistan, January 2005.
8. Ahmad Zaidan, interview by author, Islamabad, Pakistan, March 2005.
9. Hutaifa Azzam, interview by author, Amman, Jordan, September 13, 2005.
10. Essam Deraz, interviews by author, Cairo, Egypt, January 2000 and May 2005.
11. In the middle of our discussion (which took place in Islamabad, Pakistan, in July 2004) Khawaja asked me, "You want to meet Osama?" and in walked his son, Osama, a tall, lightly bearded man in his late twenties who looked like any college student dressed in a T-shirt and jeans.
12. Wael Julaidan, interview by author, Jeddah, Saudi Arabia, September 11, 2005.
13. Basil Muhammed, op. cit., p. 86.
14. Quranic verses from the Night of Power chapter: "The Night of Al-Qadr is better than a thousand months." [97:3] "The Angels and the spirit descend thereon by the leave of their Lord with every command." [97:4] "(The night is) Peace until the rising of the dawn." [97:5] Lailat al Qadr is also known as the night the Prophet Muhammad received his first revelations from the Angel Gabriel. The importance of the night is also noted in the hadith of Sunan An-Nasal [4:129]: "Verily the month of Ramadan has come to you all. It is a blessed month, which Allah has obligated you all to fast. During it the gates of Paradise are opened, the gates of Hell are closed and the devils are shackled. In it there is a night that is better than one thousand months. Whoever is deprived of its good, then he has truly been deprived."
15. Jamal Khashoggi, interview by author, London, United Kingdom, June 13, 2005.
16. Jamal Khashoggi, "Arab youths fight shoulder to shoulder with Mujahedeen," Al Majallah (Issue #430), May 4, 1988.
17. Khaled Batarfi, interviews by author, Jeddah, Saudi Arabia, September 5 and 9, 2005.
18. Jamal Khashoggi, "Interview with Prince Turki al Faisal," Arab News and MBC Television, November 4–9, 2001.
19. Arundhati Roy, "The Algebra of Infinite Justice," The Guardian, September 29, 2001.

20. Excerpt from a letter written by Michael Moore and posted to his Web site: www.michael-moore.com, September 12, 2001.
21. For more information on the CIA bin Laden unit, I recommend Michael Scheuer's *Through Our Enemies' Eyes: Osama bin Laden, Radical Islam, and the Future of America* (Washington, D.C.: Brassey's, Inc., 2002).
22. For those readers who might be interested in additional detail on this question, in my book, *Holy War, Inc.*, I devote Chapter 3 to the CIA's operations during the Afghan war. Steve Coll's book, *Ghost Wars: The Secret History of the CIA, Afghanistan, and bin Laden, from the Soviet Invasion to September 10, 2001* (New York: Penguin Press, 2004), also examines this proposition.
23. Ayman al Zawahiri, *Knights under the Prophet's Banner*, excerpts published by *Al Sharq al Awsat*, December 2001.
24. Wael Julaidan, interview by author, Jeddah, Saudi Arabia, September 11, 2005.
25. For more information on Ayman al Zawahiri, I recommend Lawrence Wright's article "The Man Behind bin Laden," *The New Yorker*, September 16, 2002.
26. Zawahiri would only be convicted of possession of a firearm.
27. Video footage, CNN, September 29, 2001.
28. Montasser al Zayyat (translated by Ahmed Fekry and edited by Sara Nimis), *The Road to Al-Qaeda: The Story of bin Ladin's Right-Hand Man* (London: Pluto Press, 2004).
29. Osama Rushdi, interview by Paul Cruickshank, London, United Kingdom, August 9, 2005.
30. Khaled al Hammadi, "Bin Ladin's Former 'Bodyguard' Interviewed on al Qaida Strategies," *Al Quds al Arabi*, in Arabic, August 3, 2004.
31. Faraj Ismail, interview by author, Cairo, Egypt, June 2005.
32. Abdullah Anas, interviews by author, London, United Kingdom, June 15, 17, and 20, 2005.
33. Guantánamo Bay tribunal transcripts, author's collection.
34. There is a fair degree of conspiratorial speculation about Salem bin Ladin's plane crash. Unfortunately, there is no National Transportation and Safety Board (NTSB) report documenting the crash in 1988 to verify the exact reasons why it occurred.
35. Khaled Batarfi, "Interview with Alia Ghanem," *Mail on Sunday*, December 23, 2001.

CHAPTER 4
1. Interview with Taysir Alouni of Al Jazeera, October 2001.
2. U.S. Treasury Department, "Treasury Designates Benevolence International Foundation and Related Entitities as Financiers of Terrorism," November 19, 2002.
3. The Tareekh Osama documents are taken from the Government's Evidentiary Proffer Supporting the Admissibility of Co-Conspirator Statements, *United States v. Enaam Arnaout*, No. 02-CR-892 (North District of Illinois, filed January 6, 2003). Some of this material can be found in the proffer. Much of the information is retained by Motley Rice, the lead law firm for the 9/11 victim's families.
4. "Muslim Charity Director Pleads Guilty to Racketeering," CNN.com, February 10, 2003.
5. Adam Curtis film, *The Power of Nightmares: The Rise of the Politics of Fear*, BBC2, October 2004.
6. Ibid.
7. Ibid.
8. "Tareekh Osama" documents, op. cit.
9. Ken Silverstein, "Official pariah Sudan valuable to America's war on terrorism," *Los Angeles Times*, April 29, 2005.

10. "Tareekh Osama" documents, op. cit.
11. Ibid.
12. At the time of Wadi el-Hage's attendance, the University of Louisiana in Lafayette would have been the University of Southwestern Louisiana, which became part of the state university system in 1999.
13. "Tareekh Osama" documents, op. cit.
14. Ibid.
15. Jamal Khalifa, interview by author, Jeddah, Saudi Arabia, September 6 and 9, 2005.
16. Jamal Ismail, interview by author, Islamabad, Pakistan, March 2005.
17. Abu Musab al Suri, "The International Islamic Resistance Call," published on the Internet, December 2004.
18. It is interesting that the same Abu Bakr, who al Suri notes "inspired" al Qaeda, once told a Muslim army setting out for battle against the Byzantine Army in Syria: *"Stop, O people, that I may give you ten rules for your guidance in the battlefield. Do not commit treachery or deviate from the right path. You must not mutilate dead bodies. Neither kill a child, nor a woman, nor an aged man. Bring no harm to the trees, nor burn them with fire, especially those which are fruitful. Slay not any of the enemy's flock, save for your food. You are likely to pass by people who have devoted their lives to monastic services; leave them alone."* Source: Quintan Wiktorowicz and John Kaltner, "Killing in the name of Islam: al Qaeda's justification for September 11," *Middle East Policy,* No. 2, Vol. 10, June 22, 2003.
19. Hasin al-Banyan, "Interview with Hasan Abd-Rabbuh al Surayhi (the Arab Afghan Veteran)," *Al Sharq al Awsat,* November 25, 2001.
20. Jamal Khashoggi, interview by author, London, United Kingdom, June 13, 2005.
21. "Tareekh Osama" documents, op. cit.
22. *U.S.A. v. Usama bin Laden,* Testimony of Jamal al Fadl, February 6, 7, 13, and 20, 2001.
23. Steve McCurry, phone interview, New York City, July 2005.
24. Peter Bergen, "Beware the Holy War: The Power of Nightmares," *The Nation,* June 2, 2005.
25. Edward Giardet, interview by author, Kabul, Afghanistan, January 2005.
26. Bin Laden was in Saudi Arabia at the time of Abdullah Azzam's death.
27. Faraj Ismail, interview by author, Cairo, Egypt, June 2005.
28. Wael Julaidan, interview by author, Jeddah, Saudi Arabia, September 11, 2005.
29. Date of article unknown.
30. Al-Banyan, op. cit.
31. Osama Rushdi, interview by Paul Cruickshank, London, United Kingdom, August 9, 2005.
32. Kamal Halbawi, interview by Paul Cruickshank, London, United Kingdom, July 25, 2005.
33. Hutaifa Azzam, interview by author, Amman, Jordan, September 13, 2005.
34. Abdullah Anas, interviews by author, London, United Kingdom, June 15, 17, and 20, 2005.
35. Ahmed Zaidan, interview by author, Islamabad, Pakistan, March 2005.
36. Noman Benotman, interview by author, London, United Kingdom, August 30, 2005.
37. *U.S.A. v. Usama bin Laden,* Testimony of L'Houssaine Kherchtou, February 21, 22, 26, 27, and April 24, 2001.
38. *Encyclopedia of Jihad,* translated by Combating Terrorism Center, United States Military Academy at West Point, New York. Author's collection.
39. Kherchtou, op. cit.
40. Ali Mohamed, military record. Author's collection.

41. Haji Deen Mohamed, interviews by author, Jalalabad, Afghanistan, June 2003, and January 16, 2005. Mohamed now serves as the Governor of Nangahar in Afghanistan.
42. Ahmad Shah Ahmadzai, interview by James Meek, Kabul, Afghanistan, August 2005.
43. U.S. State Department Background Note on Afghanistan, August 2005.

CHAPTER 5
1. Abu Musab al Suri, *The International Islamic Resistance Call,* posted on the Internet, in December 2004.
2. Abu Walid al Misri, excerpts from *Afghan Arabs,* published by *Al Sharq al Awsat,* December 2004.
3. Noman Benotman, interview by author, London, United Kingdom, August 30, 2005.
4. Essam Deraz, interviews by author, Cairo, Egypt, January 2000 and May 2005.
5. Jamal Khalifa, interviews by author, Jeddah, Saudi Arabia, September 6 and 9, 2005.
6. *USA v. Usama bin Laden,* Testimony of Jamal al Fadl, February 6, 7, 13, and 20, 2001.
7. Khaled Batarfi, interview by author, Jeddah, Saudi Arabia, September 5, 2005.
8. Jamal Khashoggi, "Former Saudi Intel Chief interviewed on Saudi-Afghan Ties, bin Laden—Part 4," *Arab News,* November 7, 2001.
9. Khaled Al-Hammadi, "Bin Laden's Former 'Bodyguard' interviewed on al Qaeda Strategies," *Al Quds Arabi,* in Arabic, August 3, 2004, and March 20–April 4, 2005.
10. Jose Pedro Castanheira and Antonio Pedro Ferreira, "Exterrorista portugues confessa-se," *Expresso,* April 13, 2002.
11. Fuad Hussein, *Abu Musab al Zarqawi: The Second al Qaeda Generation.* The book was completed in spring 2005 by Fuad Hussein, a Jordanian journalist and writer, who did extensive research on al Zarqawi and received information from three people close to him, including Sayf al Adel, to whom this chapter is attributed. The Arabic-language London-based daily *Al Quds Al Arabi* started serializing the book on May 13, 2005, and this section is the eighth in the series, published by the newspaper on May 21–22, 2005.
12. Testimony of Jamal al Fadl, op. cit.
13. Jamal Ismail, interview by author, Islamabad, Pakistan, March 2005.
14. Hassan al Turabi, interview by Sam Dealey, Khartoum, Sudan, July 8, 2005. Al Turabi was released from prison in 2003 and arrested again in 2004 before being released finally in 2005.
15. Wisal al Turabi, interview by Sam Dealey, Khartoum, Sudan, July 10, 2005.
16. Khaled al Hammadi, "Bin Laden's Former 'Bodyguard' interviewed on al Qaeda Strategies," *Al Quds Al Arabi,* in Arabic, August 3, 2004.
17. Ibrahim Mohammed al Sanoussi, interview by Paul Cruickshank, London, United Kingdom, August 2, 2005.
18. Montasser al Zayyat (translated by Ahmed Fekry and edited by Sara Nimis), *The Road to Al-Qaeda: The Story of bin Ladin's Right-Hand Man* (London: Pluto Press, 2004).
19. Hasin al Banyan, "Interview with Hassan Abd-Rabbuh al Surayhi (the Arab Afghan Veteran)," *Al Sharq al Awsat,* November 25, 2001.
20. Testimony of Jamal al Fadl, op. cit.
21. Affidavit, Minister of Citizenship and Immigration and Mohamed Zeki Mahjoub, Federal Court of Canada, September 6, 2000, signed by the defendant.
22. Abdullah Anas, interview by author, London, United Kingdom, June 15, 17, and 20, 2005.
23. Testimony of Jamal al Fadl, op. cit.
24. Wael Julaidan, interview by author, Jeddah, Saudi Arabia, September 11, 2005.
25. Essam al-Ridi, Testimony at the Southern District Court of New York, February 14, 2001.

26. Testimony of Jamal al Fadl, op. cit.
27. Sheikh Abdul Ghafar, interview by Sam Dealey, Khartoum, Sudan, August 17, 2004.
28. "Part One of Series of Reports on bin Ladin's Life in Sudan," *Al Quds Arabi,* November 24, 2001.
29. Peter Bergen, "Interview: Scott MacLeod," September 29, 1998.
30. Khaled al Fauwaz, interview by author, London, United Kingdom, April 1, 1997.
31. Keith Johnson and David Crawford, in "New Breed of Islamic Warrior is Emerging," *Wall Street Journal,* March 29, 2004, write: "Takfiri ideology originated in a similarly named sect in Egypt in the 1970s and burst into notoriety with the assassination of Egyptian President Anwar Sadat in 1981. The doctrine spread during the Afghan war in the 1980s and was brought back to North Africa by veteran Mujahedeen who preached to young people."
32. Neighbor of Osama bin Laden, interview by Sam Dealey, Khartoum, Sudan, July 2005.
33. Al Hammadi, op. cit.
34. Jamal al Fadl, op. cit.
35. Abdel Bari Atwan, interview by author, London, United Kingdom, June 2005.
36. Al Hammadi, op. cit.
37. Federal Bureau of Investigation interview, "Mohamed Sadiq Odeh," August 15–28, 1998 (transcribed August 31, 1998).
38. Testimony of Essam al Ridi, op. cit.
39. *U.S.A. v. Usama bin Laden,* Testimony of L'Houssaine Kherchtou, February 21, 22, 26, 27, and April 24, 2001.
40. FBI Affidavit on Ali Mohamed, submitted by Special Agent Dan Coleman, September 1998. Author's collection.
41. "Excerpts from Guilty Plea in Terrorism Case," *New York Times,* October 21, 2000.
42. FBI report, "Interview of Ramzi Ahmed Yousef," February 7, 1995.
43. FBI report, "Interview of Abdul Basit Mahmoud Abdul Karim," February 7–8, 1995.
44. FBI interview of Ramzi Yousef en route to the United States; February 7–8, 1995, p. 3.
45. Raghida Dergham, "Interview of Ramzi Yousef," *Al Hayat,* April 12, 1995.
46. For more information on al Hawali and al Awdah, I recommend Mamoun Fandy's *Saudi Arabia and the Politics of Dissent* (New York: St. Martin's Press, 1999).
47. Hamid Mir, interview by author, Islamabad, Pakistan, March 2005.
48. Al Hammadi, op. cit.
49. Osama bin Laden, interview by Peter Arnett (produced by the author), March 22, 1997, aired on CNN May 10, 1997.
50. Bin Ladin family statement, signed by Bakr bin Ladin, April 2004.
51. Saudi Binladin Group (SBG) Web site documents, http://binladen.com/history.htm (no longer operational), October 30, 2000.
52. Kherchtou testimony, op. cit.
53. Jamal al Fadl testimony, op. cit.
54. Probably Nigeria.
55. Jamal Khashoggi, "Former Saudi Intel Chief Interviewed on Saudi-Afghan Ties, Bin Ladin—Part 5," *Arab News,* November 8, 2001.
56. Al Hammadi, op. cit.
57. Ambassador (Ret.) Timothy Carney, e-mail to author, October 11, 2005.
58. Final Report of the National Commission on Terrorist Attacks upon the United States (New York: W. W. Norton, 2004), pp. 109–110.
59. Vahid Mojdeh, interview by author, Kabul, Afghanistan, January 2005.
60. Al Hammadi, op. cit.

CHAPTER 6

1. U.S. Department of State, Bureau of Intelligence and Research (INR), "Terrorism/ Usama bin Ladin: Who's Chasing Whom?" July 18, 1996 (declassified July 21, 2005).

2. Vahid Mojdeh, "Afghanistan under Five Years of Taliban Sovereignty," translated by Sepideh Khalili and Saeed Gangi (Kabul, 2001), pp. 20–27.

3. Abu Walid al Misri, "The History of the Arab Afghans from the Time of their Arrival in Afghanistan until their Departure with the Taliban," Serialized in *Al Sharq al Awsat*, December 8–14, 2004.

4. Hutaifa Azzam, interview by author, Amman, Jordan, September 13, 2005.

5. Osama Bin Laden, "The Declaration of Jihad on the Americans Occupying the Country of the Two Sacred Places" August 23 1996.

6. Abdel Bari Atwan, interview by author, London, United Kingdom, June 2005.

7. Khalid al Hammadi, "Bin Laden's Former 'Bodyguard' interviewed," *Al Quds Al Arabi*, August 3, 2004, and March 20–April 4, 2005.

8. Trial testimony of Abdurahman Khadr, in the Matter of a Certificate under Subsection 77(1) of the Immigration and Refugee Protection Act and Adil Charkaoui, Federal Court of Canada, July 13, 2004. His testimony was made as part of the defense for Charkaoui, who was appealing his detention by Canadian authorities. Charkaoui was granted conditional release in February 17, 2005.

9. Zaynab Khadr, interview by Terrence McKenna, Islamabad, Pakistan, "Al Qaeda Family," CBC, "Maha Elsammah and Zaynab Khadr," February 22, 2004.

10. Noman Benotman, interview by author, London, United Kingdom, August 30, 2005.

11. Ahmed Rashid, *Taliban: Militant Islam, Oil and Fundamentalism in Central Asia* (New York: I. B. Tauris, 2000), p. 178.

12. Hamid Mir, interview by author, Islamabad, Pakistan, March 2005.

13. Peter Jouvenal, interview by Paul Cruickshank, London, United Kingdom, August 23, 2005.

14. Fax from Tim Metz to Peter Bergen, April 30, 1997.

15. Osama bin Laden, interview by Peter Arnett (produced by the author), March 22, 1997, aired on CNN May 10, 1997.

16. Wadih El Hage's grand jury testimony was read in court in the case *USA v. Usama bin Laden et al.* trial in the Southern District of New York on February 15, 2001.

17. Abu Musab al Suri, statement issued from Sheikh Amr Abd al Hakeem's office (the Syrian Abu Musab), translated by Mohannad Hage Ali, January 25, 2005.

18. Abu Musab al Suri, *The International Islamic Resistance Call,* published on jihadist Web sites, 2004.

19. Vahid Mojdeh, interview by author, Kabul, Afghanistan, January 2005.

20. It's possible that these were, in fact, African-Americans who wanted to disguise their origins. Al Qaeda has recruited a small number of African-Americans.

21. Al Hammadi, op. cit.

22. *Encyclopedia of Jihad,* translated by the Combating Terrorism Center, United States Military Academy at West Point, New York. Author's collection.

23. Ibid.

24. Al Hammadi, op. cit.

25. World Islamic Front, "Statement of Jihad against Jews and Crusaders," *Al Quds Al Arabi,* February 28, 1998. Signed by Osama bin Laden; Muhammad bin Laden; Ayman al Zawahiri, amir of the Jihad Group in Egypt; Abu Yasir Rifa'i Ahmad Taha, Egyptian Islamic Group; Shaykh Mir Hamzah, secretary of the Jamiat-ul-Ulema-e-Pakistan; and Fazlur Rahman, amir of the Jihad Movement in Bangladesh.

26. CIA Counterrorist Center Memorandum, "Fatwas or Religious Rulings by Militant Islamic Groups against the United States," February 23, 1998.

27. Feroz Ali Abbasi, Guantánamo Bay Prison Memoirs, 2002–2004, author's collection.

28. Interrogation of Ahmed Ibrahim al-Sayyid al-Naggar by Captain Vasir Azzulddin of the State Security Department, Egypt, July 2, 1998.

29. U.S. State Department Report on 'The Patterns of Global Terrorism 1997," released April 1998. The report noted that bin Laden had relocated in 1997 from Jalalabad to the Taliban's capital of Kandahar and that "bin Laden continued to incite violence against the United States." The U.S. never designated the Taliban as a state sponsor of terrorism, as the Taliban were never officially recognized as Afghanistan's government.

30. Osama bin Laden, "Taliban Government Accused of Terrorism by the Americans," May 16, 1998. Author's collection.

31. Hamid Mir, interview by author, Islamabad, Pakistan July 9, 2003.

32. Nic Robertson, "Previously unseen tape shows bin Laden's declaration of war," CNN, August 20, 2002.

33. Ismail Khan, interview by author, Islamabad, Pakistan, September 1998.

34. Robertson, op. cit.

35. Ibid.

36. Rahimullah Yusufzai, interview by author, Peshawar, Pakistan, September 1998 and June 29, 2003.

37. Hamid Mir, interview by author, Islamabad, Pakistan, May, 2002.

38. Ressam testimony, The al Qaeda Documents, Vol. 2, pp. 548–552 (Alexandria, Virginia: Tempest Publishing, 2003). The Khaldan training camp graduated Ressam; one of the bombers of the U.S. embassy in Kenya in 1988, Mohamed al 'Owhali, and Raed Hijazi, a Jordanian-American convicted of terrorism in Jordan in 2002. See Holy War, Inc.: Inside the Secret World of Osama bin Laden (Touchstone, New York, 2002), p. 143.

39. Osama bin Laden, CNN 1997 interview, op. cit.

40. Reference to banner from page 9 of U.S.A. vs. Ahmed Abdel Sattar and Lynne Stewart et al. 02 Crim. 395, Southern District of New York.

41. Rifa'i Taha statement from Ayman al Zawahiri, Knights under the Prophet's Banner, serialized in Al Sharq al Awsat, December 2001.

42. Omar Abdel Rahman, "My Testimony to History," 1996. Author's collection.

43. Zawahiri, op. cit.

44. Abu Walid al Misri, The History of the Arab Afghans from the Time of their Arrival in Afghanistan until their Departure with the Taliban. Serialized in Al Sharq al Awsat, December 8–14, 2004.

45. Rick Bennett, interview by Paul Cruickshank, London, United Kingdom, July 23, 2005.

46. John Miller, interview by Peter Bergen, Washington, D.C., September 2005.

47. ABC Nightline, presented by Ted Koppel, June 10, 1998.

CHAPTER 7

1. John Miller, interview by Peter Bergen, Washington, D.C., September 2005.

2. U.S.A. v. Usama Bin Ladin, Testimony of Stephen Gaudin, March 7, 2001.

3. Federal Bureau of Investigation interview, "Mohamed Sadiq Odeh," August 15–28, 1998 (transcribed August 31, 1998).

4. U.S.A. v. Usama Bin Ladin, Testimony of Stephen Gaudin, March 7, 2001.

5. Rahimullah Yusufzai, "Osama denies hand in embassies blasts," The News, August 21, 1998.

6. Khalid al Hammadi, "Bin Laden's Former 'Bodyguard' Interviewed," Al Quds al Arabi, August 3, 2004, and March 20–April 4, 2005.

7. Khaled Batarfi, interviews by author, Jeddah, Saudi Arabia, September 5 and 9, 2005.

8. Habib Ahmed, interview by author, Peshawar, Pakistan, September 1998.

9. Abdel Bari Atwan, interview by author, London, United Kingdom, June 2005.

10. Guantánamo Bay tribunal transcripts, author's collection.

11. Sami Ul Haq, interview by author, Peshawar, Pakistan, September 1998.

12. This correspondence is slightly edited.

13. Al Hammadi, op. cit.

14. Declassified U.S. Government documents obtained through the Freedom of Information Act can be found at the National Security Archive (hosted by The George Washington University in Washington, D.C.). See the Web site http://www.gwu.edu/~nsarchiv/index.html.

15. An apparent reference to the Lewinsky affair.

16. Peter Bergen, "Bin Ladin, Taliban at Odds in Afghanistan," CNN, March 4, 1999.

17. Abu Walid al Misri, *The History of the Arab Afghans from the Time of their Arrival in Afghanistan until their Departure with the Taliban,*" serialized in *Al Sharq al Awsat,* December 8–14, 2004.

18. The UN imposed limited sanctions on the Taliban on October 15, 1999, banning commercial flights and freezing Taliban bank accounts worldwide.

19. Mullah Khakshar interviewed by author, Kabul, Afghanistan, January 2005, and by James Meek, August 2005.

20. Ahmad Zaidan, interview by author, Islamabad, Pakistan March 2005.

21. Hamid Mir, interview by author, Islamabad, Pakistan, March 2005.

22. Mohammed Atef ("Abu Hafs") internal report on the Taliban, date estimated to be 1998. Author's collection.

23. Al Hammadi, op. cit.

24. Arab News and MBC Television interview, "Prince Turki al Faisal," November 4–9, 2001 (conducted by Jamal Khashoggi).

25. Al Hammadi, op. cit.

26. Jamal Ismail, interview by author, Islamabad, Pakistan, March 2005.

27. Al Jazeera interview, "Osama bin Laden," 1998 (undated). The comments made were in response to the U.S. cruise missile strike on Afghanistan on October 20, 1998.

28. Executive Order 13129.

29. Key sections of the tapes were translated by Mohannad Hage Ali, who reports on al Qaeda for *Al Hayat* in London.

30. Indictment by Spanish Judge Garzon, issued September 17, 2003. The indictment named 35 individuals, including Osama bin Laden, and was the first indictment of al Qaeda's leader after September 11, 2001.

31. Vahid Mojdeh, *Afghanistan Under Five Years of Taliban Sovereignty,* translated by Sepideh Khalili and Saeed Gangi (Kabul, 2001).

32. Alan Cullison and Andrew Higgins, "A Computer in Kabul Yields a Chilling Array of al Qaeda Memos" and "Forgotten Computer Reveals Thinking Behind Four Years of al Qaeda Doings," *Wall Street Journal,* December 31, 2001. See also Alan Cullison, "Inside al Qaeda's Hard Drive," *The Atlantic Monthly,* September 2004.

33. Noman Bentoman, interview by author, London, United Kingdom, August 30, 2005.

34. Cullison and Higgins, op. cit.

35. Al Hammadi, op. cit.

36. Ibid.

37. Final Report of the National Commission on Terrorist Attacks upon the United States (New York: W. W. Norton, 2004), pp. 152–153.

38. Al Hammadi, op. cit.
39. Peter L. Bergen, *Holy War Inc., Inside the Secret World of Osama bin Laden* (New York: Free Press, 2001), p. 198.
40. "Bin Laden Verses Honor *Cole* Attack," Reuters, March 2, 2001.
41. Abdul Sattar Khan, "Osama urges Ummah to continue jihad," *The News,* May 12, 2001.

CHAPTER 8
1. Malika Malik, *Les Soldats de Lumière,* (Brussels: Les Ailes de la Miséricorde, 2003).
2. Khalid al Hammadi, "Bin Laden's Former 'Bodyguard' Interviewed," *Al Quds al Arabi,* August 3, 2004, and March 20 to April 4, 2005.
3. Some of what follows comes from the German indictment of Shadi Abdalla (alias Emad Abdelhadie), May 14, 2003. There are also excerpts from his interviews with German authorities that occurred between April 2002 (when he was arrested) and May 2003. Author's collection.
4. Al Hammadi, op. cit.
5. Trabelsi was questioned in French in June 2002 and the text of his interrogation was later provided in Italian to prosecutors in Milan investigating one of Trabelsi's associates. Documents acquired and translated by investigative journalist Leo Sisti of *L'Espresso.* Author's collection.
6. CBC News Online, "Singapore in the Cross Hairs," October 11, 2004. See www.cbc.ca/news/background/jabarah/singapore.html
7. Excerpts from Canadian Security Intelligence Service interrogation of "Mohammed Monsour Jabarah," 2002. Author's collection.
8. "Information derived from Mohammed Mansour Jabarah," U.S. Department of Justice, Federal Bureau of Investigation, August 21, 2002. Author's collection.
9. Feroz Ali Abbasi, Guantánamo Bay Prison Memoirs, 2002–2004. Author's collection.
10. Dipesh Gadher, "From Croydon to Kandahar: a Martyr's story," *Sunday Times* (London), November 21, 2004.
11. On June 21, 2005, a grand jury charged that Warsame provided support to al Qaeda and that he gave false statements to FBI agents. The alleged false representations concerned his travel to Afghanistan, Pakistan, and the United Kingdom before returning to Canada and the United States; maintaining contact with others who had attended the same al Qaeda camps, where he met and once dined with bin Laden; and wiring two thousand dollars to one of these individuals in Pakistan. In December 2003, Warsame agreed voluntarily to an interview with the FBI. The extract quoted includes parts of the FBI affidavit filed in support of his pre-trial detention. It reveals Warsame's close-up view of bin Laden's effect on al Qaeda recruits. His trial is expected to commence in the spring of 2006. "Affidavit in Support of Pre-trial Detention," filed by Special Agent Kiann Vandenover, U.S. District Court District of Minnesota, Crim. No. 04-29 (JRT/FLN), February 6, 2004. Author's collection.
12. FBI report, "Interview of John Philip Walker Lindh," December 9–10, 2001. Author's collection.
13. Testimony of Fouad al Rabia before U.S. Military Tribunal, Guantánamo Bay. Author's collection.
14. This extract comes from an Italian arrest warrant for four Moroccans (El Kaflaoui, Raouiane, Zergout and Ben Ali). The warrant is titled, "Tribunale di Torino, Sezione Giudici per le Indagini Preliminari—Ordinanza di Applicazione di Misure Cautelari," and was signed on May 7, 2005 by the Turin (Italy) Judge Paola Dezani. It contains information derived from the Moroccan interrogations of Nafia Noureddine in August 2003

(supplied to Italian prosecutors). Documents acquired and translated by Leo Sisti of *L'Espresso*. Author's collection.

15. The wire intercepts of Es Sayed are found in a report filed by DIGOS (the special anti-terrorist unit of the Italian police) on May 15, 2002, in Milan. The report was used in the trial against Es Sayed, Benattia Nabil, and others. Documents acquired and translated by investigative journalist Leo Sisti of *L'Espresso*. Author's collection.

CHAPTER 9

1. National Commission on Terrorist Attacks upon the United States, 9/11 Commission Final Report (2004), p. 166.
2. The tape was translated by George Michael, a translator at the Diplomatic Language Services, and Dr. Kassem M. Wahba, of Johns Hopkins University School of Advanced International Studies.
3. Ibid.
4. Jamal Ismail, interview by author, Islamabad, Pakistan, July 29, 2004.
5. Bakr Atyani, phone interview by Paul Cruickshank, Islamabad, Pakistan, August 22, 2005.
6. Vahid Mojdeh, *Afghanistan Under Five Years of Taliban Sovereignty*, Translated by Sepideh Khalili and Saeed Gangi (Kabul, 2001).
7. Abu Walid al Misri, *The History of the Arab Afghans from the Time of their Arrival in Afghanistan until their Departure with the Taliban*. Serialized in *Al Sharq al Awsat*, December 8–14, 2004.
8. Hamid Mir, interview by author, Pakistan, March 2005.
9. Peter Jouvenal, interview by Paul Cruickshank, London, August 23, 2005.
10. The video was found on a jihadist website, www.moonwarriors.com, which is no longer operational. Author's collection.
11. The letter is an edited version.
12. Mojdeh, op. cit.
13. Malika Malik, *Les Soldats de Lumière* (Brussels: Les Ailes de la Miséricorde, 2003).
14. Malika Malik, phone interview by Paul Cruickshank, Fribourg, Switzerland, September 26, 2005.
15. "Interview with Abu Haijer," *Voice of Jihad*, Issue 1 and Issue 2, October 2003 (translated by the Middle East Media Research Institute).
16. Feroz Ali Abbasi, Guantánamo Bay Prison Memoirs, 2002–2004. Author's collection.
17. Abdullah Anas, interview by author London, United Kingdom, June 15, 17, and 20, 2005.
18. Jamal Khashoggi, interview by author, London, United Kingdom, June 13, 2005.
19. National Commission on Terrorist Attacks upon the United States, 9/11 Commission Final Report (2004), p. 149.
20. Ibid., pp. 145–150.
21. Yosri Fouda, interview by author London, United Kingdom, January 13, 2003.
22. Al Jazeera documentary "The Road to September the 11th," September 11, 2002.
23. The summaries of the Ramzi Binalshibh interrogations were provided to German prosecutors on May 9, 2005, by the U.S. Department of Justice Criminal Division, Office of International Affairs. Author's collection.
24. *United States of America* v. *Ali Hamza Ahmad Sulayman al Bahlul*. Author's collection. Obtained through www.FindLaw.com. On February 24, 2004, al Bahlul became one of the first Guantánamo Bay detainees to be charged with terrorism. He is subject to a U.S. military tribunal based on President Bush's determination of July 3, 2003.
25. Feroz Ali Abbasi, op. cit.
26. Abu Musab al Suri. *The International Islamic Resistance Call*, published on jihadist Web sites, 2004).

27. Fuad Hussein, *Al Zaqawi: The Second al Qaeda Generation,* serialized in *Al Quds al Arabi,* June 8 to July 15, 2005. Fuad Hussein is a Jordanian journalist who received information from three people close to al Zarqawi, including Sayf Adel, to whom this chapter is attributed.

28. Philip Shenon and David Johnston, "A Nation Challenged: The Investigation," *New York Times,* October 4, 2001.

CHAPTER 10

 1. Osama bin Laden, "Sermon for the Feast of the Sacrifice," Middle East Media Research Institute (MEMRI), Special Dispatch Series, No. 476, March 5, 2003.

 2. Jamal Ismail, interview by author, Islamabad, Pakistan, March, 2005.

 3. Jamal Khashoggi, interview by author, London, June 13, 2005.

 4. José Pedro Castanheira and Antonio Pedro Ferreira, "Eu rezo por Bin Laden," *Expresso* (Portuguese weekly), April 3, 2002. Translation by Carmen Cruickshank-Reynders.

 5. Brian Fyfield-Shayler, phone interview by Paul Cruickshank, Devon, United Kingdom, June 2005.

 6. Bakr Atyani, phone interview by Paul Cruickshank, Islamabad, Pakistan, August 22, 2005.

 7. Guantánamo Bay tribunal transcripts. Author's collection.

 8. The full text of the Voice of America interview with Mullah Omar can be found at http://www.robert-fisk.com/voa_interview_mullah_umar_24sept2001.htm.

 9. Abu Walid al Misri, *The History of the Arab Afghans from the Time of their Arrival in Afghanistan until their Departure with the Taliban.* Serialized in *Al Sharq al Awsat,* December 8–14, 2004.

10. Rahimullah Yusufzai, interview by author, Pakistan, September 1998 and June 29, 2003.

11. *Ummat* interview, "Osama bin Ladin," September 28, 2001, conducted by a "special correspondent" (place and time not given), translated by BBC Monitoring Service.

12. Alan Cullison and Andrew Higgins, "A Computer in Kabul Yields a Chilling Array of al Qaeda Memos" and "Forgotten Computer Reveals Thinking Behind Four Years of al Qaeda Doings," *Wall Street Journal,* December 31 2001. See also Alan Cullison, "Inside al Qaeda's Hard Drive," *The Atlantic Monthly,* September 2004.

13. Faraj Ismail, interview by author, Cairo, Egypt, June 2005.

14. Faraj Ismail, "Taliban Leader Mullah Omar interviewed," *Al Majallah,* October 14, 2001.

15. Osama bin Laden, "Statement," October 7, 2001 (aired on Al Jazeera).

16. Hamid Mir, interview by author, Islamabad, Pakistan, May 11, 2002, and March 2005.

17. Khaled Batarfi, interviews by author, Jeddah, Saudi Arabia, September 5 and 9, 2005.

18. Khalid al Hammadi, "Bin Laden's Former 'Bodyguard' Interviewed," *Al Quds al Arabi,* August 3, 2004, and March 20 to April 4, 2005.

19. Ahmad Zaidan, interview by author, Islamabad, Pakistan, March 2005.

20. Associated Press, November 28, 2002. Dr Aziz, a Lahore-based physician, told the AP that he had been summoned to treat Mohammed Atef for a slipped disk a day before he was killed by a U.S. air strike. Aziz said it was the second time he met bin Laden. The first time was in 1999 when Aziz said he treated the al Qaeda leader after he hurt his back falling off a horse in southern Afghanistan. Bin Laden was in good health at both meetings, he said. Ayman al Zawahiri was also present when he treated Mohammed Atef in November 2001.

21. Osama bin Laden interview by Taysir Alouni of Al Jazeera aired on CNN on February 2002. For full transcript see http://archives.cnn.com/2002/WORLD/asiapcf/south/02/05/binladen.transcript/.

22. Aslam Khan, "Interview of Jalaluddin Haqqani," *The News,* October 20, 2001 (location of interview unknown).

23. Peter Jouvenal, interview by Paul Cruickshank, London, United Kingdom, August 23, 2005.

24. Vahid Mojdeh, *Afghanistan Under Five Years of Taliban Sovereignty,* translated by Sepideh Khalili and Saeed Gangi (Kabul, 2001).

25. Feroz Ali Abbasi, Guantánamo Bay Prison Memoir, 2002–2004. Author's collection.

26. Guantánamo Bay tribunal transcripts. Author's collection.

27. Ibid.

28. Mohamed Asif Qazizanda, interview by author, July 4, 2004, Jalalabad, Afghanistan.

29. Presidential Debate, September 3, 2004, at the University of Miami, Coral Gables, Florida. Transcript is available from the Commission for Presidential Debates at www.debates.org/pages/trans2004a.html.

30. General Tommy Franks, "War of Words," *New York Times,* October 19, 2004.

31. Cheney was speaking in Ohio on the morning of October 19, 2004. The transcript of his remarks is available on the White House Web site: http://www.whitehouse.gov/news/releases/2004/10/20041019-19.html.

32. Dan Froomkin, "Bush Buys Himself Some Time," Washingtonpost.com, October 27, 2004. President Bush was speaking on the morning of October 27 at a rally in Lancaster County, Pennsylvania.

33. "U.S. Officials Believe bin Laden Is in Tora Bora," CNN transcript, December 15, 2001.

34. Tommy Franks and Malcolm McConnell, *American Soldier* (New York: Regan Books, 2004), p. 348.

35. Gary Berntsen, *Jawbreaker: The Attack on bin Laden and al Qaeda: A Personal Account by the CIA's Field Commander* (New York: Crown, December 2005).

36. The statement was posted to al Neda, al Qaeda's main Web site at the time, on September 11, 2002.

37. "Moroccan Security Source Views Danger of Moroccans Released from Guantánamo," *Al Sharq al Awsat,* August 20, 2004.

38. Osama bin Laden, "Message to our Brothers in Iraq," Al Jazeera, February 11, 2003 (translated by ABC News).

39. Osama bin Laden videotape, Al Jazeera, November 27, 2001.

40. Abdel Barl Atwan, interview by author, London, June 2005.

CHAPTER 11

1. Rahimullah Yusufzai, "Osama bin Laden lashes out against the West," *Time* magazine, January 11, 1999 (conducted in Afghanistan's Helmand province).

2. José Pedro Castanheira and Antonio Pedro Ferreira, "Eu rezo por bin Laden," *Expresso (Portugese Weekly),* April 13, 2002, translation by Carmen Cruickshank-Reynders.

3. *U.S.A. v. Usama bin Laden,* Testimony of Jamal al Fadl, February 7 and 20, 2001.

4. Complaint, *United States v. Mamdouh Mahmud Salim,* September 25, 1998 (unsealed).

5. Osama bin Laden statement, "Dangers and Signs of the Indian Nuclear Explosions," May 14, 1998. Author's collection.

6. Amjad Bashir Siddiqi, "I Never Thought Meeting Osama, Omar Will Spell Trouble for Me," *The News,* March 19, 2002.

7. U.S. Treasury Secretary Paul O'Neill, "Remarks on New Terrorist Financing Designations," Washington, D.C., December 20, 2001. O'Neill additionally stated that "during 2001, Mahmood met with Mullah Omar and with Osama bin Laden. During a follow-up meeting, an associate of Osama bin Laden indicated he had nuclear material and wanted to know how to use it to make a weapon. Mahmood provided information about the in-

frastructure needed for a nuclear weapons program and the effects of nuclear weapons. In November 2001, the Taliban left Kabul and the workers at UTN's Kabul offices fled the area with them. Searches of UTN locations in Kabul have yielded documents setting out a plan to kidnap a U.S. attaché and outlining basic nuclear physics related to nuclear weapons."

8. Nic Robertson, "Tapes Shed New Light on bin Laden's Network," August 19, 2002.

9. Roland Jacquard, *L'Archive Secrètes d'al Qaida* (Paris: Jean Picollec, 2002), p. 281.

10. Abu Walid al Misri, *The History of the Arab Afghans from the Time of their Arrival in Afghanistan until their Departure with the Taliban,* serialized in *Al Sharq al Awsat,* December 8–14, 2004.

11. Alan Cullison and Andrew Higgins, "A Computer in Kabul Yields a Chilling Array of al Qaeda Memos" and "Forgotten Computer Reveals Thinking Behind Four Years of al Qaeda Doings," *Wall Street Journal,* December 31, 2001. See also Alan Cullison. "Inside Al-Qaeda's Hard Drive," *The Atlantic,* September 2004.

12. Abu Walid al Misri, op. cit.

13. Peter Jouvenal, interview by Paul Cruickshank, London, August 23, 2005.

14. Jacquard, op. cit., p. 291.

15. Memorandum sent by Deputy Defense Secretary Paul Wolfowitz to Deputy Attorney General James Comey on May 28, 2004, titled, "Summary of Jose Padilla's Activities with al Qaeda." Author's collection.

16. Suleiman Abu Ghaith, "In the Shadow of the Lances," The Middle East Research Institute, Special Dispatch Series No. 338, June 12, 2002.

17. Abu Musab al Suri, "A statement issued from Sheikh Omar Abdel Hakeem's office (the Syrian Abu Musab)," January 25, 2005, translated by Mohannad Hage Ali.

18. Hamid Mir, interview by author, Islamabad, Pakistan, May 11, 2002.

19. Hamid Mir, "Usama bin Ladin," *Ausaf* and *Dawn* interview, November 9, 2001 (conducted near Kabul, Afghanistan).

20. John Walker Lindh interviews, U.S. Department of Defense, December 1, 2001. Author's collection.

CHAPTER 12

1. Al Azhar Fatwah, March 9, 2003. See "Al Azhar calls for Jihad in case of Iraq war," Islam Online, March 10, 2003. www.islamonline.net/english/News/2003-03/10/article15.shtml.

2. "Lebanese Shiite Cleric Fadlallah: No Legitimacy for US-Backed Iraqi Government," *Beirut al Nahar,* April 6, 2003. In a message addressed to the Islamic nation Fadlallah exhorted, "Muslims must work to invoke their elements of strength. They must work now, as they worked in the past, to expel the colonialist."

3. Adel S. Elias, "Hezbollah's Spiritual Leader Advocates Fatwah against Terrorists," *Der Spiegel* (German weekly), 15 October, 2001. Sheikh Fadlallah told Elias, "They (the 9/11 hijackers) did not die in the course of the jihad, the Holy War. They were merely suicides. Anyone committing this kind of thing must be brought to account. And, in the case of a Muslim, he must be punished for it by an Islamic court. The attacks have been a washout, in terms of concrete results." See also, "Al Azhar Chief Says Islam Against All Forms of Terrorism." *Middle East News Agency (MENA),* September 17, 2001.

4. Susan Glasser, "U.S. figures show sharp global rise in terrorism," *Washington Post,* April 27, 2005. Statistics were not included in the U.S. State Department's mandated annual Patterns of Global Terrorism Report for 2004, a break from past practice. They were released by the National Counterterrorism Center on April 27, 2005.

5. "Rumsfeld's War-on-Terror Memo," *USA TODAY,* October 22, 2003. The memo was written by Secretary Rumsfeld on October 16, 2003, and addressed to General Richard

Myers, Deputy Secretary Paul Wolfowitz, General Peter Pace, and Under Secretary Douglas Feith.

6. Osama bin Laden, "A Message to the Iraqi People," Al Jazeera, October 18, 2003.
7. Osama bin Laden, "Audio recording," May 6, 2004. Ambassador Bremer left Iraq on June 28, 2004, the date the Coalition Provisional Authority was dissolved.
8. Osama bin Laden, "Statement," December 16, 2004, posted on the Internet (translated by BBC Monitoring).
9. Hutaifa Azzam, interview by author, Amman, Jordan, September 13, 2005.
10. Fuad Hussein, *Al Zarqawi: The Second al Qaeda Generation,* serialized in *Al Quds al Arabi,* May 15, 2005, and June 8 to July 15, 2005.
11. Some of what follows comes from the German indictment of Shadi Abdalla (alias Emad Abdelhadie), May 14, 2003. There are also excerpts from his interviews with German authorities which occurred between April 2002 (when he was arrested) and May 2003. Author's collection.
12. Colin Powell, Presentation before the U.N. Security Council, February 5, 2003. See www.whitehouse.gov/news/releases/2003/02/20030205-1.html.
13. Bundeskriminalarnt (BKA) Intelligence Report, Abu Musab al Zarqawi, April 2002, translated by Steven Arons. Author's collection.
14. Ibid.
15. Fuad Hussein, op. cit.
16. BKA Intelligence Report, op. cit.
17. Abu Musab al Zarqawi's Letter to Osama bin Laden, Coalition Provisional Authority, February 12, 2004.
18. Secretary of Defense Donald Rumsfeld, Remarks to Council on Foreign Relations, October 4, 2004. Rumsfeld claimed later that day that his remarks had been "misunderstood" (see "A Statement from Secretary of Defense Donald H. Rumsfeld," Department of Defense news release #990–04, October 4, 2004).
19. Zarqawi's pledge of allegiance to al Qaeda was posted on Mu'asker al Battar, Issue 21, October 17, 2004. See Jeffrey Pool, *Terrorism Monitor, Jamestown Foundation,* Volume 2, Issue 24 (December 16, 2004).
20. Osama bin Laden, Audiotape, Al Jazeera, December 27, 2004.
21. Abu Musab al Zarqawi letter to Osama bin Laden, dated May 2005.

CHAPTER 13

1. Scott McClellan, White House Daily Briefing, October 5, 2005.
2. Osama bin Laden, "Will," *Al Majallah,* October 27–November 2, 2002.
3. Osama bin Laden videotape, Al Jazeera, aired December 27, 2001.
4. Muhammad al Shafi'i, "A Site Close to al Qaeda Posts a Poem by bin Laden in which He Responds to His Son Hamzah," *Al Sharq al Awsat,* June 16, 2002.
5. On the evening of October 6, 2002, one day before the first anniversary of the start of the U.S. air campaign in Afghanistan, Al Jazeera aired a two-minute audiotape of bin Laden, the first he had been heard of since December 2001, stating that "the youths of God are planning more attacks against the U.S." (See Osama bin Laden audiotape, aired on Al Jazeera, October 6, 2002.) That morning, just hours before Al Jazeera received the audiotape, al Qaeda operatives launched a suicide attack on the French oil tanker *Limburg* off the coast of Yemen. On October 8, al Zawahiri released an audiotape to Al Jazeera in which he declared, "We should begin the resistance now. The interests of the Americans, British, Australians, French, Polish, Norwegians, South Koreans and Japanese are everywhere. They all participated in the occupation of Afghanistan, Iraq and Chechnya or supplied Israel with means of subsistence." (See al Zawahiri audiotape, aired on Al

Jazeera, October 8, 2002). On October 12, only days after bin Laden and Zawahiri's statements telegraphing a new wave of attacks, a disco popular with Australians and other Westerners was bombed in Bali, killing more than 200, exactly two years after the attack on the USS *Cole*. Also, al Qaeda's leaders were eager to exploit the attacks for maximum propaganda value. On October 14, a fax bearing bin Laden's signature was received by Al Jazeera declaring that, "these attacks coincide with the anniversary of the crusade [the beginning of the U.S. campaign in Afghanistan] and are a clear message that the mujahideen have not been weakened." (See Philip Smucker, "Bin Laden Gloats at Terror Attacks," *Daily Telegraph* (London), October 15, 2002. (Bin Laden did not directly refer to the Bali attack.)

6. Al Zawahiri audiotape, "Message to Muslims in Pakistan and Afghanistan," aired on Al Jazeera and Al Arabiya, September 28, 2003. Zawahiri stated, "It is Musharraf who enabled America to topple the [Taliban] Islamic emirate in Afghanistan and is seeking to send Pakistani forces to Iraq. Muslims in Pakistan must unite and co-operate to topple this traitor and install a sincere leadership that would defend Islam and Muslims." President Musharraf survived two assassination attempts in December 2003.
7. Osama bin Laden audiotape, "A message to the Americans," aired on Al Jazeera, October 18, 2003. Bin Laden stated, "We reserve the right to retaliate at the appropriate time and place against all countries involved, especially the U.K., Spain, Australia, Poland, Japan, and Italy, not to exclude the Muslim states that took part, especially the Gulf States and in particular Kuwait, which has become a launch pad for the crusading forces."
8. Ahmad Zaidan, interview by author, Islamabad, Pakistan, March 2005.
9. Osama bin Laden, "Sermon for the Feast of the Sacrifice," MEMRI, Special Dispatch Series No. 476, March 5, 2003.
10. Osama bin Laden audiotape, aired on Al Jazeera and Al Arabiya, April 14, 2004.
11. Osama bin Laden, "Statement," December 16, 2004, posted on the Internet (translated by BBC Monitoring). The 74-minute audio recording was found at www.gal3ah.net (no longer operational).
12. "Interview with Abu Hajjer," *Voice of Jihad*, Issue 1 and Issue 2, October 2003 (translation by Middle East Media Research Institute).
13. According to officials in Saudi Arabia, the Saudi cells asked for more time for their attacks, saying they were unprepared for a full assault on the Saudi government and that they feared a public backlash. After a debate in early 2003 bin Laden overruled them, ordering the attacks to begin. See Craig Whitlock, "Al Qaeda shifts its strategy in Saudi Arabia," *Washington Post*, December 19, 2004.
14. Sayf al Adel, al Batar Military Camp Publication, 2003. Author's collection.
15. Peter Bergen, "Letter from Riyadh: Are We Witnessing a Saudi Glasnost?" *National Review Online*, February 14, 2005.
16. See Susan B. Glasser, "Martyrs in Iraq mostly Saudis," *Washington Post*, May 15, 2005. See also Reuven Paz, "Arab Volunteers Killed in Iraq: an analysis," *Project for the Research of Islamist Movements*, Herzliya, Israel, Occasional Papers, Volume 3, (2005), Number 1 (March 2005). Reuven Paz found from lists of fighters killed posted on jihadist Web sites that of a sample of 154 Arabs killed in the previous six months in Iraq, 61 percent were from Saudi Arabia. Of the 33 who died in suicide attacks, 23 were Saudis.
17. CNN correspondent Barbara Starr discussed the bin Laden tape on CNN's *Wolf Blitzer Reports*, October 29, 2004.
18. Osama bin Laden videotape, aired on Al Jazeera, October 29, 2004. This translation is from CNN.

19. Bin Laden's mention of Sweden is interesting, as it is the only country in Europe he appears to have visited.
20. Noman Benotman, interview by author, London, United Kingdom, August 30, 2005.
21. Jamal Khalifa, interviews by author, Jeddah, Saudi Arabia, September 6 and 9, 2005.
22. Al Sahab ("the Clouds"), al Qaeda videotape, aired on Al Jazeera, September 1, 2005.
23. Abdel Bari Atwan, interview by author, London, United Kingdom, June 2005.

CHAPTER 14
1. See Sayyid Qutb, *Milestones* (1965) and *The America I Have Seen* (1949).
2. Osama bin Laden, "Will," *Al Majallah,* October 27–November 2, 2002.
3. Jamal Khalifa, interviews by author, Jeddah, Saudi Arabia, September 6 and 9, 2005.
4. Hutaifa Azzam, interview by the author, Amman, Jordan, September 13, 2005.
5. Abdel Bari Atwan, interview by the author, London, United Kingdom, June 2005.
6. Khalid al-Hammadi, "Bin Laden's Former 'Bodyguard' Interviewed," *Al Quds al Arabi,* August 3, 2004, and March 20 to April 4 2005.
7. Khalid Khawaja, interview by author, Islamabad, Pakistan, July 2004.
8. Jamal Ismail, interview by author, Islamabad, Pakistan, March 2005.
9. Montasser al Zayyat (translated by Ahmed Fekry and edited by Sara Nimis), *The Road to al Qaeda: The Story of bin Ladin's Right-Hand Man,* (London: Pluto Press, 2004).
10. Rahimullah Yusufzai, interviews by author, Pakistan, September 1998 and June 29, 2003.
11. Abu Musab al Suri, *The International Islamic Resistance Call,* (Published on Jihadist Web sites, December 2004).
12. Saad al Fagih, interview by author, London, September 2002. In December 2004, the U.S. Treasury designated Fagih a provider of material support and resources to al Qaeda and bin Laden. Treasury cited the allegation, developed in the U.S. embassy bombing trial, that Fagih purchased a satellite phone and had it delivered to bin Laden. But the British government has not taken legal action against him, other than freezing MIRA's financial assets, to the disappointment of the Saudi government. See U.S. Treasury Department press release titled, "U.S. Treasury Department Designates Two Individuals with Ties to al Qaida, UBL, Former BIF Leader and al Qaida Associate," December 21, 2004.
13. Noman Benotman, interview by author, London, United Kingdom, August 30, 2005.
14. Ayman al Zawahiri, *Knights under Prophet's Banner,* serialized in the *Al Sharq al Awsat* newspaper, December 2001.
15. Olivier Roy, *L'Echec de L'Islam Politique ("The Failure of Political Islam"),* (Paris: Seull, 1992).
16. See Gilles Kepel, *Jihad: Expansion et declin de l'islamisme* (Paris: Gallimard, 2000) and Gilles Kepel (translated by Anthony F. Roberts), *Jihad: the Trail of Political Islam* (New York; Belknap Press, 2002), p. 375.
17. Osama bin Laden, "Will," *Al Majallah,* October 27–November 2, 2002.

APPENDIX B
1. Michael Field, *The Merchants* (New York: The Overlook Press, 1985), p. 105.
2. Carmen bin Ladin, *Inside the Kingdom: My Life in Saudi Arabia,* (New York: Warner Books, 2004), p. 64.
3. Ibid, p. 65.
4. Khaled Batarfi, interviews with author, Jeddah, Saudi Arabia, September 5 and September 9, 2005.
5. This list was compiled from information in J.R.L. Carter's *Leading Merchant Families of*

Saudi Arabia (United Kingdom: Scorpion Publications Ltd. And D R Llewellyn Associates, 1979), and from a phone interview with Brian Fyfield-Shayler, Devon, England, June 2005.

6. Carmen Bin Ladin, op. cit., pp. 108–109.
7. Relative of Bin Ladin family.
8. Field, op. cit., p. 110.
9. Bud Kennedy, "Strange Death of bin Laden's Brother in Texas," *Ft. Worth Star-Telegram,* September 27, 2001.
10. *Who's Who in Saudi Arabia,* Third Edition (Jeddah: Tihama, 1983), p. 57.
11. Holly Stepp, "Bin Ladin's Half Brothers are University of Miami Alumni," *Miami Herald,* September 20, 2001.
12. Ibid.
13. Carmen Bin Ladin, op. cit., p. 40.
14. Ibid, p. 110.
15. Ibid, p. 80.
16. Stepp, op. cit.
17. Carmen Bin Ladin, op. cit., p. 40.
18. Georg Mascolo and Erich Follath. "Osama's Road to Riches and Terror," *Der Spiegel,* June 6, 2005.
19. Ibid.
20. Carmen Bin Ladin, p. 110.
21. Mascolo and Follath, op. cit.
22. Carmen Bin Ladin, p. 131.
23. Craig Shirley, "Harvard's Own bin Laden," *Washington Times,* October 29, 2001.
24. Abdullah bin Ladin, interview with Barbara Walters on ABC News, June 3, 2005.
25. Abdullah bin Ladin, interview with ABC News, March 29, 2002.
26. Khalid al Hammadi, "Bin Laden's Former 'Bodyguard' Interviewed," *Al Quds al Arabi,* August 3, 2004, and March 20 to April 4, 2005.
27. Hutaifa Azzam, interview by author, Amman, Jordan, September 13, 2005.
28. Jamal Khalifa, interviews by author, Jeddah, Saudi Arabia, September 6 and 9, 2005.
29. Al Hammadi, op. cit.
30. Ibid.
31. Ibid.
32. Ibid.
33. Ibid.
34. "Bin Ladin's son says father in 'safest place in the world,' " London Press Association, October 13, 2001.
35. Hutaifa Azzam interview, op. cit.
36. Ibid.
37. Douglas Farah and Dana Priest, "Son Plays Key Role in al Qaeda," *Washington Post,* October 14, 2003.
38. Abdel Bari Atwan, interview by author, London, June 2005.
39. Jamal Ismail, interview by author, Islamabad, Pakistan, March 2005.
40. "Moroccan Security Source Views Danger of Moroccans Released from Guantanamo," *Al Sharq al Awsat,* August 20, 2004.

Acknowledgments

This book could not have happened without the people who collaborated with me to make it happen. Paul Cruickshank worked on every phase, performing important interviews and research, making key editing suggestions, translating materials from French, and handling the nitty-gritty of fact checking and footnoting. In the final month of writing, Paul moved to Washington, D.C., to help; he was an invaluable collaborator. Alec Reynolds brought a great deal of focus, discipline, and creativity to the research, and made important editorial suggestions. Kelly Magsamen also provided valuable editing suggestions and vital input on fact checking and footnoting. Without Paul, Alec, and Kelly the book would not have attained its present form. Tom West also provided useful help with the research for this project. Thanks to all of you, and for your friendship.

Paul, Alec, Kelly, and Tom were all students of mine at Johns Hopkins University School of Advanced International Studies (SAIS). Thank you, Sunil Khilnani, the head of the South Asia department at SAIS, for affording me the opportunity to teach at SAIS and to work with so many excellent students. SAIS is also the provenance of Steve Arons, who worked on the German translations for this book. Georges Chebib and Mark Thomas, also SAIS graduates, took on the daunting task of summarizing and translating thousands of pages of *Jihad* magazine. Mark also undertook other important Arabic translations. Sam Dealey did the interviews on the ground in Sudan. Thanks for the fine job. James Meek also helped by doing a couple of interviews in Afghanistan. Thanks to Mohammad Hage Ali for his translation of Abu Musab al Suri's 1,500-page opus and other Arabic translations. Thanks to Amelie Reuterskiold for the Swedish translations. And a particular thank-you to Paul's mother, Carmen Cruickshank-Reynders, for the Portuguese translations.

Thanks, of course, to everyone who agreed to be interviewed for this book. Almost everyone spoke on the record and the names of those interviewees can be found by reading this book.

My colleague Henry Schuster at CNN and I have worked together on the bin Laden/al Qaeda story since 1997, and we have talked about some facet of the story most days since. Henry gave this book a through reading and it has benefited a great deal from his suggestions and from the work we have done together over the years. Also at CNN I have been the beneficiary of the work and expertise of Nic Robertson, Octavia Nasr, Phil Hirshkorn, David Ensor, and Justine Redman. Thanks also to Rick Davis for permission to quote CNN material. Thanks to Sid Bedingfield, Ken Shiffman, and Kathy Slobogin of *CNN Presents* for their interest in this project. Also at CNN thanks to Pamela Sellars, Joy DiBenedetto, Gail Chalef, Susan Walsh, Megan Hundahl, and Anderson Cooper for the interest they have taken in my work.

Thanks to Aimee Ibrahim, who helped me wade through *Jihad* magazine early on and helped to flag important passages. Thanks also to Lauren Gaum for help in organizing my research. Stephen Glain and Anatol Lieven made helpful comments on the manuscript. Thanks to N. C. Aizenman, the *Washington Post*'s Afghanistan correspondent in 2005, for a careful reading of the manuscript and for your years of support. Also to Shaun Waterman of UPI for reading the manuscript and for your friendship.

A number of institutions were helpful in making available material from their archives. In particular, I would like to thank the law firm of Motley Rice, which represents many of the 9/11 families and possesses one of the world's most important libraries of al Qaeda material. Thanks to Ron Motley, and a particular thanks to Michael Elsner, and to Lisa Saunders. Thanks also to West Point's Center on Combating Terrorism for making available thousands of pages of al Qaeda's *Encyclopedia of Jihad*. Thanks in particular to Jarrett Brachman, the director of the center. Thanks also to Vanessa Blum of *Legal Times* for making available Guantánamo materials. Thanks to MEMRI for its Arabic translations.

Al Qaeda is a global organization and so reporting on it necessitates a global approach. For help with German materials, thanks to George Mascolo of *Der Spiegel* and Andreas Schulz, the German lawyer for the 9/11 families. Thanks to Stewart Bell, Canada's foremost reporter on terrorism, for his help with some of the Canadian material in this book. Thanks to Karen Greenberg at New York University's Center on Law and Security for all the work that you do and for your friendship, and thanks to Stephen Holmes of NYU. Through Karen I had the good fortune to meet Leo Sisti of *L'Espresso* magazine, one of Italy's leading investigative journalists, who provided me with invaluable help with the Italian research for the book. For help with Spanish research and translations, thanks to Pablo Pardo and to Juliana Silva. Hans Lindquist, Ann-Mari Johansson, Anders Hansson, and Peter Carlson were helpful in Falun, Sweden. In Belgium, thanks to Marc Eekhaut, of *De Standaard* newspaper, and Alain Grignard, who heads Belgian counterterrorism efforts.

In Afghanistan, thanks to Khalid Mafton, Yusuf Massoud, and Hamid Hamidullah for all your help on research and translation. Thanks also to the staff at Gandamack Lodge, especially Kawoos Rahman and Fatima Syed. Thanks also to owners Peter and Hassina Jouvenal. Thanks also to Scott Wallace for the most enjoyable trip we took to Afghanistan in 2003, and your photos in this book. Thanks to "the Bookseller of Kabul," Shah Muhammad Rais, for pointing me in the direction of *Jihad* magazine. And thanks to Hekmat Karzai, Jake Sutton, and Richard Mackenzie for your expertise on Afghanistan. Thanks to Vahid Mojdeh for permission to quote from his book on the Taliban. And thanks to Malika Malik for the quotations from her book about her life in Afghanistan. In Pakistan, thanks for repeated help over the years to journalists Rahimullah Yusufzai, Ismail Khan, and Jamal Ismail.

In Yemen, thanks to Khaled al Hammadi of *Al Quds Al Arabi* newspaper for all your help over the years and for the illuminating interview with Abu Jandal that was used in this book. Thanks also to Abdel Bari Atwan of *Al Quds Al Arabi,* who gave permission for the Abu Jandal interview to be used, and who is himself interviewed in this book. Thanks to Dr. David Hoile and Milt Bearden for your efforts on my behalf regarding a trip to Sudan. In Jordan, thanks to Ranya Kadri. Thanks to the Jordanian journalist Fuad Hussein for permission to quote from his book on Zarqawi. Professor Jack Kalpakian of Al Akhawayn University was helpful in Morocco. Thanks to Adel Jubeir and Nail Jubeir for easing the way for my trip to Saudi Arabia. A big thank-you to Essam Al-Ghalib of *Arab News* for his help in Jeddah. And thanks to Khaled Al-Meena, the editor of *Arab News,* for permission to quote material from his newspaper. Thanks also to Wendell Belew Jr. for his advice on Saudi Arabia. Thanks for the hospitable welcome I was given in Jeddah by Khaled Batarfi and Abdul Aziz Raheem. Thanks also to Michael Petruzello and Matt Lauer of Qorvis Communications. In Egypt, thanks to Mandi Mourad for help on translation and research and for your friendship. And thanks to Reem Nada. It's been a pleasure to know you for the past six years.

In the United Kingdom, thanks to Brian Fyfield-Shayler, who was extraordinarily helpful, and to John Carter. Thanks also to Nick Fielding of the *Sunday Times,* Yosri Fouda of Al Jazeera, Osama Rushdi, and Kamal Halbawi, all of whom helped with aspects of the book. Also in London, thanks to Abdullah Anas, who provided a great deal of his time and expertise. Thanks to Mohammed al Shafey of *Al Sharq al Awsat* newspaper for much valuable guidance and also thanks to Tariq Alhomayed the editor of *Al Sharq al Awsat* for allowing material from his newspaper to be quoted in the book. Thanks to Satnam Matharu, head of international media relations, and Wadah Khanfar, the managing director of Al Jazeera, for permission to use material from their network. Thanks also for their help on permissions to Ruth-Ellen Soles at CBC, and Kerry Glencourse.

I have also benefited from both the work and friendship of Steve Coll, Dan Benjamin, Steve Simon, Marc Sageman, Mike Scheuer, Jason Burke, Paul Eedle, Zachary Abuza, Bruce Hoffman, and Larry Wright. Thanks to Carsten Obleander of Storyhouse Productions for the three documentaries we have made together about al Qaeda since 9/11. And thanks also to John King and Vicky Matthews of Storyhouse. Making those documentaries helped shape my thinking about al Qaeda. Some of the ideas or reporting for this book first took shape in a number of different magazines and newspapers. Thanks to Cullen Murphy, Toby Lester, and Bessmarie Moll at *The Atlantic,* Adam Shatz at *The Nation,* Gideon Rose at *Foreign Affairs,* Marie Arana and Warren Bass at the *Washington Post,* David Shipley and James Gibney at the *New York Times,* and Monika Bauerlein at *Mother Jones.*

At *Vanity Fair,* thanks to Graydon Carter and Chris Garrett for taking a continuing interest in my work on bin Laden and for excerpting this book. I am especially grateful to Wayne Lawson for the work he has done editing my work for *Vanity Fair.*

Thanks to FBIS, FindLaw.com, and Cryptome.org, institutions that provided the tools to make some of the research possible in this book. At the FBI, thanks to Richard Kolko. And for all the work he has done, thanks to Dan Coleman. Thanks to Laurie Garrett, David Fidler, and Dawn Hewett for tolerating my absences caused by writing this book as we worked together on the Princeton Project. I learned a lot from you. Federal News Service did the bulk of the transcriptions for this book and I am very grateful to Bob Lee and his team Joseph B. Trapple, Kimberly K. Trapple, Carrie L. Mitchell, Leticia A. Watson, and Jordan D. White. Thanks to Fernando Batista for his work on www.peterbergen.com. Thanks also to George Vassiliou, Clark Forcey, and Chris Clifford.

I would like to thank Pam Hill and John Lane, my longtime bosses at CNN, who indulged my interest in bin Laden at a time when he was more or less unknown. In 1997 I visited Afghanistan with Peter Arnett and Peter Jouvenal to interview bin Laden. Thanks to you both for making the interview happen.

Friends were supportive in the time I spent reporting and writing this book—Trish Enright, Cindy Balmuth, Nir and Tiffany Rosen, Rachel Klayman, Christina Davidson, Quil Lawrence, Andrew Boord, George and Pauline Case, Andy Marshall, Paul and Yasmin Berczeller, Jenny Rees-Tonge, Tom Rhodes and Deborah Lee, Narisara Murray and John McDermott, Bill and Wendy Smee, Graham Messick, Tom Carver and Katty Kay, Kate Boo, and Neil Barrett. Marla Ruzicka was killed in Iraq by a suicide bomber in April 2005. I miss her a great deal.

Thanks to Martha Levin and Free Press for supporting my work over the past several years. Thanks also to those at the Free Press who speeded this book to publication: Carol de Onís, Elisa Rivlin, Karolina Harris, Eric Fuentecilla, who designed the handsome jacket, and Shilpa Nadha. Thanks to Kathryn Higuchi for the fine job on the copy editing. Thanks to Carisa Hays for excellent advice about publicizing the book. Thanks to Jeffrey Ward who made the map. Thanks to my editor, Dominick Anfuso, who believed in the book's potential and had a number of valuable ideas about how it should be shaped. Dominick also brought a great deal of calm to a frenzied production schedule that involved completing my work in early November 2005 and having it in bookstores two months later. Wylie O'Sullivan, Dominick's assistant, was invaluable.

Also, thanks to the New America Foundation, which has provided me such a friendly and congenial home to work on this book. Thanks to Ted Halstead, Steve Clemons, Sherle Schwenninger, Hannah Fischer, Lucinda Toliver, Michael Lind, Jeanette Warren, Jenny Buntman, Sameer Lalwani, Preethi Guniganti, and Simone Frank. Thanks also to Bernard Schwartz, whose generosity funds my position at New America. Thanks to Erica DeBruin of New America for her input on the manuscript.

My literary agency, Janklow & Nesbit, was vital to all phases of this project. Tina Bennett is simply the best agent imaginable. She made this project happen and it is a great pleasure to work with her and to count her as a friend. Also at Janklow, thanks to Richard Morris, Svetlana Katz, Ed Roque, Cullen Stanley, and to Tif Loehnis, who helped me so much with my first book.

Finally, thanks to my family: Tom Bergen, who gave this book a careful reading. To Sarah Lampert Bergen, Katherine Bergen and Nick Wood, Margaret Bergen and John Fielding, and the McCanns— Charlotte, Isobel and Brendan—for their support. Thanks also to Carolina Bergen. And most of all, thanks to Juliana Silva, to whom this book is dedicated. Without your love and support there would be no book.

Index